U.S.S. Barb (SS-220)
American Submarine
War Patrol Reports

Also from Riverdale Books

American Submarine War Patrol Reports Series

U.S.S. *Cod* (SS-224)
ISBN: 1-932606-04-1

U.S.S. *Wahoo* (SS-238)
ISBN: 1-932606-07-6

U.S.S. *Tang* (SS-306)
ISBN: 1-932606-05-X

Submarine Fiction

Bacalao
J.T. McDaniel
ISBN: 0-9712207-5-1 (Trade Paperback)
ISBN: 1-932606-03-3 (Hardcover)

With Honour in Battle
J.T. McDaniel
ISBN: 0-9712207-3-5

U-859
Arthur Baudzus
ISBN: 0-9712207-7-8

Non-Fiction

The Submariner's Dictionary
Ron Martini
ISBN: 1-932606-14-9

U.S.S. *Barb* (SS-220)
American Submarine War Patrol Reports

Foreword by
Everett P. "Tuck" Weaver

J.T. McDaniel,
Editor

Riverdale Books
Riverdale, Georgia

U.S.S. Barb (SS-220): American Submarine War Patrol Reports
New content © 2006, Riverdale Books. All rights reserved.

This book contains both copyrighted and public domain material. For information, contact the publisher.

Riverdale Books
is an imprint of

Riverdale Electronic Books
PO Box 962085
Riverdale, Georgia 30296
www.riverdaleebooks.com

ISBN: 1-932606-10-6

Library of Congress Control Number: 2006900901

Printed in the United States of America

Contents

Foreword	vii
Introduction	xiii
Patrol One, 20 October 1942 – 25 November 1942	1
Patrol Two, 16 December 1942 – 18 January 1943	12
Patrol Three, 1 February 1943 – 9 March 1943	34
Patrol Four, 1 April 1943 – 14 May 1943	56
Patrol Five, 8 June 1943 – 24 July 1943	68
Patrol Six, 30 September 1943 – 28 November 1943	74
Patrol Seven, 2 March 1944 – 23 April 1944	95
Patrol Eight, 21 May 1944 – 9 July 1944	122
Patrol Nine, 4 August 1944 – 3 October 1944	179
Patrol Ten, 27 October 1944 – 25 November 1944	244
Patrol Eleven, 19 December 1944 – 15 February 1944	290
Patrol Twelve, 8 June 1945 – 2 August 1945	350

Foreword

The United States Submarine Service, frequently referred to as the Silent Service, had a lot to be silent about in the first year of the war against Japan. Six or seven U-boats operating off the east coast of the United States sank approximately as many ships and tons each month as our 45 submarines, arrayed against Japan, sank during the first year of hostilities.

We had three problems: the torpedoes, the boats and the training of the commanding officers. Not wishing to spend $10,000 to explode a torpedo in peacetime, no live ones were fired, and we entered the war unaware of three different problems causing them not to work. It took nearly two years to identify and correct these problems.

We started the war with about a fifth of our fleet being S-class subs, first built in World War I, and unfit for combat in the forties. For various reasons, including sub-standard engines, most of the later ones were not much better until 1938, when the Navy started building the "fleet boats," which used diesel electric power plants of the type used to power railroad locomotives. This design became standard, and boats were built during the war at four main production facilities. It was several years before the fleet boat became the majority of our force.

The third problem, the training of the commanding officers, could not have been more unrealistic. Not wishing to spend the money to explode depth charges near submarines—depth charges were believed to be far more dangerous than they were—caused the skippers to become so cautious that sinking a target was almost an accident. The preferred method was to attack by sound at fifty feet below periscope depth. Of the thousands of ships eventually sunk by subs, not one was sunk by that method. The turnaround came after about a third of the skippers were relieved during the first year and replaced by a younger breed who, with torpedoes that worked and better boats, eventually sank about 60% of the Japanese freighters and tankers, and nearly 40% of the warships, which all U.S. forces destroyed during the war.

Gene Fluckey spent the early part of the war on a sub in Panama, where there was no action. Then followed a year in the States, taking a post graduate course in electrical engineering. He arrived in the Pacific War zone in February 1944. Many of his contemporaries at Annapolis had already been there for a year or two. He was assigned to be Prospective Commanding Officer aboard *Barb*, a trial cruise to test his suitability for command. The Commanding Officer, eight years his senior, was commencing his sixth (and last) patrol as CO. In the wardroom, when the conversation turned to tactics, the two were polar opposites, not agreeing on anything, yet Lieutenant Commander Fluckey possessed the rare ability to disagree with his superior without being disagreeable, and the two got along fairly well on a personal basis.

Lieutenant Commander Fluckey was full of new ideas that were either out of step with, or one step ahead of existing doctrine. He had calculated that one submarine on the surface during the daytime in the patrol area could cover as much ground as a dozen submerged boats. The periscope, instead of being three feet above the surface of the water, was about 45 feet above the ocean, and with the world being round the visibility was about ten times as far. The radar, inoperative under water, could pick up objects twenty miles away when the boat was on the surface. But to operate on the surface in Japanese water in daylight was considered both dangerous and foolhardy.

Lieutenant Commander Fluckey talked about subs being the ideal launching platforms for spiral rocket missiles, as the boat could get close to land based installation unobserved, fire their missiles, and disappear, leaving the Japanese to wonder where the missiles had come from. He repeatedly asked the commander's permission to take one of the boat's scuttling charges ashore on Formosa (now Taiwan) in a rubber boat to blow up a railroad bridge that could be seen near the shoreline. Per the CO, a foolish idea. He might be captured and reveal important military secrets. Permission denied, and stop bringing up the matter.

Unknown to those on the boats at that time was the fact that our codebreakers had broken the Japanese *Maru* (merchant) code. The boats were receiving Ultra messages giving the location, course and speed of Japanese convoys, and about half of the sinkings by submariners during the war came as a result of these Ultras. On Lieutenant Commander Fluckey's PCO patrol, as *Barb* was nearing its patrol area, an Ultra was received describing a convoy headed for a Japanese island harbor. It was calculated that by going 19 knots (full speed) for twelve hours we could intercept the convoy just before it reached the harbor. About five hours into the chase we were spotted by a Japanese Mavis patrol plane, which dropped three bombs after we had submerged, doing no damage. The Captain ordered 150 feet in depth for three hours, meaning we would lose our chance at the target.

The openings of the officers' quarters staterooms had no doors, just curtains that provided visual privacy, but no soundproofing. Right after the dive the Captain went to his quarters and Lieutenant Commander Fluckey followed him and spent about ten minutes trying to persuade the Captain to surface and resume the chase. Across the passageway in our small quarters, with the curtain closed, junior officers Paul Monroe and I heard the conversation, and when the skipper was starting to remind Lieutenant Commander Fluckey who was in command of the boat, we slipped out of our quarters into the wardroom just forward of our space. A minute or so later Gene (we called him that on his PCO run) left the Captain's quarters, saw us in the wardroom, and asked if we had heard the exchange. We said we had, and then he told us that if he ever got command of *Barb* and stayed down more than 15 minutes for an airplane we were to give him a swift kick in the rear end, and that was an order.

After the war I got all of Barb's patrol reports on microfilm and found that during the three patrols I made under his command, we dived for planes 78 times, were bombed five times, suffered no damage, and never stayed down more than 15 minutes.

He had unique programs, which I had not heard of being used on other boats. It was customary for two officers to be on watch at the same time on the same shifts, four hours on and eight hours off. With all the practice drills and routine job responsibilities it was difficult to get enough sleep. A person who is tired should not be on watch on a boat on the surface during the daytime. He changed the schedule from four on and eight off to four on and sixteen off, with only one officer on watch at a time. Now we were all wide awake in looking for planes and periscopes.

Another effective program, which may have saved us twice, was the constant helm steering while on station. To successfully bomb or torpedo a target one has to know which way it is going. If the general direction was to be north, we would put the rudder over about five degrees until our heading was east and then reverse it until we were going west, averaging north, but constantly changing direction. On two occasions planes coming out of the sun were not seen by us until we heard them nearly directly overhead, but their bombs missed because we had changed direction when they first sighted us.

Gene told us it was safe to do the totally unexpected, but dangerous to keep repeating it. Three examples are the Nam Kwan Harbor attack; the only U.S. landing on mainland Japan, which blew up a railroad train; and the destruction of factories near the shoreline with rocket missile attacks. Submarines of all nations avoided operating in shallow water because, if sunk, the enemy could salvage the boat and get valuable proprietary information. Thus, convoys felt very comfortable anchoring in harbors where the water was shallow, secure in the belief that no sub would venture in to attack them.

Captain Fluckey, while patrolling off China on patrol number eleven, became aware of a large convoy anchored in Nam Kwan Harbor. To get there the boat would have to travel about 15 miles in water too shallow to dive. His observations convinced him that he would not run into opposition either going in, or getting out. Travelling with *Picuda*, he invited that boat to join him, but the *Picuda*'s skipper's reply was, "Get lost." The venture was successful. Every torpedo hit an anchored ship and earned for Commander Fluckey the Medal of Honor.

On patrol twelve, near the end of the war and with few Japanese ships left to sink, he sent a group of saboteurs ashore in northern Japan in the sub's rubber boats with a scuttling charge and blew up a railroad train. A prisoner of war captured a few days later said the local papers had attributed the disaster to a lucky hit by an airplane. Similarly, when *Barb* was bombarding the north coast of Japan with rockets (the only sub to use them during the war) the locals believed the attacks were coming from Halsey's battleships.

When he came aboard as PCO Gene Fluckey, instead of spending a lot of time in the wardroom playing cribbage, hearts, and gin rummy with the off duty officers, began circulating among the crew. He would ask them to explain their jobs so he could learn more about them and then follow up by questioning them about their life aspirations. When you consider that in World War II about 15,000 men placed their lives in the hands of their submarine's commanding officers (and 22% paid the ultimate price) it was very appealing to an enlisted man to have the captain know who he is.

In writing his book (*Thunder Below!*, 1992, University of Illinois Press) he mentioned the name at least once of nearly everyone who had served with him on *Barb*. After he got command of *Barb* (he was no longer Gene to the officers, but Captain) one of the first things he did was throw the Mast Book over the side, announcing there would be no need for it on *Barb*. There wasn't. Beginning with the *Hunley* in the Civil War, which lost three different crews due to operational mishaps, it became widely recognized that submarines are dangerous to operate, and one mistake by one man can lose the boat. In wartime especially, there was no room for or tolerance of misbehavior while at sea, so the crew became self-enforcers of good, safe conduct.

On the matter of commanding officer personalities, of the living former *Barb* officers, two served only on *Barb* and under Captain Fluckey. One served under *Barb*'s original skipper and Captain Fluckey. My experience was different, in that I made war patrols under five different commanding officers on three different boats. Gene Fluckey was totally unlike the others—all capable men, somewhat austere and rigid, conscious of their rank and not always easy on the nerves. Gene was informal and upbeat in manner. There was something about him that made people feel good to be around him. It was quite common, when people were rotated off *Barb*, particularly those he had worked closely with, for him to thank them for doing a good job and telling them he would like to keep in touch with them after the war—something he actually did. A few did not want to leave *Barb* when they got the call to go back to the States for a new construction submarine. He was generous in the credit he gave to others. Post war, when he was giving speeches around the country, he would say others played significant roles in his military successes. He would say the only thing he ever accomplished all by himself, with no assistance from others, was to win a smile contest when he was ten years old.

One of the post war surprises for all of our military services operating in the Pacific theater was the JANAC report. This stands for Joint Army Navy Assessment Committee. They reevaluated the war based on access to Japanese records. All of the services combined claimed, during the war, to have sunk about three times as many ships as Japan ever had, and the size (tonnage) of the ships claimed sunk was about twice what they actually were. The overestimates during the war were about evenly balanced among the services. The submarines, which according to JANAC sank about 60% of the merchant fleet and nearly 40% of the warships, had claimed to have sunk everything Japan ever had in terms of numbers of ships and gross tonnage.

For a sub skipper to win a Navy Cross, the criteria was to sink four ships on his first patrol and five thereafter. One winner of five Navy Crosses had never sunk more than two ships on any one patrol according to JANAC. There were other ways to win a Navy Cross, such as sinking a battleship or carrier or some other notable accomplishment, such as evacuating MacArthur from the Philippines in a PT boat.

The original skipper of the *Barb* had not sunk an accredited ship prior to Gene Fluckey coming aboard as PCO. (He did damage a tanker belonging to a neutral country by mistake, but that was expunged from the records.) Of the five high awards won by Gene, three were unrelated to the number of ships he sank (sixteen, according to JANAC). One was for the carrier on patrol nine, one for the Nam Kwan Harbor raid, and one for the train destruction and the rocket attacks.

When Gene was given command of Barb after his PCO run, he was one of the least experienced persons to get a command, and Admiral Lockwood (ComSubPac) came out to Midway to look him over. As soon as they met, Gene asked the Admiral how many ships he wanted Gene to sink. When the Admiral did not immediately respond, Gene asked if five would be enough. He then asked what kind of ships the Admiral would like sunk. The Admiral wished him Godspeed and told him to get going. The five ships he sank on that patrol were done in daylight and photographed as they were going down, thus standing up to the JANAC test. No skipper had a better ratio of claims vs. sinkings than Gene. According to JANAC, Gene sank more Japanese tonnage than any other skipper. After the war, Admiral Lockwood wrote in his memoirs that Gene was the only skipper to tell him in advance how many ships he was going to sink and then went out and did it.

The claims to sinkings problem was more prevalent by the Japanese than by U.S. forces. They claimed to have sunk 894 of our subs, whereas we lost only 52, and of those nearly a dozen were not sent down by the Japanese. They were lost to grounding, friendly fire, collision, errant torpedoes and operational error.

Everett P. Weaver
Winnetka, Illinois

Introduction

The U.S.S. *Barb* (SS-220) was laid down on 7 April 1941 at the Electric Boat Company yard on the Thames River in Groton, Connecticut. She was launched on 2 April, sponsored by Mrs. Charles A. Dunn, and commissioned 8 July 1942, under the command of Lieutenant Commander John R. Waterman.

Barb was a *Gato* class fleet type submarine, 311' 9" overall, with a 27' 3" beam, and an average surface draft of 17'. As built, she was armed with a 4"/50 deck gun and ten 21" torpedo tubes, distributed six forward and four aft. In addition to the ten torpedoes in the tubes, *Barb* was designed to carry 14 reloads. She was also armed with machine guns and various small arms.

The *Gato* class boats were the second most numerous class of American submarine in World War II, with 73 commissioned. Their number was exceeded only by the 122 boats of the *Balao* class, which was essentially a *Gato* with a tougher pressure hull, allowing an extra 100 feet of rated diving depth, and an extremely cut down conning tower fairwater to minimize surface silhouette.

Following shakedown and training, *Barb* was assigned to SubRon 50, based at Rosneath, Scotland. Her initial patrol was taken up with reconnaissance and serving as a beacon submarine for Operation Torch, the Allied landings in North Africa. This initial patrol was under U.S. control, after which the squadron was placed under the operational control of the Royal Navy's Flag Officer (Submarines).

Barb made a total of five war patrols with SubRon 50. Four of these were under Waterman's command. Patrol number four was made under the command of Nicholas Lucker, Jr., one of the squadron's staff officers, who took temporary command as part of a squadron rest program for commanding officers. Lucker's patrol was in Norwegian waters. The other patrols were conducted primarily in the Bay of Biscay, mostly off Spain. *Barb* made only one attack during the European deployment, unfortunately against a Spanish tanker, which was mistaken for a German ship. While it was believed by the crew that the tanker had been sunk, she actually made it into port.

The entire episode was removed from the patrol report, and the Spanish, when they protested to the British, were simply told that no British submarine was involved. True enough, though the implication of the denial—that it was probably a German submarine—obviously wasn't. The deleted portion of the patrol report, retained in Admiralty files in London, remained classified until the 1970s.

Barb's record in SubRon 50 was typical for the squadron, which conducted numerous patrols to little effect. There was simply not enough German shipping in the Atlantic to provide worthwhile opportunities for the big American submarines. During her fifth patrol, *Barb* was ordered back to the United States. After refitting in Groton, she was sent to the Pacific.

Waterman made two more patrols out of Pearl Harbor, after which he moved up to a Division command. He was replaced by Lieutenant Commander Eugene B. Fluckey, a 1935 Naval Academy graduate. Fluckey was in command during *Barb*'s last five war patrols. During the course of five patrols, Fluckey earned four Navy Crosses and the Medal of Honor, in the process sinking 25 Japanese ships (reduced to 16 1/3 by JANAC), for a total of 179,700 tons (95,360 tons JANAC).

After the war ended, Fluckey served in a number of important posts, including Commander SubDiv 52. Promoted to rear admiral in 1960, he then served as Commander Amphibious Group 4, and Commander, Submarines, Pacific. He retired in 1972. Fluckey Hall at the Navy submarine Combat Systems Training Center at the Submarine Base, New London, is named after Admiral Fluckey, the only building on the base to be named after a living person. His Medal of Honor and four Navy Crosses make him the most highly decorated living American.

♦   ♦   ♦

The editorial process involved in producing the published version of *Barb*'s twelve war patrols is relatively straightforward. The microfiche copies of the original mimeographed reports are transcribed into a commercial typesetting program, where they may be edited. My editorial policy is generally to do as little as necessary to produce a readable book. Obvious typographical and spelling errors are corrected, though I generally leave spelling idiosyncrasies alone. Thus, in several reports "en route" is spelled "enroute," as it appeared in the originals. Some words that were abbreviated in the original, such as "yds." for "yards," and "ft." for "feet," are generally spelled out in full in the body text, but left as is in tables.

Numerous footnotes have been added, where it was thought necessary to explain or define references in the reports that would be familiar enough to World War II submariners, but not necessarily so to modern readers. These include things such as explaining the American code names for various Japanese aircraft, and various fittings and pieces of equipment found in submarines. For this volume, we also include a Foreword by former *Barb* officer Tuck Weaver.

> J.T. McDaniel, series editor
> American Submarine War Patrol Reports
> 1 December 2005
> Riverdale, Georgia

Patrol One, 20 October 1942 – 25 November 1942

SS220/A16
Serial (026)

U.S.S. *Barb*
c/o Fleet Post Office
New York, New York

C-O-N-F-I-D-E-N-T-I-A-L   November 26, 1942.

From: The Commanding Officer.
To: The Commander Submarine Squadron Fifty.

Subject: First War Patrol – Report of.

References: (a) Comsubron 50 Conf. ltr. FC5-50/A16(4)
                    Serial 061 of November 24, 1942.

Enclosure: (A) Subject Report.

1. In accordance with Reference (a), Enclosure (A) is forwarded herewith.

                                J.R. Waterman

DECLASSIFIED - ART. 0445, OPNAVINST 5510.IC
BY OP-09B9C   **DATE** 5/23/72

SS220/A16   U.S.S. Barb
Serial (026)   c/o Postmaster,
                          New York, N.Y.

CONFIDENTIAL   November 25, 1942.

Report of First War Patrol – Period Oct. 20, 1942 to Nov. 25, 1942.

PROLOGUE

Commissioned July 9, 1942. Conducted training operations in vicinity of New London, Conn. until departure on patrol. This period included forty-seven operating days, a twelve day docking, and a three week engine overhaul for renewal of crankshaft and replacement of all cylinder liners with chromium plated liners, followed by a run in period.

1. NARRATIVE

October 20, 1942 – November 5, 1942 – Uneventful except as noted.

2200 Queen[1], 20th – Took departure seven miles east of Montauk Point.

0230 Queen, 21st – Radar contact bearing 216° relative[2] at 14,000 yards. Range increased and bearing moved aft.

0130 Queen, 22nd – Radar contact bearing 036° at 10,000 yards. Bearing moved aft and contact lost at 16,000 yards.
Encountered heavy head seas, which continued until October 27, 1942.

0335 October 27th – Radar contact bearing 020° relative at 5,200 yards in rain squall. Range decreased to 2,900 yards and was lost in direction of rain squall. No sight contact.

0325 October 28th – Sighted smoke on port bow and discerned masts of steamer on opposite course passing abeam hull down.

---

[1] Queen: Navy time zone "Q," or Greenwich Mean Time minus 4 hours. The U.S. Atlantic time zone.

[2] Sightings and radar bearings can be given as either Relative or True. Relative bearings are based on the ship's bow being 000°, with the bearing angle relative to that constant. This is usually the most convenient way to report a sighting, as it allows the report to be made without the necessity of referring to a compass. True bearings report the target's actual compass bearing from the ship, without regard for the viewer's own ship's bearing. True bearing are most commonly used in written reports, after conversion from relative bearings.

1917 November 4th – Surfaced and sighted very bright lights of two vessels astern about one mile. They had not been heard on sound gear or seen during periscope sweep prior to surfacing. Submerged at 1918 and inspected. Decided lights were on fishing craft and surfaced at 1930 and proceeded.

Night of November [4]th

Approaching Safi[3] on surface by D.F[4]. No accurate fix for two days. Heavy rain, rough sea.

Sighted vessel showing two bright all around lights in estimated position 15 miles west of Safi. Assumed to be station ship, but not subsequently located.

November 5th

Submerged in rough sea at 60 fathom curve and proceeded eastward. Sea rising, making depth control at periscope depth uncertain.

After sunrise tentatively identified Cape Kantin, Square Tower on Point de la Tour, and town of Safi. Cut using these fixed position six miles north west of Safi.

Increasing southwest seas, scattered clouds, high southwest wind prevented repeated periscope observations from being successful. Withdrew westward until noon. Reversed course and closed shore in heavy rain. Visibility one mile. Continued eastward until water shoaled. Reversed course and repeated for remainder of daylight. Rain continued and visibility reduced to 300 yards. Surfaced after dark in heavy rain and rough sea. Weather cleared and sea abated about 2100. Fix obtained.

Observed numerous lighted craft proceeding on southerly courses. Observed beam of searchlight in vicinity of Cape Kantin repeatedly transmitting letters "VA."

Proceeded southwest to a position ten miles west of Safi.

November 6th

Submerged at 0440 and proceeded east at periscope depth.

Identified Cape Kantin Lighthouse and Square Tower. Safi obscured by glare of sun directly behind.

Weather clear, light westerly wind, slight chop, low long swell, ground haze.

Cleared Safi Harbor and observed breakers on breakwater. No activity evident. No ships visible in harbor.

Set 075 drift, .45 knots on flood tide. Gun battery observed on Point de la Tour. Maintained position off Safi, off shore. Conducted practice approach.

---

[3] The city of Safi is located on Morocco's west (Atlantic) coast, about 125 miles south of Casablanca.

[4] DF: Direction finder. *Barb* was homing in on a radio station in Safi.

1330 Commenced closing Safi Harbor. Tide ebbing, set 210° true, drift .6 knots.

No evidence of net or boom tender. Harbor appears bare of shipping. Took still and motion pictures. Remained in vicinity of Safi until after dark to identify any light which may show.

Loss of one day due to rain does not leave sufficient time to reach Jorf el Mahudi at slow speed submerged. Long range observation, six miles, shows no activity. Surf and shoals as elsewhere on coast.

At 1300 sighted large liner approaching from south west on course 046° at 8½ knots. About three miles off shore she hoisted calls letters, changed course to 350° true and proceeded past Cape Kantin. Vessel was black and white with red trim and had large French flags painted on sides. No escorts. The movements of this vessel seem to be conclusive evidence of the lack of any mine fields in the immediate vicinity of Safi.

Just prior to sunset sighted two vessels approaching from the southwest. Appeared to be a 20,000, 2 stack liner with a trawler type escort. Course 030° true, speed 10 knots. Passed between liner and escort and identified as *Porthos* (15,500 tons)[5]. Prepared to surface when sound reported ship crossing astern. Distinguished another large vessel crossing astern about 2,000 yards. On surfacing sighted five smaller vessels on various bearings. All seemed to proceed on northeasterly courses past Cape Kantin.

Proceeded westward to put in battery charge. All navigational aids and town lights of Safi blacked out. Searchlight on Cape Kantin again active. Searchlight on Point de la Tour also active transmitting letters "SC."

An additional five vessels sighted during night. All on northerly courses and showing lights. All coastal shipping appears to pass five to eight miles off shore.

November 7th

Submerged at 0520 and closed Safi.

Weather clear, slight chop and low swells.

At 1205 observed 5,000 ton merchant vessel under way from Safi Harbor. Vessel emerged on course 270° true for about one mile, changed course to 292° true. This vessel must have been alongside the east-west dock in Safi and was therefore not visible from seaward. Identified by name on side "*Sac Z Espana*" but flags appeared to be Austrian.

At 1300 took course 310° to assume position for approach to night station.

---

[5] *Barb* was patrolling off Safi in preparation for Operation Torch, the Allied invasion of North Africa, where she was to serve as a beacon ship for the Safi invasion force. The diplomatic situation, with the Allies hoping that the Vichy French forces in Morocco would change sides once confronted by the invasion force, precluded making any attacks on shipping in *Barb*'s patrol area, as did security considerations.

SS *Porthos* was en route to Casablanca. Her reprieve was only temporary, as she would be sunk at her berth alongside the Môle during the invasion.

At 1530 sighted fishing drifter of about 200 tons on a northerly course. Passed close aboard.

At 1830 observed a string of about seven white lights in Safi Harbor. Estimated to be on warehouse on north side of harbor. Also one white light which appeared to be on white tower in center of town.

Night of November 7th
Surfaced at 1915 and started battery charge.

About 2100 assumed station on point JR 2.6 miles from Point de la Tour. Eight to ten lights showing in town of Safi. Identified position of brightness and used as navigational aid to maintain station.

At 2338 disembarked Lieutenant Duckworth[6], U.S. Army, and scouts. Followed movement of rubber boat by radar until well clear. Rigged infra-red lamp and started transmission.

During period 2300 to 0400 made a sight or sound contact with numerous units, which formed rough semi-circle around *Barb*, distance 200 yards to 6,000 yards to seaward. It appeared as though ships were taking bombardment stations from our position.

0330 Identified assault boats proceeding shoreward.

0427 Bombardment commenced. Answering fire from shore. Continued infra-red transmissions.

0450 Two large caliber shells exploded close astern. Observed several aircraft overhead burning navigation lights—too large to be ship based. Gunfiring to seaward. Observed ship bombed and burning.

0530 Secured infra-red transmissions.

0537 Ahead 2/3 on all engines.

0550 All hands on bridge observed glow which appeared to be tracers heading toward us from our own ships. In same line of sight there was a series of blinding flashes. Submerged. Periscope observations all clear.

0555 Surfaced. Proceeded on course 340° true gradually increasing speed.

0603 Observed U.S.S. *New York* on converging course. Exchanged recognition signals and informed of our intention to submerge to northward.

0628 Passed between two patrolling destroyers and changed course to west.

0536 Submerged and proceeded clear of area. U.S.S. *New York* observed continuing bombardment. Explosions and smoke columns on Point de la Tour. During forenoon numerous explosions were heard through the hull. These were of

---

6   Lieutenant Willard G. Duckworth and four Army scouts were put off in a rubber boat, at a position *Barb* had determined to be 3½ miles off shore. The fix proved to be inaccurate and the scouts had to paddle nearly seven miles to reach shore. It took them six hours to reach the breakwater, by which time the bombardment had started. Duckworth and his men survived, but they never reached their assigned position and their backup had to handle their assigned task.

varying intensity, but more appeared close. Destroyer pinging on constant bearing astern. Finally disappeared on 201° relative.

1914 Surfaced and proceeded to patrol station.

2130 Radar contact astern 12,000 yards. About four vessels. Range decreased and drew aft. Identified as friendly through reception of muffled TBS[7] transmission. Increased speed and continued course.

2325 Sighted lighted merchant vessel hull down on northerly course. Assumed neutral and continued course.

November 9th

Arrived on patrol station at 0300. Sighted lights of fishing craft enroute. Submerged at 0333 and conducted periscope patrol on east-west courses from six miles off Cape Sim to fourteen miles off Cape Sim. Nothing sighted. Surfaced at 1910 and conducted patrol at 5 knots on north-south courses. Sighted numerous lighted craft. Closed first two and investigated. Identified as small fishing trawlers or drifters. Decided to keep clear of others sighted in order to remain undetected.

November 10th and 14th

Conducted periscope patrol during daylight. Uneventful except:

November 12th at 0200 Received Comtaskfor 34 secret despatch 111918.

November 12th at 2400 Received Comtaskfor 34.11 confidential despatch HS 462 2349Z/11.

November 14th at about 0230 and 0430 Received Comsubron 50 despatches HS 496 1201 Z/13 and HS 497 1219 E/13 respectively.

November 14th at 0330 departed Patrol Station for Base.

November 14th to 17th

Uneventful.

November 18th

Proceeding at 17 knots in heavy swells endeavoring to comply with Flag Officer, Submarines British 2141 A/17.

At 1150 lookout reported searchlight signals dead astern. OOD[8] discerned vessel, which he tentatively identified as U.S. Submarine. Received correct challenge and gave reply and counter challenge. No reply and vessel lost to view. Slowed to 2/3 speed to allow him to overtake. Had occasional glimpses of him astern. Rain set in and when it cleared one hour later vessel was no longer in

---

[7] TBS: Talk Between Ships. A low powered voice radio intended for short range communication between vessels operating together.

[8] OOD: Officer of the Deck. The officer in charge of the operation and navigation of the ship during a particular watch. Assisted by the JOOD (Junior Officer of the Deck).

sight. Resumed speed.

At 2121 obtained fix through rifts in clouds and found it impossible to comply with Flag Officer, Submarines British 2159 A/18. Transmitted *Barb* 2221 Z/18 and slowed to ten knots. During most of the day and night we had been making turns for 17 knots into a head sea. Speed through the water averaged 14 knots. Due to the pounding main ballast tanks gradually filled and the low pressure blower[9] had to be used every two hours.

November 19th
Commenced daylight submergence and surface running at night. FO S/M 1634 A/19 received at 2000. Increased speed to 17 knots (rpm). FO S/M 0334 A/19 (received at 0400 19th), but not addressed to this vessel, was decoded after submergence on 20 November in accordance with FO S/M 1241 A/19, which was received on 20 November.

November 20th
Continued submerged as FO S/M 0334 A/19 was then over a day old and surface running in present position is not considered feasible.

At 1015 heard loud roar through hull, which sounded like a torpedo passing overhead. This occurred again at 1145 and changed to a series of heavy thumps at 1400. Periscope search revealed nothing. Concluded that noise was caused by subterranean disturbance. This continued throughout the afternoon.

November 21st
At 2120 sighted small lighted merchant vessel. Identified as *City of Antwerp*. Did not molest.

November 22nd
Uneventful.

November 23rd
Contacted H.M. Trawler *Silsdean* ten miles south of Lizards Head and escorted towards Falmouth. Transferred to escort of H.M. Sloop *U-92* with U.S.S. *Shad* and U.S.S. *Herring* in company, proceeding to Base II, Rosneath, Scotland.

November 24th
__1933 Ancho__red Rothesay Bay.

[9] A fleet type submarine's low pressure blower was a Roots type compressor (similar to a race car supercharger), with a standard output pressure of ten pounds. This was used to complete the blowing of ballast tanks after the submarine was on the surface. Initial blowing of ballast was with high pressure air stored in the submarine's air banks, which had to be replenished. Using the low pressure blower conserved the HP air in the air banks, reducing the amount of time needed to replenish them.

November 25th
  Arrived Base II, Rosneath, Scotland.

2. WEATHER

The weather in general was excellent in the patrol area except for the particularly rough seas and rain encountered the first day on station.
Visibility was exceptional and stars appeared brighter than normal.
Westerly winds were the rule.
Long swells caused too great a periscope exposure when in the trough.

3. TIDAL INFORMATION

During ebb tide the set is along the Moroccan coast in a general southerly direction and the drift average about .5 knots. During flood tide the set shifts to eastward.

4. NAVIGATIONAL AIDS

Chart soundings in the Patrol Area are not considered accurate enough to be relied upon. All navigational lights blacked out. Silhouette sketches in Coast Pilot are antiquated as towns have grown considerably since sketches were made.
The Navigator, Lieutenant [illegible] Lawrence, U.S. Navy, did an exceptional job under adverse conditions. The bubble octant is of doubtful value, although not given a fair try. Satisfactory results were obtained using a high grade sextant for night sights.

5. DESCRIPTION OF ENEMY VESSELS SIGHTED

None.

6. DESCRIPTION OF AIRCRAFT SIGHTED

  a. 6 aircraft over task force at Safi. Not identified due to darkness.
  b. Aircraft of all types in vicinity of Falmouth and enroute to Clyde Area, none enemy.

7. PARTICULARS OF ATTACKS

None.

8. ENEMY ANTI-SUBMARINE MEASURES

None.

9. DESCRIPTION OF ENEMY MINE-SWEEPING OPERATIONS

None.

10. MAJOR DEFECTS EXPERIENCED

No major defects were experienced.

Minor defects consisted primarily of trouble with sound gear training gear equipment including a burned out armature in QC[10] training motor.

Attached salt water circulating pump on #3 main engine gave evidence of fore and aft motion of impeller shaft. This engine was kept in reserve from 18 November awaiting thorough investigation of trouble.

7 out of 11 pairs of binoculars had loose prisms and all 11 flooded when used in heavy weather. This was a serious handicap but was partially overcome by disassembly and repair aboard.

Automatic by-pass valve in hydraulic manifold stuck open a number of times. Disassembled and found frozen dash pot plunger. Freed and returned to use.

Radar operation was excellent. No major defects experienced.

Radio transmitter generator pilot circuit has a 240 volt ground, but operation not affected. Decided to await return to disassemble and repair.

Search light bracket carried away submerged. Light lost.

11. RADIO RECEPTION

Radio reception was poor in the African area due to static but improved steadily as we proceeded north.

12. SOUND CONDITIONS AND DENSITY LAYERS

No density layers were encountered. Sound reception was poor with maximum JK reception of propeller sounds at 3,550 yards. Echo ranging was not used.

---

[10] The JK/QC sonar head was mounted on a retractable shaft on the port side of the keel. The JK half was listening only; the QC half was capable of active pinging. The active QB head was mounted on the starboard side of the keel, also on a retractable shaft. The shafts and training motors were located in the forward torpedo room, just forward of the after bulkhead. The remote controls and receiver/amplifier units for the JK/QC and QB sonar were located in the conning tower.

13. HEALTH AND HABITABILITY

Health and habitability were excellent. Air conditioning kept the boat comfortable but made sound reception difficult. Units were secured when cruising below periscope depth.

Common colds were entirely absent but chronic seasickness was more or less prevalent, causing the vomiting of blood in one case.

On the 14th day of the patrol one man developed a throat infection that in two days swelled the membranes of the throat to such an extent that swallowing of any solid food was impossible. Temperature ranged from one to two degrees of elevation. Sulfathiazole therapy and mouth washes of diluted vinegar at regular intervals were used effectively and two days later temperature returned to normal. Condition of throat was greatly improved and one week after initial symptoms recovery was complete.

The following cases were treated.

NUMBER OF CASES	CAUSE	DAYS LOST
2	Boils	0
5	Lacerations	0
24	Constipation	0
15	Headache	0
2	Urethritis	0
7	Colds	0
2	Gingivitis	0
1	Ringworm	0
1	Infection, Throat	3
2	Burns, 2nd degree	0
1	Toothache	0
9	Fungus Infection	0
3	Seasickness (Acute)	1
	Total days lost due to sickness	4

14. MILES STEAMED SURFACE AND SUBMERGED

710 miles submerged
6,499 miles surfaced

15. FUEL OIL EXPENDED

67,245 gallons

16. FACTORS OF ENDURANCE REMAINING

>Fuel – 20 days.
>Provisions – 40 days.
>Personnel – Indefinite

17. FACTORS OF ENDURANCE CAUSING END OF PATROL

>None. Recalled by order of Comtaskfor 34.

18. REMARKS

It is considered that the use of submarines in landing operations has infinite possibilities, however, the value of reconnaissance conducted just prior to the assault phase is believed to have negative value only. The fact that no messages were transmitted was an indication to the Force Commander that there were no changes of major importance and the presence of the beacon submarine on station was proof that mine fields did not exist. Other information compiled, including pictures, would be of little value in current operations when received so late.

Communications difficulties caused most trouble and worry. During submerged patrol despatches were normally received from 36 to 48 hours after time of origin. The code in use is cumbersome and takes too long to decode.

In attempting to transmit acknowledgements of CSS 50 1219E/13 November it was impossible to raise Gibraltar or Whitehall and message was finally broadcast. In order to transmit *Barb* 2202 16th November Gibraltar and Whitehall were called repeatedly from 2230 – 16th November to 1510 – 17th November. At this time decided to place "O" (Urgent) in call up. Received immediate answer. During the period 15th and 17th many hours were spent looking for transmitter trouble. Excessive work, worry and transmissions were caused. A more efficient and direct method of communication with submarines would be highly welcome.

Trimming down on very dark nights is considered of doubtful value. The considerable increase in phosphorescence caused by the swells breaking through the deck over compensates for the reduction in silhouette.

Sub-Lieutenant F. Bradley, RNVR, was a distinct addition to the wardroom. He was a considerable help with communications as well as watch standing. His performance of duty was of the highest order, and his continued presence aboard is desirable.

It is recommended that the efforts of Lieutenant W. Duckworth, U.S. Army, and the Army scouts be recognized by the Navy as considered appropriate.

Length of patrol 33 days, of which 24 days were spent submerged and 11 days surfaced.

Editor's Note: Endorsements for this patrol report are not available.

Patrol Two, 16 December 1942 – 18 January 1943

SS220/A16　　　　　　U.S.S. *Barb* (SS220)
Serial (01)　　　　　　c/o Fleet Post Office
　　　　　　　　　　　New York, New York

U.S CONFIDENTIAL – BRITISH SECRET　　　　　　　　January 18, 1943
C-O-N-F-I-D-E-N-T-I-A-L

From:　　　　　The Commanding Officer.
To:　　　　　　The Commander Submarine Squadron Fifty.

Subject:　　　Report of the Second War Patrol of the U.S.S. Barb. Period from December 16, 1942 to January 18, 1943.

Reference:　　(a) Comsubron Fifty Conf. ltr. Serial 061 of November 24, 1942.

Enclosure:　　(A) Report of the Second War Patrol of the U.S.S. Barb. Period from December 16, 1942 to January 18, 1943. Area – Vigo, Spain. Operation Order CSS 50-4-42.

　　1. In accordance with reference (a) enclosure (A) is submitted herewith.

　　　　　　　　　　　　　　J.R. Waterman

PROLOGUE

The period since last patrol was spent at Base II for upkeep, overhaul, provisioning, leave and recreation. Most of the work was accomplished by the ship's force with assistance rendered by U.S.S. *Beaver*[1], tender.

1. NARRATIVE

December 16, 1942

1156 Underway from Base II in accordance with Comsubron 50 Operation Order 4-42 in gale of gradually increasing intensity. Formed on escort HMS *Sardonx*[2], U.S.S. *Herring* in company, proceeding to point of departure 12 miles south of Bishop Rock. Heavy gale continued throughout the night.

December 17, 1942

1328 In approximate position 51-30 N., 05-02.45 W., sighted large floating mine about 300 yards on starboard bow. Maneuvered to avoid and fired 20 MM in direction of mine to indicate position to U.S.S. *Herring*. Could not depress gun sufficiently to explode mine and suggested to escort that *Barb* return and accomplish this. Was advised not to do so by escort.

December 18, 1942

0010 Parted company with HMS *Sardonyx* and U.S.S. *Herring* and took route as ordered by FOS 1504, 12 December 1942. Attempting to make good 15 knots into heavy head seas. At this time sighted white airplane flare dead ahead. During next four hours approximately thirty flares were seen in the same general position and numerous planes were observed overhead. Concluded planes were exercising and held course and speed.

December 19, 1942

0800 Bombing restriction in area expired. Submerged five miles outside next area. Gale continued and depth control at periscope depth very difficult. Surfaced after twilight—seas undiminished. Proceeded at 16 knots, making good 12-13 knots.

---

[1] U.S.S. *Beaver* (AS-5), was built by Newport News Shipbuilding and Drydock Company in 1909, and purchased by the Navy in 1917. She was converted for use as a submarine tender by Mare Island and commissioned on 1 October 1918. She served as tender for SubRon 50 at Rosneath from October 1942 until July 1943.

[2] HMS *Sardonyx* was an old S Class destroyer, built in 1919 by Alexander Stephen & Sons, Glasgow. She was scrapped in October 1945.

December 20, 1942
Still unable to maintain periscope depth at less than standard speed. About 1000 heard two distant detonations. Surfaced at twilight and proceeded at best speed (making good a very uncomfortable 13 knots).

December 21, 1942
Uneventful.

December 22, 1942
Approaching patrol area on surface.
0216 Sighted lighted craft on southerly course. Closed to 3,000 yards and identified as trawler type vessel.
0415 – 0420 Sighted lights of ships close together, distant about seven miles and on northerly courses respectively. Closed to final range of 4,000 yards and tentatively identified as *Castillo Bellver* and *Marquis De Urquijo*. Reference FOS 1428 – 20 December (RS 525). Moon was full and passing squalls made visibility vary from bad to exceptional. Identified Cape Finisterre Light, Cape Corrubedo Light, and Point Carreiro Lights. Obtained fix and continued toward patrol point. Submerged at 0738. Conducting submerged patrol with observations every 15 to 30 minutes.
1355 Sound contact bearing 300° relative, fast screw drawing aft. Identified as 100 ton trawler. Unable to close sufficiently to determine nationality.
1751 Sighted drifter standing toward Vigo at 7 knots and carrying Spanish flag.
1932 Surfaced in bright moonlight. Sighted two lighted fishing vessels distant three and seven miles respectively and bearing 050° true and 322° true. Put closer vessel astern and observed second vessel until identified. Both still toward Vigo.
2228 Sighted lights of 4 small craft between bearing 078° true and 081° true on southerly courses. Unable to draw sufficiently to positively identify.
2332 Sighted lights of vessel hull down bearing 059° true. Identified as fishing craft.

December 23, 1942
0040 Sighted lighted fishing craft rounding Cape Finisterre.
0600 Sighted lighted trawler bearing 098° true. We were silhouetted against bright moon and submerged at 0609 to escape detection. Vessel passed on southwesterly course. Spanish colors were illuminated.
1015 Sighted motor sailing ketch crossing astern. Photographed it at one mile.
1124 Sighted sailing vessel at long range.
1931 Surfaced.
2010 Sighted fishing vessel.

2109 Sighted lighted ship bearing 044° true—8 miles. Went ahead standard speed and drew ahead so that ship would cross in bright moon path. Identified as Spanish by illuminated colors but could not read name. Vessel was approximately 3,000 tons and probably *Cabo Caovera* (FOS HS 461/22).

December 24, 1942

0137 Radar contact ahead at 6,000 yards. Closed to investigate and sighted a large trawler with dim lights.

0147 Sighted lighted ship on northerly course and commenced surface approach. Identified as steamer of about 3,000 tons with illuminated colors, probably *Miere* (FOS HS 451/22). During approach sighted a small steamer or trawler and two lighted fishing craft, which greatly interfered with undetected approach.

0600 Sighted lighted ship on northerly course and commenced approach. Sighted lighted fishing craft between us and ship. Closed slowly and failed to positively identify, but ship carried same illuminated markings as other sighted. Broke off approach due to beginning of twilight and submerged at 0735 and conducted periscope patrol. No sightings during daylight. Surfaced at 1929 and commenced patrolling parallel to shipping lane.

1950 Sighted small craft ahead. This craft seemed to patrol or fish in the same spot and was still present in the morning.

2107 Sighted lights of ship bearing 120° true on northerly course. Proceeded to investigate. Identified as *Babo Ortegal* (FOS 1749/A24).

2126 Sighted lights of ship bearing 019° true on southerly course. Commenced approach as vessel first appeared to be a tanker. Paced to obtain course and speed.

December 25, 1942

0029 Identified ship as *Gayarre* (FOS 1749/24) and broke off approach.

0421 Sighted ship on westerly course north of Cape Finisterre. Answered description of *Zorroza* (FOS 1749A/24).

0731 Submerged with three small craft in sight.

1040 Sighted 150 ton drifter crossing astern. Photographed.

1931 Surfaced and commenced surface patrol along shipping lane in vicinity of patrol point.

2046 Sighted lighted trawler bearing 016° true.

2145 Sighted lighted small vessel bearing 083° true.

2150 Sighted lighted small vessel bearing 036° true.

2205 Sighted lighted small vessel bearing 141° true.

2259 Sighted lighted small vessel bearing 324° true.

December 26, 1942

0008 Sighted two ships bearing 030° true, one small vessel and one steamer. Commenced approach. Steamer proceeded to westward of shipping lane on southerly course and therefore appeared suspicious. Trailed to determine course and speed until 0156, at which time it was decided that his tonnage was considerably less than 2,500 so broke off approach and returned to patrol lane.

0045 Sighted ship on northerly course, but did not identify due to fact we were trailing first ship.

0300 Sighted small ship bearing 153° true.

0535 Sighted small ship bearing 062° true.

0540 Sighted small ship bearing 039° true.

0600 Sighted about ten trawlers or fishing vessels on various courses and bearings.

0641 Submerged to escape detection.

0742 Sound contact — trawler lights.

0750 Sound contact — trawler lights.

Remained in contact with from two to six craft until 0910 (sunrise). Came to periscope depth and sighted six trawlers on various bearings and courses, all within 2,500 yards. Put nearest astern and drew clear. The tactics of these craft indicated some sort of crude sound screen, similar to that described in S.I.S., as they seemed to work in pairs on perpendicular courses. Details of craft could not be ascertained due to fogged periscope, but believe I saw Spanish flag.

1450 Sighted smoke bearing 343° true and drawing to westward. Commenced approach.

1530 Identified as trawler and broke off approach.

1929 Surfaced.

> **Editor's Note:** At 2313 on 26 December, *Barb* fired two torpedoes at what was believed to be a German tanker in position 41°55.5 N., 09° 00 W. Missing with this salvo, *Barb* fired another torpedo at 2314 and hit the tanker in the stern. The tanker was down by the stern, and *Barb* attempted to finish her off with a fourth torpedo at 2327. Instead of finishing off the tanker, the torpedo made a circular run and very nearly hit the submarine.
>
> Unfortunately for *Barb* and Waterman, the ship proved to be the Spanish tanker *Campomanes*. The story has come down that *Camponanes* was sunk in this attack, but in fact she made it into Vigo. The entire record of the attack was excised from the patrol report, and when Spanish authorities protested the attack to the British, the British responded (truthfully) that none of their submarines had been involved, but neglected to mention any possible American role. The hope, presumably, was that the Spanish would conclude a German boat was the culprit.

December 27, 1942

0445 SD[3] contact 19 miles, closed to 13 miles.

---

[3] SD radar was an omni-directional air warning radar. The SD unit gave the target's range, but could not provide a bearing to the target. Localization of the target still depended upon visual sighting.

0621 SD contact 19 miles, closed to 15 miles.
0709 Submerged about forty miles from patrol point. An uneventful day.
1930 Surfaced.

December 28, 1942
0550 Sighted small craft bearing 108° true.
0715 Submerged. Surfaced 1929. Uneventful.
2035 Sighted lights of small vessel.
2156 Sighted lights of small vessel.
2220 Sighted lights of two small vessels.

December 29, 1942
0023 Sighted lights of small vessel.
0025 Sighted lights of ship; commenced approach. Identified as small Spanish steamer. Broke off approach.
0512 SD radar contact which moved in rapidly to five miles. Submerged. During night there had been three other contacts, but they had not moved in closer than 12 miles.
0730 Sound contact 047° relative. Periscope search revealed nothing. Bearing drew aft and suddenly disappeared at 110° relative.
1009 Sound contact bearing 062° relative. Periscope search revealed nothing, but visibility was not good. Put contact astern. Bearing remained constant and was very loud. Commenced evasive tactics, running silent. Went to 110 and attempted to get on estimated beam of target. Considered possibility of target being submerged U-boat and planned to maneuver until continued change of bearing was obtained, then fire sound shot. These maneuvers continued until 1245, when sound suddenly disappeared. At the same time sound of our own propellers could no longer be heard, indicating abrupt change in sound conditions. This contact was definitely propeller beats at 90 RPM and the intensity did not vary over a period of two hours. We were definitely being trailed and were unable to turn the tables and reach a firing position. Continued running silent for another thirty minutes and then came up for observation. Nothing in sight.
1930 Surfaced and set course for Cape Finisterre.
2238 Sighted lights of three vessels on northerly courses. Vessels quite small so did not approach.
2236 Sighted lights of two vessels on northerly courses.
2344 Sighted lights of two vessels on northerly course. Commenced approach. Small Spanish steamers.

December 30, 1942
0151 – 0540 Sighted lights of seven vessels. Five were fishing craft and two steamers. These approached until Spanish colors were readily discernable and

the approach was broken off. In so doing we were boxed in by small craft and possibly sighted in moon path. One of these small craft appears to be in the same approximate position every night and cruises around on various courses. He does not appear to be fishing and may be a Spanish patrol, however he is quite close to point QQ and has managed to add to the difficulties of a number of our approaches.

0706 Submerged. Patrolling through QQ on north and south courses. The sea has made up considerably and periscope observations will be difficult.

1223 Sound contact dead ahead drawing slightly to starboard. Periscope observation revealed nothing but high seas prevented satisfactory observation. Contact making 90 RPM sounded very close and suddenly stopped. Not subsequently heard. During afternoon heard a number of loud rumbles as if large volume of air were escaping. These can best be described as sounding like gigantic belches.

1930 Surfaced.

2303 Sighted lights of vessel on northerly course. Commenced approach. Broke off when vessel was seen to be quite small.

December 31, 1942

0014 Sighted lights of fishing craft.

0235 Sighted lights of vessel on northerly course. Commenced approach.

0335 Identified as neutral. Broke off approach.

0600 Sighted small ship on southerly course. Did not approach.

0640 SD radar contact moving in rapidly. Submerged.

1018 Sound contact 090° relative. Sighted trawler at 3,800 yards. Crossing astern.

1625 Sighted steamer bearing 315° true. Commenced approach. At 2,500 yards identified as Spanish steamer of about 2,500 tons, probably *Simancas*. Broke off approach.

1630 Received FOS 1512A/31.

1927 Surfaced and proceeded at 15 knots en route to new position.

1950 Sighted small steamer on southerly course.

2020 Sighted small steamer on southerly course.

January 1, 1943

1100 Arrived on station and commenced surface patrol to west in accordance with FOS despatch 0719A/1.

1250 Reversed course as directed in FOS 1151A/1.

1600 Increased to full speed.

1625 SD contact moving in rapidly. Submerged to 100 feet.

1650 Sound reported fast screws astern. Sighted Sunderland[4] flying boat

---

[4] The Short Sunderland was a large, four-engine maritime patrol aircraft, and was used extensively for anti-submarine patrols. Sunderlands had an endurance rating of 20 hours, and

astern. At same time sighted HMS *Scylla*[5] on slightly diverging course, overtaking at 28 knots.

1651 HMS Scylla passed close aboard to port.
1712 Surfaced.
1834 SD contact moving in rapidly. Submerged.
1846 Surfaced.
1849 Submerged when plane returned.
1910 In attempting to extend SD mast while submerged depth control was lost and we came up to about 35 feet. At this time periscope observation revealed bright blinking light on our port beam. Regained depth control and ran silent. No sound contact. Assumed to be either friendly submarine or U-boat, which submerged.
1924 Surfaced with nothing in sight. Continued at full speed.
2016 Sighted flash of light on port quarter covering large area and well over the horizon.
2037 Abandoned search in accordance with FOS despatch 1923A/1 and stood towards Vigo at 16 knots.

January 2, 1943
0435 SD contact. Did not close to less than 11 miles.
0705 Submerged in patrol area, proceeding toward Vigo. Uneventful.
1927 Surfaced.
2113 Sighted small vessel on northerly course.
2124 Sighted lights of vessel on southerly course. Commenced approach. Identified as neutral.
2235 Sighted lights of vessel on southerly course. Commenced approach. Identified as less than 1,500 tons.

January 3, 1943
0140 Sighted lights of vessel on southerly course. Commenced approach. Identified as neutral.
0310 Sighted lights of vessel on southerly course. Commenced approach. Identified as less than 1,500 tons.
0412 Sighted small vessel on southerly course.
0514 Sighted two fishing craft on southerly course.
0704 Submerged.

---

could carry up to 2½ tons of ordnance in the form of bombs and depth charges. Starting in 1940 all were radar equipped. Prudence dictated diving even for "friendly" aircraft unless the submarine's captain could be assured that the pilot knew who he was. At least one American submarine, *Dorado*, is believed to have been sunk by friendly aircraft.

[5] HMS *Scylla* was a Dido class light cruiser, commission 22 June 1942. Her active service ended when she hit a mine off Normandy on 23 June 1944. Later used as a target, *Scylla* was scrapped in 1950.

1105 Sighted small steamer of about 500 tons on easterly course.
1520 Sighted steamer of about 1,500 tons on northerly course.
1806 Sighted two trawlers using same tactics as those of December 26th.
1950 Surfaced.
2049 Sighted lights of small vessel. Southbound.
2154 Sighted lights of small vessel. Southbound.
2224 Sighted lights of fishing vessel.
2358 Sighted lights of small vessel.

January 4, 1943
0023 Sighted lights of vessel. Commenced approach. Identified as neutral.
0030 Sighted steady white light.
0420 Sighted Vigo pilot boat.
0710 Submerged.
0925 Sighted 1,500 ton steamer on northerly course. Spanish colors visible.
1125 Sighted trawler hull down to northwest.
1144 Sighted five small vessels on southerly course.
1939 Surfaced.
1953 Sighted lights of small vessel 208° true.
2243 Sighted lights of small vessel on southerly course. Made identification approach.
2316 Sighted lights of vessel on northerly course. Made identification approach.
2345 Sighted lights of two small vessels.

January 5, 1943
0017 Sighted three white lights bearing 047° true.
0250 Sighted lighted vessel on northerly course. Made identification approach. About 2,000 tons.
0515 Sighted a small craft bearing 103° true.
0551 Sighted two vessels bearing 138° true and 151° true on northerly course. One of these was a small steamer and the other was a small craft, which steered various courses in approximately the same spot.
0630 Sighted lighted vessel on northerly course. Approached and identified as small steamer of about 2,000 tons.
0716 Submerged. The sea had made up considerably and the wind risen.
0907 Unable to control boat at periscope depth. Increased depth to 100 feet and carried out listening patrol.
1143 Sound contact. Recognized typical trawler screw.
1259 Sound contact. Recognized typical trawler screw.
1607 Sound contact. Recognized typical trawler screw.
1941 Surfaced.

2048 Sighted lights and identified as small vessel.
2050 Sighted lights and identified as small vessel.
2117 Sighted steamer lights. Started approach.
2220 Sighted lights of fishing craft.
2335 Broke off approach.

January 6, 1943

0102 Sighted steamer lights bearing 235° true. Started approach.

0108 Sighted fishing craft bearing 191° true. Approached lighted steamer on port quarter. This vessel had blinding lights and no colors were visible. Tonnage hard to estimate as hull not visible through glare. Determined to attack, when at range of 2,000 yards vessel was silhouetted by Cape Finisterre light. She was then seen to be an old coal burner of much less tonnage than estimated. Badly illuminated Spanish colors aft were then discerned and approach broken off.

0556 Sighted small steamer on northerly course.
0559 Sighted small steamer on northerly course.
0646 Sighted small steamer on northerly course.
0716 Submerged.
0914 Sighted small steamer on northerly course. Sighted five small trawlers and drifters on various bearings and courses.
0939 Sighted trawler on southwest course.
0957 Sighted drifter.
1014 Sighted two drifters.
1820 Sighted smoke. Small ship on southerly course.
1944 Surfaced.
1946 Sighted lights of small vessel on northerly course.
2021 Sighted lights of small vessel on northerly course.
2355 Sighted lights of vessel bearing 055° true. Commenced approach. Neutral.

January 7, 1943

0030 Sighted lights of vessel bearing 285° true. Commenced approach. Small craft.

0209 Sighted vessel bearing 331° true—small craft. Sighted vessel bearing 004° true—commenced approach. This vessel was hugging the coast and appeared rather large. He was well lighted but we could not make out his colors. Went ahead 15 knots to intercept south of Vigo, but never made contact as he abruptly changed course and entered Vigo. By this time we were on the edge of territorial waters. Started to withdraw west as fishing fleet stood out. We were required to evade numerous craft.

0726 Submerged with about ten craft in sight.
1026 Sighted small steamer on southerly course.

1203 Sighted drifter.
1318 Sighted two trawlers—046° true and 032° true.
1550 Sighted trawler—023° true.
1830 – 1855 Heard heavy detonations at long range in two groups—one of two and one of four.
1933 Surfaced.
2024 Sighted lights of small vessel on northerly course.

January 8, 1943
0053 Sighted lights of small vessel on southerly course.
0500 Sighted fishing fleet of ten craft standing to westward.
0533 Sighted vessel on southerly course.
0719 Submerged.
0849 Sound contacts on six separate bearings.
0921 Sighted six trawlers and drifters on various bearings. Maneuvered to clear.
1018 Sighted small steamer carrying Spanish colors.
1135 Sighted drifter—starboard beam.
1147 Sighted drifter astern and another ahead.
1222 Sighted trawler—by this time we were surrounded by six vessels on various courses, which were changed at frequent intervals. Maneuvered to clear unsuccessfully and finally increased depth to 110 feet and drew clear.
1937 Surfaced.
2155 Sighted lighted vessel. Commenced approach. Vessel appeared small but colors could not be distinguished until range was reduced to 1,900 yards. Broke off approach.
2210 Sighted small vessel. Identified after approach as neutral.

January 9, 1943
0103 Sighted ship. Identified as neutral.
0130 Sighted ship. Identified as neutral.
0317 Sighted small vessel.
0350 Sighted small vessel.
0430 Sighted trawler.
0614 Sighted trawler.
0652 Sighted fishing craft—about six.
0720 Submerged.
0837 – 0900 Numerous sound contacts. At sunrise.
0910 Sighted three fishing craft on various bearings. One was very close and necessitated our going deep. These and a few more remained in sight and sound contact until 1238 when we drew clear. The sea was making up and shifting through west toward south.

1214 Sighted drifter.
1437 Surfaced.
2020 Sighted lighted vessel. Small craft.

January 10, 1943
0135 Sighted lighted vessel and made identification approach. Small neutral.
0627 Sighted lighted vessel. Identified as small neutral.
0649 Sighted trawler.
0730 Submerged.
0858 Sound contact drawing aft to starboard.
0901 Sound contact drawing aft to starboard.
0930 Attempted to run periscope patrol, but rough seas prevent proper depth control. Increased depth to 100 feet.
1315 Two sound contacts—distant.
1934 Surfaced in heavy sea. Visibility low, intermittent rain.

January 11, 1943
0715 Sighted small steamer on northerly course. Fishing craft did not stand out.
0725 Submerged. Unable to conduct periscope patrol. Went to 100 feet.
1935 Surfaced in heavy sea. Visibility about 500 yards with a driving mist obscuring all navigational lights.
2217 Sighted lighted steamer and commenced approach. Identified as 3,000 ton neutral with well lighted colors.

The seas continued to increase in height and became mountainous. The wind was of whole gale force, reaching 70 MPH at times.

January 12, 1943
0734 Submerged heading for point of departure. The heavy swell dragged us back to the surface immediately and depth control at 120 feet was impossible at slow speed. Increased depth to 145 feet, where boat became manageable.
1935 Surfaced. Although swell was undiminished, gale had spent itself and sea was much less rough. Turns for 14 knots made good 9.5–10 knots.
2330 Shipped heavy sea, which partially flooded conning tower, control room, forward engine room and ventilation system. No damage.

January 13, 1943
0815 Submerged about twenty miles behind schedule. Since the designated speed is not possible in heavy seas it was necessary to surface early and submerge late in order to prevent dropping behind progressively.
1945 Surfaced. Sea still extremely rough. Turns for 16 knots made good 12

knots. Ship pounded severely.

January 14, 1943
    0814 Submerged.
    1740 Heard about six distant heavy detonations.
    1947 Surfaced. Sea had abated somewhat.

January 15, 1943
    0815 SD contact moving in rapidly. Submerged.
    1945 Surfaced. Proceeding at 17 knots.

January 16, 1943
    1100 Arrived rendezvous, awaiting escort and *Blackfish*.
    1615 Formed on HMS *Swallow* with *Blackfish* in company and commenced passage to Base II at 14 knots.

January 18, 1943
    Arrived Base II, Rosneath, Scotland.

2. WEATHER

Throughout patrol period heavy swells were the rule making depth control at periscope depth difficult. Mountainous seas were experienced. Driving gales and winds above 70 knots experienced.

During the period of full moon the visibility was exceptional as the sky was cloudless.

3. TIDAL INFORMATION

In accordance with *Coast Pilot*.

4. NAVIGATIONAL AIDS

All navigational lights on the coast of Spain were in operation. Cape Finisterre light was extinguished one morning and was irregular in characteristics at other times.

The DRA proved of inestimable value, especially during operations of 1 January.

5. DESCRIPTION OF ENEMY WARSHIPS OR MERCHANT VESSELS

None to report.

6. DESCRIPTION OF ALL AIRCRAFT SIGHTED

1 January – Sunderland flying boat.
SD radar eliminated plane sightings on station. Numerous Allied craft of all types sighted in the vicinity of the British Isles.

7. PARTICULARS OF ATTACKS

None to report.

8. ENEMY A/S MEASURES

The tactics of the trawlers sighted on various operations were probably coincidence, but these tallied with the description given in S.I.S.

9. DESCRIPTION OF ENEMY MINESWEEPING OPERATIONS

None.

10. MAJOR DEFECTS EXPERIENCED

    a.   The trim pump has grown progressively louder and is considered a menace to any submarine. It will be removed from the ship and completely overhauled, but a new design pump is considered essential. Instruction books and prints have not been supplied.
    b.   Binoculars continue to be a major worry. Although excellent optical instruments, our 7x50 binoculars are much too fragile and easily flooded. A light knock will disarrange the prisms and one wave or heavy rain will flood them.
    c.   Radar failure of December 25th was traced to a defective tube.
    d.   H.P. air compressor 3rd stage air cooler developed a leak. No spares available. The cooler (spiral tubing) was removed and the defective part served with copper wire and soldered. This has proved satisfactory as a temporary repair, but replacement is required. Since this is the third occrrence of this casualty, it is recommended that a spare coil be supplied each boat.

11. RADIO RECEPTION

Radio reception was excellent. At periscope depth Rugby schedules were normally copied but faded if depth increases from 63 to 65 feet. Communications as a whole were quite satisfactory with the exception of the delay in receiving information if unable to copy while submerged. A complete schedule at 2030 would be helpful.

On January 15th it was not possible to raise Whitehall on 4740 kcs and shift was made to 6300 kcs with success..

12. SOUND CONDITIONS AND DENSITY LAYERS

In position 42-22 N. and 9-28 W. there appears to be a series of water strata greatly affecting the sound conditions. As the vessel passed through these strata even the sound of our own propellers faded completely. At the same time additional rudder was required to maintain course, indicating currents rather than density layers.

13. HEALTH AND HABITABILITY

A mild epidemic of colds was experienced at the beginning of the patrol, which increased in intensity until nearly 100% of the crew were affected. After long periods submerged the dampness becomes increasingly troublesome and colds are hard to combat. Although air conditioning equipment was kept in operation mildew was prevalent and the after torpedo room soggy.

The effect of 29 days submergence on the personnel was apparent in reduced efficiency and lowered resistance.

NUMBER OF CASES	CAUSE	DAYS LOST
1	Sinusitis	0
1	Lacerations, face	0
1	Lacerations, wrist	0
3	Urethritis	0
35	Constipation	0
11	Sore throat	0
3	Gingivitis	0
9	Coughs	0
1	Sprain, foot	0
2	Pediculosis	0
3	Conjunctivitis	0
17	Headache	0
4	Ringworm	0
1	Gastritis	0
2	Foreigh Body, eye	0
1	Ear-ache	0
1	Furuncle	0
1	Pleurisy	0

14. MILES STEAMED SURFACE AND SUBMERGED

    a.   Surface –   4,685 miles
    b.   Submerged –   864 miles

15. FUEL OIL EXPENDED

45,139 gallons

16. FACTORS OF ENDURANCE REMAINING

    a.   Torpedoes – 20[6]
    b.   Fuel – 42,000 gallons
    c.   Stores – 40 days
    d.   Personnel – Undetermined

17. FACTOR OF ENDURANCE CAUSING END OF PATROL

None. Patrol terminated by FOS despatch 1636 A/8 January.

18. REMARKS

    During the patrol off Vigo we made actual sight contact with 224 vessels. Although a large percentage were small craft the considerable remainder required in each case a decision as to enemy character and in practically every case an approach or evasion. All ships sighted were carrying lights and it was necessary to close well in before the hull could be seen through the glare of lights. During the period around full moon this was an uncomfortable procedure.

    Most approaches were complicated by the presence of one or more trawlers or fishing craft. These craft apparently cruised aimlessly and often made abrupt changes of course at unpredictable times. One in particular seemed to camp in immediate vicinity of our designated patrol point.

    The forecasts of neutral shipping provided us merely with the approximate number and tonnage of expected sightings as no pictures or silhouettes of these vessels are aboard. Therefore, as a definite policy it was decided to sink:

    a.   All tankers.
    b.   Ships making over 12 knots.
    c.   Ships obviously over 5,000 tons unless specifically notified to the contrary.

---

[6] While the section concerning the attack on the *Campomanes* was removed from the report before it was distributed, someone missed this clue. The normal torpedo load for a *Gato* class submarine was 24, and if there were no attacks that number should still have been aboard.

All other ships not of the fishing or trawler class, were identified as to size, type, and neutral markings and, if these checked, were considered neutral.

During the search for *Rhakotis*[7] on 1 January submarines were cautioned to remain undetected by submerging on SD contacts (FOS 2014A/31). As a result of this we were forced down three times by planes, presumably our own. This caused us to lose one and one half hours surface running time when we were closest to the enemy's estimated position. Under the circumstances, i.e., operating in conjunction with aircraft and surface vessels, it is believed that a patrol line 45° to the enemy's estimated course, with submarines patrolling normal to the enemy's course, would have provided greater probability of contact.

On passage to the patrol area we encountered head seas continually. In attempting to make good 15 knots, as required by our operation orders, the vessel took considerable pounding and the topside watch was useless, being constantly drenched. It is believed that this speed is too strenuous into a rough sea. Turns for 17 knots gave us 13 knots through the water and we soon dropped behind the bombing restriction[8]. Under these conditions 10 or 11 knots is our best speed made good.

It is recommended that this vessel be supplied with a satisfactory type of trim pump immediately. The one now supplied is considered to be a menace to safe submarining and could not possibly be used when in contact with A/S forces[9].

Although our air conditioning plant was kept in constant operation it was impossible to keep down the excessive dampness. The after torpedo room was especially damp and unhealthful.

The increased familiarity with British procedure eliminated most of the communications difficulties experienced last patrol. The fact that all schedules were received from the same transmitting station was a distinct advantage. Submerged

---

[7] *Rhakotis* was German passenger/freighter belonging to the Hamburg-Amerika Line, attempting to return to Germany from Japan. In addition to her crew, *Rhakotis* was carrying a number of Norwegian seaman who had been crew members of the ships sunk by the German surface raider *Michel*. Spotted on 1 January 1943 by a British Sunderland, she was caught by HMS *Scylla* later in the day and sunk. The survivors took to the ship's boats, landing in Spain on 3 January.

[8] As a submarine passed through areas where Allied air patrols were in operation, it was supposed to stay within a bombing restriction area, inside which bombing of submarines was forbidden. This was essentially a rectangular box that moved along the sub's projected course through the area. If a boat could not maintain its projected speed of advance, it would inevitably fall behind the advancing restriction area and find itself in an area where it was liable to be bombed by friendly aircraft.

[9] American fleet submarines were initially supplied with a reciprocating trim pump, essentially a slightly updated version of a pump originally installed in World War I German U-boats. It worked better than the old American design, but it was noisy and likely to attract the attention of escorts if it had to be used during evasion. These would eventually be replaced with a centrifugal type that was both more efficient and much quieter.

reception was quite satisfactory on the few days of smooth weather when a constant depth of 63 feet could be maintained. When depth increased to 65 feet, reception was poor.

Contrary to the general belief this type of boat is not well suited for periscope patrol in a heavy swell. Due to its length depth control is more difficult and unreliable than in S class submarines.

SUBMARINE SQUADRON FIFTY
FC5-50/A16   U.S.S. *Barb*, Flagship

Serial (09)   c/o Fleet Post Office,
U.S. CONFIDENTIAL – BRITISH SECRET   New York, New York
C-O-N-F-I-D-E-N-T-I-A-L

From: The Commander Submarine Squadron Fifty.
To: The Commander-in-Chief, U.S. Fleet.
Via: (1) The Admiral (Submarines).
               (2) The Admiralty.
               (3) The Commander, U.S. Naval Forces in Europe.

Subject: U.S.S. *Barb* – Report of Second War Patrol.

1. The Second War Patrol of the U.S.S. *Barb* is forwarded herewith. The length of patrol was thirty-four days, of which twenty-four were spent on station.

2. The Barb made over two hundred contacts and showed aggressiveness in developing these contacts. Those vessels which were closed sufficiently were identified as neutral. There is considerably more traffic through the patrolled areas in the Bay of Biscay than is reported in the forecasts of neutral shipping, which raises a very strong suspicion that the enemy is making use of neutral colors, markings and territorial waters. It is believed that, unless and until a blockade is established along the northern Spanish coast between the Portuguese and French borders, the enemy will continue to receive war materials in quantity. The nature of the waters along the coastline of northern Spain make them particularly good hunting grounds for submarines. Submarine Squadron Fifty, brought up to full strength, could if a blockade were established, effectively deal with the situation.

3. The material defects noted will be corrected by the tender prior to the departure of the *Barb* on her next patrol. Trim pump noise has been minimized. It is hoped that these harrowing noise makers will be replaced by the new design at an early date.

4. The last statement of the commanding officer under "Remarks" is not concurred in. It is of such common knowledge throughout the submarine service that the fleet-type submarine is greatly superior in all respects to the S-class that comment is superfluous. By copy of this endorsement the commanding officer is advised that better functioning of his depth control party will improve depth control.

5. It is believed that the homing procedure could have been used effectively during the search for the *Rhakotis* on January 1st.

                                 R.S. Ives

DISTRIBUTION:

The Admiralty
The Admiral Submarines
Comnaveu
Cominch (2)
VOpnav
Cincpac
Cinclant
Comsopac
Comsowespac
Comsubpac
Comsublan (2)
Comsubsopac
Comsubsowepac

UNITED STATES FLEET
UNITED STATES NAVAL FORCES IN EUROPE
20 GROSVENOR SQUARE
LONDON, W.1.

Please refer to file:

A16-4
Serial 0250
First Endorsement to
ComSubRon 50 Serial 09
dated 4 Feb. 1943

From: Commander, U.S. Naval Forces in Europe.
To: Commander in Chief, U.S. Fleet.

Subject: U.S.S. *Barb* – Report of Second War Patrol.

1. Ten advance copies of subject patrol report are forwarded for distribution to U.S. Navy commands listed in basic letter except Commander Submarines, Atlantic Fleet.

2. By copy of this letter two copies of subject patrol report are being forwarded direct to Commander Submarines, Atlantic Fleet.

J.G. Bray, Jr.
By Direction

Copy to:
Comsublant (with 2 copies basic report)
Comsubron 50 (less basic report)

From **ADMIRAL (SUBMARINES)**
　　　　Northways, London, N.W.3

Date　　11th March, 1943　　　No. SM4343/40

To　　Commander U.S. Naval Forces in Europe
　　　　(Copy to: Commander U.S. Submarine Squadron 50)

　　1.　The following additional remarks on U.S.S. *Barb*'s report of 2nd war patrol (Commander U.S. Submarine Squadron 50's No. FC5-50/A16, Serial (09) of 4th February 1943) are forwarded in continuation of my minute No. 313/SM.4343 of 7th February 1943.

　　2.　Paragraph 2 of Comsubron 50's letter has been studied by the Director of Economic Warfare Division Admiralty, who remarks that the "forecasts of neutral shipping" referred to are confined to Spanish shipping of *over* 2,500 tons G.R.T. This figure is considerably lower than the G.R.T. of any Far East blockade runner and the forecasts therefore serve their purpose. (within a limited degree of accuracy) of helping to distinguish between a legitimate neutral passing through the Biscay area and the blockade runner. To include ships of less burthen could only cumber the plots unnecessarily; in any case, forecasts of movements of such small ships would probably be inaccurate and misleading as they do not run to schedule but sail when they have secured a cargo.

　　3.　With reference to paragraph 18 of the Commanding Officer's report, it is assumed that the qualification "unless specifically notified to the contrary" refers to (a) and (b) as well as (c). Spanish tankers sometimes proceed to Ferrol, Vigo and Bilbao as did *Campomanes* last December; as also do certain Spanish passenger ships such as Marques de *Comillas* and *Magellanes*, both of which are 16 knot ships. The latter cleared Trinidad for Bilbao on 27th February. Subject to that, and to the exercise of reasonable discretion, the Commanding Officer's policy was substantially correct. Detailed orders on the subject have been issued since.

　　　　　　　　　　　　　　　　　　　[signed]
　　　　　　　　　　　　　　　　　　　Rear Admiral

Patrol Three, 1 February 1943 – 9 March 1943

SS220/A16
Serial (03)

U.S.S. *Barb* (SS220)
c/o Fleet Post Office
New York, New York

March 9, 1943

C-O-N-F-I-D-E-N-T-I-A-L

From: The Commanding Officer.
To: The Commander Submarine Squadron Fifty.

Subject: Third War Patrol of the U.S.S. Barb – Period from February 1, 1943 to March 9, 1943. Area K-505 and vicinity of Vigo. Operation Order CSS 50 3-43.

Reference: (a) Sublant X-18, November 15, 1942.

Enclosure: (A) Report of the Third War Patrol of the U.S.S. *Barb*.

1. In accordance with reference (a) enclosure (A) is submitted herewith.

J.R. Waterman

CONFIDENTIAL
Report of the Third War Patrol of the U.S.S. *Barb*

PROLOGUE

The period since the last patrol was spent at Base II for upkeep, leave and recreation. No operations were undertaken and repairs were routine. Arrived Base II January 18, 1943 and departed February 1, 1943.

1. NARRATIVE

February 1, 1943
1100 Underway from Base II in accordance with CSS 50 Operation Order 3-43. Formed on escort, H.M.S. *Shikari*[1], U.S.S. *Blackfish* in company.
1425 Trim dive.

February 2, 1943
0510 Shipped heavy sea, which injured two lookouts.
1210 Sighted floating mine 500 yards on port bow.
1930 Released escort.
1949 Took departure from Wolf Rock. On changing course to westward heavy seas prevented our making required speed. Slowed to 13 knots, making good about 10 knots.
2141 Transmitted *Barb* 2116 A/2 requiring extension of bombing restrictions.
2245 Unable to maintain turns for 13 knots. Slowed to 12 knots, making good 7.5 to 8.5 knots.

February 3, 1943
0725 Submerged.
1140 Heard two distant explosions in rapid succession.
2000 Surfaced. Seas abating. Increased speed to 16 knots. Received FOS 1139 A/S. Reduced speed to 12 knots.

February 4, 1943
0730 Submerged.
2030 Surfaced. Zig-zagging at 12 knots. Seas abated to such an extent that maximum speed would have been possible.

---

[1] HMS *Shikari* was an S-class destroyer, launched in 1919 and commissioned in 1924. Noted as the last ship to leave Dunkirk, *Shikari* was scrapped in 1945.

February 5, 1943

0645 Submerged. Sky overcast. We have been running on DR[2] since taking departure from Wolf Rock.

2045 Sound contact moving aft on port side. Nothing in sight through periscope.

2100 Surfaced. Radar search failed to get contact. Due to northerly course or sound contact and possible proximity of U.S.S. *Herring,* decided against search.

February 6, 1943

0230 Received FOS 0031 A/6.

0700 Submerged. Poor fix indicated that we were 30 miles south of our E.P.[3] and outside of bombing restrictions. Proceeded northeast to rectify position. This will put us close to 1900 E.P. of 3 DDs reported in FOS 1124 A/5.

1540 Struck submerged object with dull thud, but little shock. Not metallic, probably log.

1906 Electric control on bow planes went out. Broken contactor. Shifted to hand power. Repaired at 1958.

2017 Surfaced, proceeding at 16 knots in order to make land fall before submerging.

February 7, 1943

0340 Sighted loom of Cabo Villano Light bearing 179° true.

0420 Sighted loom of Islas Sisargas Light bearing 160° true.

0444 Sighted Point Herminio Light bearing 120° true. Obtained fix and set course for Cabo Prior. It has been decided to patrol off Cabo Prior for a day or so until ship lanes and fishing areas have been determined.

0511 Sighted small lighted vessel.

0515 Sighted two small lighted vessels.

0528 Sighted small lighted vessel.

0554 Sighted two small lighted vessels.

0627 Sighted two small lighted vessels.

0635 Submerged.

0750 Sound contact—trawler.

0820 Sound contact—large trawler.

0915 Sound contact—fishing vessel.

0925 Sighted small steamer carrying Spanish colors.

0930 Sighted trawler on SW course. Two or three trawlers or drifters were in sight continuously. They appeared to be fishing to seaward of us near the 100 fathom curve.

---

[2] DR: Dead Reckoning. Determining current position by calculation based on speed, distance run, and course since the last accurate fix.

[3] E.P.: Estimated Position.

1255 Sighted two small steamers on northerly courses. Spanish markings.
1656 Sighted small steamer on southerly course. Spanish markings.
2034 Surfaced. Sighted three lighted trawlers to seaward.
2106 Sighted two fishing craft.
2133 Sighted one fishing craft.
2235 Sighted two fishing craft.

February 8, 1943
0100 Sighted small vessel.
0655 Submerged. Before daylight had sound contact with two trawlers.
0821 Sound contact. Sighted four trawlers on SW courses.
1900 Sighted small launch at very close range. It is possible that our periscope was sighted by them.
2040 Surfaced. Patrolling between Cape Prior and Cape Ortegal about two miles from territorial waters. There is no intelligence indicating enemy shipping in Ferrol, so this appears a more likely station. The beach is plainly visible from here.
2116 Sighted six small craft to northwest.

February 9, 1943
Total number of small craft (trawlers and drifters) sighted will be entered at end of each day.
Sea has made up considerably, wind has increased to force 4[4] and a rain has set in.
0700 Submerged.
0901 On attempting to run periscope patrol heavy seas caused broaching even though negative tank was flooded. Increased depth to 100 feet feet and commenced listening patrol.
1315 Periscope depth. Made observations and went deep.
1337 Heard three loud explosions in rapid succession.
2033 Surfaced. Wind had subsided and sea had shifted, diminishing slightly. Commenced patrol toward Corunna. During day sighted 4 fishing craft.

February 10, 1943
0436 Sighted lighted vessel on easterly course. Commenced approach. Closed to 2,900 yards and distinguished well illuminated colors. Identified as tanker *Campanario*, one day over schedule (FOS 1831 A/6). Broke off approach.
0653 Submerged. Periscope patrol four miles off Cape Prior.
1055 Commenced approach to Ferrol. Shore fog obscured landmarks so returned to Cape Prior patrol.

---
[4]   Force 4: Wind 11 – 16 knots. Sea condition small waves, frequent white horses.

1244 Sighted vessel hull down. Commenced approach. Vessel passed 700 yards abeam and was well marked Spaniard of about 2,000 tons.

1545 Sighted vessel on NE course. At 900 yards identified as *Castillo Ampudia*, which had not been listed in FOS forecast of neutral shipping. Vessel was plainly marked with flags and name.

2035 Surfaced.

2145 Received FOS 1804 A/10 forecasting passage of *Campanaria* and *Castillo Ampudia*, which had passed 17 hours and 6 hours earlier, respectively.

2300 Sighted ship on westerly course. Spanish markings.

Sighted 15 small craft during day.

February 11, 1943

0649 Submerged.

0912 Heard distant detonations.

1012 Sound contact. Nothing in sight. Visibility poor due to heavy haze.

1024 Sound contact.

1940 Heard two heavy explosions. These did not have the metallic clang of underwater explosions, but vibrated the boat noticeably.

2040 Surfaced. Heavy fog covered the shore and large patches covered the patrol area. These patches cleared abruptly at irregular intervals then set in again during the night.

2226 Radar contact astern at 11,000 yards. Commenced approach. Indentified as Spanish steamer on course 045° true.

Sighted 11 small craft during day.

February 12, 1943

0020 Sighted vessel on NE course. Identified as Spanish steamer.

0130 Sighted vessel on SW course showing Spanish markings.

0453 Sighted vessel on NE course and identified as Spanish steamer of about 2,000 tons.

0614 Sighted vessel on SW course and commenced approach. Identified vessel as Spanish freighter of about 3,000 tons.

0658 Submerged. Fog patches dissipated during morning. Conducting periscope patrol.

1629 Heard heavy detonation. Sighted small tanker, empty, identified as either *Fernando L de Yabarra* or *Marques de Chavarri*.

1637 Sighted unidentified freighter with Spanish markings on SW course.

1707 Sighted vessel on SW course. Identified as *Gayarre*.

1728 Sighted 1,500 ton vessel. Spanish markings.

2037 Surfaced.

2055 Sighted lighted vessel—Spanish markings.

2146 Sighted vessel—Spanish markings.

Sighted 5 small craft during day.

February 13, 1943
    0649 Submerged.
    0800 High speed screw on 206° true.
    1125 Heard two detonations.
    1802 Sighted 1,500 ton freighter with Spanish markings.
    2039 Surfaced.
    2145 Sighted lights of vessel. Started approach. Identified as Spanish freighter.
    Sighted 21 small craft during day.

February 14, 1943
    0158 Sighted vessel and commenced approach. Spanish markings.
    0335 Sighted vessel and commenced approach. Spanish markings.
    0537 Sighted freighter. Spanish markings.
    0637 Submerged.
    1624 Sighted vessel and started approach—Spanish markings.
    2046 Surfaced.
    2225 Sighted vessel and commenced approach—Spanish Markings—possibly *Motomar*.
    2227 Sighted vessel of 2,000 tons with Spanish markings.
    Sighted 21 small craft during day.

February 15, 1943
    0647 Submerged. During the night the visibility had been exceptional with bright moonlight. Towards morning a shore haze set in.
    2041 Surfaced. Sea making up, moon bright.
    2236 Sighted vessel, Spanish markings.
    Sighted 25 small craft during day.

February 16, 1943
    0648 Submerged. Sea continued to build up. Periscope depth maintained with difficulty throughout the day.
    1255 Received FOS 0821 A/16 reporting departure preparation of *Nord Atlantic*. Took up approach for close patrol of Ferrol.
    1600 Received FOS 1522 A/16 and FOS 1523 A/16.
    2040 Surfaced. Proceeding to vicinity of Latitude 42-30 N., Longitude 09-15 W. in accordance with FOS 1523 A/16 at 15 knots.
    Sighted six small craft during day.

February 17, 1943

0030 Sighted vessel on SW course.

0300 Arrived in Lat. 43-30 N., Long. 09-15 W. and commenced surface patrol.

0645 Submerged. Sighted lights of vessel. Observed as range decreased. From position of lights vessel appeared to be a tanker. At this time we were in the midst of 18 fishing boats, but decided that detection was secondary to destruction of *Nord Atlantic.*

0725 Surfaced and commenced approach on vessel. At range of 2,800 yards the vessel was identified definitely as a tanker, at 6½ knots, of the *Marques de Chavarri* class. This vessel was expected about this time, but should have been on opposite course.

0745 Submerged and reversed course. We have no doubt been detected, but it is hoped we were mistaken for a U-boat. Patrolling along shipping lanes between Long. 09-09 W. and 09-15 W. on course 160° true and reverse.

2023 Sighted lighted vessel on southerly course.

2036 Surfaced. Commenced approach. Vessel identified as another tanker of the same class as that sighted in the morning. This epidemic of tankers does not agree with the forecasts of shipping, but they are easily identified as neutral through markings and silhouettes. Broke off approach. Commenced NW – SE patrol through point 42-30 N,. 09-15 W.

Sighted 24 fishing craft during day.

February 18, 1943

0645 Submerged.

0835 Sighted plane circling trawlers. Identified as Heinkel 111[5] flying at about 500 feet. When plane headed in our direction, lowered periscope. On next observation it was not in sight.

1020 Sighted vessel of about 500 tons showing Spanish markings and on SE course. Made practice torpedo approach. As we broke off approach this vessel changed course 90° right and stopped her propeller, then changed course to NW and proceeded for one hour. She then changed course to south until opposite entrance to Vigo, where she changed course east for ½ hour, then changed course to west. Her speed was 7 knots and there was no evidence of fishing. She is undoubtedly conducting some type of patrol.

1340 Sighted aircraft patrolling along coastal waters. Identified as Focke-Wulf Kurier[6]. Altitude 1,000 feet. It appears as though our presence has been reported or that a patrol is being made preparatory to the sailing of the Nord Atlantic.

---

[5] Heinkel 111: The Heinkel 111 was a twin-engine, low wing, medium bomber, with a 1,400 pound maximum bomb load and a range of about 750 miles. These bombers were also flown by Spain, where they remained in production until 1956.

[6] Focke-Wulf 177 Kurier: For the military version, correctly the Focke-Wulf 200 Condor, a 4-engine maritime patrol bomber. The "Kurier" was the airliner version.

1640 Sighted small steamer with Spanish colors similar in appearance to SS *Duero*.

1722 Sighted small steamer similar to *Achuri*—Spanish colors.

1807 Sighted large vessel and commenced approach. Identified as *Marques de Comillas*, 10,000 T.G.

1817 Sighted steamer with Spanish markings similar to *Monte Iciar*.

1940 Sighted 500 – 1,000 ton steamer believed to be same one at 1020, whose movements were suspicious. This vessel proceeded to the north, reversed course, and headed for Vigo. Similar to SS *Soton*.

2049 Surfaced. Wind force 4 from NE. Sea very choppy. There was not even a trace of cloud and it appeared like midday.

2347 Sighted two small steamers standing out of Vigo.

Sighted 34 fishing craft during day.

February 19, 1943

0640 Submerged.

1735 Sighted same steamer patrolling N & S. Photographed[7].

1742 Sighted steamer and commenced practice approach. Identified as *Castillo Tarifa*. Photographed at 700 yards.

1815 Sighted 2,000 ton steamer, Spanish markings, which stood into Villagarcia.

2048 Surfaced. Sea calm. Visibility unlimited. Sighted steamer standing out of Vigo. Identified as *Plus Ultra*. Sighted steamer to seaward on southerly course and one on northerly course. Spanish markings, and about 5 fishing craft on various bearings. We were well boxed and had to maneuver to get clear.

2145 Finally cleared all craft and stood towards entrance to Vigo.

2159 Sighted large plane heading towards us, distant about 4 miles. Submerged.

2204 Heard 4 explosions, not very close.

2219 Heard 3 explosions, farther away.

2303 Surfaced.

2336 Sighted ship, Spanish markings.

Sighted 34 fishing craft during day.

February 20, 1943

0220 Sighted small steamer, Spanish markings.

0416 SD radar contact at 14 miles closed in to 7 miles and then opened out. Visibility was so good that the hulls of ships could be seen at 12,000 yards.

---

7   After photographs obtained through makeshift camera-periscope lash ups proved of value, submarines were provided with a camera that could be attached to the periscope in place of the eye buffer. The resulting photographs could be used for intelligence purposes, as here, and in some cases provided dramatic visual confirmation of sinking claims.

0433 Sighted ship, Spanish markings.
0440 SD radar contact at 10 miles. This moved steadily in to 4 miles.
0443 Submerged and conducted periscope patrol.
0637 Sighted two steamers, Spanish markings.
0750 Sighted ship, Spanish markings.
1131 Sighted steamer. Identified as *SAC 4* and photographed at 200 yards.
1220 Sighted steamer similar to *Mina Piquera.*
1254 Sighted steamer—*Castillo Montiel.* Photographed.
1533 Sighted small steamer—our usual patroller.
1734 Surrounded by numerous fishing craft. Unable to avoid them all, so went deep to keep from fouling nets.
1937 Sighted steamer—Spanish markings.
1943 Sighted steamer—Spanish markings.
1952 Heard six loud but distinct explosions. Vibrations felt in boat.
2107 Surfaced with 1 fishing craft and the usual small steamer in sight. This patroller remained in the same position all night and forced us to seaward of our desired patrol line.
2116 Sighted steamer—Spanish markings.
Sighted 33 fishing craft during day.

February 21, 1943
0050 Sighted steamer—Spanish markings.
0100 SD radar contact at 8 miles. This moved in to 4 miles and then moved out.
0422 SD radar contact—2 planes, which moved in rapidly to 3 miles. Submerged as it was almost bright as midday.
0706 Sighted steamer, Spanish markings.
0838 Sighted patrolling steamer.
0927 Heard 4 loud explosions.
0939 Heard 4 loud explosions.
1006 Heard 6 loud explosions.
1300 Heard 1 loud explosion.
During and after each of the above a careful periscope search revealed nothing. Sea was calm and visibility excellent.
1315 Sighted two vessels standing out of Vigo. One appeared to be a tanker. Commenced submerged approach. These vessels were soon identified as the *Campomanes* in tow of the *Monte Castillo*. Examined and photographed both at close range. They were three days behind schedule and if they had passed at night the tanker would probably have been torpedoed. (FOS 2201 A/21 reported this sailing and was received at 2300 A/21 st.)
1623 Sighted plane flying north. Unidentified.
1630 Heard 4 detonations.

1648 Heard 2 detonations.
2045 Sighted 2 vessels, approached—Spanish markings.
2051 Sighted vessel, approached—Spanish markings.
2144 Sighted vessel, approached—Spanish markings.
2245 Sighted vessel, approached—Spanish markings.
2329 Sighted vessel, approached—Spanish markings.
Sighted 16 fishing craft during day.

February 22, 1943
0043 Sighted vessel—Spanish markings.
0533 SD radar contact moved in rapidly to 5½ miles and then moved out.
0633 Submerged. Fishing fleet standing out.
1230 Heard 2 explosions.
1340 Heard 9 explosions. These were rather loud and vibrations were noticeable.
Sighted 16 fishing craft during day.

February 23, 1943
0523 Sighted steamer—Spanish markings.
0553 SD radar contact moving in slowly to 13 miles, and then out.
0636 Submerged. Uneventful. Sighted 2 vessels with Spanish markings and heard 9 explosions.
2047 Surfaced. Sighted patrol steamer.
2331 Sighted lights of large ship near entrance to Vigo and commenced approach.
Sighted 13 fishing craft during day.

February 24, 1943
0012 Lights indicted vessel to be a tanker. Close examination of forecasts of neutral shipping indicated that the only tanker, *Campuzano*, should have arrived at Bilbao 3 or 4 days previously (FOS 1746 A/19). Closed at 15 knots, in bright moonlight, to 2,900 yards. Vessel was heavily loaded and Spanish colors were plainly visible on the side and aft. Bow was straight and stern counter, which did not agree with *Nord Atlantic*. Broke off approach at 0140. These evident discrepancies in forecasts of neutral shipping can easily result in the sinking of a neutral or allow an enemy to pass unmolested.
0101 Sighted ship on southerly course, Spanish markings.
0218 Sighted ship on northerly course—Spanish markings.
0508 Aircraft contact on SD radar, which moved in rapidly to 3 miles. Submerged.
2051 Surfaced. The usual patrol vessel was lying to, 2,300 yards astern.
2216 Sighted ship—Spanish markings.
Sighted 20 fishing craft during day.

February 26, 1943

0058 Sighted dark object close aboard on port bow. Maneuvered to avoid and examined. It was a launch of about 30 feet, darkened and lying to. The flare of a match in the cabin was observed. When clear reversed course with the intention of "accidentally" ramming. Fishing craft interfered with approach and when they were clear the launch could not be located.

0257 Sighted Spanish steamer.

0400 Sighted dark object. Appeared to be a roll of fish netting floating on the surface.

0536 Sighted Spanish steamer.

0623 Submerged.

1200 Received FOS 1151 A/26 placing us under operational control of C in C Plymouth.

1945 Sighted tanker on northerly course. Visibility through periscope was not good enough to positively identify, yet was too light to surface. Took normal approach course until it got darker.

2027 Surfaced and commenced closing tanker at 15 knots. Identified as Spanish tanker of *Campilo* class.

2051 Sighted Spanish ship.

2117 Broke off approach. Later we received FOS 1749 A/26 forecasting passage of *Campilo*.

2143 Sighted Spanish ship.

2347 Sighted Spanish ship.

Sighted 23 fishing craft during day.

February 27, 1943

0000 Received FOS 2308 A/26 shifting patrol area.

0410 SD radar contact, which moved in to 7 miles.

0458 Sighted 2 Spanish ships.

0520 SD radar contact, which moved in rapidly to 3 miles.

0522 Submerged.

0951 Sighted and photographed Spanish SS *Fantastico*.

2046 Surfaced.

2200 Sighted Spanish steamer. Left station, shifting patrol to area K 505.

Sighted 49 fishing craft during day.

February 28, 1943

0045 Sighted Spanish steamer.

0340 Sighted Spanish steamer.

0344 Sighted Spanish steamer.

0437 Sighted Spanish steamer.

0629 Submerged on station off Cape Prior.

0810 Heard 3 detonations.
0949 Sighted Spanish steamer—1,500 tons.
2050 Surfaced.
2339 Sighted ship and commenced approach. Closed to 2,000 yards before dimly lighted colors were visible.
Sighted 5 fishing craft during day.

March 1, 1943
0254 Sighted small Spanish steamer.
0604 Sighted 2 steamers. Spanish markings.
0621 Submerged.
0740 Sighted large plane at altitude of 500 feet. Not identified due to glare of sun.
2048 Surfaced.
2104 Sighted 2 Spanish ships.
Sighted 10 fishing craft during day.

March 2, 1942
0023 Sighted Spanish steamer.
0617 Sighted Spanish steamer.
0618 Submerged—uneventful.
2049 Surfaced.
2054 Sighted 2 Spanish steamers.
2100 Sighted 1 Spanish steamer.
2101 Sighted 1 Spanish steamer.
2138 Sighted 1 Spanish steamer.
2352 Sighted 1 Spanish steamer.
Sighted 17 fishing craft during day.

March 3, 1943
0223 Sighted Spanish steamer.
0510 Sighted Spanish steamer.
0620 Submerged.
0747 Sighted and photographed Spanish steamer.
0954 Sighted Spanish steamer—*Cabo Razo.*
1104 Sighted large plane at 500 feet. Not identified due to haze.
2049 Surfaced.
2105 Sighted 2 ships. Identified as Spanish.
2118 Sighted Spanish steamer.
Sighted 10 fishing craft during day.

March 4, 1943
    0020 Sighted Spanish steamer after radar contact. Visibility 2,000 yards due to rain.
    0335 Sighted small steamer.
    0619 Submerged.
    1000 Sighted and photographed Spanish steamer.
    1255 Received FOS 1234 A/4 terminating patrol. Took course for point X.
    1331 to 1500 Heard repeated rumblings like distant explosions.
    1820 Sighted large 4 engine bomber at 500 feet heading directly for periscope. Identified as Focke-Wulf 177 Kurier and increased depth to 120 feet and evaded.
    2033 Surfaced.
    Sighted 6 fishing craft during day.

March 5, 1943
    0832 Submerged.
    1700 to 2100 Heard series of approximately 25 sharp explosive sounds. These were similar to those previously heard, but seemed louder and all appeared to originate below and to port. Doubt exists as to whether they have external or internal causes. Careful inspection has failed to reveal an internal cause.
    2123 Surfaced.

March 6, 1943
    Uneventful.

    March 7, 1943
    Uneventful.

March 8, 1943
    Sighted numerous aircraft while approaching and at rendezvous.
    1204 Arrived at Rendezvous.
    1751 Formed astern of HMS *La Capricieuse*, U.S.S. *Herring* and U.S.S. *Shad*.
    1804 U.S.S. *Herring* and U.S.S. *Shad* left formation. Commenced passage to Base II

March 9, 1943
    2101 Arrived at Base Two.

2. WEATHER

    Weather was exceptionally good and seas unexpectedly calm.

3. TIDAL INFORMATION (IF ABNORMAL)

Normal.

4. NAVIGATIONAL AIDS

Same as last reported.

5. DESCRIPTION OF WARSHIPS SIGHTED

None.

6. DESCRIPTION OF AIRCRAFT SIGHTED.

TYPE	POSITION	COURSE	ALTITUDE	TIME & DATE
Heinkel 111	42-30 N 09-15 W	Circling	500'	0835 Feb 18
Focke-Wulf 177	42-30 N 09-11 W	South	500'	1340 Feb 18
4 Eng. Bomber	42-30 N 09-15 W	West	500 – 1,000'	2159 Feb 19
Unidentified	42-30 N 09-15 W	North	500 – 1,000'	1623 Feb 21
Unidentified	43-44 N 09-08 W		500'	0740 Mar 1
Unidentified	43-44 N 08-08 W		500'	1104 Mar 3
Focke-Wulf 177	43-40 N 08-08 W	West	500'	1820 Mar 4

Numerous planes of all types in vicinity of British Isles.
SD radar contacts between 0400 – 0600 daily.

7. SUMMARY OF ATTACKS

None.

8. ENEMY A/S MEASURES

None except plane patrols.

9. ENEMY MINE SWEEPING OPERATIONS

None.

10. MAJOR DEFECTS EXPERIENCED

None. Numerous small electrical and mechanical parts have worn out indicating approaching need for overhaul.

11. RADIO RECEPTION

Excellent. Last consecutive message HS 467 of 3-9-43.

12. SOUND CONDITIONS

Fair.

13. HEALTH AND HABITABILITY

Very good.
Following cases received for treatment.

DIAGNOSIS	NUMBER	DAYS LOST
Sprain, back	1	0
Sore throat	14	0
Colds	12	0
Coughs	10	0
Constipation	22	0
Gastritis	8	0
Gingivitis	2	0
Vincents Angina	1	0
Toothache	2	0
Headache	32	0
Pediculosis[8]	3	0
Fungus Infection	6	0

14. MILES STEAMED

1,183

15. FUEL EXPENDED

40,075

16. FACTORS OF ENDURANCE REMAINING

Torpedoes	Fuel	Provisions	Fresh Water	Personnel
24	50,374	40 days	Unlimited	20 days

---

[8] Pediculosis: Lice.

17. FACTOR OF ENDURANCE CAUSING END OF PATROL

None. Recalled by FOS 1234 A/4 March.

18. REMARKS

Because of the heavy traffic encountered, this patrol was at least extremely productive in experience in surface and submerged ship handling for all watch standers. Trawler and fishing craft contacts number 485 and 127 larger vessels were sighted, the majority of which passed fairly close aboard. Our patrol point was well chosen with respect to shipping lanes, but was also directly in the lane and area used by the fishing fleet. Consequently, in order to observe shipping and elude small craft, we were forced to maneuver radically and often. The presence of these small craft at night presented the major difficulty in making undetected approaches during the period of full moon. During this period the sea was glassy and there was not a trace of cloud in the sky.

Recurrent plane contacts indicate a regular early morning and late evening patrol. Information regarding British ferry schedules through this area would be helpful in evaluating contacts.

The numerous inaccuracies and omissions in the forecasts of neutral shipping prevent night approaches from being carried to the conclusion of attacks if Spanish colors are displayed. Positive identification of an individual ship, particularly distinguishing one tanker from another at night, is practically impossible unless the ship has outstanding characteristics. The vessel approached on the morning of February 24 was assumed to be *Campuzano*, but positive identification was impossible at 2,900 yards in bright moonlight. Illuminated colors, a straight bow and counter stern were the principle distinguishing features, but these appearances could easily be obtained by the clever application of a little paint. A defiant policy of sinking unreported neutrals would go far towards clearing up this situation.

In view of the reported preparations of the *Nord Atlantic*, that vessel appeared to be our primary objective, consequently any engine aft vessel received particular attention. The following vessels of that type, whose presence had not been forecast or who were long overdue, were sighted as follows.

10 Feb.	*Campanario* – 1 day late.
12 Feb.	*F.L. de Yabarra* – not listed.
16 Feb.	*Marques de Chavarri* type – not listed.
16 Feb.	*Marques de Chavarri* type – not listed.
21 Feb.	*Campomanes* – 3 days late.
23 Feb.	*Campuzano* type – not listed.
26 Feb.	*Campilo* – forecast received during approach.

The feeling of futility engendered by such numerous contacts which failed to develop into attacks was hard to overcome. The tendency was to become lax and the effect on morale was noticeable.

The steamer which was observed almost every day patrolling off Vigo was a duplicate of the 1,000 ton trawler shown on page 23 of CB 3075 and mentioned in FOS 1038 A/1. Repeated observations of this vessel failed to show any positive evidence of fishing. The trawler was well marked with Spanish flags, and no guns were visible. However, it is believed that she is conducting an anti-submarine or observation patrol. W/T equipment was not obvious, but may have been present.

Contrary to the opinion expressed in Radar Information Note #3, December 1, 1942, a condition of hazy atmosphere or light fog produces phenomenal radar results. On the evening of March 2nd with overcast sky and heavy ground haze contacts at 22,000 yards were obtained on medium sized ship usually picked up at from 12 to 14 thousand yards. These contacts confirmed the previously formed impression.

The explosions following the plane contact on the evening of February 19th were undoubtedly aircraft bombs and had the characteristic clang of underwater explosions. The other repeated rumbles or explosions cannot be explained. They were thought to be caused by submarine volcanic disturbances or ore blasting ashore until those on March 5th were experienced. Twenty-two U-boats were reported in our general area at that time and it is possible that we heard attacks against them. However, as all appeared to emanate from below and to port, the impression was that they originated within the ship. Careful inspection internally failed to verify this, but tank and exterior inspections will be made during upkeep period. At no time was the trim on the boat affected.

FC5-50/A16   SUBMARINE SQUADRON FIFTY
U.S.S. *Barb*, Flagship

Serial 022

                                                               c/o Fleet Post Office,

U.S. CONFIDENTIAL – BRITISH SECRET   New York, New York

C-O-N-F-I-D-E-N-T-I-A-L

From:	The Commander Submarine Squadron Fifty.
To:	The Commander-in-Chief, U.S. Fleet.
Via:	(1) The Admiral (Submarines).
	(2) The Admiralty.
	(3) The Commander, U.S. Naval Forces in Europe.
Subject:	U.S.S. *Barb* – Report of Third War Patrol
Enclosures:	(A) Track Charts (to Admiral (Submarines) only).

     1. The Third War Patrol report of the *Barb* is forwarded herewith. The length of the patrol was thirty-eight days, of which twenty-eight were spent on station.

     2. The material condition of the ship was excellent upon her arrival in port. The ship's morale was high, considering that *no targets were presented*. It will be noted that *over six hundred sight contacts were made* by the *Barb* and that *none* of the surface ships were *legitimate prey* within the meaning of paragraph six of F.S.L. 2. The intelligence information obtained will be useful. It appears that morning and evening twilight air patrols are maintained in addition to sporadic off-harbor A/S patrols by converted trawlers of the *Heimdall* class. This, coupled with probable misuse of Spanish colors and markings within territorial limits, and by failure of Spanish authorities to supply accurate forecasts of shipping to the Admiralty, constitutes a serious situation. If the wording of paragraph 6(iii) of F.S.L. 2 were altered to permit the sinking on sight of *unreported* vessels within the patrol areas, the situation would improve.

     3. It is believed that the detonations heard so frequently by the Barb may have been plane attacks on submarines by own or enemy planes. The Admiral (Submarines) is requested to coordinate the times that these explosions were heard with reports of attacks delivered by the Coastal Command. It appears that the submarine may have been attacked by aircraft on 19, 21 and 22 February.

     4. The excellent reception obtained with the D/F loop while submerged reflects credit on the radio operating personnel of the Barb.

     5. The commanding officer again displayed an aggressive spirit in covering his patrol area. His remarks are concurred in. He is advised that there are no ferry

flights over the patrol area.

    6.   Because of the restriction placed on the distribution of U.S. Submarine patrol reports by the Commander-in-Chief, U.S. Fleet, it is requested that subordinate commands be furnished with only such extracted information as is considered necessary.

                                          H.S. Ives

DISTRIBUTION:

The Admiralty
The Admiral (Submarines)
Comnaveu
Cominch (2)
VOpnav
Cincpac
Cinclant
Comsopac
Comsowespac
Comsubpac
Comsublant (2)
Comsubsowespac.

UNITED STATES FLEET
UNITED STATES NAVAL FORCES IN EUROPE
20 GROSVENOR SQUARE
LONDON, W. 1

Please refer to file:

First Endorsement to
ComSubRon 50 serial 022
dated 12 Mar. 1943

March 18, 1943

CONFIDENTIAL

From: Commander, U.S. Naval Forces in Europe.
To: Commander in Chief, U.S. Fleet.

Subject: U.S.S. *Barb* – Report of Third War Patrol.

1. Nine advance copies of subject patrol report are forwarded for distribution to U.S. Naval commands listed in basic letter except Commander, Submarines, Atlantic Fleet.

2. By copy of this letter two copies of subject patrol report are being forwarded direct to Commander Submarines, Atlantic Fleet.

J.G. Bray, Jr.,
By Direction

Copy to:
Comsublant
(with 2 copies of basic report)
Comsubron 50 less "   "

From **ADMIRAL (SUBMARINES)**
	Northways, London, N.W.3

Date   27th March, 1943   No. SM. 4343/456

To   Air Officer Commander-in-Chief, Coastal Command

U.S.S. *Barb* while on patrol off Spain, reported hearing many unidentified explosions. It would be appreciated if you could state from your records whether any of those coincided with any attacks made by our own aircraft on U-boats within 120 miles of Cape Finisterre.

Date	Time (all times B.S.T.)
11th February	0912
	1940
12th "	1629
13th "	1125
19th "	2204
	2219
20th "	1952
21st "	0927
	0939
	1006
	1300
	1630
	1648
22nd "	1230
	1340
28th "	1810
4th March	1331 – 1500
5th "	1700 – 2100

(sgd)   S.M. Raw
          for Rear Admiral

234814M Wt. 10361/90S 46,000 Pads 6/40 W&S Ltd. 51-6897.

Form 348 (small)
(pads of 100 interleaved)

ROYAL AIR FORCE

From: Headquarters, Coastal Command.

To: Admiral (Submarines), Northways, London, N.W.3

Date: 31st March, 1943

Ref: CC/S.705/21/Air   S E C R E T

SECRET(U.S. CONFIDENTIAL)

With reference to your memo No. SM. 4343/456, dated 27th March, 1943, a careful examination of the records at this Headquarters has shown that there is no connection between the explosions reported by U.S.S. Barb and any attacks on U/Boats in this area by Coastal Command aircraft.

                        Air Marshall
          Air Officer Commanding-in-Chief
                <u>COASTAL COMMAND</u>

Patrol Four, 1 April 1943 – 14 May 1943

SS220/A16
Serial (04)

U.S.S. *Barb* (SS220)
c/o Fleet Post Office
New York, New York

U.S. CONFIDENTIAL – BRITISH SECRET 14 May, 1943.

CONFIDENTIAL

From:	The Commanding Officer.
To:	The Commander Submarine Squadron Fifty.
Subject:	Report of the fourth war patrol of the U.S.S. *Barb*.
Reference:	(a) Sub lant X-18 of November 15, 1942.
Enclosure:	(A) Report of the fourth war patrol of the U.S.S. *Barb* (SS220)

1. In accordance with reference (a) enclosure (A) is submitted herewith.

N. Lucker, Jr.

SS220/A16
Serial (04)

U.S.S. *Barb* (SS220)
c/o Fleet Post Office
New York, New York

CONFIDENTIAL

Report of the Fourth War Patrol of the U.S.S. *Barb*. Period from 1 April 1943 to 14 May 1943. Area K-193 and Area Line "X". Operational Order CSS 50 5-43.

PROLOGUE

Arrived at Base II March 6, 1943 and departed April 1, 1943. The period since the last patrol was spent at Base II for upkeep, leave and recreation. Repairs effected were routine and were accomplished by ship's force assisted by tender. Operations were conducted one day, March 28, 1943, during which sound tests were made in conjunction with HMS *P-238*[1]. Two practice approaches were made on the HMS *La Capricieuse*. A total of four dives were made during this day. On 26 March 1943 Lieutenant Commander N. Lucker, Jr[2]., U.S.N. reported aboard for temporary duty as Commanding Officer as relief for Lieutenant Commander J.R. Waterman, U.S.N.

1. NARRATIVE

April 1, 1943
    1230 Underway from Base II in accordance with CSS 50 Operation Order 5-43.
    1450 Trim dive.
    1500 Formed on escort HMS *Rhododendron*[3], HMS *Severn*[4] in company.

April 2, 1943
    1520 Sighted floating mine 500 yards on port bow.
    1635 Sighted floating mine 500 yards on starboard bow.

---

1   HMS *Stubborn* (P-238), was an S-class British submarine launched in 1942. She was sunk as a target in 1946.
2   Nicholas Lucker, Jr. had previously made four war patrols in command of U.S.S. *S-40*, operating out of Manila, Java, and Australia. He assumed command of *Barb* as part of a program in SubRon 50 in which a staff officer would relieve an operational commander for one patrol to allow for an extended rest period.
3   HMS *Rhododendron* (K-78) was a Flower class corvette, built in 1940 by Harland & Wolff, Belfast.
4   A Thames class fleet submarine, HMS *Severn* entered service in 1934. She was the ninth Royal Navy vessel to bear that name.

April 3, 1943
    0720 Took departure from Nuckle Flugga.
    1240 Arrived at beginning of route, set course, speed 15 knots.

April 4, 1943
    0001 Commenced using zone minus two time.
    0512 Submerged.
    0700 Surfaced.
    1840 Heavy sea "pooped" over cigarette deck and bridge causing an extremely large amount of water to flood both conning tower hatches and main induction; ship's ventilation hull flapper had been kept in the closed position as a precautionary measure. Only damage; grounded SJ motor generator set in Forward Engine Room and the Conning Tower heater. Both grounds were cleared and units were ready for use in ten minutes.

April 5, 1943
    0431 Submerged.
    0619 Surfaced.
    0725 Sighted floating mine 400 yards off port beam. Lat. 69°-23'.45 N., Long. 08°-30'.00 E.[5]
    0840 Sighted floating mine 800 yards broad on port bow. Lat. 69°-30'.00 N., Long. 08°-45'.00 E.
    1130 Sighted floating mine 800 yards off starboard beam. Lat. 69°-55'.00 N., Long. 10°-40' E.
    1938 Sighted floating mine 800 yards off port beam. Lat. 71°-18'.45 N., Long. 12°-16'.20 E.
    2145 Arrived in patrol area.
    Sighted five floating mines during the day, four before reaching area.

April 5 – 23, 1943
    Conducted surface patrol in assigned area, making short dive each day. Sighted 52 floating mines during this period. Mines were of various type and most of them appeared to have been in the water for some time. Fired at them with the rifle, machine gun and the 20 millimeter and though many hits were obtained, the mines neither exploded nor sank[6]. This helped to relieve the monotony of

---

[5]   This position is in the Norwegian Sea. For this patrol, *Barb*'s area was to be off the North Cape.

[6]   Anchored naval mines are designed to float a few feet below the surface, connected to a heavy anchor on the seabed by a cable. If the anchor cable breaks, a safety mechanism is supposed to be engaged. This is to prevent the destruction of friendly shipping if the mine floats into the cleared lane through the minefield. As often as not, the safety mechanism failed and the mines remained armed. Just as often, the safety did work properly, as testified by numerous war patrol reports citing a large number of hits that failed to detonate the mine.

the patrol and provided a small amount of training for the crew. At 1700 April 23rd received FOS 231428 changing our patrol area to line "X."

April 24, 1943
 0001 Left station for new patrol.
 0512 Submerged due to sighting plane bearing 150° true, altitude 1°, distant about 10 or 12 miles in Lat. 71°-32' N., Long. 11°-15' E. Plane's course approximately 330° true; not identified due to distance.
 1145 Surfaced.
 1210 Submerged due to sighting plane bearing 300° true, altitude 1°, distant about seven miles. Lat. 71°-27' N., Long. 10°-30' E.
 1256 Made periscope observation, sighted plane circling, distant about four miles; identified as Blohm and Voss (BV138) 3-engine single wing flying boat.
 1310 Plane disappeared over horizon on course 100° true.
 1416 Surfaced.
 Sighted 10 floating mines during day.

April 25, 1943
 Received FOS 251219 changing patrol line to line "Y."
 1459 Submerged.
 2400 Surfaced.

April 26, 1943
 Enroute new patrol line.
 0314 Submerged.
 2350 Surfaced.

April 27, 1943
 Enroute new patrol line.
 0401 Submerged.
 1350 Surfaced.
 1900 Received FOS 271644 giving date of *Barb* leaving patrol area as May 6th and directing us to obtain information as to southern limits of ice fields.

April 28, 1943
 0550 Arrived at northern limit of new patrol line.
 0554 Submerged.
 1527 Surfaced to obtain sun line.
 1530 Submerged.
 1859 Surfaced.
 2215 Submerged. Lookout sighted 4 planes bearing 045° true, altitude 2°, distant about 8 miles; planes' course approximately 225° true; ship's position Lat.

68°-10' N., Long. 016°-07' W. Planes not identified. After fifteen minutes at 100 feet, made observation at periscope depth, no planes in sight. (Conning tower periscope can only be used in *Low Power* due to derangement of optics or shifting linkage.)

2250 Surfaced.

2253 Submerged. While on course 270° true blowing up to remain on surface, one lookout and the Officer-of-the-Deck sighted a periscope bearing 230°, distant 500 yards. Went to 150 feet, rigged for silent running and listened on sound gear but could not hear anything. Ship's position (determined from later fix, 0230/29 April, and run back, was Lat. 68°-10.7 N., Long. 16°-13.8 W.

2327 Came to periscope depth for observations and remained there.

April 29, 1943

0030 Received FOS 28133 changing date of leaving patrol to May 8.

0221 Surfaced.

0400 Submerged.

Rigged Control Room periscope for use in Conning Tower[7]; this makes conning tower periscope inoperative, but in view of the derangement and difficulty of maintaining trim in rough weather at 56 feet, plus the increased distance of Conning Officer from fire control instruments, it was decided that one good periscope in the Conning Tower is better than one in Low Power only.

2357 Surfaced.

April 30, 1943

0401 Submerged.

1555 Surfaced to ventilate boat and get sun line.

1605 Submerged.

2351 Surfaced.

May 1, 1943

0400 Submerged.

1552 Surfaced to ventilate boat and get sun line.

1613 Submerged.

2350 Surfaced.

---

[7] *Gato* class submarines were built with both periscopes located in the conning tower. By unbolting and lowering the portion of the periscope well that went from deck to overhead in the control room, however, it was possible to use one of the periscopes from the control room, at the cost of needing to be closer to the surface during observations and the loss of the watertight isolation of the conning tower and control room. Nevertheless, many captains chose to go this route, as it allowed more room in the conning tower when both periscopes were in use.

May 2, 1943
    0508 Submerged.
    1455 Surfaced to ventilate boat and get sun line.
    1506 Submerged.
    2344 Surfaced.

May 3, 1943
    0359 Submerged.
    1559 Surfaced to ventilate boat and get sun line.
    1615 Submerged.
    1730 Recieved S9's 031545 giving routing instructions and orders to leave patrol May 7.
    2345 Surfaced.

May 4, 1943
    0502 Submerged.
    1615 Surfaced to ventilate boat and get sun line.
    1633 Submerged.
    2145 Received S9's 041535 extending date of leaving patrol to May 8.
    2350 Surfaced. Headed north to determine position of ice fields as per FOS 271644.

May 5, 1943
    1843 Reversed course to 180° true. Seas still full of floating ice. Sighted large icebergs on horizon. Water temperature 28° F. Air temperature 15° F. Ship completely iced over. Floating ice deemed dangerous. Pitometer log rodmeter[8] bent due to hitting ice cake, putting Pitometer log out of commission. Ship's position Lat. 70°-48' N., Long. 16°-04' W.

May 6, 1943
    0752 Submerged.
    1652 Surfaced to get sun line.
    1705 Submerged.
    2254 Surfaced.

May 7, 1943
    Ran surface patrol due to heavy sea and frequent snow storms. Top side completely iced over.

---

8   The Pitometer Log was the submarine's speedometer. The rodmeter (sometimes referred to as the "sword") projected below the hull and registered speed through the water. The rodmeter was vulnerable to being bent if the boat ran over anything in the water, and this was by no means an unusual event.

1210 SD radar contact 25 miles, plane moved in to 23 miles then faded out; visibility still bad. Average air temperature for today 20° F. Received S9's 071221 changing routing instructions.

May 8, 1943
   0759 Submerged.
   1300 Surfaced. Left patrol area and headed for point "P."

May 9, 1943
   0432 OOD sighted periscope. Lat. 66°-19' N., Long. 8°-16' W. Submerged.
   0453 Surfaced.
   1425 Submerged.
   2051 Surfaced.

May 10, 1943
   1100 Passed 100 fathom curve.
   1330 Sighted land bearing 199° true. Later determined to be Nuckle Flugga.
   1640 Sighted escort vessel, Norwegian MTB[9].
   1650 Formed astern of escort.
   1808 Anchored in South Harbor, Lerwick, Shetland Islands.

May 11, 1943
   2235 U.S.S. *Blackfish* anchored.

May 12, 1943
   1004 Underway enroute Base II, Rosneath, Scotland in company with escort HMS *La Capricieuse*, HMS *Usurper*, and U.S.S. *Blackfish*.

May 13, 1943
   Uneventful.

May 14, 1943
   1522 Arrived at Base II, Rosneath, Scotland.

2. WEATHER

Area K193 – Except for time enroute to this area and the first few days in area the weather was good and the seas calm. Many snow and hail storms were experienced but except for one or two they were of short duration.

Line W – The weather in this area was excellent until May 5th when we started

---

[9]   MTB: Motor Torpedo Boat. The British terminology for a PT Boat.

north to look for ice. The sea was calm but the skies were overcast, as a result of which only one fix was obtained while in this area. The injection temperature averaged 30° F. On the run north heavy winds and seas were experienced and the ship was completely covered with ice. At Lat. 70°-48' N., Long. 16°-04' W., heavy floe ice was encountered and large icebergs were seen on the horizon.

3. TIDAL INFORMATION

No Remarks.

4. NAVIGATIONAL AIDS

None.

5. DESCRIPTION OF WARSHIPS SIGHTED

Periscope sighted at 2253 on April 28th was of small diameter, with a spherical lens piece.

6. DESCRIPTION OF AIRCRAFT SIGHTED

Type	Position	Course	Alt.	Time – Date
Unidentified	71°-32' N., 11°-15' E.	330°	500'	0612/4-24
Blohm & Voss (BV138)	71°-27' N., 10°-30' E.	100°	500'	1210/4-24
4 Unidentified	68°-10' N., 16°-07' W.	225°	500'	2215/4-28

7. SUMMARY OF TACTICS

None.

8. ENEMY A/S MEASURES

None except plane patrols.

9. ENEMY MINE SWEEPING OPERATIONS

None.

10. MAJOR DEFECTS EXPERIENCED

One main engine cylinder liner was cracked. This was believed to be due to a small amount of water leaking by the outboard exhaust valve and upon preparing to surface, the engine was not completely drained, the excess water caused the casualty.

The optical shifting linkage in #2 periscope became deranged to the extent that the periscope could only be used in low power. No. 1 periscope was rigged for Conning Tower operation.

Latitude correction for Arma Gyrocompass only can be set up to 70° of latitude. In Area K 193, trouble was experienced in maintaining a slow enough armature speed on the gyro motor generator set, and twice the control panel rheostat burned out. A makeshift resistor was substituted that could withstand more current. This proved satisfactory.

11. RADIO RECEPTION

Excellent. Last consecutive message HS 256.

12. SOUND CONDITIONS

No remarks.

13. HEALTH AND HABITABILITY

Very good. The following cases were received for treatment.

DIAGNOSIS	NO. CASES	DAYS LOST
Headache	37	0
Constipation	32	0
Colds	13	0
Coughs	10	0
Sore Throats	8	0
Cat. Fever, acute	2	2
Tonsillitis, acute	1	7
Vincent's Angina	3	0
Sinusitis	1	0
Gastritis	4	1
Burns	2	0
Lacerations, Fingers	4	0
Fungus Infections	8	0
Pediculosis	5	0
Conjunctivitis	2	0
Backache	1	0
Boils	6	0

Cellulitis, Wrist	1	3
Ringworm	2	0
Urethritis	3	0
Gonococcus Infection, Urethra	1	0

14. MILES STEAM ENROUTE

Total miles to and from station – 3,730.

15. FUEL EXPENDED

89,255 gallons.

16. FACTORS OF ENDURANCE REMAINING

TORPEDOES	FUEL	PROVISIONS	FRESH WATER	PERSONNEL
24	19,694 gal.	20 days	Unlimited	20 days

17. FACTOR OF ENDURANCE CAUSING END OF PATROL

None. Recalled by FOS 271644 of April 1943.

18. REMARKS

The Commanding Officer recommends that our submarines use the same camouflage painting as the British submarines as it was noticed that they were very difficult to see, even at short distances in northern waters. Our silhouette will not allow us to obtain as good results but this change should be a decided improvement.

Because of sighting a periscope on our patrol line and probably presence of enemy submarines it was decided to conduct a periscope patrol with hopes of finding a U-boat for a target. Dives were made for 20 hours duration, with a short surfacing in order to obtain a noon line. These dives were not unduly hard on personnel, but were made for nine days only and undoubtedly would have become so.

As on previous patrols the only complaints are a lack of targets and the fact that the patrol areas are not very suitable for this type of submarine. With our large silhouette and with the continual daylight experienced in these areas, we are at a definite disadvantage compared to the smaller U-boats. This disadvantage was only partially nullified by the exceptionally long dives.

FC5-50/A16 SUBMARINE SQUADRON FIFTY
Serial 068

c/o Fleet Post Office,
New York, New York.

U.S. CONFIDENTIAL – BRITISH SECRET
C-O-N-F-I-D-E-N-T-I-A-L

From:	The Commander Submarine Squadron Fifty.
To:	The Commander-in-Chief, U.S. Fleet.
Via:	(1) The Admiral (Submarines)
	(2) The Admiralty.
	(3) The Commander, U.S. Naval Forces in Europe.
Subject:	U.S.S. *Barb* – Report of Fourth War Patrol
Enclosure:	(A) Track Chart (to Admiral (Submarines) only).

 1. The report of the Fourth War Patrol of the U.S.S. *Barb* is forwarded herewith. The duration of the patrol was forty-four (44) days. This patrol was conducted off the coast of Norway and north of Iceland.
 2. The material condition of the submarine and the physical condition of the crew was of the same excellence that has obtained on all previous patrols.
 3. Air temperature from 18 to 28 degrees Fahrenheit obtained throughout the patrol but no difficulty was experienced in operation of any of the equipment or machinery. The Squadron Commander is of the opinion that in conducting patrols in high latitudes with long daylight hours, the patrol should be carried out diving as much as possible. This will nullify the disadvantage of a large silhouette. Surface patrol should be carried out at 50% or 60% battery reserve. It is believed that this routine would be most effective in keeping the efficiency of the crew at its highest.
 4. The decrease in the directive force of the Arma gyrocompass in high latitudes is noted. Manual input of "own ship's course" into the Torpedo Data Computer with consequently slight decrease in the ease of operation must be accepted.
 5. Because of the restriction placed on the distribution of U.S. submarine patrol reports by the Commander-in-Chief, U.S. Fleet, it is requested that subordinated commands be furnished only with such extracted information as is considered necessary.

N.S. Ives

DISTRIBUTION:

The Admiralty	–	The Admiral (S)
Comnaveu	–	Cominch (2)
VOpnav	–	Cincpac
Cinclant	–	Comsopac
Comsowespac	–	Comsubpac
Comsublant (2)	–	Comsubsowespac.

UNITED STATES FLEET

UNITED STATES NAVAL FORCES IN EUROPE
20 GROSVENOR SQUARE
LONDON, W.1

Please refer to file:

A16/3
Serial 0996
1st Endorsement to:
Comsubron 50 serial (068)
of May 18, 1943.

CONFIDENTIAL

From: Commander, U.S. Naval Forces in Europe.
To: Commander in Chief, U.S. Fleet.

Subject: U.S.S. *Barb* – Report of Fourth War Patrol.

    1. Nine advance copies of subject patrol report are forwarded herewith for distribution to the U.S. Naval commands listed in the basic letter except Commander Submarines, Atlantic Fleet.
    2. By a copy of this letter, two copies of the subject report is being forwarded direct to Commander Submarines, Atlantic Fleet.

                                  J.G. Williams,
                                  By Direction.

Copy to:
  Comsublant (with 2 copies basic report)
  Comsubron 50 (less basic report)
  CO USS *Barb*   "   "   "

Patrol Five, 8 June 1943 – 24 July 1943

SS220/A16
                U.S.S. *Barb* (SS220)
                c/o Fleet Post Office
                New York, New York

                                            July 24, 1943.

CONFIDENTIAL

From:	The Commanding Officer.
To:	The Commander Submarine Squadron Fifty.
Subject:	Report of the Fifth War Patrol of the U.S.S. *Barb*.
Reference:	(a) SubLant X-18, Nov. 15, 1942.
Enclosure:	(A) Report of the Fifth War Patrol of the U.S.S. *Barb*.

  1. In accordance with reference (a) enclosure (A) is submitted herewith.

                                            J.R. Waterman

SS220/A16   U.S.S. *Barb* (SS220)
                    c/o Fleet Post Office
                    New York, New York.

CONFIDENTIAL

Report of the Fifth War Patrol of the U.S.S. *Barb*. Period from 8 June 1943 to 24 July 1943. Area E-2. Operation Order CSS50 11-43.

PROLOGUE

The period since last patrol was spent at Base II for upkeep, leave, and recreation. On May 14, 1943 Lieut-Comdr. J.R. Waterman, U.S.N. resumed command, relieving Lieut-Comdr. N. Lucker, Jr., U.S.N. Repairs effected were routine and accomplished by ship's force assisted by tender repair force. Practice gun firing was conducted and two torpedo approaches were made on HMS *Otus*.

1. NARRATIVE

June 8, 1943
   1600 Underway from Base II in accordance with CSS 50 Operation Order 11-43 in company with U.S.S. *Blackfish*.
   1700 Rendezvoused with HMS *Cuttysark* and commenced passage.
   1850 Trim dive.

June 12, 1943
   1015 Commenced diving by day enroute. The following routine was followed daily while diving by day enroute and on patrol:
   Submerged about 0600 daily. Surfaced about 1700 to ventilate and take sun sight. Submerged about 1720 – 1730 and surfaced about 0100. All days were completely uneventful except as noted below:

June 14, 1943
   2030 Sighted masts of merchant vessel. Unable to close.
   2135 Sighted vessel hull down. Made submerged approach and identified as *Johnson A. Balboa*, Sweden. Photographed.

June 19, 1943
   1030 Received FOS 181926, 181929, 182036, 182041, 190024 assigning new patrol area.
   1230 Surfaced and commenced passage to new patrol area.

June 22, 1943
   0700 Commenced diving by day with same routine.

June 23, 1943
   0543 Lookout reported periscope close aboard to starboard. Officer-of-the-Deck saw wake about 100 yards on starboard bow and turned to ram but object was inside the turning circle. Submerged and rigged for silent running—possibly large fish.

June 24, 1943
   Sighted empty carlin [sic] raft[1].

July 1, 1943
   1700 Received FOS 011520, 011521, and 011536 directing *Barb* proceed to New London.

July 2, 1943
   1710 Sighted object dead ahead which, on inspection, appeared to be a large wood raft on matting covered drum floats, well barnacled. In center of raft was a sheet metal well.

July 3, 1943
   1200 Left station maintaining same routine of submergence while enroute diving by day.

July 11, 1943
   0436 Sighted lighted vessel, approached and identified as Portuguese.

July 15, 1943
   0430 Sighted lighted vessel, approached and identified as Spanish.

July 17, 1943
   0900 Sighted large metal spar buoy.

July 19, 1943
   0400 Surface running to 0500 July 22, making daily trim dive, then to 2200 July 23, same submerged routine. During 22nd and 23rd of July, strong currents

---

1   The Carley raft or Carley Float was named for its inventor, Horace Carley (1838-1918). The standard design was an elongated octagonal hollow copper float, covered with cork and bound in canvas. Carley floats were normally lashed to steeply inclined racks along the sides of a ship, and could be quickly launched by cutting the lashings, dropping them into the water. As a life-saving device, they were much more easily deployed than a ship's lifeboats, making them particularly useful in the sudden emergencies that accompanied U-boat attacks.

combined with the lack of sights necessitated piloting by fathometer alone. On reaching 50 fathom curve—it was followed until surfacing at 2100 July 23rd.

1019 Moored Sub Base, New London, Conn.

2. WEATHER

Weather was phenomenally good throughout. Seas were glassy calm the majority of days.

3.

4.

5.

6.

7.

8.

9.

10. MAJOR DEFECTS

Salt water circulating pump on Nos. 1 and 2 main engines had hot bearings and had to be renewed. This is the third occurrence of this casuality suffered in 2,000 hours of operation with chrome liners.

11. RADIO RECEPTION

Variable.

12.

13. HEALTH AND HABITABILITY

DIAGNOSIS	NO. OF CASES	DAYS LOST
Constipation	44	0
Colds	4	0
Headache	58	0

Lacerations	12	0
Fungus Infections	33	0
Vincent's Angina	3	0
Gastritis	4	0
Gastro-Enteritis	1	2
Gingivitis	2	0
Cellulitis, Foot	1	6
Sore Throat	6	0
Measles	1	4
Urethritis	3	0
Conjunctivitis	4	0
Ingrown toenail	1	0
Ulcer, penis	2	0
Ulcer, abdomen	1	0
Foreign Body – Eye	2	0
Cyst, eyelid	1	0

14.

Miles steamed surface: 5,527
Miles steamed submerged: 1,110.2

15.

Fuel expended: 70,826 Gal.

16. FACTORS OF ENDURANCE REMAINING

Torpedoes – 24
Fuel – 19,064 Gal.
Provisions – 25 days.
Fresh Water – Indefinite.
Personnel – 10 days.

17. FACTOR CAUSING ENDING OF PATROL

Order FOS.

18. REMARKS

None.

A16-3(5)   SUBMARINES, ATLANTIC FLEET
(0939)   c/o Fleet Post Office, New York, N.Y.

CONFIDENTIAL   26 July 1943

From: The Commander Submarines, Atlantic Fleet.
To: The Commander in Chief, U.S. Fleet.
Via: The Commander in Chief, U.S. Atlantic Fleet.

Subject: U.S.S. *Barb* – Report of Fifth War Patrol.

Reference: (a) Cominch/Opnav FF1/A16-5 Ser. 01529 of 17 May 1943.

Enclosure: (A) Subject report.

     1. On 8 June 1943 U.S.S. *Barb* departed Base Two for a patrol in the North Atlantic. The Flag Officer Commanding Submarines ordered the patrol terminated on 1 July and *Barb* then proceeded to the Submarine Base, New London, arriving 24 July.
     2. No contacts were made with the enemy. The Commanding Officer has stated that he considers the periscope and wake, reported as having been sighted on 23 June, to have been a disturbance caused by some specie of marine life.
     3. *Barb* has been granted availability for upkeep and engine repairs from 25 July to 7 August at the Submarine Base, New London, Connecticut. A study will be made during refit period to determine the cause and remedial action required in connection with the hot bearings reported on main engine circulating water pumps.
     4. The form for war patrol reports prescribed by reference (a) was not followed by the *Barb* due to non-receipt prior to departure from Base Two.

DISTRIBUTION   F.A. Daubin
  The Admiralty – The Admiral (S)
  Comnaveu – Cominch (10)
  VOpnav – Cincpac – Cinclant –
  Comsopac – Comsowespac –
  Comsubpac – Comsubsowespac –
  Comsubron 50
  CO *Barb*

L.S. Parks,
Flag Secretary

Patrol Six, 30 September 1943 – 28 November 1943

SS220/A16   U.S.S. *Barb* (SS220)
                             c/o Fleet Post Office
Serial 0223   San Francisco, Calif.

CONFIDENTIAL   28 November 1943

From: Commanding Officer, U.S.S. *Barb*.
To: Commander in Chief, United States Fleet.
Via: Commander Submarine Division Sixty-One.
            Commander Submarine Squadron Four.
            Commander Submarine Force, Pacific Fleet.

Subject: U.S.S. *Barb*, Report of War Patrol Number Six

Enclosure: (A) Subject Report.

    1. Enclosure (A), covering the sixth war patrol of this vessel conducted in the Formosan[1] area during the period 30 September 1943, to 28 November 1943, is forwarded herewith.

J.R. Waterman

---

[1] Formosa: Taiwan, at that time a Japanese colony.

SS220/A16

CONFIDENTIAL

U.S.S. *Barb*, Report of War Patrol Number Six

(A) PROLOGUE

The period since last patrol was spent enroute from New London, Connecticut to Pearl Harbor, T.H., plus a ten day refit by SubBase, Pearl Harbor. Extensive work was undertaken including addition of two 20 MM guns and shifting of 3" gun forward. A three day training period followed during which time six torpedoes and all guns were fired.

(B) NARRATIVE

30 September
2230z[2] Departed Pearl Harbor under escort of U.S.S. *Allen*[3], in accordance with Comtaskfor 17 OpOrd 221-43 and commenced passage to operating area via Midway.

1 October
0530z Parted company with escort.
Sighted large bomber on westerly course, distant 10 miles (Contact #1).

3 October
0130 Sighted large bomber on easterly course, distant 12 miles (Contact #2).

4 October
1800z Arrived rendezvous and contact plane escort.
2105z Moored to nest alongside *Sperry*[4] and commenced exchange of exploder mechanisms.

6 October
1951z Underway from Midway. Commenced passage to area.

---

[2] Time Zone "Z," or "Zebra" in the World War II phonetic alphabet ("Zulu" in the modern military phonetic alphabet). Greenwich Mean Time. Most submarines in the Pacific operated on local time, as would *Barb* on subsequent patrols.

[3] U.S.S. *Allen* (DD 66). A *Sampson* class destroyer built in 1916, *Allen* was a survivor of the Pearl Harbor attack. She remained at Pearl for the rest of the War and was scrapped in 1946.

[4] U.S.S. *Sperry* (AS 12).

7 October

0340z Sighted large bomber, distant 12 miles, on opposite course (Contact #3).

0840z Lookout reported periscope 1,000 yards on starboard beam. Placed astern and went to flank speed. Not sighted by OOD or CO (Contact #1).

14 October

0645z Sighted Haha Jima bearing 300(T) distant about 35 miles.

15 October

1245z Commenced surface patrol on east-west courses in vicinity Long. 137-44 E. in accordance with Comsubpac directive.

16 October

1012z Sighted lights of a vessel. Closed to investigate and obtained radar range at 25,000 yards. After two hours at full power we closed sufficiently to identify a properly marked hospital ship. Broke off approach[5] and returned to patrol line (Contact #2).

18 October

1952z At the beginning of morning twilight, made radar and sight contact with large passenger freighter of *Heian Maru* type and two large DD[6] escorts emerging from a rain squall (Contact #3) Went to radar depth at range of 12,5000 yards and soon sighted target, which passed into another rain squall. Intermittent sightings after going to periscope depth until range was reduced to about 4,800 yards with 10° starboard angle. At this time one DD passed within 800 yards but we held fire for main target. It was our last chance as formation changed about 120° away at this time. Maneuvers appeared to consist of constant helm imposed on zig plan. Both screens were on starboard bow of target. Four torpedoes flooded, so commenced routining as formation was drawing away. Lost contact. Completed routining and commenced full speed pursuit but failed to regain contact. Broke off pursuit at 0700z on 19th and resumed passage to area. Formation must have made radical change of base course after contact was lost.

21 October

0443z Entered patrol area.

22 October

0645z Made landfall on Miyako Jima. Decided to patrol north Miyako Jima light before proceeding to Eoka Sho.

---

[5] Hospital ships are legally considered non-combatant vessels, and may not be attacked as long as they comply with international law regarding proper marking and operation.

6   DD: Destroyer.

2330z Sighted convoy consisting of two medium sized freighters and four small ships, possibly escorts, plus plane escort. Attempted to gain position ahead on the surface, but plane's approach drove us down. Approached at high speed for three hours, but gradually lost distance. Surfaced at 0300z, 23rd and attempted end around. Convoy and plane escort were sighted at intervals as we drew ahead. At 0700z, sighted plane approaching in glide astern. Submerged and took one depth bomb. On return to periscope depth, saw that plane had been joined by others. They were making intensive search of area and kept us submerged until after dark. On surfacing, decided further pursuit would be a waste of fuel as they were already out of our area and their base course was uncertain (Contact #4). (Plane Contacts #5 & 6).

23 October

1445z Unable to raise NPM[7] to send report.

1920z Obtained radar contact at 3,900 yards on some small craft, which approached at high speed to 2,500 yards. Submerged and tracked by sound. Never sighted (Contact #5).

24 October

0320z While surfacing, periscope watch sighted two SC[8] type patrol craft in formation 10,000 yards on port beam. Submerged. Not seen again (Contact #6).

25 October

0340z Sighted smoke while submerged. After determining direction of bearing change, came to normal approach course and ran at high speed. Finally sighted three large transports with DD and plane escort (Contact #7) (Plane Contact #7), but angle on the bow was 90° starboard. Two zigs toward put us dead ahead at 12,000 yards, but all other zigs were away and formation passed out of range. Base course appeared to be 050(T) but when last sighted the formation had again come right. With this in view, it was decided to report contact on base course 060(T) for use of submarines in northern areas, but to proceed on course 090(T) in the event last indicated course proved to be correct. This would pass convoy through point where contact #4 passed; convoy passed out of sight 1½ hours before sunset but air escort kept us down. After sunset, surfaced and proceeded at full speed. Sent contact report, *Barb* Serial #2.

25 October[9]

1711z Radar contact at 3,700 yards with two small craft. Detoured and did not sight.

---

[7] The Navy radio station at Pearl Harbor.
[8] SC: Sub Chaser. Small, usually wood-hulled anti-submarine vessel.
[9] Date in original. Probably a typo and actually 26 October.

1930Z Discontinued search and slowed down. Proceeding to southern part of area for a few days.

27 October
2105z Sighted Seikoo Road Light at 15 miles. Conducted submerged patrol along shore. Heavy but passing rains, overcast sky and rough seas made observations difficult. During the afternoon, a steady rain set in and visibility became worse. Surfaced and proceeded east to transmit *Barb* Serial 3, thence between Yonakuni Jima and Iriomote Jima to Hoka Sho.

31 October
Patrolling this area. Overcast skies with numerous rain squalls continue to be prevalent and when not in sight of land navigation is next to impossible. Radar fixes prove invaluable. Rough seas continue. In view of the bad weather conditions combined with the strong currents encountered, it has been decided to continue patrolling these eastern areas rather than enter Formosa Channel, until the weather improves. No evidence on Hoka Sho of the radar suspected by *Sculpin*.

0430z Periscope watch sighted nine large bombers on westerly course, flying in formation. Disappeared in overcast (Contact #8).

1500z Sighted lights on horizon, which were soon identified as properly marked hospital ship on course 060(T). This contact tends to verify our belief that traffic is being routed further east (Contact #9).

3 November
Rough seas and bad visibility continue unabated. Inshore submerged patrol not feasible so continuing surface patrol between Hoka Sho and Sento Shosho.

0216z SD radar contact at 6 miles moving in. Submerged and searched by periscope. Not sighted due to overcast (Contact #9).

0700z SD radar contact at 8 miles moving in. Submerged. Evidently a regular air patrol is maintained here (Contact #10).

4 November
0145z SD radar contact at 8 miles, which moved in rapidly. Submerged (Contact #11).

5 November
Conducting inshore patrol at Seikoo Road. Weather has improved and seas abated somewhat, however, squalls and overcast continue.

6 November
Will return to Hoka Sho and attempt to intercept convoy reported heading south.

7 November

Patrolling NE of Hoka Sho. Set during the night was 29 miles to the eastward.

8 November

Just prior to surfacing, the boat suddenly took a down angle and descended rapidly to 95 feet. A bubble in safety[10] checked the descent and the cause was evident on the bathythermograph[11], which showed extreme gradient plus and minus. A down current probably exists here and the surface is cut up by its rip tides.

Patrolling northern Formosa Straits. The weather has cleared for the first time and the sea is glassy.

9 November

All night run at standard speed put us in noon position of reported convoy. Patrolled that area during daylight without results. Assumed that convoy had hugged island chain, continued south, and would then cut sharply northwest. Proceeded toward Yonakuni Island to intercept.

1519z Radar contact at 11,000 yards in the midst of a rain squall (Contact #10). Tracked to obtain course and speed and commenced end around. Extremely heavy seas held our speed down to 11 to 13 knots, but finally gained position on port bow of formation and commenced surface radar approach. The night was black as a fathom up a chimney and nothing was sighted until the range was reduced to less than 3,000 yards. We were making approach on largest ship in center of formation when shapes suddenly loomed up at 1,600 yards broad on starboard bow. We were on a collision course, so changed rapidly towards and took these two overlapping ships as targets.

At 2017z fired four torpedoes from bow tubes (Attack #1) and observed two hits in large AK[12] (8,000 T) and one in medium AK similar to *Heiyo Maru* (5,624 T). Immediately four vessels turned on strong searchlights and one fired a gun. Swinging to bring on stern tubes or shift to other flank, as feasible, when a DD or torpedo boat suddenly appeared around the sterns of the torpedoed AKs and at 1,600 yards headed for us.

As we passed 60 feet, one heavy explosion was heard combined with a series

---

[10] The Safety Tank was an internal ballast tank, with the same liquid capacity as the conning tower. It was normally kept flooded when the submarine was submerged. In the event the conning tower flooded, safety could be blown to maintain trim or, as here, safety could be partially blown to compensate for a sudden loss of buoyancy.

[11] Bathythermograph: A recording thermometer/depth recorder. A stylus traced a depth/temperature record on a graph card. Temperature layers will deflect or reflect sonar pings, so knowing where the layers exist allowed the submarine to hide below them.

[12] AK: Freighter, from the hull number prefix assigned to Navy cargo ships (Auxiliary, Cargo). The "K" is employed because "C" indicates a "Cruiser."

of noises which we believed to be the vessel breaking up. The loud explosion was more like a surface detonation or one at shallow depth, lacking the usual depth charge bang. It could not possibly have come from the DD or torpedo boat.

About an hour later there were three very heavy explosions and loud rumblings at a good distance, which also lacked the characteristic depth charge bang. These may have been exploding boilers. The type of explosions and noises heard, plus the observed hits and extremely heavy seas from ahead convinced us that at least one of the vessels sank.

On submerging into the heavy seas excessive water had to be taken in and she went down like a rock. Safety was blown and the boat checked at 375 feet. She was tight except for #1 MB tank riser[13] and conning tower cables, but valuable time was lost in regaining trim. Commenced retirement as seas were much too heavy for periscope observations in approaching twilight and we were too close to the beach to surface.

Although the formation was never seen, it appears from radar information to have consisted of four medium to large cargo vessels in two columns, with one escort ahead, one astern, and one on each flank. No pinging was heard, and the rough seas prevented their making contact by sonic listening[14].

11 November
Proceeding to eastern edge of area preparatory to departing for Midway. Making good seven knots on turns for ten knots. If head seas persist, fuel will become a problem.

12 November
Enroute position Lat. 20-00 N., 137-00 E. as directed by Comsubpac.

14 November
0604z Transmitted *Barb* Serial #5.

15 November
Patrolling designated area.

---

[13] Number 1 main ballast tank is located in the single-hull section at the forward end of the boat, under the forward torpedo room. Because of the location of the tank, it is connected to the vents by risers located inside the pressure hull in the forward torpedo room. These risers were always considered a potential problem, as a rupture could open the FTR to the sea. Number 7 main ballast tank, also in a single-hull section under the after torpedo room, is vented in the same manner. The vent risers for the other main ballast tanks are located under the superstructure, outside the pressure hull.

[14] Sonic listening: Sound search using hydrophones listening for sound in the normal human hearing frequency range (below 15,000 Hz). Listening for sound above 15,000 Hz is called "super-sonic," and requires special equipment to make the sounds audible to the sonar operator. Most ship noises are in the sonic range; active sonar is normally in the super-sonic range.

16 November

1100z Hydraulic plant binding has grown progressively worse. It is secured all night and has to be secured during day at intervals for oiling. While plant was secured for this purpose, sighted float type plane crossing astern at five miles (Contact #12). Rang diving alarm, but #2 MB vents failed to open. Finally got pressure built up and vents open and commenced to submerge. Periscope reported plane's wing over and dive. His first drop exploded fairly close as we passed 50 feet and his next while at 140 feet. Only his poor marksmanship saved us from a bad shaking up. As we were within sight of both Kito Iwo Jima and Haha Jima decided to stay submerged until dark.

[17 November]

0454z During periscope sweep sighted single engine monoplane headed directly for us (Contact #13). Probably not sighted as nothing was dropped. Surfaced after dark and proceeded at two engine speed. The brilliant phosphorescence on the glassy sea made it appear as though we had on contour lights. If our pals hadn't been averse to night flying, they couldn't have failed to spot us.

1505z Sighted blinking light on horizon, headed toward it and soon sighted two other lights. They were all similar, but had slightly different characteristics. One gave a dot and long dash, the other two, other combinations of dots and long dash. No ship's hulls could be seen even though there was a brilliant moon. Since our presence in the vicinity was known, decided not to investigate further as lights were probably either a decoy or signals from fishing vessels or small boats. Resumed course (Contact #11).

19 November

0205z Sighted lights on horizon and closed. A line of three lighted craft were stationed about 3 miles apart and appeared to be patrolling on course 030(T) and reverse. They were due north of Marcus Island. Unable to make out hull in bright moonlight, but obtained weak radar contact at 3,000 yards. Decided that the possibility of fishing craft operating from Marcus Island was remote, so detoured and proceeded.

24 November

0210z Contacted plane, escorted.
0420z Moored alongside tender at Midway.

26 November

Underway enroute Pearl Harbor.
2155z Sighted PBM patrol plane[15] and exchanged recognition signals.

---

[15] PBM: Martin Mariner, twin-engine seaplane patrol bomber.

27 November

Sighted steamer bearing 062(T). Opened range to south to remain undetected. This vessel was in sight the remainder of daylight and was contacted by radar after dark.

28 November
2200z Moored at Submarine Base, Pearl Harbor, T.H.

(C) WEATHER

At this season of the year the weather in the Formosan area is either bad or worse. During the entire time in the area there were only three days of good weather. Calm seas and clear skies were experienced on a few other days, but these conditions never lasted more than a few hours. Frequent rain squalls, fresh northeast winds, a complete overcast, and rough seas were the rule. This applied when west of the Bonin Islands. Between these islands and Midway, the weather was excellent.

(D) TIDAL INFORMATION

In general, tidal conditions conformed to data supplied by charts and H.O.[16] publications. On a few occasions, however, current varied by 90° from that charted.

(E) NAVIGATIONAL AIDS

Navigational lights were on but not at full brilliance on Formosa Island. No lights were sighted in the Saki Shima Gunto group.

(F) SHIP CONTACTS

No.	Time-Date	Lat. Long.	Type(s)	Initial Range	Est. Course Speed	How Contacted	Remarks
1.	2040z 7 Oct	25-59 N 176-43 E	Periscope	(Yards) 1,000	—	SD	
2.	1012z 16 Oct	25-20 N 137-45 E	Hospital Ship	23,000	310(T) 15 kts.	SD	Properly lighted

---

[16] H.O.: The U.S. Hydrographic Office (renamed U.S. Naval Oceanographic Office in 1962), was responsible for oceanographic surveys, and produced the Navy's nautical charts and other related publications.

U.S.S. *Barb* (SS-220)   83

No.	Time Date	Lat. Long.	Type		Est. Course Speed	How Contacted	Remarks
3.	1952z 18 Oct	25-31 N 137-42 E	11,600 T AK & DD	14,000	340(T) 13 kts	R, SN	Unable to close
4.	2330z 22 Oct	25-20 N 125-26 E	Convoy 2 AK, 4 small vessels	23,000	050(T) 3 kts	P, SD	Air Escort
5.	1920z 23 Oct	25-07 N 124-38 E	Unknown	3,900	—	R	Not sighted
6.	0320z 24 Oct	25-07 N 124-18 E	Two Patrol Craft	10,000	270(T)	P, SD	—
7.	0340z 25 Oct	25-30 N 122-30 E	Three transports	20,000	060(T) 12 kts	P	Unable to close
8.	1711z 25 Oct	25-31 N 122-50 E	Small craft	3,700	—	R	Not sighted
9.	1500z 31 Oct	25-54 N 122-50 N	Hospital Ship	20,000	060(T) 15 kts	SN	Properly lighted
10.	1519z 9 Nov	24-37 N 122-58 E	Convoy: 4 AK 4 Escorts	11,000	300(T) 7 kts	R	Attacked at 2017z
11.	1505z 17 Nov	26-11 N 143-02 E	Blinking Lights	12,000	—	SN	Decoy or Fishing boats
12.	0206z 19 Nov	27-48 N 134-32 E	Lighted Patrol Craft	12,000	030(T) 210(T)	SN	—
13	1920z 27 Nov	21-10 N 163-40 W	Friendly AK	30,000	110(T) 12 kts	SD	High Periscope

(G) AIRCRAFT CONTACTS

No.	Time - Date	Lat. Long.	Type(s)	Initial Range (Miles)	Est. Course Speed	How Contacted	Remarks
1.	1 Oct	25-30 N 162-50 W	—	10	Westerly	SD	—
2.	1500vw 2 Oct	27-07 N 167-47 W	Large Bomber	10	Easterly	SD	U.S. Army
3.	1540y 6 Oct	28-00 N 179-01 W	Large Bomber	12	Easterly	SD	
4.	2330z 22 Oct	25-20 N 125-26 E	Sally	12	Various	SD	Escorting Convoy
5.	0700z 23 Oct	25-35 N 126-04 E	Sally	5	050(T)	SD	Dropped bomb
6.	0930z 23 Oct	25-35 N 126-00 E	Sally Jake	5	Various	P	Searching

7.	0340z 25 Oct	25-30 N 122-30 E	Nell	5	Screening	P	Escorting transport
8.	0430z 31 Oct	25-50 N 122-10 E	9 Large bombers	5	Westerly	P	—
9.	0216z 3 Nov	25-43 N 122-41 E	—	6	—	R	Not sighted
10.	0700z 3 Nov	25-25 N 122-42 E	—	8	—	R	Not sighted
11.	1045z 4 Nov	23-25 N 122-02 E	—	8	—	R	Not sighted
12.	0200z 17 Nov	25-00 N 142-00 E	Float	6	180(T)	SD	Bombed twice
13.	0545z 17 Nov	25-55 N 142-08 E	Small Monoplane	4	000(T)	P	Headed at periscope
14.	2155z 26 Nov	22-46 N 168-35 E	PBM	10	270(T)	SD	Exchanged Signals

(N) ATTACK DATA

U.S.S. *Barb*　　Torpedo Attack No. (1)　　Patrol No. (6)
Time: 0517　　Date: 10 November 1943　　Lat. 24-41 N., Long. 122-11 E.

Target Data – Damage Inflicted

Description: Attack made on convoy on surface, approach using radar with final bearings by TBT[17]. Contact by radar. Seas extremely rough and very dark night.
Ship(s) Sunk: 8,000 ton unidentified AK
Ship(s) Damaged }
Probably Sunk } 5,624 ton similar to *Meiyo Maru*[18]
Damage Determined by: Three hits observed and heard. Times agree with torpedo run. Heavy explosions and breaking up noises heard after submerging.
Target Draft: —　Course: 300(T)　Speed: 7 kts.　Range: 2,200 yards (at firing)

Own Ship Data

Speed: Steerageway　Course: 005(T)　Depth: Surface　Angle: —

---

[17] TBT: Target Bearing Transmitter. Early in the War, a special pelorus with a fitting into which a pair of binoculars could be clamped. Later a pair of pressure-proof binoculars, fitted with cross hairs and a lighted reticle, were built into the unit. Used to determining target bearing during surface attacks. Pressing a button on the handle transmitted the bearing to the conning tower.

[18] Elsewhere in the report and endorsements shown as *Heiyo Maru*.

Fire Control and Torpedo Data

Type Attack: Radar – Surface.

	No. 1	No. 2	No. 3	No. 4
Tubes Fired				
Track Angle (Torp)	140 P	145 P	137 P	143 P
Gyro Angle	335	329	337	323
Depth Set	10	10	10	10
Power	High	High	High	High
Hit or Miss	------------ 3 hits, one miss ------------------			
Erratic	No	No	No	No
Mark Torpedo	14-34	14-34	14-34	14-34
Serial No.	23656	25401	25421	25445
Mark Exploder	6-1	6-1	6-1	6-1
Serial No.	6960	6011	12328	12332
Actuation Set	-------------- Contact Only -------------------			
Actuation Actual	---------------- Contact ---------------------			
Mark Warhead	16	16	16	16
Serial No.	9771	10497	3806	6151
Explosive	TPX[19]	TPX	TPX	TPX
Sea Conditions	4	4	4	4
Overhaul Activity	------------ SubBase, Pearl Harbor ------------			

Remarks: Exploders fitted with lightweight firing pins[20] and modification A, B, C, D, E in accordance with SubBase, Pearl Harbor E&R Dept. Dwg. No. XA49 dated 9/28/43.

(I) MINES

(J) ANTI-SUBMARINE MEASURES AND EVASION TACTICS

Plane patrols are evidently maintained in the Formosan area, but fly high enough to be detected by radar. The Bonin air patrol is conducted by slow float type planes and their charges are not very heavy.

---

[19] TPX: Torpex, a mixture of TNT, RDX (cyclonite and cyclomethane trinitramine) and aluminum powder. This was first used in American torpedoes in 1943. The mixture is about 50% more powerful than TNT alone.

[20] This was the so-called Pearl Harbor Modification to the Mark 6 exploder. As originally designed, the firing pins (there were two) were made of steel. Inertia would cause these to hang up on the guides on impact, with the result that the guides were often distorted by the impact before the firing pins could hit the primers. Experimentation at Pearl Harbor disclosed the problem, and lightweight aluminum firing pins were produced, which accelerated faster upon release and were thus able to strike the primers before the guides distorted. The number of successful attacks increase dramatically from that point.

Both convoys sighted during daylight had plane escorts, which proved very efficient in forcing us down and keeping us there before attack positions could be reached. These planes patrol around the convoy not more than 3 miles abeam, but up to twenty miles ahead and astern. Small patrol craft were sighted only on the line between Miyako Jima and Sento Shosho where three contacts were made. The absence of these craft in the vicinity of Hoka Sho was a surprise.

The convoy attacked on November tenth fired the usual gun signal and swept the area with four powerful search lights.

(K) MAJOR DEFECTS

The main hydraulic plant was a constant source of trouble throughout the patrol. This condition is serious and came close to causing the loss of the boat. The accumulator was removed from the vessel and overhauled at Pearl Harbor, but the binding and pounding returned after two weeks operation. It was necessary to shut down the plant during the night to avoid unnecessary operation and at intervals during daylight it had to be secured for oiling. The cause of the trouble is not definitely known but appears to be a lack of tolerance between the air plunger and the air cylinder bushing. Excessive oil temperature and unsatisfactory hydraulic packing are probably contributory causes. It is believed that a completely new unit should be installed unless the cause can be definitely determined and rectified.

Main engine mufflers corroded through.

Main vents leak and require complete overhaul.

A very loud groan, accompanied by a grinding noise, has again developed in the rudder post or steering gear rams. The cause of this is also not definitely known, although it disappeared for a few days after the rams were repaired at Pearl Harbor. It is believed that the rudder should be unshipped for inspection.

One day out of Pearl Harbor a fuel oil leak developed from FBT through the check valve and LP blower stops to turbo blow accumulator. The blower lines were removed at Midway and blanked off.

The QB sound equipment, repaired many times, leaked badly in the hydraulic system. Excessive leakage of oil past the drift stop control valves causes overloading and consequent overheating of the main hydraulic plant. There appears to be a binding between the piston and cylinder in the main shaft. On rotation this causes the smaller shaft to shear the locking key and unscrew the smaller shaft. The unit should be removed for complete overhaul.

#2 periscope has given trouble since this ship has been in commission and was pulled for the 12th time while in Midway. Grinding still exists as well as fogging in high power. Scores developed and were stoned at regular intervals, but gradually returned. New bushings and a new periscope should be installed as this one has never been satisfactory.

Bow plane magnetic brake failed. Planes now coast to some extent.

Leak developed in 4th stage H.P. AC cooler. Spare cooler installed.

Vapor compression still coils developed leak. Repaired. Valves to fresh water system also had to be overhauled.

Pit log has been kept in operation by almost daily repair.

#1 MB tank riser developed flange leak due to deep submergence (375 feet).

Altered pilot house has a synchronous vibration, which caused excessive noise at submerged speeds above 2/3.

Aux. engine in need of overhaul. Grommet leaks and governor trouble predominated.

Outboard exhaust valves leak excessively.

(L) RADIO

Radio reception was good except on a few nights. One Serial was missed. On one occasion it was impossible to raise NPM.

(M) RADAR

There were no radar casualties and results were excellent.

(N) SOUND GEAR AND SOUND CONDITIONS

Sound conditions were fair to good.

(O) DENSITY LAYERS

Enroute to area, distinct density layers were experienced from 100 feet to 230 feet. All temperature layers were of a negative character. No density layers were found in the area except in the vicinity of the Koka Sho Light.

At Lat. 23° 33' N., Long. 122° 33' E. encountered a very extreme negative temperature gradient upon two occasions in which the temperature dropped 5° to 10° with no depth change. On one of these occasions, down currents were in evidence as depth control was impossible and Safety Tank had to be resorted to in checking descent. During descent the gradient approached an isothermal character. In this area strong rip tides were in evidence.

(P) HEALTH AND HABITABILITY

The physical condition of the crew was excellent. It is quite apparent that patrols in these areas are much less a physical strain than those made in the European theater.

Summary of cases requiring medical attention during patrol:

	No. Cases	Days Lost
Constipation	34	0
Fungus infection, feet	21	0
Fungus infection, groin	10	0
Headache	78	0
Colds	4	0
Coughs	1	1
Burns, second degree	1	0
Neuritis, left arm	1	0
Laceration, finger	4	0
Backache	1	0
Cold Sores	3	0
Earache	2	0
Mastoiditis	1	2
Vincent's Angina	2	0
Boils	1	0

(Q)

Personnel reacted excellently under combat conditions as well as maintaining morale during the longer periods of boredom. This is the sixth war patrol of this vessel and many of those aboard have made them all. The cumulative effect is becoming apparent in some cases in the form of slacking interest or increased nervousness.

(R) MILES STEAMED – FUEL USED

Base to area	4,432.3 miles	34,442 gals.
In Area	4,085.6 miles	38,260 gals.
Area to base	4,557.0 miles	34,354 gals.

(S) DURATION

Days enroute to area	15 days
Days in area	20 days
Days enroute to base	9 days
Days submerged	15 days

(T) FACTORS OF ENDURANCE REMAINING

Torpedoes	Fuel	Provisions	Personnel Factor
20	4,826 gals.	20 days	20 days

Limiting factor this patrol – Fuel.

(U) REMARKS

At this season of the year weather appears to be the most annoying antagonist to be met in the area. Rough seas, complete overcast, and frequent rain squalls persisted for all except three days. Efficient close inshore submerged patrol was not possible except during the rare occasions of improvements in the weather and those were of such short duration as not to be worthwhile.

All traffic seems to be in convoy and round about routes are employed. The convoy attacked on 10 November had come south close inshore along the chain of island, passed south of Yonakuni Islands, then northwest toward Kiirun.

SUBMARINE DIVISION SIXTY-TWO

FB5-61/A16-3

Serial (027)

Care of Fleet Post Office,
San Francisco, California,
29 November, 1943.

First Endorsement to
U.S.S. *Barb* Sixth War Patrol,
dated 28 Nov 43.

C-O-N-F-I-D-E-N-T-I-A-L

From: The Commander Submarine Division Sixty-One.
To: The Commander-in-Chief, United States Fleet.
Via: (1) The Commander Submarine Squadron Four.
        (2) The Commander Submarines Force, Pacific Fleet.

Subject: U.S.S. *Barb* Sixth War Patrol – Comments on.

1. The sixth war patrol of the *Barb* was the first conducted in the Pacific area, the first five having been conducted in the European theater. The patrol extended over a period of sixty days, of which twenty-two days were spent in the patrol area and six additional days patrolling stations outside the area.

2. The *Barb* had four contacts with enemy ships worthy of attack with torpedoes:

(a) 19 October – At the beginning of morning twilight made contact with a *Heian Maru* type passenger-freighter escorted by two large destroyers. Intermittent rain squalls prevented continuous sighting after it was necessary to go to periscope depth. When the range was 4,800 yards, 10° on starboard bow of the large ship, one escort passed within 800 yards. The Commanding Officer, seeing his excellent position on what was apparently an important target, withheld fire. Both screens were on the starboard bow of the target. At this time the formation, which had been zig-zagging, made a change of course 120° away and all chance for attack was lost. The value of the target, as evidenced by the heavy screening vessels, and the position of the screens lead to a logical conclusion that the *Barb* was in a good position to attack the main target. It is believed that the Barb might have had another chance for attack had she surfaced sooner and maintained sight contact while making an end-around run. Contact was lost and not regained.

(b) The contact with the convoy during the morning of 23 October was aggressively pursued but was frustrated by planes, which caused the *Barb* to submerge twice. The last plane contact dropped on depth bomb and, with others, patrolled the vicinity until after dark. A further chase of this low speed convoy after dark might have proved worth while although the base course was uncertain.

(c) About noon, 25 October, another convoy was sighted but despite use of high speed the radical zigs of the formation kept it out of torpedo range of the *Barb*. Air escort kept the *Barb* submerged until after sunset. Pursuit was then made to eastward, the last indicated course, but contact was not re-established. Later contact by other submarines indicates that the base course was about 060°T. The choice for the enemy was to go westward or southward of an island group. The *Barb* guessed wrong, but supplied information which assisted other submarines to make contact.

(d) On the night of 9 November, the *Barb* had difficulty in getting ahead of a low speed four ship, four escort convoy. A PPI[21] would have been a great help for accurately locating ships and escorts. In a night surface attack four torpedoes were fired at overlapping ships resulting in two hits on one AK and one hit on the other. The explosions and noises heard after the attack indicate the sinking of one of the ships. Escorts forced submergence and the proximity to destination prevented further attack.

3. Only one day was spent patrolling in the Formosa Strait, the majority of the time being spent in the vicinity of Hako Sho, which area has proved fruitful of contacts in the past year. Rough weather influenced the Commanding Officer in remaining where he could occasionally get a radar fix on islands rather than to venture into the area where the position would be unknown for long periods.

4. The *Barb* has had no Navy Yard overhaul since commissioning. Many small defects indicate that overhaul at this time is very desirable. The main hydraulic plant was a constant source of trouble and a thorough overhaul, or replacement, is required.

5. The Commanding Officer, officers and crew are congratulated on the success of their first patrol in Pacific waters.

6. It is recommended that the *Barb* be credited with inflicting the following damage on the enemy:

SUNK

| One Freighter (unidentified) | 8,000 tons |

DAMAGED

| One Freighter (*Heiyo Maru* class) | 5,624 tons |

C.C. Smith

---

21   PPI: Plan Position Indicator. A type of radar display in which the ship is always at the center of the screen, with targets represented by pips around it. The type of display seen in most film depictions of radar. The original SJ display provided range and bearing, but was considerably more difficult to interpret at a glance.

FC5-4/A16-3   SUBMARINE SQUADRON FOUR   18/mg

Serial 0312   c/o Fleet Post Office,
                                           San Francisco, Calif.
C-O-N-F-I-D-E-N-T-I-A-L
                                           2 December 1943
Second Endorsement to
U.S.S. *Barb* Report of
Sixth War Patrol,
of 28 November 1943.

From: The Commander Submarine Squadron Four.
To: The Commander-in-Chief, United States Fleet.
Via: (1) The Commander Submarine Force, Pacific Fleet.
               (2) The Commander-in-Chief, Pacific Fleet.

Subject: U.S.S. *Barb* Sixth War Patrol – Comments on.

    1. Forwarded concurring in the remarks of Commander Submarine Division Sixty-One.

    2. The Commander Submarine Squadron Four congratulates the Commanding Officer, officers and crew on the successful completion of their first patrol in Japanese waters.

C.B. Momsen[22]

---

[22] Charles B. "Swede" Momsen (1896-1967) was the developer of the Momsen Lung submarine escape breathing apparatus. He directed the rescue of the survivors from the *Squalus* (SS192) in 1939, as well as the salvage of the submarine, which was repaired and recommissioned as U.S.S. *Sailfish*. During the war Momsen took the lead in diagnosing and fixing the problems with the mechanical detonator in the Mark 6 exploder. He commanded both Submarine Squadrons Two and Four. He also commanded the first American wolf pack, and exerted a strong influence on American wolf pack tactics. The Momsen Lung was used only once during the war, when eight men used it to escape after the sinking of U.S.S. *Tang* (SS306). Despite his nickname, Momsen was of German-Danish ancestry, not Swedish.

FF12-10/A16-3(8)/(16)   SUBMARINE FORCE, PACIFIC FLEET   ld

Serial 01816   Care of Fleet Post Office,
                                            San Francisco, California,
CONFIDENTIAL   3 December 1943.

Third Endorsement to   NOTE: THIS REPORT WILL BE DESTROYED
Barb Report of   PRIOR TO ENTERING PATROL AREA.
Sixth War Patrol.

ComSubPac Patrol Report No. 316
U.S.S. *Barb* – Sixth War Patrol.

From: The Commander Submarine Force, Pacific Fleet.
To: The Commander-in-Chief, United States Fleets.
Via: The Commander-in-Chief, U.S. Pacific Fleet.

Subject: U.S.S. *Barb* (SS220) – Report of Sixth War Patrol.
            (30 September to 28 November 1943).

    1. The *Barb*'s sixth war patrol was its first in the Pacific Ocean Area. The patrol was conducted in areas off the China Coast and north of Formosa.
    2. Much of *Barb*'s patrol was hampered by poor weather and faulty material.
    3. Of the six contacts made worthy of torpedoes, two were hospital ships. One was closed for attack. This attack was aggressively conducted in spite of extremely rough weather and resulted in damage to the enemy.
    4. The *Barb*'s contact reports sent for the benefit of the coordinated attack group in areas north of her resulted in successful attacks being made by that group.
    5. This patrol is considered successful for Combat Insignia Award.
    6. The Commander Submarine Force, Pacific Fleet, congratulates the Commanding Officer, officers and crew for having inflicted the following damage upon the enemy:

SUNK

1 – Freighter (class unknown)   8,000 tons

DAMAGED

1 – Freighter (*Heiyo Maru* class)   5,628 tons

C.A. Lockwood

DISTRIBUTION:
(Complete Reports)
Cominch	(5)
CNO	(5)
Cincpac	(6)
Intel. Cen. Pac. Ocean Areas	(1)
Comservpac (Adv.Base Plan. Unit)	(1)
Cinclant	(2)
Comsublant	(8)
S/M School, NL	(2)
Comsopac	(2)
Comsowespac	(1)
Comsubsowespac	(2)
CTF 72	(2)
CTF 16	(1)
Comsubpac	(20)
SUBAD, MI	(2)
ComsubspacSubordcom	(3)
All Squadron and Div. Commanders, Subspac	(2)
Comsubstrainpac	(2)
All Submarines, Subspac	(1)

J.A. Woodruff, Jr.
Flag Secretary

Patrol Seven, 2 March 1944 – 23 April 1944

SS220/A16
Serial 0226

U.S.S. *Barb* (SS220)
c/o Fleet Post Office
San Francisco, Calif.

CONFIDENTIAL

From: The Commanding Officer, U.S.S. *Barb*.
To: The Commander-in-Chief, United States Fleet.
Via: Commander Submarine Division Sixty-One.
          Commander Submarine Squadron Six.
          Commander Submarines, Pacific Fleet.

Subject: U.S.S. *Barb*, Report of War Patrol Number Seven.

Enclosure: (A) Subject Report.
           (B) Track Chart, ComSubPac only.

1. Enclosure (A) covering the seventh war patrol of this vessel conducted in the area west of the Mariannas between Longitude 140° and 143° E. and Latitudes 16° and 22° north, and in the Formosan area during the period 2 March to 23 April 1944, is forwarded herewith.

J.R. Waterman

CONFIDENTIAL

U.S.S. *Barb* – Prologue of Seventh War Patrol

(A) PROLOGUE

Nov. 28
Arrived Pearl Harbor after Sixth War Patrol.

Dec. 2
Departed for Mare Island Navy Yard to conduct major overhaul.

Feb. 15
Arrived Pearl Harbor. Assigned three days voyage repairs and seven days training during which three Mark XIV[1] and one Mark XVIII[2] exercise torpedoes were fired. Dry-docked to replace damaged propeller. Lieutenant Commander E.B. Fluckey, U.S.N., reported aboard for temporary duty as P.C.O[3].

(B) NARRATIVE

Mar. 2, 1944
1700(V-W) Departed Pearl Harbor for patrol in accordance with T.F. 17, Op Order No. 73-44 in company with U.S.S. *Snapper*, escorted by *PC*[4]-*379*, Vice Admiral Lockwood aboard for passage to Midway.
2000 Released escort.

Mar. 3
0800(W) Parted company with U.S.S. *Snapper*.

---

[1] The Mark XIV torpedo was the standard wet-heater (steam) torpedo used by fleet type submarines. During the first 20 months of war it suffered from numerous problems with depth keeping, and with the magnetic and contact features of the Mark 6 exploder. By this time these had been diagnosed and fixed and the torpedo had become highly reliable. It remained in service through the late 1970s.

[2] The Mark XVIII was an electric torpedo, the principle advantage of which was that the electric motor did not create the bubble wake of a wet-heater torpedo. Reverse engineered from a captured German G7e electric torpedo, the Mark XVIII had a few problems of its own, mostly with erratic guidance. At least two American submarines, U.S.S. *Tang* (SS306) and U.S.S. *Tullibee* (SS284), are known to have been sunk by circular runs of their own Mark XVIII torpedoes.

[3] Prospective Commanding Officer. A command qualified officer placed aboard a submarine as an observer prior to taking command of his own boat.

[4] PC: Patrol, Coastal. A small, steel hulled anti-submarine ship, designed as a coastal escort.

School opened for all non-qualified men, with leading Chief and First Class Petty Officers acting as instructors. Daily drills for the fire control party will be held between 1800 and 1700.

Mar. 5

1053(X) Sighted and exchanged recognition signals with U.S.S. *Snapper*.

Encountered moderately heavy seas from ahead, shipping some water into engine induction. Auxiliary generator cables shorted out causing a fire (See K).

Mar. 6

1730(Y) Moored at submarine pier, Midway Island. Vice Admiral Lockwood left the ship. Commenced making voyage repairs.

Mar. 7

1315 Departed Midway for patrol escorted by *PY-27*[5]. Made trim dive, received indoctrinational depth charge, and released escort upon surfacing.

Encountered heavy seas from ahead, which reduced speed to six knots pit. During the night increased wind velocity and mountainous seas slowed us to 4.5 knots.

Mar. 8

Making little more than steerageway into fifty to sixty foot waves. Shipping very little water due to slow speed.

Mar. 10 (L)

Steerageway only, into seventy foot waves and seventy knot gale. Sent *Barb* Serial One to ComSubPac.

Mar. 11

No change in weather. Water taken down conning tower hatch grounded out 7MC[6] (See K). Speed now two knots.

Mar. 12

Wind and seas have abated sufficiently to make turns for 13 knots. Commenced using constant helm zig zag plan during daytime and making three training dives daily. At standard and full speeds submerged a shaft squeal can be heard plainly through the hull.

---

[5] PY: Patrol Yacht. A large civilian power yacht converted for Naval use. *PY-27* (*Girasol*) was built by Krupp Iron Works, Kiel, Germany, in 1926 and acquired by the Navy and commissioned in March 1942.

[6] 7MC: Two-way announcing system.

Mar. 13
    1130 Received ComSubPac's Serial Four Zebra. Set course for new patrol area. Seas are getting rougher.

Mar. 14
    Seas still heavy. Submerged to 120 feet to routine torpedoes. At this depth the ship is rolling ten degrees a side. The shaft squeal has gotten worse and can now be heard through the hull at all speeds except dead slow.

Mar. 15
    Weather has moderated. Long swells from the northwest, sky overcast.
    1120 Noticed definite interference on SD radar. Tune CUO to SD frequency. No signal.
    1134 Indistinct pip on SD at 4 miles. Dove, had lunch, and at
    1213 surfaced. Interference still present. It may be the *Grouper*.

Mar. 17
    Commenced routining torpedoes submerged.
    1600(K) Sighted small trawler crossing our stern on a northerly course.
    1700 Could not close sufficiently to determine whether it had armament.

Mar. 18
    Steaming at 15 knots until area is reached in order to make up for mileage lost during rough weather.

Mar. 19
    Received ComSubPac's Serial Two Seven Oboe.

Mar. 20
    Patrolling northeastern sector of area on surface.
    1030 SD contact 26 miles, steady. Did not dive.
    1300 SD contact 23 miles. Opened to 38 miles. Did not dive.
    1340 SD contact 29 miles, opening slowly to 33 miles. Did not dive.
    These contacts indicate a possible ferry route between Iwo Shima and Saipan, as our positions were roughly 25 miles from that line at the time of contact.

Mar. 21
    Conducting surface patrol at 10 knots on diagonal SE–SW course.

Mar. 22
    Sighted oil drum Lat. 18-55, Long. 140-42. Unable to hoist it aboard to obtain sample.

2200 Converted #4 FBT to MBT[7].

Mar. 23

No contacts after covering three-fourths of area on diagonal courses. Have decided to concentrate on a 100 mile line across Guam, Saipan, and Truk great circle routes from major Japanese ports as all previous contacts in the area have been in this lane.

1120 Sighted oil drum, brought it aboard, and took two quart sample of high test gasoline for shipment to experiment station. Drum had no markings and appeared to have been in the water about three weeks.

Mar. 24

0930 Changed course to 115° and went to four engine speed in attempt to intercept reported convoy.

1400 Sighted Mavis[8] patrol plane heading in, distance 7 miles. Submerged to 140 feet in glassy sea.

1409 Received two bombs, which broke a light bulb. Believe he used an oil slick from #4 MBT as his point of aim. Went to 175 feet.

1520 Starting up for a look.

1524 Another bomb, not close, probably just to let us know he is still there.

1640 Periscope depth, nothing in sight. Surfaced and continued chase.

1930 Called *Stingray* on 450 KC. No answer. Sent message blind asking if she had made contact with convoy. No reply.

2103 Sent *Barb* Serial Three to ComSubPac.

2130 Discontinued search and set course for new area in accordance with previous orders.

Mar. 26

Enroute area. In view of the importance of the phosphate plant on Okino Daito Shima (East Island), which exports over 300,000 tons annually, have decided to reconnoiter the island. The installations may be suitable for bombardment or an ore ship might be loading.

Missed ComSubPac's Serial "Yoke."

---

[7] A submarine's range could be extended by using certain ballast tanks as fuel ballast tanks. While employed for this purpose, the vents were disconnected to prevent accidental opening, and the flood valves were kept shut. When the fuel was consumed, the vents were reconnected so that the tanks could be used as normal main ballast tanks. While this extended the boat's range, converting the tanks at sea meant that crew members had to work under the superstructure, always with the knowledge that they would probably drown if the boat had to make an emergency dive. It was also difficult to insure that all of the fuel oil had been flushed from the empty tank, as *Barb* discovered two days later.

[8] Mavis: Kawanishi HK6, Type 97 flying boat.

Mar. 27
Sent Barb Serial Four to ComSubPac.

Mar. 28
Made radar contact on Rasa Island at 19,000 yards.
0224 Sighted island at 12,000 yards, closed to 9,000 yards and commenced patrolling off the southwest and waiting for daylight.
0444 Started closing the island.
0503 Radar contact, 4,500 yards. Not the island.
0513 Dove.
0532 Sighted patrol boat.
0541 Sighted ship about 1,600 yards west of the island on a northerly course. Commenced closing and identified ship as *Syowa Maru*. We assumed he[9] was about to moor, thus giving us a chance to attack. However, he continued his course and circled the island, smoking intermittently. His actions indicated a listening patrol. No guns or depth charge throwers were evident, but there were unidentified structures aft and amidships. Decided he was a Q-ship[10] as he was too large for patrol craft, although definitely on some type of patrol. Continued to close the island, but heavy seas made periscope observations extremely difficult. At range of 4,500 yards observed a considerable expansion of facilities over those described in ONI 50.

The 204 foot radio masts seen in November 1943 have been removed. The west end of the island slopes gradually to the water and contains virtually all of the island's installations. A group of new buildings, which look like barracks, are located on the northwest point. The residential area, just to the south, is closely packed and much of it appears new. South of the residential district is the industrial section, consisting mainly of a large roasting or processing plant with numerous chimneys. The dock is due west of the plant and is flanked by a good-sized steel loading hoist with endless belt conveyor. Between this plant and the dock are six long, low buildings covering a large area. They appear to be warehouses. Photographed island facilities but in doing so broached in plain view of the town. Retired to await sunset. Developed films only to find we had drawn a bad roll.

1920 Surfaced. Seas still too rough for bombardment so commenced 4 hour approach on *Syowa Maru*, whose actions were unique to say the least. When range closed to 4,300 yards he secured from his circular patrol and commenced an ir-

---

[9] In English, ships are usually referred to as "she." When "he" is used, as here, it may generally be presumed that the writer is referring to the ship's captain and not to the vessel.

[10] Q-Ship: A merchant type vessel mounting concealed guns and depth charges, intended to lure a submarine in close before opening fire. The Japanese were believed to have built several ships with extremely shallow draft hulls for this purpose. Q-Ships were most effective during World War I, when it was still common for submarines to make gun attacks on merchantmen sailing alone. They were far less effective in World War II, when most attacks were made with torpedoes at periscope depth or at night.

regular routine of continual course changes up to 270° with speed variations of from 6 knots ahead to 3 knots astern. We stopped whenever he did, but every time we took an attack course he made some change, which forced us to start all over again. We felt he could hear us but could not see us, and that he was cunningly drawing us closer to the beach, possibly for searchlights and shore batteries. Finally at

2355 he gave us a zero then 90° starboard angle, stopped, then started.

2357 Fired tubes 3, 5 and 4 at range of 2,200 yards; depth setting six feet.

2358:20 First torpedo hit aft, second one passed astern, and third one hit under the stack. A loud explosion and a shower of sparks followed the second hit, which broke the target in two, the stern sinking in 20 seconds and the bow going down half a minute later. Opened out at flank speed as we were very close to the beach. The island started transmitting on 3730 kc, the frequency listed in ONI 50, and for which we had prepared. Effectively jammed it for twenty minutes. Took course for area. The overly-innocent appearance and peculiar actions of the target left no doubt in my mind that she was a Q-ship.

Mar. 29

Proceeding on surface towards southern tip of Nansei Shoto.

After an analysis of recent reports it has been decided to patrol the Nansei Shoto passes, the Manila route as given by the Air Force, and the eastern Formosa shoreline. This should cover all possible routes left open in the area.

Mar. 30

Patrolling across Manila–Japan shipping lanes enroute Yonakuni Pass. No fix since leaving Rasa Island.

Mar. 31

Patrolling submerged south of Yonakuni Pass, exact position uncertain.

1430 Sighted sampan on southwesterly course, speed 5 knots. Took parallel course and decided to attack with deck gun after sunset.

1822 Surfaced and ran up track at 13 knots. Visibility very poor due to heavy mist and contact not regained in spite of four hour search.

2240 Set course for Yonakuni Island.

Apr. 1

Soundings indicated land should be within radar range.

0200 Examination of SJ shows it to be out of order, which explains how the sampan got away.

0400 SJ back in commission. Radar contact on land bearing 270° True.

0520 Identified land as Suo Wan and obtained our first fix in four days. Submerged and proceeded towards Yonakuni.

Apr. 2 – 3

Patrolling north of Yonakuni Island and along north side of Nansei Shoto. Current sets have varied from 270°T through North to 160°T. The drift has been approximately as indicated. Position can be maintained only through sight and radar contact with the islands as the sky has been overcast continuously.

Apr. 4

Patrolling off Hadarusa Jima submerged. Just after sunset heard pinging on sound gear, which did not sound like supersonic search, but consisted of irregular transmissions of dashes and letters of equal strength on all bearings. Surfaced and conducted four hour search amidst continuous pinging. As our mystification increased we discovered that securing the SJ radar stopped the pinging. Evidently a receiver circuit is oscillated by energy received on the radar. An investigation will be made.

2300 An uncertain radar pip at 39,000 yards bearing 230°T. Ran towards it at increased speed until 0300. No further contact. Concluded it was an ionized cloud or squall, broke off the search, and headed towards Yonakuni for fix.

Apr. 5

No contacts after five days in Nansei Shoto–Yonakuni Pass indicate that traffic has been shifted from this route, at least temporarily. Proceeding towards Formosa in hopes that some shipping will be using the Formosa coastal route.

1104 Sighted unidentified plane, which quickly disappeared into overcast.

Apr. 6

Patrolling submerged off San Sondai Light, working northward along the coast. This light was burning last November but is now blacked out. The current set us off shore all day at about 2.1 knots.

1700 Surfaced and took course for Longitude 128° E. in accordance with directive. Tried unsuccessfully to contact *Grouper* on 450 KC.

Apr. 7

Enroute to position at two engine speed.
2330 Arrived Longitude 128° E. and headed south.

Apr. 8

Reached Latitude 22° 10' N and began patrolling east and west across 128° E. Longitude till daylight, then commenced search to northward. At Latitude 23° 10' N. commenced east–west patrol. Unlimited visibility. Surface periscope watch can see at least 20 miles in all directions.

2100 Took course to return to Sakishima Gunto after having covered positions from plus seven hour to minus eleven hours.

Apr. 9

Patrolling on surface in dense fog. SJ radar out of commission. This set, when operating properly, has given phenomenal results, but has been a constant source of trouble. Only the expert knowledge and tireless efforts of Lt.(jg) R.H. Barnes have kept it operating.

2200 After 24 hours of steady work the SJ is back in commission with six separate troubles remedied.

2300 Radar contact on Iriomoto Jima at 70,000 yards. Took course to pass Hadoruma Jima at 4 miles enroute Yonakuni Pass.

Apr. 10

Patrolling Yonakuni Pass submerged.

Apr. 11

Patrolling northern part of area. This sector, as all others, is completely devoid of traffic.

Apr. 12

Patrolling 50 miles southwest of Mayoyama Rhetto across Manila–Japan route.

1150 SD contact 24 miles. Closed to 21 miles, then opened. Did not dive.

In view of the *Flying Fish*'s report of traffic through Yoron Jima Pass, will spend last 2 days in area patrolling across line from this pass to Palau.

Apr. 13

Enroute new position proceeding through points of contact from previous patrols.

1306(I) Sighted unidentified plane. Dove without being sighted. He seemed too far from land for a routine patrol. Decided to remain submerged for a few hours in hopes that he was sweeping ahead of a convoy.

1635 Surfaced.

1745 JOOW sighted formation of 12 to 15 planes at 8 miles on starboard bow heading northwest. They turned toward us as we submerged to 150 feet, but no attack materialized. JOOW stated they "looked small and brown."

1810 Periscope depth, nothing in sight. Surfaced at sunset. An all-night search at two engine speed netted nothing.

Apr. 14 – 15

Patrolling 15 miles either side of line from Yoron Jima Pass to Palau.

Apr. 16

Proceeding toward departure point.

1106 Sighted Mavis patrol plane on northerly course emerging from clouds at 4 miles. Submerged to 140 feet.

1123 Periscope depth, plane still in sight. Commenced routing torpedoes.

1128 Plane disappeared into clouds.

1455 Completed routing torpedoes. Surfaced. Took course for Rasa Island to conduct bombardment.

2000 Sent *Barb* Serial Six to ComSubPac.

2104 SJ radar interference bearing 065°T.

Apr. 17

0010 Rasa Island picked up on radar bearing 030°T, 14 miles.

0020 Radar contact bearing 355°T, distance 10,000 yards.

0030 Exchanged recognition signals with U.S.S. *Steelhead* and proceeded to clear vicinity of Rasa Island in order to transfer our SJ radar range unit to the *Steelhead*, whose unit was inoperative. *Steelhead* offered to join forces for bombardment.

0300 Commenced exchanging range units and planning joint bombardment.

0432 Exchange completed. Parted company with *Steelhead*. Too late to close Rasa on surface for submerged reconnaissance but did not feel this necessary as we reconnoitered the island on March 28, and the *Steelhead* looked it over yesterday, reporting patrol boat and large plane circling the island.

2135 Contacted *Steelhead* who formed in column 1,000 yards astern.

2332 Arrived on designated line 5,000 yards bearing 230°T from Rasa Island chimneys, and took course north at 5 knots. The night was dark but clear and cloudless. Although the island and installation were clearly visible from the bridge, only a vague outline could be seen through gun telescopes. Closed to 3,400 yards and commenced fire with 4" gun. First shot was a hit in congested area of island. Steelhead opened up with her 3" gun immediately and did some nice shooting. Continued closing to 2,300 yards and opened up with our four 20 mm and two .50 caliber guns. Steelhead joined with automatic guns and a respectable barrage resulted.

The effectiveness of this fire was above expectations. Small fires were started but none took hold. During the first pass, two or three rounds were short, all others were hits. One shell was a direct hit in the main installation, toppling the large steel conveyor loading hoist. Another hit on the island center caused a large blue-white flare over 100 feet high, followed a few seconds later by a tremendous explosion. It must have been explosive or chemicals. Point detonating shells were seen to hit in the warehouse area, spreading considerable debris. What appeared to be automatic weapon fire was noted from the north point but was ineffective.

Apr. 18

Completed first pass and changed course to 130°T for closer run. The difficulty of seeing the target after gun flashes resulted in a slow rate of fire for the 4" gun. Both ships resumed fire. During this run there were 4 shorts, and the remainder were hits. Automatic weapons were again extremely effective. There were two more explosions with bluish flare as on first pass.

0019 Four inch gun jammed. Continued firing small guns until two 20 mm guns had stoppages and the barrels of the .50 calibers were white hot.

0023 Both ships ceased fire and *Barb* took course to clear island to eastward.

0031 Extracted jammed case and fired clearing charge to remove stuck projectile. Transmitted Serial Seven. As we drew away from the island occasional small flames and four distinct explosions were observed, the last of which occurred over one hour after bombardment had ceased. The patrol boat did not make his appearance. Frantic signals using letters ESM–SM–SM were heard on 8470 kc. Nothing on 500 kc. Only 38 rounds of 4" were fired due to gun stoppage, but 2,000 round of 20 mm and .50 cal. weighing 1,000 pounds were poured into the island by *Barb*. The *Steelhead* fired considerably more 3" and less automatic.

It is believed that the export of refined phosphate from this important plant will cease for a considerable period, and that expensive repairs will be required.

19 – 24 April

Uneventful.

25 Apr.

1130(M) SD contact 3½ miles, closed until pip merged with outgoing signal. SJ radar picked up contact and followed it out to 21,000 yards. Contact never sighted in low overcast.

25 Apr.

0530 Crossed International date line and repeated this date.

26 Apr.

1705 Moored Midway.

(C) WEATHER

To the westward of the Mariannas the weather was uniformly good with moderate warm breezes and clear days and nights. In the Formosa–Sakishima Gunto area, the sky was continually overcast in the vicinity of the Japan Stream, but cleared partially about one day in three in parts of the area not traversed by this current. Wind there always less than force 3, which was in sharp contrast with the heavy seas and strong winds encountered here last October and November. Average temperature was 75° F.

(D) TIDAL INFORMATION

Currents in the vicinity of Sakishima Gunto were strong, variable, and unpredictable. They did not agree with the current chart for April in most cases. The table covers currents observed between accurate fixes, but must be used with caution as the set changes at about the same time of high and low water at Karimata Anchorage, Miyako Shima. The current off the east coast of Taiwan was found to be as described in the *Coast Pilot* and current charts.

CURRENT

Current observed between: Actual   Predicted

Lat.	Lon.	Lat.	Lon.	Force	Set	Force	Set	Remarks
24-35	123-00	24-43	125-10	1.4	274	1.3	040	Submerged
24-44	124-02	24-41	123-47	.9	102	1.2	050	Submerged
23-30	128-00	23-30	123-00	.8	270	Var	270	Submerged
24-32	123-00	24-44	124-03	.5	160	1.2	050	Surfaced
24-41	123-47	23-55	123-42	1.0	294	1.2	030	Surfaced
23-55	125-42	24-02	123-56	.4	270	0.1	000	Submerged
23-30	123-25	23-36	123-36	1.5	084	1.0	030	Submerged
23-00	121-38	23-20	121-45	2.5	032	2.5	016	Submerged

(E) NAVIGATIONAL AIDS

1. Lights. No navigational lights were observed burning.
2. When in the Formosa–Sakishima Gunto area, the sky was completely overcast as long as we were in the Japan Stream. When clear of this current, sun sights and evening stars were available 50 percent of the time and a morning fix could be obtained on four days out of 19. Radar fixes on the islands were used successfully, making frequent use of tangents from the PPI combined with closest and farthest ranges. Sounding between Yonakuni Jima and Taiwan agreed with the chart.
3. The 6x30 monocular fitted to the sextant is of assistance when observing stars under unfavorable light conditions.

(F) SHIP CONTACTS

No.	Time-Date	Lat. Long.	Type(s)	Initial Range	Est. Course Speed	How Contacted	Remarks
1.	3-17	25-00 N 153-15 E	100 ton Trawler	8,000	350 8 kts	PD	
2.	3-28	24-18 N 131-11 E	Q-Ship	4,500	000° 5 kts.	PD	Sank at 2337
3.	3-31	23-51 N 123-E	100 T Sampan	3,000	240° 5 kts.	PD	
4.	4-16	23-51 N 131-00 E	SS	9,600		R	*Steelhead*
5.	4-17	24-20 130-00	SS	13,000		R	*Steelhead*

(G) AIRCRAFT CONTACTS

No.	Time-Date	Lat. Long.	Type(s)	Initial Range	Est. Course & Speed	How Contacted	Remarks
1.	3-20	21-55 N 142-28 E	—	26 mi.	—	R	Did not dive
2.	3-20	21-50 N 142-04 E	—	23 mi.	—	R	" " "
3.	3-20	21-49 N 143-56 E	—	29 mi.	—	R	" " "
4.	3-24	18-59 N 142-14 E	Mavis	7 mi.	305° 200 kts.	PD Surface	Bombed
5.	4-5	18-59 N 123-13 E	—	15 mi.	N.	PD	
6.	4-12	23-34 N 123-26 E	—	24 mi.	—	SD	Did not dive
7.	4-13	23-23 N 128-00 E	—	10 mi.	W	SD	Submerged, not sighted.
8.	4-13	24-00 N 128-19 E	About 15 planes	8 mi.	NW	SD	A V formation which turned towards, no attack.
9.	4-16	24-14 N 129-30 E	Mavis	4 mi.	N	SD	Submerged, not sighted

(N) ATTACK DATA

U.S.S. *Barb*   Torpedo Attack No. 1   Patrol No. 7
Time: 2337   Date: 28 March 1944   Lat. 24-25 N.   Long. 131-11 E.

Target Data – Damage Inflicted

Description: Attack made on *Syowa Maru* class "Q" ship by surface.
Approach: Contact made by radar, approach made using radar ranges and bearings and TBT bearings. Dark night, moderate sea.
Ship Sunk: *Syowa Maru* class – 2,221 Ton "Q" ship.
Damage Determined by: 2 hits observed by CO and bridge personnel. Sinking observed by CO and bridge personnel. Stern sank in 20 seconds and bow in 50 seconds.

Target Draft: 10'   Course: 110   Speed: 1¼   Range: 2,200 yards.

Own Ship Data

Speed: 5   Course: 028   Depth: Surface   Angle: 0°

Fire Control and Torpedo Data

Type Attack: Radar, surface. Target went ahead 6 kts, stopped, backed and constantly made course changes up to 180 degrees.

Tubes Fired	#6	#3	#4
Track Angle	98 S	98 S	102 S
Gyro Angle	348	359	003
Depth Set	6 Ft.	6 Ft.	6 Ft.
Power	High	High	High
Hit or Miss	Hit	Miss	Hit
Erratic	No	No	No
Mark Torpedo	14-3A	14-3A	14-3A
Serial No.	25979	26171	40730
Mark Exploder	6-4	6-4	6-4
Serial No.	3010	1507	14732
Actuation Set	--------------- Contact ------------------		
Actuation Actual	--------------- Contact ------------------		
Mark Warhead	16-1	16-1	16-1
Serial No.	3052	3176	10387
Explosives	Torpex	Torpex	Torpex
Firing Interval	—	13 Secs.	8 Secs.
Type Spread	--------------- Divergent ----------------		
Sea Condions	------------------ 3 --------------------		
Overhaul Activity:	Submarine Base, Pearl Harbor		

Remarks: Target apparently heard us during entire approach, but could not see us. Target made continuous radical course and speed changes, backed down, stopped, circled, but did not attempt to escape.

U.S.S. Barb   Gun Attack No. 1   Patrol No. 7
Time: 2346   Date: 17 April 1944   Lat. 24-28 N.   Long. 131-11 E.

Target Data – Damage Inflicted

Bombardment of Rasa Island phosphate plant, warehouse, and loading installations. Destroyed large steel endless belt loading hoist, and damaged or destroyed warehouses, refinery, and sections of phosphate plant installation. Damaged sections of town, starting small fires. Probably many casualties.

Damage Determined by:

Approximately 30-4" hits observed in phosphate plant and warehouse area, including direct hits on loading hoist, warehouses, and adjacent buildings. Hundreds of 20 MM hits observed in plant and warehouse area, and in town. Many large explosions heard during and after firing and numerous small fires started. Three large persistent bluish explosions observed from plant and warehouse area. Observed toppling of conveyor hoist.

Details of Action

Bombardment conducted on dark clear night. Commenced attack in column formation, U.S.S. *Steelhead* 1,000 yards astern of *Barb*, on northerly heading, speed 5 knots. At range of 3,600 yards *Barb* commenced firing 4" common and H.C.P.D.[11] and *Steelhead* 3". When range decreased to 2,900 yards commenced firing 4 20 MM and 2 .50 cal., *Steelhead* opening fire with automatic weapons at same time. Upon passing northern extremity of island abeam, reversed course and resumed fire as before. Ceased fire with 4" due to stoppage when second pass approximately completed, but continued automatic fire until 2 20 MM guns jammed and .50 cal. barrels were white hot.

Ammunition expended: 11 rounds 4" 50 Cal.[12] common[13], 27 rounds 4" 50 Cal. H.C.P.D., 1,000 rounds of 20 MM, and 1,000 round of .50 cal.

Performance of guns and ammunition in general was excellent. Approximately 10% of the tracers in 4" 50 Cal. ammunition failed to function. Although all 4" 50 Cal. ammunition was flashless pellet powder, occasional flashes blinded the gun's crew. The jamming of the 20 MM guns was caused by faulty magazines, and the 4" 50 Cal. gun stoppage by small burr in chamber.

(I) MINES

None.

---

[11] High Capacity, Point Detonating. A high explosive shell designed to detonate on impact, and primarily used as an anti-personnel round, or for blowing up unarmored vessels or structures.

[12] 4" 50 Cal.: Naval rifles are classified by bore diameter and barrel length. A "4/50 Caliber gun has a bore of four inches and a barrel length of 4" times 50, or 200" (16' 8").

[13] Common: Standard high-explosive anti-shipping rounds. The fuses have a slight time delay to allow the shell to penetrate the hull before exploding.

(J) ANTI-SUBMARINE MEASURES AND EVASION TACTICS

None.

(K) MAJOR DEFECTS AND DAMAGE

1. Serious grinding and squealing of starboard propeller shaft at speeds greater than 80 RPM. Rewooding probably required[14]. Port shaft also noisy but to a lesser degree. These shaft noises could be heard through the hull without the aid of listening devices.
2. No. 2 periscope hoisting panel was grounded out almost continuously during rough weather. It is recommended that the panel be relocated to the pump room.
3. Voycall system grounded out due to water down the hatch.
4. Auxiliary generator terminal board grounded out from water down the main induction, resulting in a fire. These terminals should be made completely drip proof.
5. QB Sound Gear. Loud groan and humming vibration appears in upper bearing when gear is trained in lowered position.
6. No. 2 periscope: Grinding noise plus seizing at bearing makes No. 2 periscope hard to turn.

(L) RADIO

Reception was very good throughout the patrol except for a few hours every day at dawn. Only one serial was missed.

All transmissions were made without difficulty. Receipts did not come out on the schedule for *Barb* Serial Two and Three. Serial Three was taken by radio New Zealand, who gave us the proper authentication, but the message failed to reach ComSubPac.

(M) RADAR

The SJ-A radar set performed very satisfactorily when it could be kept operating, but required considerable servicing throughout the patrol, with the largest share of the troubles developing in the Transmitter-Receiver Unit.

---

[14] The propeller shafts exit the hull through packing glands, which use rings of lignum vitae wood as packing material. This is a very dense, naturally oily wood. Shaft seal pressure is always a compromise between allowing minor seepage and clamping the gland down so tightly that the shaft is unable to rotate. If the wooden packing rings dry out enough friction is created to make noise. The only cure is to replace the packing. Modern vessels use a synthetic material.

The following are some of the more outstanding defects found: The present motor generator set[15] is not large enough for the added load of the PPI Unit and new transmitter. A defective socket on the 5D21 tube caused a loss of grid bias. A defective 721-A tube caused failure of crystal detector, these tubes having been found to have a nominal life of about 200 hours for reliable operation rather than the 300 hours recommended. The receiver tuning potentiometer burned out, possibly due to a shorted reflector bias cable between the range indicator unit and transmitter unit, which was found at the same time. Condenser[16] C-22A in the transmitter biasing circuit shorted out. It is known that this fault has occurred in other sets and the recommendation is made to use a higher voltage condenser in this circuit. Two 706-AY tubes were found to develop erratic frequency characteristics, the changes of frequency being great enough to cause large reflection echoes to appear on the screen at ranges between 1,200 and 2,000 yards. With the tubes in this condition subsequent tuning of the wave guide would remove the standing wave echoes from the indicator screen but no position of the tuning stubs would give a standing wave change from maximum to minimum of less than seven scale divisions as measured with a 60ABM wave meter. The output of the 706-AY tubes was apparently of normal power but showed a fluctuation of three to five scale divisions on the 60 ABM. This is a new experience and no comments are offered beyond the possibility of the internal straps burning off and allowing the tubes to pass from one side to another. Two 726-E tubes developed frozen tuning screws, making it impossible to tune them to match a different 706-AY tube. The main switch on the control unit burned out. Tube failure in the standard tubes types were possibly a little more numerous than normally might be expected but presented no difficulty of replacement through on board spares. The appearance of spurious echoes at the end of the 5,000 yard sweep was traced to a poor IF cable ground at the AFC circuit panel.

One peculiarity occurred which took place for a period of about three hours one night and has not been repeated since. The sound gear picked up signals of a sharply tunable frequency of 28 kilocycles, these signals were apparently pinging from some source and in very readable Morse code. Various letters of the alphabet were heard and often repeated. No bearing of train could be found for these signals, however. The signal strength was practically constant around the dial. When the SJ-A set was turned off the signals ceased and began again when the SJ-A was put back in operation. No explanation is offered, but one would be appreciated.

15 Motor Generator Set: A fleet submarine's main generators supplied direct current for running the propulsion motors and charging batteries. Much of a submarine's equipment runs on DC, but radar, radios, and other electronic equipment required Alternating Current. A motor generator set was a DC motor driving an AC generator, which was used to supply the needed AC current. Rather than a single, large unit supplying the entire boat, several motor generator sets were provided where needed.

16 Condenser: Old name for a capacitor.

(N) SOUND GEAR AND SOUND CONDITIONS

None.

(O) DENSITY LAYERS

None.

(P) HEALTH AND HABITABILITY

The ship's company showed few signs of fatigue at the end of this long patrol and appears to have an indefinite limit of endurance under the conditions experienced in this area. The favorable temperature and comparatively large amount of time on the surface are the biggest reasons for this. Only one day was lost from sickeness.

Summary of cases requiring medical attention during patrol:

	No. of Cases	No. of Days Lost
Abscess, scrotum	1	1
Boils	2	0
Constipation	12	0
Fungus infection, feet	3	0
Fungus infection, groin	1	0
Gingivitis	2	0
Headache	10	0
Otitis Media (external L. ear)	1	0
Pitriasis Rosea	1	0
Ringworm	1	0
Scabies	1	0
Shoulder dislocation	1	0
Sprain ankles, left	2	0

The food was exceptionally good. Even after fresh foods were gone, frozen foods, fine meat, and remarkably good baking maintained a very high standard in our commissary. The ice cream freezer is a most welcome addition and the supply of ice cream mix will be doubled on the next patrol.

(P) PERSONNEL

The *Barb* experienced an unusually large turnover in personnel while undergoing regular Navy Yard overhaul. Between the sixth and seventh war patrols, 26 men were transferred, including 5 Chief Petty Officers and 8 First Class POs. In return, 30 men were ordered to the ship, including 1 CPO and 3 first class petty officers. Since few of the replacements could fill billets vacated by the transferees, a general fleeting up of responsibility was necessary, giving an ever larger proportion of men new to their jobs.

While in Mare Island every training opportunity was utilized. Men attended schools as follows:

Air and Surface Craft Recognition (10 day course)	10 men.
Night Lookout (4 day course)	18 men.
Mk 18 Torpedo School (1 week)	9 men.
Gunnery (20 MM and .50 Cal.) (6 day)	13 men
	1 Off.
Gunnery (20 MM and .50 Cal.) (6 day)	15 men.
S/M Training Device (10 hours per man)	16 men.

In addition special training was obtained by selected individuals in gas welding, optical repair, gyro repair, and sound repair. The fire control party spent 7 periods on the attack teacher with noticeable benefit.

While training at sea following overhaul it was found that our new men, though proficient at school, needed the practical work aboard to become useful and dependable submariners. The submarine training device taught the mechanics of planes handling to the new men, for example, but it took many dives before new planesmen could be depended upon to anticipate the ship's movements, which they found quite different from the reactions of the training device.

We proceeded to sea on the *Barb*'s 7th patrol with 26 non-qualified men, 18 of whom had never been to sea before on any type of ship. While on patrol the newcomers turned to with remarkable enthusiasm, which was soon reflected in the efforts of the old timers to help them along. 18 of this group qualified under strict requirements prior to returning to port. In addition, 35 men were advanced in rating while on this patrol.

The conduct of Officerss and crew was exemplary. Special credit is due Lt.(jg) R.H. Barnes, USNR, whose untiring efforts and expert knowledge solved the numerous difficult problems of a very cranky SJ-A radar.

Data required by ComSubPac Serial 276 of 8 Feb. 1944.
(a) Number of men on board during this patrol	71
(b) Number of men qualified at start of patrol	45
(c) Number of men qualified at end of patrol	63
(d) Number of men unqualified making 1st patrol	20
(c) Number of men advanced in rating this patrol	33

(R) MILES STEAMED – FUEL USED

Pearl Harbor to Area	5,608.8 miles.	46,720 fuel, gals.
In Area No. 1	1,123.8 miles.	7,980 fuel, gals.
In Area No. 2	3,591 miles.	27,315 fuel, gals.
Area to Midway	3,271.0 miles.	41,529 fuel, gals.

(S) DURATION

Days enroute to area	–	18 days.
Days in area	–	28 days.
Days enroute to base	–	9 days.
Days submerged	–	20 days.

(T) FACTORS OF ENDURANCE REMAINING.

Torpedoes Number	Fuel Gals.	Provisions Days	Personnel Factor Days
21	4,500	20	20

Limiting factor this patrol – provisions of operations order.

(U) REMARKS

It is recommended that the eastern limit of this area be extended to Longitude 132° E. to include Rasa and Borodino Islands in view of the expansion and increased activity noted.

Priority was given to the southwestern tip of the Nansei Shoto because of recent successes in the vicinity. Possibly because of these successes this route has apparently been abandoned for the time being.

The addition of 18 to 20 rounds of star shell to the ammunition allowance would be a decided advantage. If these had been available on April 17th a much higher rate of fire with increased accuracy would have resulted.

Performance, Care and Upkeep of Mark XVIII Torpedoes with Recommendations and Comments

Performance: No remarks as none fired.

Care and Upkeep: The routine followed was to shift torpedoes in tubes with those in the rack about every seven days, weather and tactical conditions permitting. Torpedoes were completely routined prior to loading into the tubes, charged within a day of removal from tubes, and again one or two days before loading regardless of gravity.

Two torpedoes required watering after 32 days, 4 charges, and the other six torpedoes after 34 days, 8 charges since test discharge in shop.

Securing battery charges on constant gravity reading rather than the constant voltage was used.

The following defects were found.
- (A) Upon receipt from shop.
    1. One battery cell strap disconnected from terminal, with connecting nut and bolt resting on top of terminal.
    2. Rubber balloon replacement plug not in one cell, but found lying on top of the adjacent cell.
    3. Extra nuts, bolts and washers found in motor compartment of two torpedoes.
- (B) During patrol.
    1. One electrolyte ground. Eliminated by washing with soda solution and drying.
    2. One internally discharging cell and a 110 volt positive 42 volt negative ground in torpedo #53629. Cause not determined.
    3. Sealing compound between top plate and jar cracked in two cells in torpedo #53895. Electrolyte was bubbling out of these cracks on cell tops. Caused by sticky vent plugs; stuck in closed position.
    4. Spilling of electrolyte through vent plugs in extreme weather.

Recommendations: Alter battery vent plugs so as to prevent spillage of electrolyte on to cell tops in rough weather. Replace rubber washer between plunger point and barrel of the plug casing with composition washer unaffected by temperature and action of electrolyte.

Include the following in Mark XVIII spare parts:

1. 2 foot hard rubber extension for air hose with a 1" right angle nipple for reaching inaccessible portions of battery compartment when drying off cell tops.

2. 4" scribed, flexible, transparent tube for measuring height of electrolyte in all cells. All cells do not require full ounce of water when watering batteries.

Comments: No remarks.

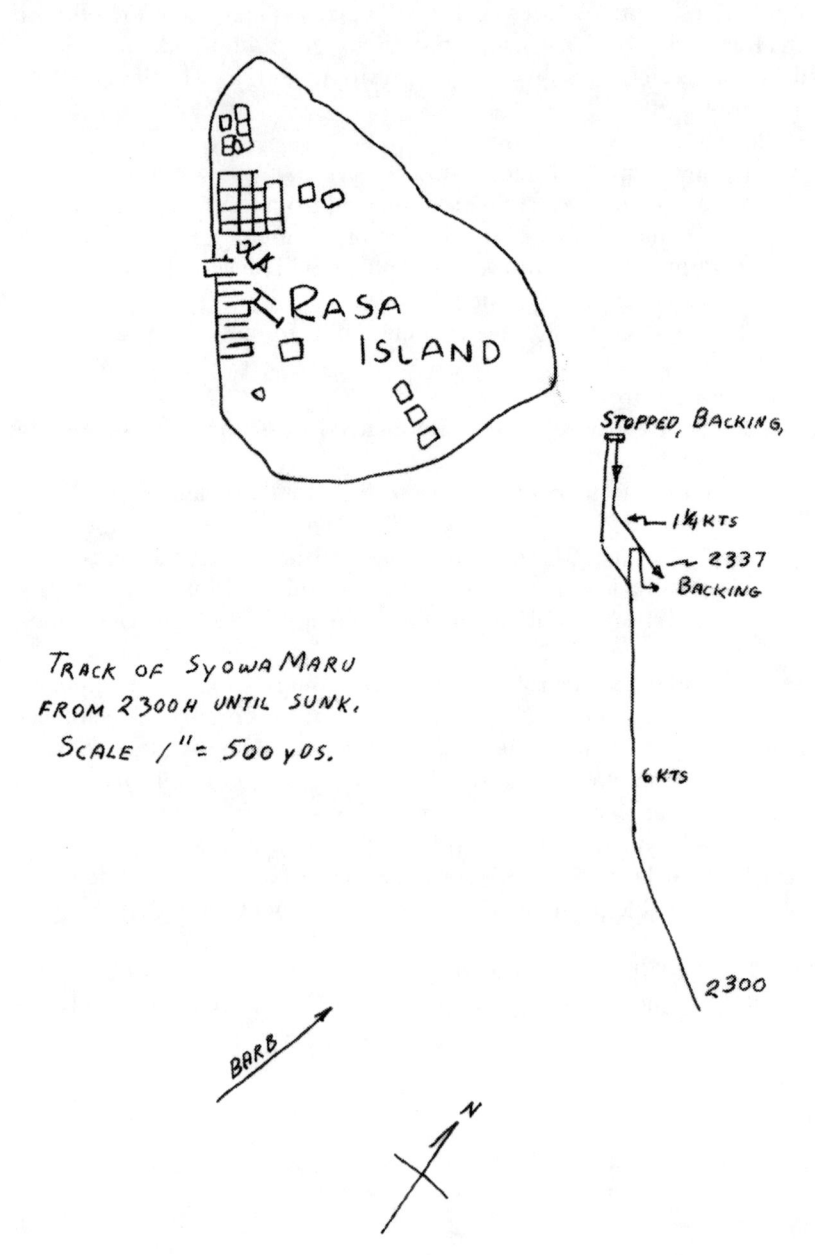

Track Chart, Syowa Maru attack

SUBMARINE DIVISION SIXTY-ONE (fcw)

FB5-61/A16-3

Serial: 071

Care of Fleet Post Office,
San Francisco, California,
27 April 1944.

CONFIDENTIAL

First Endorsement to
U.S.S. *Barb* Report
of Seventh War Patrol.

From: The Commander Submarine Division Sixty-One.
To: The Commander-in-Chief, United States Fleet.
Via: (1) The Commander Submarine Force, Pacific Fleet,
                 Subordinate Command, Navy No. 1504.
             (2) The Commander Submarine Force, Pacific Fleet.
             (3) The Commander-in-Chief, U.S. Pacific Fleet.

Subject: U.S.S. *Barb* (SS220) – Report of Seventh War Patrol.

1. The seventh war patrol of the *Barb* covered a period of fifty-five days of which twenty-eight days were spent in the assigned areas west of the Mariannas and in the Formosan area. Patrol was terminated by the provision of the operation order.

2. There was only one contact worthy of torpedo fire and this developed into a successful attack and sinking. Rasa Island was reconnoitered in detail and a successful bombardment was directed against the phosphate plant, warehouses and settlement in company with, and assisted by, the U.S.S. *Steelhead*.

3. The single torpedo attack was made on a ship of the *Syowa Maru* class, which was conducting what appeared to be an anti-submarine patrol off Rasa Island. The attack was a night surface attack following four hours of approach complicated by erratic speed and course changes on the part of the target. The target seemed to be aware of the *Barb*'s presence and not unwilling to make contact under conditions favorable to the target, leading to the conclusion that she was a Q-ship. At the opportune moment *Barb* fired three torpedoes at a range of 2,200 yards for two hits. Target was seen to break in two and sink within fifty seconds.

4. The bombardment of Rasa Island was a well coordinated attack and resulted in considerable observed damage.

5. Health and morale of officers and crew on return from patrol were excellent. The material condition of the Barb is excellent except for propeller shaft noises, which will be thoroughly investigated during the current refit.

6. The Command Officer, officers and crew are congratulated for the damage inflicted upon the enemy during the bombardment of Rasa Island and for the sinking of a target particularly obnoxious to submarines.

SUNK	TONS
1 – Q-Ship (Similar to *Syowa Maru*)	2,211

W. I. Hoffheins

Copy to:
 CO U.S.S. Barb

A16-3   COMMANDER SUBMARINE FORCE, PACIFIC FLEET   (Mc)
          SUBORDINATE COMMAND, NAVY NO. 1504
                                         Care of Fleet Post Office,
C-O-N-F-I-D-E-N-T-I-A-L   San Francisco, California,
                                         28 April 1944.

From: The Commander Submarine Force, Pacific Fleet,
             Subordinate Command, Navy No. 1504.
To: The Commander-in-Chief, United States Fleet.
Via: (1) The Commander Submarine Force, Pacific Fleet.
          (2) The Commander-in-Chief, U.S. Pacific Fleet.

Subject: U.S.S. *Barb* (SS220) – Report of Seventh War Patrol.

1. Forwarded, concurring in the remarks contained in the first endorsement. The lack of contacts in the area, previously productive, indicates more frequent changes in enemy convoy routes are to be expected.

2. The Commanding Officer, officers and crew are congratulated for the damage inflicted upon the enemy.

                              C.D. Edmunds

SUBMARINE FORCE, PACIFIC FLEET   hch
FF12-10/A16-3(15)/(16)
                                    Care of Fleet Post Office,
Serial 0845   San Francisco, California,
                                    4 May 1944.

CONFIDENTIAL

Third Endorsement to
U.S.S. *Barb* Report of   NOTE: THIS REPORT WILL BE
Seventh War Patrol   DESTROYED PRIOR TO
                                           ENTERING PATROL AREA.
ComSubPac Patrol Report No. 412
U.S.S. *Barb* – Seventh War Patrol

From: The Commander Submarine Force, Pacific Fleet.
To: The Commander-in-Chief, United States Fleet.
Via: The Commander-in-Chief, U.S. Pacific Fleet.

Subject: U.S.S. *Barb* (SS220) – Report of Seventh War Patrol
             (2 March to 25 April 1944)

1. The seventh war patrol of the *Barb* was conducted in the waters west of the Mariannas and east of Formosa.
2. Although good area coverage was maintained, the *Barb* made only one contact worthy of torpedoes. This was a small ship, apparently on anti-submarine patrol, and was attacked by the *Barb* and sunk.
3. The reconnaissance of Rasa Island and subsequent joint bombardment of the phosphate plant, warehouses, and loading installations by the *Barb* and *Steelhead* (SS280) was outstanding. The coordinated attack was carried out close enough to the island to enable both ships to fire all mounted guns aboard.
4. This patrol is designated as successful for Combat Insignia Award.
5. The Commander Submarine Force, Pacific Fleet, congratulates the Commanding Officer, officers, and crew for this successful war patrol. The *Barb* is credited with having inflicted the following damage upon the enemy.

SUNK

1 – Anti-Submarine Vessel (*Syowa Maru* class) – 2,221 tons (Attack No. 1)

DAMAGED

1 – Phosphate Plant by Gunfire.

J.H. Brown, Jr.

Distribution:
(Complete Reports)

Cominch	(5)
CNO	(5)
Cincpac	(6)
Intel.Cen.Pac. Oceans Areas	(1)
Comservpac (Adv.Base Plan Unit)	(1)
Cinclant	(2)
Comsublant	(8)
S/M School, NL	(2)
Comsowespac	(1)
Comsubsowespac	(2)
CTF 72	(2)
Comnorpac	(1)
Comsubspac	(40)
SUBAD, MI	(2)
ComsubspacSubordcom	(3)
All Squadron and Division Commanders, Subspac	(2)
Comsubstrainpac	(2)
All Submarines, Subspac	(1)

E.L. Hynes, 2nd,
Flag Secretary

Editor's Note: This was the final war patrol for Commander John R. Waterman, who was slated to move up to a Division command. He had commanded *Barb* on all but one of her seven war patrols.

Discussing his own arrival aboard in his book *Thunder Below! The U.S.S. Barb Revolutionizes Submarine Warfare in World War II* (1992, University of Illinois Press), Eugene Fluckey related that Waterman had requested he do his PCO cruise in *Barb* in order to take some of the pressure off Waterman, with the promise that he would take command after the patrol. As it happened, while *Barb* was at sea, John K. Fyfe was assigned as her next commander. This situation required a certain amount of finagling to get Fluckey the command. An appeal was made to ComSubPac, Vice Admiral Charles Lockwood, who had ridden *Barb* to Midway at the beginning of the patrol and was consequently aware of Waterman's plan for Fluckey.

With Lockwood's help, Fluckey got command of *Barb*, and Fyfe was given *Batfish*, where he ran up a wartime credit of 11 ships sunk during four patrols.

Patrol Eight, 21 May 1944 – 9 July 1944

U.S.S. *Barb*
SS220/A16
Serial 0228

                                                    Care of Fleet Post Office,
                                                    San Francisco, California,
                                                      9 July 1944

CONFIDENTIAL

From:	The Commanding Officer, U.S.S. *Barb*.
To:	The Commander in Chief, United States Fleet.
Via:	Commander Submarine Division Forty-One.
	Commander Submarine Squadron Four.
	Commander Submarines, Pacific Fleet.
Subject:	U.S.S. *Barb*, Report of Eighth War Patrol
Enclosure:	(A) Subject Report.
	(B) Track Chart, ComSubPac only.

    1. Enclosure (A) covering the eighth war patrol of this vessel conducted in the area along the Kurile Island Chain, north coast of Hokkaido and in the Sea of Okhotsk during the period 21 May 1944 to 9 July 1944, is forwarded herewith.

                                          E.B. Fluckey.

CONFIDENTIAL

U.S.S. *Barb* – Report of Eighth War Patrol

(A) PROLOGUE

April 25
Arrived Midway after Seventh War Patrol.

April 26 – May 11
Normal refit accomplished by SubDiv 61 Relief Crew and Sub Base Midway. An excellent job.

April 28
Commander John R. Waterman was relieved as Commanding Officer by Lt. Comdr. Eugene B. Fluckey. Transferred two officers. Received two new Submarine School graduates.

May 14 – 16
Conducted training exercises. Fired five torpedoes. Fired all deck guns. Training facilities were excellent and well coordinated.

(B) NARRATIVE

May 21
1630(Y) Departed Midway in accordance with CTF 17 Operation Order No. 164-44.

May 22
Omitted. Crossed date line.

May 23
Commenced daily training consisting of section dives, drills, fire control drills, enlisted school for qualification, Officers school for department qualification.

May 24
Occasional patches of heavy fog.

May 25
Solid fog. Visibility 300 to 700 yards.
1835(L) Periscope sighted by OOD, lookout and quartermaster on starboard beam, range about 500 yards. Turned away at flank speed and lost periscope

quickly in fog. After opening for three minutes turned around, stopped and attempted to make contact by radar or sound. Returned to position of sighting and searched area for 20 minutes. Possibly a Blackfish.

All reports jibed in that 1½ to 2 feet was exposed for about 10 seconds. Lat. 38-24 N., Long. 166-57 E.

May 26

Barometer took a skid, waves bounced up to 35 feet and wind to 60 knots. Slowed to 6 knots.

0645(L) Trim dive. Wild and wooly, but good experience for the new diving section.

1400(L) As barometer commenced to rise, believed we could take advantage of temporarily heavy sea, so submerged to routine all torpedoes and water batteries.

1800(L) Surfaced. Seas were dying down, wind had calmed, barometer was climbing. Within an hour speed was built up to 15 knots.

May 27

Heavy fog.

May 28

0400(L) Entered area.

1050(L) Picked up Jap Zoomie rubber boat. No survivors. Lat. 44-20 N., Long. 53-10 E.

1650(L) Picked up a large inflated airplane inner tube of Goodyear vintage. Japs must be running short of rubber boats. Lat. 44-45.6 N., Long. 161-30.1 E.

2120(K) Radar contact on Uroppo To, 60,000 yards.

2330(K) Passed through Yetorofu Strait. During night had innumerable radar contacts at ranges less than 3,000 yards. One of these was visually identified as a sea parrot when tracked in to 430 yards. For non-ornithologists sea parrots are 14 inches long and have a heavy body with a stubby red beak (All times King unless otherwise noted).

May 29

0535 Detoured to northward of large ice floe, length unknown, width at northern end five miles, peaks on floe were to 50 to 100 feet high.

1100 Lat. 45-02 N., Long. 145-05 E. Commenced patrolling on course 350°T and reverse in accordance with directive, covering area 16 miles north and 15 miles south of position.

2315 Commenced hourly zig changes on courses 320°T to 200°T down the track to obtain position check on Karafuto.

May 30

0240(K) Sighted light and closed contact (Ship Contact #1).

0300(K) Determined contact to be a properly marked Russian[1] ship estimated to be a small tanker about 275 feet long on course 215°T, speed 10 knots. Lat. 46-06 N., Long. 144-12.5 E.

0315(K) Checked navigational position on Karafuto, show current in Okhotsk Sea to be negligible.

0413(K) Back on the track, course 079°T, speed 15 knots.

0500(K) Having covered area for 20 hours changed course to 054°T heading for new station, patrolling along probable convoy lane.

May 31

0030(K) Commenced patrolling new station. Fairly dense fog.

0100(K) Radar contact at 17,000 yards (Ship Contact #2). Lat. 48-18 N., Long. 150-05 E. Commenced approach. Single large pip. Decided to make first pass for observation to make sure it was not the *Herring*, since we were in her area. Had no radar interference, but it was possible her radar may be *hors de combat*. At slow speed while target passed 2,600 yards ahead without being seen. Tracked on course 020°T, speed 8.25 knots.

0139 Eased out for end around and a closer look at slow speed, since water was highly phosphorescent.

0147 Target changed course to 041°T and speed to 11.8 knots. This convinced me, however attempted to contact *Herring* by voice on 450 KCS in vain. Commenced approach.

0230 Stopped on 20 port track, 2,000 yards distance to track and made ready the bow tubes. As gyros were approaching zero commenced easing in to get one quick look and start shooting, then at

0236 with zero gyros, 1,400 yard run, a beautiful tanker loomed out of the fog at 1,800 yards with Russian lights. Binocular formula checked by OOD and Captain gave her length at 560 feet, (filled binoculars at 1,400 yards), estimated tonnage 12,000, slightly raked bow, cruiser stern. Frankly I was tempted to order the lookouts to about face and let go anyhow. However we sat and watched her quickly pass into the fog, then swung in on her port quarter to make a course check because she appeared similar to the *Sinkoku Maru*. Course 041°T was correct for Russian shipping lane (also Paramushiru).

0250 Fog closed in tight and at 900 yards on her quarter could barely make out her lights when OOD said he heard a shot. Knowing the armament of large Jap tankers, decided there wasn't a lot we could do except feel we had been had, so turned away and returned to patrol station.

---

[1] While an American ally in Europe against Germany, the Soviet Union remained a neutral in the Pacific until a few days before the Japanese surrender. Their ships were common in the Sea of Japan and along the Russian Pacific coast.

0400 Commenced patrolling. Ceiling zero. Lat. 48-24 N., Long. 150-02 E.

0600 Headed for new patrol station.

0800 Radar interference. Probably *Herring*.

0956 Radar contact, 8,500 yards (Ship Contact #3). Commenced pulsing letter B on radar transmission by varying pulse rate, by varying the high voltage stop valve. We had wanted to try this system for recognition and had arranged with *Herring* to send H. The H's were clearly received on both PPI and A-scope. *Herring* later reported clearly receiving our B's.

1013 Sighted *Herring* on surface at 6,000 yards in the fog.

1015 Lost sight and radar contact.

1022 Sighted *Herring* again. She was at radar depth now, range 3,200 yards. Sent recognition signals by sound. Not received. Sent recognition signals by searchlight.

1038 *Herring* surfaced. Closed her to 100 yards.

1035[2] Held megaphone conference. Decided *Barb* would cover area south and west of lane, *Herring* to north and east of Matsuwa. Tested our voice sets on 450 kc at 100 yard at better than 2 amp output. No reception either way.

1120 Secured conference and headed south for roving patrol along lane.

1212 Headed east.

1222 Radar contact 21,000 yards, commenced approach. Went ahead full and worked ahead. Splotchy fog. Smoke visible at times.

1242 (Ship Contact #4) Haze lifted suddenly leaving us with a stripped feeling. Large merchant ship in full view. Dove.

1244 (Plane Contact #1) Bomb, not close. Single air cover must have spotted our wake. Kept going to 90 feet to get rid of the plane.

1246 Returned to periscope depth.

1252 Depth charge. Distant. *Herring* must be at work.

1315 Fired three torpedoes from bow tubes, 90 track, 5° gyros, 1,400 yards range.

1316 Observed first hit, which split side of freighter open just abaft funnel. Streams of steam gushed out of side. Heard muffled explosion. Observed second hit forward of bridge. Loud explosion. Observed third hit about 15 yards aft of bow. Loud explosion. Ship began settling by bow. Took pictures.

1320 Ship sank. Lat. 48-21.1 N., Long. 151-19.6 E.

1330 (Ship Contact #5) Sighted medium sized merchant ship hull down. *Herring* must have scattered convoy. Too distant to close. Estimated range 14,000 yards. As haze was commencing to settle again decided to remain submerged and maintain contact for end around upon surfacing.

1400 Ship barely visible. Surfaced. Upon reaching bridge one of two power landing barges (Army type A), which had floated off sinking ship and were now

---

[2] Time in original.

jammed with survivors, opened up with machine guns. Had observed them before surfacing, but it was disconcerting to put my head over the bridge rail looking for planes and have bullets whiz overhead. Other ship had disappeared in haze, so decided against gun action now target had been eliminated. Our primary job at the moment is maintenance of contact. Went ahead full on engines and conned ship clear from crouched position on bridge. That ostrich feeling.

1410 Commenced end around on target who was heading southwest. Was afraid he would make one of the island passes or air coverage so ended around to port at 12,000 yard permitting him a good look at us at 8,000 yards on his port quarter, to make him realize his danger of trying to make the Kurile chain. Target seemed to agree for he gradually headed southwest toward La Pérouse. As fog closed down again let him think himself secure and ended around.

1659 Visibility 2,000 yards in patchy fog with light haze overhead. Nearly ahead of target for approach position when at

1700 (Plane Contact #2) Radar contact 3,000 yards closing fast. At 1,000 yards pulled the plug. Submerged. No bombs.

1710 Radar depth. Set up looked good so decided it was good chance to expend fish aft.

1730 Periscope depth. Range 4,000 yards.

1740 Target came out of fog just in time to stop us from surfacing for another end around.

1742 Single ping range, which checked within 10 yards of generated range.

1743 Fired three torpedoes from stern tubes, 95° track, 4° gyros, 1,685 yard range.

1744 Observed first torpedo hit two thirds of way from funnel to stern. Loud explosion.

Observed second hit under funnel. Loud explosion.

Observed third hit two thirds of way from funnel to bow. Loud explosion. Lat. 47-52 N., Long. 151-02 E.

1745 Took pictures. Target uptailed and sank.

1746 Two bombs close. Went deep. Breaking up noises.

1749 Two more bombs, not close.

1904 Surfaced, returned to scene of sinking in heavy fog.

1932 At wreckage. Decided we could use a prisoner who knew Matsuwa and Paramushiru, also information on remainder of convoy. No lifeboats had gotten away and most of the remaining survivors on flotsam were far gone in the icy water. Took most likely looking prospect aboard in a collapsed condition.

2200 Revived prisoner. Questioned on convoy. *Herring* had sunk escort. Three freighters had scattered. Original destination La Pérouse. One evidently remained.

2215 Headed for La Pérouse area.

June 1

0901 Made trim dive to routine flooded torpedoes.

1003 Surfaced.

1230 Now ahead of and to eastward of freighter's possible routes so headed west to southwest tip of Karafuto.

June 2

0101 (Ship Contact #6) Radar contact 10,500 yards. Visibility about 6,000 yards. High speed target. Commenced approach.

0205 Sighted target. A lone *Chidori*[3]. Would like magnetic exploders for this one.

0219 Fired three torpedoes from bow tubes, 120 track, 0° gyros, range 3,190 yards, depth 6 feet. Set up clicking. Disliked this long range, but we were approaching minefields and patrol boat lanes, so was forced to accept it.

0221:30 All torpedoes missed. Believe they passed under *Chidori*. A hard one to take.

0222 *Chidori* turned away following down torpedo tracks with guns blazing, side throwers and racks in action. Twelve depth charges were dropped. Target took off for La Pérouse leaving us in his dust.

0305 (Ship Contact #7) Radar contact, closing. Dove. Went to 250 feet. Depth charge, not close, closing. Rigged for depth charge and silent running.

0307 Screws passed up port side. Sounds like a spitkit.

0312 Lost screws.

0325 Periscope depth. Commenced reload and routine of torpedoes forward. Visibility zero.

0451 Distant depth charge.

0641 Screws closing. Commenced evading. Another spitkit.

0740 Lost screws.

0758 Surfaced. Headed north for patrol off Naka Shiretoko Misaki.

1715 Sighted large ice field along east coast of Karafuto. Calculated height 120 feet. Atmosphere cleared completely leaving us 14 miles off Karafuto, 9 miles off the ice field in bright sunshine. Sun was scintillating off the ice, so figured shore observers would be blinded.

1905 (Plane Contact #3) Sighted plane. A Pete[4]. Range 5 miles. Went to 140 feet.

1915 Periscope depth.

1917 SD depth. All clear.

---

[3] *Chidori* class torpedo boat. A relatively small (269', 600 ton), fast (30 knot) anti-submarine and escort ship. Armed with three 120 MM (4.7")/45 cal guns (originally 127/50), two 530 MM (21") torpedo tubes, and depth charges.

[4] Pete: Mitsubishi F1M1, Type 0 reconnaissance seaplane. A single-engine, central float biplane.

1922 Surfaced. Secured SD.
2211 (Plane Contact #4) Visibility zero. Plane heard passing down port side, by all hands on bridge.
Dove to 135 feet.
2218 Periscope depth.
2225 SD depth, all clear.
2227 Surfaced. Secured SD. With twenty hours of daylight we can't afford to stay submerged any longer than absolutely necessary.
2343 Headed south for Abashiri, Hokkaido, planning to work along north side of Hokkaido and then through Kunashiri Suido. If Abashiri looks like a good set up may give her a hit and run bombardment.

June 3

0818 Sighted Hokkaido. Visibility clearing. Surface haze only.
0902 (Plane Contact #5) Sighted plane, range 5 miles. A Sally[5]. Dove. Periscope depth.
0913 SD depth, all clear.
0915 Surfaced. Secured SD.
0933 (Plane Contact #6) Sighted plane, range 6 miles. A Sally. Dove. Periscope depth.
1000 SD depth. All clear.
1004 Surfaced. Secured SD.
1115 (Ship Contact #8) Sighted trawler too close to beach. Eased around on edge of visibility circle. Low surface haze was decreasing. Lighthouse was plainly visible, but we wanted to get further in Abashiri Wan before diving and approaching Abashiri. All mountains around are snow capped.
1215 Surface haze suddenly lifted leaving us nude 5 miles off Notoro Misaki Light with trawlers all around. Dove heading for Abashiri.
Experienced 3 knot current and tide rips setting us away. 12° temperature gradient while at 63 feet. Hoped the haze would drop again so we could surface.
1445 Nine fishing vessels within 2,500 yards. Had a field day on sound training.
1800 Haze dropped again.
1810 Surfaced. All trawlers had returned to port. Decided against bombardment Abashiri, having been unable to reconnoiter. P.O.W. said seven major air bases within 50 miles would give us the works. Headed for Konashiri Suido.
2235 Radar broke down. A bit trying with heavy fog and an ice field which we had spotted on May 20 about 60 miles ahead and 15 miles off our track. Commenced injection check, every five minutes[6].

---

[5] Sally: Mitsubishi Ki-21, twin-engine Army "heavy" bomber.
[6] Sea water temperature normally drops in proximity to ice, so monitoring water injection temperature can be used to give a warning.

June 4
0350 Headed for Paramushiru–La Pérouse convoy lane to patrol new station. Injection remaining constant at 38°F. Ice field must have moved on. Visibility 1,000 yards.
0945 Radar back in commission.

June 5
0200 Commenced patrolling across convoy lane at high speed. Visibility 600 yards. Lat. 49-48 N., Long. 147-28 E.
1200 Splotchy fog. Visibility varying from 100 to 13,000 yards.
1845 Having patrolled station for 20 hours headed for new station.

June 6
0058 On station Lat. 49 N., Long. 146-33 E. Commenced patrolling across lane.
0954 Headed towards Siberia for transmission.
1823 Passed large icefield on port beam. Injection dropped from 37° to 34°. Lat. 49-45 N., Long. 145-09 E. Decided to close the Russian Coast and follow down 1,000 fathom curve to Cape Patience in hopes of spotting a floating Jap cannery or Jap fisherman.
2119 SJ contact on Russian Sakhalin at 73,000 yards. Injection remaining constant. Slowed to 5 knots. Visibility 800 yards.
2125 Radar contact 1,100 yards on drift ice. Avoided. Commenced avoiding small chunks of drift ice 5–10 feet high with 10–30 feet below water. Converted #4 FBT.

June 7
Approached to within 12 miles of Karafuto dodging through continued drift ice until we got tired of broken field running and opposition increased to a wonderland of 50-60 foot columns and pinnacles with seals basking on the smaller chunks. Worked in and out down coast on edge of ice field. Injection remained constant at 34°. Visibility 700–50,000 yards. Good maneuvering practice for OOD. Radar never picked up ice beyond 3,500 yards. After sun up with sun obscured encountered several arctic mirages. A 20–30 foot solid pack of ice was sighted at 5–6,000 yards with a kaleidoscope of light being reflected off its side. Maneuvered ship to parallel. After passing along its side for 20 minutes all hands on the bridge sighted masts and funnels of four trawlers apparently ice bound. Lookout reported smoke from one funnel. Decided to close for gun shoot to lob a few over at some really fast ships from edge of field. Upon closing, ice field backed away and trawlers disappeared. An unbelievable mirage. OOD said he must have been out on patrol too long and requested a relief. New OOD arrived thinking we were a bit touched. A short while later he reported an icefield on the

opposite bow. The captain, now feeling like a grizzled arctic veteran who knew all about mirages, took a good look through his binoculars, ascertained it to be another mirage, and so told the OOD—who immediately wagered a quart of whiskey. Considering the present scarcity, and to teach the OOD a lesson, the bet was made, and we approached the mirage confidently, only to find it was the real McCoy. Captain retired to the wardroom. A few minutes later a messenger reported, twelve o'clock, all chronometers are round. At this the captain decided to turn in and take stock of himself.

1530 Headed for new patrol area.

2100 Commenced patrolling across lane. Lat. 48-55 N., Long. 146-33 E.

June 8

0816 Headed for new patrol station.

1118 On station commenced patrolling across lane Lat. 48-30 N., Long. 145-40 E.

1510 (Ship Contact #9) SJ contact 15,000 yards. Visibility 10,000 yards. Commenced end around on starboard at 11,000 yards, sighting large freighter at intervals, during which we turned away and hid in the steam from our exhausts. Target changed course from 045°T to 000°T, speed 9.75 knots, which lengthened end around.

1630 Visibility increased to 18,000 yards.

1823 Ahead of target. Dove. Commenced approach. Sunset at 2001. Twilight till 2200.

1825 JP[7] picked up target at 18,000 yards. Turn count 90 RPM. JK picked up target at 4,800 yards. Rigged for silent running. Visibility decreased to 8,000 yards.

1913 At 1,700 yards with gyros approaching zero, bow tubes ready, 105 starboard track, a matter of seconds before firing *Russian* flag on side was seen. Pictures were taken. Target was estimated at 10,000 tons, 540 feet. Guns fore and aft with numerous 20 MM AA mounts all over topside. These ships in the Okhotsk Sea should burn running lights day and night.

1922 Surfaced. Headed for Kunashiri Suido, where we have planned to bombard the Kurile cable link at Kushibotsu on Yetorofu Jima, then run around to Naval Base at Hito Kappu Wan and perhaps get a shot at whatever they send out after us.

---

[7] JP: The JP hydrophone was a long, trainable horizontal bar mounted on a short, post-like support on the forward upper deck. The bar had a magnetized iron core, wrapped with copper wire, and with sound deadening material covering the back side, making it into a directional magnetic microphone. JP was operated from the forward torpedo room and trained by hand. One distinct advantage of the JP over a fleet sub's other passive sound gear was that, being mounted on the upper deck instead of alongside the keel, it could be used when the boat was sitting on the bottom.

2330 New patrol station assigned, which cuts our time short for free lance movement. However, we may still be able to squeeze the bombardment in, but Hito Kappu Wan is out and the chance for taking trawler or patrol boat prisoners as requested.

June 9

1704 Radar contact on Yetorofu Jima 6,500 yards. Visibility 500 yards. Headed into Tannomoyo Wan for investigation of Kushibetsu Cable station prior to bombardment.

2002 Fog disappeared completely except over Kushibetsu, leaving us 4 miles off the beach in bright sunlight. Dove. Started single ping on fathometer at intervals to check chart. Readings appeared to be 30 to 40 fathoms shallower than shown on chart, beyond 100 fathom curve.

2051 Light surface haze set in. Surfaced. Low fog on beach.

2104 (Ship Contact #10) Radar contact 5,000 yards about 2,000 yards off point south of Cable station. Tracked northward along beach and closed. Possible patrol boat, speed 7 knots.

2145 Crossed 100 fathom curve. Fathometer going continuously now, because of chart discrepancy. Speed 5 knots.

2152 Inshore fog. Target not visible at 2,700 yards. Beach 3,300 yards. Shoaling rapidly, 18 fathoms—left full rudder.

2153 Sounding 8 fathoms—all back full—5 fathoms—4 fathoms. A breathless moment. Then deep water. Target now coincided with beach. Chart shows nothing less than 50 fathoms at our 4 fathom spot. Pulled a mile out in Kunashiri Suido and stopped. Decided to wait for moon rise and fog to lift over cable station. Meanwhile watching movements of patrol craft. CUO sweep, all clear.

2215 A full moon popped over the volcanic peaks like a Japanese postcard. All haze and fog disappeared with the exception of a thick blanket about 1,000 yards long and 100 feet high directly over our gun target. What a break! All other shore lines were plainly visible, also our patrol craft, an 80 foot spitkit, which quickly spotted us and commenced blinking recognition signals at us—individual "G"s at intervals. An impasse was reached. The fog wouldn't lift over target. The patrol craft hung onto the beach.

2330 Situation remains the same, with the exception of volcanic flashes appearing over one peak at irregular intervals and a new fog bank rolling in. Shoved off for Taraika Wan.

June 10

1327 (Ship Contact #11) Smoke sighted by high periscope watch. Closed until upper works were visible. A long torpedo boat making 15 knots headed for La Pérouse. Commenced end around at full speed. Visibility unlimited.

1546 Sighted patrol plane (Emily[8]). Distance 8 miles. Evidently we had not been sighted, so kept going because we had a struggle picking up bearing.

1548 Patrol plane headed toward us. Dove.

1610 Plane shoved off.

1617 Surfaced.

1624 Sighted same plane distance 10 miles. Did not dive. Continued end around. A task to pick up the valuable bearing we had lost, for it was now a race to see who could reach the mine field first. Prayed for a fog.

1830 Torpedo boat won the race and, as he turned away for Haka Shiretoko Misaki we gave up. Had thought we could have him with torpedoes set on 5 feet.

2300 Sighted Airo Misaki light (dimmed). Headed up along coast to Sakeyehama for a night look in at the anchorage.

June 11

0304 Harbor vacant. Headed for Kita Shiretoko Misaki (Cape Patience).

0330 Started fathometer for readings across unsounded section of Taraika Wan.

1000 Ice fields again. Maneuvered to parallel.

1110 (Ship Contact #12) Sighted trawler about 3,000 yards inside field working among the icebergs, probably after seal.

1150 Manned gun stations. Laid ship 10 yards off the ice field. Commenced firing the 4 inch. An odd practice with the target weaving his way slowly in and out among the bergs. Fired 31 rounds of 4 inch at ranges from 3–4,000 yards with many near misses and range spots down to 25 yards after straddling continuously.

1216 Frankly don't believe we ever got a direct hit, but shrapnel from the near misses and flying pieces of ice finally sank the trawler and destroyed numerous icebergs.

1233 (Ship Contact #13) Sighted another trawler, distant 8,000 yards, who started a race for the protection of the icefield.

1248 Fired a magazine of 20 mm to find out what armament he had. No reply. Decided to set him on fire with automatic weapons.

1252 At 500 yards opened up with our four 20 mm (620 rounds) and two .50 cal. machine guns (700 rounds). Could not set him on fire, incendiaries having no effect. He had just entered ice field so at

1258 Commenced firing 4 inch at 850 yards, which systematically cut his hull to pieces with 15 rounds high capacity. Target sank.

---

[8] Emily: Kawanishi H8K flying boat. A four-engine, long-range maritime patrol aircraft, the Emily was designed as a replacement for the Kawanish H6K (Mavis), and had an endurance of up to 24 hours. Generally considered the most advanced flying boat design built until well after World War II. A Mavis could carry up to 4,000 pounds or bombs of torpedoes in wing racks, and later versions were equipped with radar.

1332 (Ship Contact #14) Sighted two smoke streaks. Tracked and commenced end around at full speed. Targets at 11 knots, heading to southward. One large AP or AK, one medium. Anticipated a change in his base course to westward towards Sakaychama, so at

1604 Base course changed to West, angle on bow zero, range 20,000 yards. Dove.

1620 Visibility reduced to 8,000 yards. Rain. Targets disappeared.

1630 Still no targets. Came to radar depth. No pips.

1640 Surfaced. Targets visible in haze heading south.

1645 Targets headed west again. Figured we had been on extreme end of new base course zig, so ran on till we had a 15° port angle on bow.

1652 Dove. Commenced approach. Visibility unlimited. Sea glassy. Target changed his mind again and started a new series of zigs to southwest. Could not surface due to visibility and he still had to head west for his port.

2000 A three hour race at standard speed when he finally headed west and slid across 7,000 yards ahead of us. However we had some consolation in still having contact with sunset approaching.

2049 Surfaced with target in sight at 20,000 yards.

2050 Visibility dropped to 5,000 yards. Headed down his tracks.

2143 Radar contact on targets. Commenced end around to starboard at 7,000 yards in the blackest night we had ever seen. Rich phosphorescence.

2330 Ships in echelon with leading ship 300 yards to starboard of larger second ship. Size of second ship made it seem the reverse from the bridge.

2334 Fired 1-2-3 bow tubes at leading ship. Two misses.

2336 First hit in stern of second ship. Second hit about two thirds of distance between stern and funnel. Another miss. Second ship commenced sinking stern first with whistle blowing, and blinking (I hope) furiously at us. First ship was turning away. Couldn't afford to let such prey get away crippled, so swung hard left at full speed in a tight circle and headed for him. Made ready stern tubes.

2339 Cripple kept swinging left having nearly completed an 180° turn. Range closed to 780 yards. Cripple opened fire from midships gun. Believed he had seen our phosphorescent wake so slowed to standard with right rudder and had lookouts and quartermaster take cover. Passed him at 680 yards. Radar operator swallowed his chewing gum. Ship shuddered once from nearby explosion. Possibly a near miss, possibly second ship breaking up as he sank.

2343 Cripple was now evidently stopped and coasting with right rudder. Firing ceased.

2343 Backed down to get in position for another attack.

2345 Fire control party did a remarkable job of getting a new setup. Target at ½ knot speed. Angle on bow 90 starboard.

2347 Commenced twisting to get better gyro angles.

2349 Fired 7-8-9 stern tubes, 80 track, zero gyros, range 1,900 yards. Other ship had now sunk.

2350 Three hits, one aft, one under funnel, one forward. One must have touched off his magazine for suddenly he blew sky high. We were alone again.

2354 Took the D.R. the cripple had given us over 500 kc, before his transmission was interrupted, and set course for Paramushiru. Lat. 46-54 N., Long. 144-38 E. This was one time I was glad I had selected the bridge as my night approach station. The conning tower party was entirely lost after our 360° turn, the target's 180° turn left and 90° right turn punctuated by explosions; whereas from the bridge I had the complete picture, complete control of the situation, and was able to quickly position the ship for the final attack.

June 12
Enroute Paramushiru, covering convoy lanes.

June 13
Enroute Paramushiru, covering convoy lanes.

1713 (Ship Contact #15) Sighted smoke. Commenced end around to starboard. Target constant helming, base course 205°T.

1745 Whitish visibility conditions. Tied bedsheet tightly around our dark gray #1 periscope shears to increase camouflage.

2036 Ahead of target, waiting for darkness, change of base course.

2115 Target changed base course to 250°, speed 14 knots, and commenced new zig plan, which included 70° course changes and some 3 minute legs. A short end around.

2147 End of twilight, and the worst phosphorescence we had experienced. The loom of this on the steam from our exhaust gave the impression we had two searchlights trained aft. Decided we would have to shoot a stern tube shot on a sharp track from a stopped position. Night was clear, with partial overcast. Torpedo boat escort worked from port to starboard quarter. CUO sweep, all clear.

2223 Stopped dead ahead of target, range 3,700 with stern tubes on a 20° port track, holding our breath for the expected zig away. Bow wave of target looked tremendous bearing down on us. Target zigged 40° away and at

2231 Fired 9-10 stern tubes (our last 2 aft) on a 60° port track, 3° gyro angle, torpedo run 1,475 yards, range 1,770.

2232 Observed two hits, one in stern, which blew off part of his fantail, one halfway between stern and funnel. Target stopped and settle aft, whistle blowing.

2233 All ahead full. Radar jamming. Here comes the escort. Depth charges started. Range to escort kept decreasing during escape. Finally, at 2,600 yards, the escort turned away while he was winning the race, so at

2238 Stopped to observe target. CUO sweep, all clear.

2241 All ahead full. Escort came after us again. More depth charges. Range decreased again, then escort turned off. Still having radar jamming.

2247 Stopped. Depth charging continuing at intervals. Range to target 8,000 yards. Watched escort rejoin target on PPI, then work away at intervals to drop depth charges. Target pip growing smaller.

2305 Commenced working around target, waiting for him to sink. Escort pinging, radar interference, depth charges.

June 14

0003 With less than two hours of darkness remaining decided we couldn't wait any longer. Target pip now same size as escort. Headed in for coup de grace.

0016 Target pip disappeared. Target had sunk at last. Escort headed down our old track, desperately depth charging, while we passed 1,000 yards from where target had been with nothing in sight. Dropped punctured 5 gallon can of oil over side to give *Chidori* a target for his depth charge.

0030 Set course for lower Kamchatka to cover convoy lanes and a quick sweep for possible floating canneries.

0315 Depth charging ceased. (Total charges dropped—38)

1036 (Plane Contact #8) Sighted plane, distant 8 miles. Dove. Routined 4 torpedoes left forward.

1320 Surfaced.

1835 Sighted Araido To bearing 150°T, distant 90 miles.

June 15

0030 Radar contact on Kamchatka at 26,200 yards. Closed to 5 miles and headed down 20 fathom curve towards Shimushu.

0912 (Plane Contact #9) Sighted plane. Pete type, distant 8 miles. Dove.

0924 Radar depth. All clear.

0927 Surfaced. Secured SD.

1403 (Plane Contact #10) Sighted plane. Dove. Believed him to be covering nearby convoy departure points, so decided to remain submerged for a while.

1450 Sighted plane through periscope. Identified as Russian reconnaissance type MBR-2.

1445 Radar depth. All clear.

1447 Surfaced.

1508 (Plane Contact #11) Sighted plane. Russian MBR-2. Dove.

1531 Periscope depth.

1649 Radar depth.

1650 Surfaced. Secured SD.

1658 (Ship Contact #16) Sighted ship, distant 14 miles. Commenced end around.

1706 Ship kept zigging toward. Now more angle on bow. Kept range open to observe future zigs.

1726 No more zigs. Probably a Russian. Dove. Commenced approach.

1805 Identified liberty ship as a properly marked Russian on course 359°T.

1818 Surfaced. Headed down Kamchatka coast about 7 miles off the beach.

2130 Closed coast to 5 miles. No signs of fishing vessels or floating canneries. Numerous shore canneries.

June 16

0145 Abeam Mys Sivuchi. Headed for patrol point between Shimushu, Paramushiru, Araido To covering all western exits from Paramushiru Kaikyo.

0300 Commenced surface patrol. Daylight.

0315 Intermittent fog. Visibility varying between 400–14,000 yards in less than one minute. Tried hugging fog banks for a while, but it ruined our area coverage.

0400 Patrolling on easterly and westerly courses keeping ten miles off Araido To and Paramushiru. No radar interference. CUO sweep. All clear.

0410 SJ radar out of commission. Slowed for sound protection.

1440 Radar in commission.

1200 Visibility 200 yards. Heavy fog.

1311 SJ radar out of commission.

1355 (Ship Contact #17) Radar in commission. Radar contact 11,000 yards. Worked ahead of target, which was not zigging. Possibly a Russian, but how to identify in a fog this thick was a problem.

1830 No change in visibility, the heaviest fog yet. Now had target speed to thousandths of knots. Decided to close target on quarter and identify or shoot him the minute the fog broke. Target course 293°T.

1909 Radar contact on another target at 13,000 yards. Tracked him for future possibilities.

1922 On starboard quarter of first target at 2,000 yards.

1954 Target changed course to 240°T. Swung with him and decided to maintain position until dark for we probably would see the loom of his identification lights as soon as he turned them on. Ship was sounding fog signals. P.O.W. says Japs do also in heavy fog.

2009 Sunset.

2130 Still no lights visible. Now fairly dark. We could not spend the whole patrol on an unidentified ship, so commenced closing on starboard quarter, from downwind.

2205 At 510 yards, lights became visible and identified target as a properly marked Russian. After deck filled binocular. Shoved off to regain other contact.

2220 (Ship Contact #18) SJ contact at 16,560 yards. Closed on his starboard side.

2321 Crossed astern of him at 1,500 yards. Unable to identify. Heard weak air powered fog signals.

2335 Closed from downwind on his port quarter to 515 yards before making out his lights. Identified as properly marked Russian. Our patrol off Paramushiru Strait had thus been fruitless, due to Russians cutting the corner after passing through Shimushu Strait instead of staying on Russian lanes. With dangerous disadvantage of having to identify targets, decided to shift to patrol station off Kakumabetsu Wan where any good sized pip was a shooting target.

June 17

0040 (Ship Contact #19) Radar contact 16,500 yards. Closed.

0110 Crossed target's stern at 1,200 yards. Identified target by smell, his course prescribing exactly with Russian lane, no zigs, speed steady. Headed for Kakumabetsu Wan. This steady course speed combination is odoriforous.

0450 Commenced patrolling on surface 6 miles northwest of Kakumabetsu Naval Base on course 125 and 305 covering inside track between Araido To and Paramushiru, to commence close in surface patrol 7 miles off Paramishiru Strait and 7 miles from Araido To.

June 18

0010 Commenced patrolling. Visibility 1,000–10,000 yards, variable.

0902 Fog disappeared. Dove.

1515 (Ship Contact #20) Radar contact 17,200 yards. Tracked on Russian course, 2 miles to south of Russian track. Had planned this patrol to come no closer than 18,000 yards to Russian track, to avoid them. Plotted his track to Shimushu Strait and secured approach.

1645 (Ship Contact #21) Horizon cleared to west, land still fog bound. Sighted smoke to westward, range 30,000 yards. Worked ahead. This fellow was well clear of Russian track.

1713 Dove. Commenced approach.

1758 Identified as Russian, range 8,000 yards. He had evidently cut the corner of his prescribed dog leg track. A dangerous short cut. Turned approach over to torpedo officer and advanced other officers in station for training.

1830 Took pictures instead of shooting.

1837 Surfaced. Returned to patrol station.

2005 (Ship Contact #22) Sighted two patrol vessels off Araido To. Avoided.

2036 As fog set in attempted to regain contact in vain.

2202 Assumed Jap ships have been cleared of this area since Matsuwa bombardment on June 12–13 by surface craft and planes. We had sunk one big fast one at night on the 13th, which our P.O.W. had seen at Paramushiru. Decided to proceed to Matsuwa via convoy lanes, in hopes they would need some urgent spare parts there.

June 19
  Patrolling convoy lanes on route Matsuwa.

June 20
  Nearing Matsuwa via convoy lanes.
  0353 Renewed pit log blade. This had been bent after last sinking, evidently from passing through wreckage. A complete stricture finally resulted. We were fortunate to have a spare blade aboard.
  1059 Radar contact, 46,000 yards, on Chirihkotan.
  1333 Radar contact 70,000 yards, on Matsuwa.
  1831 Fog lifted over Banjo To and Matsuwa anchorage with us 6,000 yards off Banjo To. Headed away. Took a good look at anchorage, which was bare with the exception of one patrol boat. No structures on eastern side of Banjo To.
  1834 Dove. Headed in for observation of Matsuwa.
  1840 Found both periscopes to be completely fogged. Headed clear to southward waiting for scopes to clear.
  1915 JP picked up small boat screws crossing our stern. Periscope still fogged. Rigged for silent running.
  1916 JP lost sound of screws.
  1945 One periscope cleared sufficiently around edges to show us visibility had dropped to about 8,000 yards. Came to radar depth. All clear on SJ and SD.
  1952 Surfaced. Secured SD.

June 20
  2000 Decided to chalk a day off our patrol on possibility of making a photographic reconnaissance of Matsuwa for determination of damage done by surface force bombardment on June 12–13. Commenced circle of island looking for patrol boat in hopes of obtaining requested prisoner.
  2030 While passing westward between Matsuwa and Rashuwa gave chase to radar contact at 18,000 yards astern of us twice. This disappeared after turning both times, then reappeared after we had resumed our course. From analysis of its ranges with those of the two high islands we were passing between it appeared to be a distinct vectoral combination of their backlobes. Radar officer says it can't happen.
  2100 Tested both periscopes. Pressure zero. Recharged with nitrogen.

June 21
  0353 Circling Matsuwa. Passed between Saikoke and Matsuwa.
  0400 Encountered eddies and whirlpools 200 yards across. These heeled ship 5° to 6°.
  0520 Visibility 1,000 yards. Passed Banjo To at 3,000 yards. No break in fog.
  0600 Commenced patrolling shipping lane to and from Matsuwa.

0800 Visibility 5,000 yards. Light haze overhead.

0815 (Plane Contact #12) SJ contact closing fast. Lost contact at 2,600 yards.

0831 Started keying SD for 5 seconds every half hour to determine what planes were doing. Appeared to be three planes undergoing training. They stayed within 21 miles.

1131 Picked up SD interference at half hourly keying. Checked it, then secured SD. We were DF conscious[9].

1400 Fog thinning. Commenced working in towards Matsuwa south of Banjo To to obtain good diving position for reconnaissance if fog dispersed. Chose this position because it would give us a 3,000 yard range to Banjo To sono station, a fair position for photography, with an exodus without grounding if we were fogged out during approach with a strong current.

1458 Fog jumped up. We jumped down. Dove. Matsuwa 6,000 yards away. Rigged for silent running.

1545 Tagan Kaku distant 4,000 yards, took 7 pictures, depth 64 feet. Lat. 48-01.3 N., Long. 155-19.7 E.

1611 Tagan Kaku distant 1,900 yards, took 22 pictures. Depth 65 feet. Sea calm. Lat. 48-02.6 N., Long. 153-16.3 E. Headed out. Visual observation subject of special report.

1621 Fog dropping. No further navigational fixes. Passed within 1,500–2,000 yards of sono station, whispering. Hope the soundings on this chart are correct.

1847 Radar depth. All clear SD and SJ.

1849 Surfaced. A fortunate reconnaissance in a land of 21 hours daylight with only a 4 hour dive.

June 21

1900 There must be some Japs somewhere. Decided to circle all islands and investigate all anchorages listed on route Musashi Wan Naval Base.

2030 Nothing at Raikoke.

2330 Nothing in anchorages around Shasukotan.

June 22

0100 Rounded Yekaruma at 6,000 yards. Nothing there or around Chirinkotan. A crystal clear night.

0300 Passed through Shasukotan Strait. Whirlpools and eddies. Ran into fog bank.

---

[9] It was commonly believed among submarine officers that the Japanese were able to pick up and home in on the signals emitted by the SD radar. Some captains preferred to keep the SD secured (shut off) and rely on lookouts to warn of enemy planes. Other captains used the SD only sparingly, while others ran it almost continuously. Results shown in patrol reports of various submarines are, at best, inconclusive on this point.

0500 In Harumkotan Strait. Nothing at patrol base in the Hakuchi. Currents up to 6 knots, variable. Steered 30° to right of course to make good desired course.

0605 Fog lifted. Speeded up to get clear of this unproductive spot.

0608 (Plane Contact #13) Started SD. Plane contact moving from 21 miles to 17 miles. Keying SD at half hour intervals.

0707 Secured SD.

0800 Visibility unlimited. Land 90 miles distant sighted. Decided to patrol on surface 15 miles east of Onekotan and 35 miles south of Musashi Wan (Paramushiru). With the visibility we had we could cover a tremendous area. Expected aircraft trouble so slowed to 10 knots.

1017 (Plane Contact #14) Sighted 2 planes over Paramushiru. Believe it or not this distance was close to 36 miles. Watched these planes conduct training in dog fights.

1020 Sighted another section of 4 planes over Paramushiru.

1027 Sighted 2 more planes over Paramushiru.

1028 Sighted 5 more planes over Paramushiru, conducting training.

1041 Took panoramic movies of Harumkotan, Onekotan and Paramushiru. Lat. 49-22.7 N., Long. 155-18.3 E.

1048 Sighted 2 more planes over Paramushiru engaged in dog fighting.

1100 Shifted patrol to north–south line to keep small angle exposed to Paramushiru. Slowed to 8 knots to reduced wake.

1600 Volcano getting more active on Paramushiru. Putting out black smoke, which formed a low, dark haze around island. Probably volcanic ash is what is termed a dust fog in these regions.

1607 Sighted 2 planes over Paramushiru.

1626 Heard noises that sounded like gun practice from Paramushiru.

1700 Headed north to close Musashi Wan Naval Base.

2105 Four miles off Naval Base. Nothing in the anchorage. Headed for anchorage at Otomae Wan.

2227 (Ship Contact #23) Radar contact 2,200 yards. Sampan. Avoided.

2239 Radar contact 3,200 yards. Sampan. Avoided.

2246 Radar contact 3,700 yards. Sampan. Avoided.

2252 Radar contact 2,600 yards and 3,800 yards. Sampans. Avoided.

2324 Radar contact 4,300 yards. Sampan. Avoided.

2337 Radar contact 4,500 yards. Sampan. Avoided.

2340 Off Otomae Wan. Nothing in anchorage. Headed for Suribachi Wan Air Base anchorage.

2354 Radar contacts 4,000 yards on each beam. Sampans. Avoided.

2359 Radar contacts 3,500 yards and 3,300 yard. Sampans. Avoided.

June 23

0004 Radar contact 3,400 yards. Sampan. Avoided. *Whew!*

0005 Radar contact 5,000 yards. Sampan. Avoided.
0010 Off Suribachi Wan. Nothing in anchorage. Headed for patrol off Higashi Banjo Suido.
0011 Radar contact 4,100 yards. Sampan. Avoided.
0012 Radar contact 2,500 yards. Sampan. Avoided.
0014 Radar contact 3,500 yards. Sampan. Avoided.
0015 Radar contact 3,200 yards. Sampan. Avoided.
0016 Radar contacts 2,550 yards and 4,750 yards. Sampans. Avoided.
0017 Radar contact 2,850 yards. Sampan. Avoided.
0018 Radar contact 4,160 yards. Sampan. Avoided.
0021 Radar contact 3,650 yards. Sampan. Avoided.
0022 Radar contact 3,450 yards. Sampan. Avoided.
0024 Radar contact 4,000 yards. Sampan. Avoided.
0026 Radar contact 3,450 yards. Sampan. Avoided.
0027 Radar contact 3,500 yards. Sampan. Avoided.
0029 Radar contact 2,900 yards. Sampan. Avoided.
0033 Radar contact 4,150 yards. Sampan. Avoided.
0034 Radar contact 3,100 yards. Sampan. Avoided.
0037 Radar contact 3,350 yards. Sampan. Avoided.
0053 Radar contact 5,100 yards. Sampan. Avoided.
0055 Radar contact 4,400 yards. Sampan. Avoided.
0101 Radar contact 3,600 yards. Sampan. Avoided.
0105 Radar contact 2,950 yards. Sampan. Avoided.
0107 Radar contact 2,550 yards. Sampan. Avoided.
0126 Radar contact 1,850 yards. Sampan. Avoided.
0144 Radar contact 2,200 yards. Sampan. Avoided.
0154 Dawn. Sampans all around. Dove. Looks like our first submerged day will be a long one. In view of Saipan operations and present emptiness of area, decided to patrol off Higashi Banjo Suido, which is a warship lane, in hopes of contacting a submarine leaving Kataoka Submarine Base for Midway and points east or returning from patrol.
0407 Sighted five sampans.
0705 Sighted small trawler or patrol vessel.
1050 Sighted small trawler or patrol vessel.
1340 (Plane Contact #15) Sighted aircraft, distance 10 miles. Unidentified.
1712 Sighted sampan.
1730 Sighted sampan.
1953 Heard rubbing and clanking noises against hull.
1955 Sighted 2 red flags astern. Looks like we've picked up a net. Started fathometer. Depth 45 fathoms. Went to 150 feet. Still clanking and scraping noises all over hull. Went to 200 feet and backed down for 10 minutes. Cleared net and at
2024 Returned to periscope depth.

2028 Sighted sampan.

2128 Sighted sampan.

2131 Radar depth. Picked up another fishing net, banging, clanking and scrapings all over hull. Getting dark.

2141 Surfaced, armed with knives. Cut our way through nets, which covered the bridge, shears and deck. Headed for Onekotan Strait to patrol other side of Paramushiru.

2143 Sighted Sampan. Avoided.

2147 Radar contact 1,550 yards. Sampan. Avoided.

2150 Radar contact 3,000 yards. Sampan. Avoided.

2152 Radar contact 3,400 yards. Sampan. Avoided.

2212 Radar contact 7,400 yards. Sampan. Avoided.

2215 Radar contact 6,400 yards. Sampan. Avoided.

2225 Finally cleared all fish nets off topside. These were buoyed with wood and weighted with lead pellets and rocks.

June 24

0038 Twilight again. Land plainly visible. Prayed for an early fog so we could make the Strait.

0100 Our fog arrived.

0400 Passed through Onekotan Strait.

0930 Visibility increased to 8,000 yards. Looked in at Kujira Wan. Nothing in anchorage.

1100 Off Kakumabetsu Naval Base. Nothing in anchorage. The area is truly deserted since our attack on Saipan.

1155 Sighted small ice in Araido Strait. Light fog commenced clearing. We cleared the Strait and opened out from land.

1627 Visibility 40 miles. Took pictures of Araido To.

1811 Visibility 50 yards. Heavy fog.

2020 (Ship Contact #25) Radar contact 16,000 yards. Commenced tracking. Target on steady course, 35° from prescribed Russian course.

2049 Commenced identification approach.

2125 Closed to 950 yards on starboard quarter of target. Sighted hull fifteen seconds before sighting Russian identification lights. Secured approach. Headed for north convoy lane from Paramushiru.

June 25

Patrolling northern Jap convoy lane from Paramushiru. Nothing seems to be leaving Paramushiru and this will ensure us an attack position for anything entering and keep us clear of Russians.

0305 (Ship Contact #26) Radar contact 12,000 yards. Commenced tracking. Heavy fog.

0600 Still escorting target. Visibility 50 yards. Waiting for 2,000 yards visibility for attack.
0659 Dove. Commenced approach. Visibility 1,500 yards, clearing. On starboard bow of target.
0712 Sighted target, a merchant ship, estimated 3,000 tons. Well off expected bearing showing port angle on bow.
0718 Target zigged, giving us starboard angle on bow. Spotted Russian side markings at 1,600 yards. This fellow was lucky, if visibility had not cleared prior to 0900 I intended to make daylight surface attack in fog shooting on radar bearings. He followed the Jap convoy lanes and courses, including 85° change closer than the Japs do. His speed was 13 knots. I anticipated a destroyer.
0744 Surfaced.
2108 Radar interference on SJ. Apparently coming from a bearing aft. Something must be catching up to us.
2123 Commenced stationary patrol across convoy track.
2127 Lost interference. Possibly one of our planes circling around waiting for dark before bombing Shimushu.

June 26
0012 Secured stationary patrol. Heading down convoy lane toward Airo Misaki. Requested two day extension patrol.
1300 Working on periscope #1 empty. #2 water on lens.

June 27
Patrolling Okhotsk Sea convoy lanes.

June 28
0657 Radar contact on Airo Misaki. 48,000 yards. Poor SJ performance.
0730 Heading for Kunashiri Strait.
0845 (Ship Contact #26) Sighted ship coming out of hazy section of horizon at 16,000 yards. Dove.
0931 Surfaced for end around. Ship appeared to be a liberty ship, so made daylight surface approach.
1059 At 9,000 yards identified ship as Russian. These boys are every place.
1603 (Ship Contact #27) Ship sighted at about 30,000 yards. Closed.
1615 SJ radar and PPI contact on same ship 36,850 yards. Still don't believe this, but I saw it. Radar officer had been working on the set since poor results this morning. The bearing was correct, the target tracked properly, but the ranges were phenomenal and unbelievable. At 30,000 yards by radar range the silhouette was identified as Russian liberty ship. Secured approach. Radar followed this ship to 41,000 yards before losing it.

2055 Radar contact on land over 80,000 yards. Shortly after this the phenomena ended and the radar gave up and quit, undoubtedly exhausted.

2206 Sighted Yetorofu. Headed for Kushibetsu for bombardment.

June 29

0030 Passing through Kunashiri Strait. Visibility clear except for bombardment target, which seems to have its own perpetual blanket of low, heavy fog. Gave up bombardment, but it is still a good target.

0230 Completed passage of strait, having encountered currents up to 7 knots.

0300 A clear twilight. If any Jap lookouts are up we should be spotted. Anticipate plane trouble from Hitokappu Wan, distant 50 miles.

0400 Patrolling north of Ashikotan. Broken clouds. Am tempted to use SD, am certain it would bring planes from the air bases close by.

1200 Patrolling outer lanes.

2230 Departed area. Great circling[10] to Midway.

June 30–July 4

Enroute Midway. Had two July 4th's.

1757(Y) Moored Midway. Received usual excellent welcome with all facilities available.

July 5

1530(Y) Enroute Pearl in company with *Gar* and *Swordfish*. Conducted tests with *Gar*, using SJ radar for transmision and reception of message both visually on A scope and by listening using a phone connected circuit rigged by Radar Officer. To the best of my knowledge the listening and keying feature of SJ message reception was developed by Williams, B., RT1c at Submarine Base, Midway.

July 9

Arrived Submarine Base, Pearl Harbor.

(C) WEATHER

In general the weather in the Sea of Okhotsk and in the vicinity of the Kurile chain was favorable for submarine operations between 28 May and 29 June, the period covered by this report. Winds never exceeded Force 3, calms being predominant; temperatures were low but not uncomfortable. However fog with vary-

---

[10] A "great circle" route is the shortest distance from one point on the globe to another. So called because the route looks like a deep arc when laid out on a flat map or chart due to the inherent distortion necessary to depict a spherical planet on a flat surface. On a globe the same course will appear as a straight line.

ing density was with us for at least part of every day. Average injection temperature was 37° F, dropping sharply to 34° when in the vicinity of drift ice.

The fogs are low and extremely dense. It was necessary to close one Russian vessel to 310 yards to make out her hull identification lights. Volcanic ash and dust from numerous active craters undoubtedly account for the "dusty thick" fogs, mentioned in the sailing directions. Visibility often changes with great rapidity from zero to horizon, particularly near land and on the Pacific side of the Kuriles. Mountain tops usually show above the fog, when not hidden in the clouds.

Drift ice, collected in limited fields, was found in the following locations:

Date	Lat.	Long.	Location	Description
29 May	43°-45' N	146°-30' E	N.W. of Etorofu	Field at least 5 miles wide. Peaks 50-100 feet high.
2 June	46°-10' N	143°-10' E	Karafuto	Huge field, appeared 120 feet high.
6 June	50° to 49° N	142°-20' to 145°-10' E	Karafuto	Loosely packed drift ice, floes 2-30 ft thick maximum.
11 June	48°-20' N	144°-30' E	Taraika Wan	Loose drift ice, limits unknown.

Note: Radar could not detect this ice inside of 3,500 yards.

Embarrassing phosphorescence was encountered several times in the Sea of Okhotsk. Lat. 49-45, Long 144-38, and Lat. 51, Long 152. This phenomena was most noticeable with a wind of Force 2 and slight chops, although usually it appeared only with a calm surface.

Remarkable refraction effects were noticed on 21 June when the fog suddenly cleared with a light northerly breeze and nearly all of Araido To's 7,655 feet could be seen from Lat. 52-16, Long. 154-32, a distance of 91 miles. At that range only the top 1,300 feet should have been over the horizon. A few minutes later the sun set and strata of varied density caused the red ball to elongate to an ellipse, then break into a jagged edged symmetrical pagoda, finally sinking below the horizon in two separate sections. Believe it or not; we didn't, even though we saw it.

The extraordinary clarity of the atmosphere on these occasions was again demonstrated on 22 June when planes were observed dogfighting with each other over Paramushiru at a range of 38 miles.

(D) TIDAL INFORMATION

In the open area of the sea of Okhotsk currents were negligible. This was true also off the coast of Kamchatka north of 54°-15' N, and the coast of Karafuto and Sakhalin except near the capes guarding Taraika Wan. In the vicinity of the Kurile

Straits, however, currents were of high velocity and unpredictable set. We were unable to predict times of flood and ebb from tidal data available. The most violent currents were encountered in Harumukotan Strait, 5 miles NE of that island where variable currents of up to 8 knots required steering 30 degrees off course to make good the track laid down. Whirlpools and eddies several hundred yards in width were encountered in the middle of Shasukotan Strait and in Matsuwa Strait. These caused the ship (on the surface) to heel 3 to 5 degrees while passing through them.

Detailed observations on currents are listed in the following table. Radar fixes obtained as described in Section E of this report were compared with dead reckoning analyzer positions to establish current. Speed input to this instrument is from the pit log, which has been very accurate. Wind during these observations was negligible. Results are probably accurate to ¼ knot and ten degrees.

CURRENT OBSERVATIONS

Time (−10 zone) Time Date 1944	Time relative high water at "Shakotan"	Set	Drift	Lat.	Long.	Location
0315 : May 30	+5 hrs. 43 min.	165	.2 kt.	46-06	144-12	SE of Karafuto
1230 : June 3	+11 hrs. 45 min.	026	1.2	44-12	144-29	Abashiri Wan
2000 : June 3	+5 hrs. 49 min.	072	3.1	44-10	144-40	Abashiri Wan
2352 : June 11	+3 hrs. 39 min.	160	1.2	50-08	145-50	Hiro Masaki
1718 : June 20	+43 min.	307	1.2	48-16	153-23	NE of Matsuwa
1821 : June 20	+1 hr. 46 min.	337	1.7	48-07	153-23	E of Matsuwa
2127 : June 20	+[?] hrs. 52 min.	095	1.3	47-53	153-21	SE of Matsuwa
2355 : June 20	+7 hrs. 20 min.	086	1.8	47-56	153-10	S of Matsuwa
0030 : June 21	+7 hrs. 55 min.	050	3	47-57	153-01	SW of Matsuwa
0203 : June 21	+9 hrs. 28 min.	065	.5	48-06	152-34	W of Matsuwa
0245 : June 21	+10 hrs. 10 min.	165	2.8	48-09	153-01	NW of Matsuwa
0340 : June 21	+30 min.	135	4.1	48-12	153-10	N of Matsuwa
0432 : June 21	+1 hr. 22 min.	202	.8	48-09	153-18	N of Matsuwa
0653 : June 21	+3 hrs. 43 min.	162	2.5	48-09	153-29	NE of Matsuwa
1321 : June 21	+10 hrs. 11 min.	—	0	48-04	153-36	E of Matsuwa
1431 : June 21	+11 hrs. 21 min.	—	0	48-00	153-26	SE of Matsuwa
0130 : June 22	+8 hrs. 15 min.	045	1.3	49-03	153-48	NW of Shasukotan
0241 : June 22	+9 hrs. 26 min.	300	1.8	49-03	154-09	N of Shasukotan
0340 : June 22	+10 hrs. 25 min.	—	0	48-57	154-30	S of Harumukotan
0855 : June 22	+5 hrs. 5 min.	255	1.7	49-23	155-18	E on Onekotan

1833 : June 22	+39 min.	030	1.4	49-37	155-15	NE of Onekotan
2209 : June 22	+4 hrs. 15 min.	060	.6	49-56	155-30	Musashi Wan
0908 : June 23	+4 hrs. 39 min.	—	0	50-16	156-27	E of Paramushiru
0900 : June 23	Negligible			50-20	156-30	E of Paramushiru
2300						
0700 : June 24	+1 hr. 55 min.	150	1.7	49-52	154-30	Onekotan Kaifyo
0846 : June 24	+3 hrs. 41 min.	190	.6	50-10	154-40	N of Shurinuito
1023 : June 24	+5 hrs. 20 min.	185	.8	50-25	155-22	W of Paramushiru
1123 : June 24	+6 hrs. 19 min.	270	2.2	50-32	153-34	W of Paramushiru
1333 : June 24	+8 hrs. 29 min.	075	1.6	50-38	155-15	W of Paramushiru
0035 : June 29	+4 hrs. 15 min.	220	3.1	44-35	145-48	Kunashiri Suido
0059 : June 29	+4 hrs. 39 min.	037	7.0	44-32	146-45.8	Kunashiri Suido
0117 : June 29	+4 hrs. 37 min.	345	4.6	44-29	146-45	Kunashiri Suido
0136 : June 29	+5 hrs. 16 min.	038	2.7	44-25	148-48	Kunashiri Suido
0203 : June 29	+3 hrs. 48 min.	310	3.8	44-21	146-54	Kunashiri Suido

(E) NAVIGATIONAL AIDS

Fog and overcast prevented celestial observation in this area and the proximity to enemy bases frequently rendered use of the fathometer inadvisable. Reliance was placed in radar fixes, which were very accurate and easier to obtain than the usual visual cuts on uncertain contour tangents.

The method used in the *Barb* is one similar to that described by the Commanding Officer of the U.S.S. *Mayrant* in *Radar Information Notes No. 8*, of 1 April 1944. A plotting board was manufactured for us by Sub Base Midway of 1/16" Lucite about 20 inches square, sand blasted on one side to take pencil marks and a hole drilled for the pivot of a plotting arm. The scale of this arm is laid off from the latitude scale of the chart in use. A compass rose is mounted under the arm.

Data for the plotting is taken from the PPI, which was prepared by inserting a cellulose acetate disc scribed with 8 concentric rings, under the viewing glass, so that ranges may be quickly estimated during a search at slow speed. The Navigator during a sweep past land calls "mark" at points where a noticeable change in contour appears on the scope and reads out the minimum range at this point in fractions of a range ring, as 3.8, 2.5, etc., and an assistant records this data together with the true bearing at the "mark." Referring to a calibration table for the range scale in use, the ring readings are converted, plotted, and faired in, giving the line of closest land as shown on the PPI, but to the scale of the chart. The transparent board then is oriented on the chart with true north, corrected for radar bearings and gyro error, and moved about until the faired outline coincides with the shore contour visible to the radar at that distance. The fix is marked by pricking the chart through the center of the pivot and is, in effect, the locus of the intersection of a great number of ranges and bearings. The entire process takes three to five minutes and is extremely accurate when charts are available which show inland contours. In this connection the confidential Japanese Aviation Charts V6–1, 2 and 6 were invaluable. The faired outline often followed valleys, bays, bluffs and peaks with a fidelity which suggested it had been traced from the chart.

Fixes obtained by this method permitted continuous plotting of the ship's position when running the Kurile Straits, where currents up to 7 knots were encountered, and enable the ship to quickly and safely reconnoiter the enemy's many anchorages on the surface at night and in the fog, from close inshore.

Only one navigational light was observed burning. Airo Misaki Lighthouse on Sakhalin Island showed the correct characteristics at reduced brilliance being visible at ten miles on June 10, 1944.

Injection temperatures were logged every five minutes in the vicinity of ice. A drop in temperature from 37° to 34° always indicated the proximity of the field. Individual growlers or small bergs were not always picked up by radar.

The pit log gave us very good service, possibly due to our care in securing it below 100 foot depths. The blade was bent on June 20 and was renewed from inboard with no variation in the accuracy of the instrument.

The fathometer was out of commission for a few hours while a faulty tube was located and necessary soundings at that time were taken by housing the QC projector and reading the depth in yards with single pings on the bottom.

Soundings were taken at 15 minute intervals while crossing an unsounded portion of Taraiko Wan, and the record forwarded separately to the Hydrographic Office.

The portfolio of charts are generally accurate, but land shifts due to volcanic action undoubtedly have occurred, which alter contours and offshore depth. In particular the following were noted.

H.O. Chart No.	Lat.	Long.	Remarks
5820	52° N	156° E.	Soundings off coast of Kamchatka agree.
5820	52-28 N	157-26 E	Sopka Opalmaya appears to be 7 miles to the northward.
6527 (Plan of Tannamoyo Wan)	44-34.4 N	146-55 E	Soundings outside 100 fathom curve were 40-50 fathoms shallower than shown. 7 fathom depth encountered at 44° 34.4 N., 146° 55.2 E. where chart shows about 50. A high bluff of island also appeared on the shore about east of this point.

5324		48-04 N	153-14 E		Periscope cuts on contours of Matsuwa agree with charted tangents.	
V6-6 (Jap Aviation Chart conf)		44-00 N	144-30 E		Soundings in Abashiri Wan agree.	
V3-2 (Jap Aviation Chart conf)		48-18 N	153-15 E		Raikoku To appears to be 1.8 miles to S.E. of its charted position.	

(F) SHIPS CONTACTS

No.	Time Date	Lat. Long.	Type(s)	Initial Range	Est. C/S	How Contacted	Remarks
1.	0240(K) 30 May	46-06 N 144-12.6 E	Tanker (R) 275 ft. long	14,000	215 10	SN	Properly marked Russian
2.	0100(K) 31 May	48-18 N 130-04.6 E	12,000 tons (R) Tanker	16,000	041 11½	R	Carried USSR ID lights.
3.	0956(K) 31 May	48-28 N 151-04 E	U.S.S. *Herring*	8,500	090 10	R	Rendezvoused
4.	1224(K) 31 May	48-21.1 N 151-19.6 E	AP	21,000	190 9 ¾	R	3 hits, sank. Attack # 1.
5.	1330(K) 31 May	48-31.1 N 151-20 E	AP	14,000	250 11	P	3 hits, sank. Attack # 2.
6.	0100(K) 2 June	45-32 N 144-29 E	*Chidori* Cl. Torpedo Boat	10,500	265 16	R	Missed. Attack # 3.
7.	0305 2 June	45-47 N 144-17 E	Patrol Boat	3,000	090 5	JP	
8.	1115 3 June	45-02 N 144-31 E	Trawlers & Sampans	7,000	070 3	SD	
9.	1510(K) 8 June	48-31 N 143-36 E	AK (R)	13,000	000 9 ¾	R	Carried USSR identification.
10.	2104 9 June	44-29 N 143-36 E	Patrol Boat	6,000	020 7	R	
11.	1335(K) 10 June	47-00 N 145-05 E	Torpedo Boat	20,000	200 15	SD	Unable to close.
12.	1110(K) 11 June	48-20 N 144-22 E	Fishing Trawler	9,000	Stopped	SD	Destroyed by gunfire.
13.	1248(K) 11 June	48-21 N 144-23 E	Fishing Trawler	8,000	300 7	SD	Destroyed by gunfire.
14.	1322(K) 11 June	48-19 N 144-32 F	2 AK in company, smoking	20,000	200 10	SD	6 hits, sank. Attack # 4, 5, 6.

15.	1713 13 June	51-37 N 152-13.6 E	1 AK & Escort.	30,000	280 14	SD	2 hits, sank. Attack # 7
16.	1536 15 June	52-11 N 156-04 E	1 AK (R)	24,000	310 12	SD	Carried USSR identification.
17.	1330 16 June	51-05.6 N 155-01.8 E	1 AK (R)	10,500	240 7	R	Carried USSR identification.
18.	2220 18 June	51-17.0 N 154-46.0 E	1 AK (R)	16,350	240 7	R	Carried USSR identification.
19.	0040 17 June	31-00 N 154-31 E	1 AK (R)	16,300	126 10	R	Identified Russian.
20.	1516 18 June	50-57 N 155-56 E	1 AK (R)	17,200	030 10	R	Identified Russian.
21.	1645 18 June	51-01 N 155-55 E	1 AK (R)	25,000	123 9	SD	Identified Russian.
22.	2003 18 June	50-58 N 155-53 E	2 Patrol Craft	10,000	353 6	SD	
23.	2252 22 June	49-56 N 155-40 E	Numerous Fishing boats	5,000	Lying to	R	About 58 encountered.
24.	2020 24 June	51-27 N 155-15 E	AK (R)	15,000	090 9	R	Russian
25.	0303 25 June	52-11 N 155-44 E	AK (R)	12,900	176 12.5	R	Russian
26.	0846 28 June	46-40 N 144-09 E	AK (R)	19,000	050 8½	SD	Russian
27.	1603 28 June	45-56 N 145-30.6 E	AK (R)	40,000	050 9	SD	Russian

(G) AIRCRAFT CONTACTS

	Contact No.	1	2	3	4	5	6	7
S U B M A R I N E	Date	5-31-44	5-31-44	6-2-44	6-2-44	6-3-44	6-3-44	6-10-44
	Time (Zone)	1244	1700	1905 (–10)	2211 (–10)	0901 (–10)	0953 (–10)	1548 (–10)
	Position (Lat) (Long)	48-21 151-20	47-52 151-02	46-07 144-03	46-13 144-06	44-50 144-05	44-24 144-08	46-43 144-36
	Speed	6	10	10	5	10	10	10
	Course	280	290	280	100	180	160	230
	Trim	63 ft.	Surf.	Surf.	Surf.	Surf.	Surf.	Surf.
	Min. since last SD search	Not in use.	Not in use.	Not in use.	Not in use.	Not in use.	Not in use.	Not in use.
A I R C R A F T	Number	1	1	1	Unk	1	1	1
	Type	Unk.	Unk.	Pete	Unk.	Sally	Sally	Sally
	Probable Mission	H	H	Unk.	Unk.	Unk.	Unk.	Unk.
	How Contacted	Bomb	SJ	Sight	Heard	Sight	Sight	Sight
	Initial Range	2.5	1.5	5 mi.	Unk.	5 mi.	6 mi.	8 mi.
	Elevation Angle	Unk.	Unk.	10°	Unk.	4°	2°	3½°
	Range and Rel. Br. when it detected S/M	Unk.	N.D.	N.D.	N.D.	N.D.	N.D.	N.D.
C O N D I T I O N S	Sea (State – Beauf.) (Direction)	0 —	0 —	0 —	0 —	0 —	0 —	0 —
	Clouds (Ht. in ft.) (overcast)	— 0	Low fog Lt. haze	6,000 30°	— Low fog	— Lt. haze	— Lt. haze	12,000 —
	Moon (Bearing(R)) (Angle) (Illum.)	— — —	— — —	Day — —	090 50° 50%	— — —	— — —	— — —

Type S/M Camouflage on this patrol – Haze Gray 32/3SS/B

	Contact No.	8	9	10	11	12	13	14
S U B M A R I N E	Date	6-14-44	6-15-44	6-15-44	6-15-44	6-21-44	6-22-44	6-22-44
	Time (Zone)	1056 (−10)	0910 (−10)	1402 (−10)	1508	0815	0608	1017
	(Lat) Position (Long)	52-05 152-29	52-58 155-55	52-16 156-05	52-12 156-06	48-22 153-27	49-00 154-46	49-26 155-[?]
	Speed	15 k	10 k	10 k	10 k	10 k	10 k	10 k
	Course	085	180	160	160	090	150	227
	Trim	Surf.	Surf.	Surf.	Surf.	Surf.	Surf.	Surf.
	Min. since last SD search	Not in use.	Not in use.	272	21	Not in use.	0	100
A I R C R A F T	Number	1	1	1	3	1	1	17
	Type	Unk.	Pete	MBR-2 Russ.	MBR-2 Russ.	Unk.	Unk.	Unk.
	Probable Mission	Unk.	Unk.	Pat.	Pat.	Unk.	Patrol	Trg.
	How Contacted	Sight	Sight	Sight	Heard	SJ	SD	Sight
	Initial Range	8 mi.	8 mi.	8 mi.	4 mi.	8.5 mi.	21 mi.	38 mi.
	Elevation Angle	½°	½°	½°	3°	Unk.	Unk.	4°
	Range and Rel. Br. when it detected S/M	N.D.	N.D.	N.D.	4 mi. 270	N.D.	N.D.	N.D.
C O N D I T I O N S	(State – Beauf. Sea (Direction	0 —	1 045	1 070	1 070	0 —	0 —	0 —
	(Ht. in ft. Clouds (overcast)	2,000 98	3,000 90	— 0	— 0	Fog 100	Haze 100	— 0
	(Bearing(R) Moon (Angle) (Illum.)	— — —	— — —	— — —	— — —	— — —	— — —	— — —

Type S/M Camouflage on this patrol – Haze Gray 32/3SS/B

Aircraft Contact No. 15

Submarine: Date: 6-23-44; Time (zero) 1340; Position – Lat. 59-29 Long. 156-29; Speed 2 k,; Course 000; Trim – 63 ft; Min. since last SD search – Not in use.

Aircraft: Number – 1; Type – Unk.; Probable Mission – Unk; How Contacted – Periscope; Initial Range – 10 miles; Angle – 2°; Range and relative bearing when it detected S/M – N.D.

Conditions: Sea – State (Beauf) 0 – Dir. Rel. —; Clouds – Ht. in ft. —; Overcast —; Moon – Bearing —; Angle —; Illum. —.

U.S.S. *Barb* (SS220)　　　　Torpedo Attack No. 1　　　　Patrol No. 8

Time: 1316(K)　　Date: 31 May 1944　　Lat. 48-21.1 N., Long. 151-19.6 E.
Target Data – Damage Inflicted
Description: 1 AP – Similar *Kasima Maru* (in ballast) pg. 29, ONI 208-J[11]. Length 490–495 feet as computed from measurement of developed picture, position of torpedo hits and spread. P.O.W. stated that he did not know name or displacement but that ship was an Army transport.
Ship Sunk: 1 AP – Similar *Kasima Maru* – Pg. 29, ONI 208-J.
Damage Determined by: Three hits observed. Sinking observed by all conning tower fire control party. Pictures of sinking taken. Ship sank in about three minutes.
Target Draft: 15'　　Course: 190T　　Speed: 9 ¾　　Range: 1,400 yards (At firing)
Own Ship Data
Speed: 2.2　　Course: 088 T (A)　　Depth: 63'　　Angle: 0 (At firing)
Fire Control and Torpedo Data
Type Attack: Submerged

Tubes Fired	No. 6	No. 5	No. 4
Track Angle	80½ S	87½ S	94½ S
Gyro Angle	2½ R	7½ R	12½ R
Depth Set	6'	6'	6'
Power	High	High	High
Hit or Miss	Hit	Hit	Hit
Erratic	No	No	No
Mark Torpedo	14-3A	14-3A	14-3A
Serial No.	40759	25540	26576
Mark Exploder	6-4	6-4	6-4
Serial No.	8682	7839	7809
Actual Set	Contact	Contact	Contact
Actuation Actual	Contact	Contact	Contact
Mark Warhead	16-1	16-1	16-1
Serial No.	3476	3823	11740
Explosive	TPX	TPX	TPX
Firing Interval	0 Sec.	8 Sec.	8 Sec.
Type Spread	------------ Divergent ----------------		
Sea Conditions	2	2	2
Overhaul Activity	Submarine Base, Midway		

Remarks: Approximately 100 survivors seen in two Army type A landing craft after sinking of ship. Upon surfacing, survivors opened fire with light machine guns. No damage. Wreckage included extremely large DF loop. Spread computed for 30 yards between torpedoes along the target.

---

[11]　*ONI 208-J: Japanese Merchant Ships, Recognition Manual.*

U.S.S. *Barb* (SS220) Torpedo Attack No. 2 Patrol No. 8

Time: 1743(K)   Date: 31 May 1944   Lat. 47-52 N., Long. 151-02.0 E.

Target Data – Damage Inflicted

Description: 1 AP – *Koutou Maru* (not in ONI 208-J) – Length 330' as computed from measurement of developed picture, position of torpedo hits and spread. Average displacement for ships of this length 4,000 tons, as taken from ONI 208-J. P.O.W. taken from this ship stated he did not know the displacement, but ship was a naval transport. Length 130 meters.

Ship Sunk: 1 AP – *Koutou Maru*.

Damage Determined by: Three hits observed. Target observed to sink by all conning tower fire control party. Pictures of sinking taken. Ship sank in about 1 minute. P.O.W. taken.

Target Draft: 15'   Course: 250T   Speed: 11   Range: 1,685 yards (At firing)

Own Ship Data

Speed: 3   Course: 342T   Depth: 63'   Angle: 0 (At firing)

Fire Control and Torpedo Data

Type Attack: Submerged.

Tubes Fired	No. 7	No. 8	No. 9
Track Angle	91 S	96½ S	100 S
Gyro Angle	½ R	4 R	9½ R
Depth Set	6'	6'	6'
Power	High	High	High
Hit or Miss	Hit	Hit	Hit
Erratic	No	No	No
Mark Torpedo	14-3A	14-3A	14-3A
Serial No.	40799	26552	26242
Mark Exploder	6-4	6-4	6-4
Serial No.	2057	701	8603
Actuation Set	Contact	Contact	Contact
Actuation Actual	Contact	Contact	Contact
Mark Warhead	16-1	16-1	16-1
Serial No.	11575	3262	12718
Explosive	TPX	TPX	TPX
Firing Interval	0 Sec.	8 Sec.	7 Sec.
Type Spread	------------ Divergent ----------------		
Sea Condition	2	2	2
Overhaul Activity	Submarine Base, Midway		

Remarks: Visibility 1,500 – 10,000 yards depending on fog banks. Final bearings by periscope when target came out of fog at 1,700 yards. Check range by single ping. Spread computed for 30 yards between torpedoes along target.

U.S.S. *Barb* (SS220)   Torpedo Attack No. 3   Patrol No. 8

Time: 0157(K)   Date: 2 June 1944   Lat. 45-22.4 N., Long. 144-29.9 E.

Target Data – Damage Inflicted

Description: 1 *Chidori* Class Torpedo Boat.
Ship(s) Damaged or Probably Sunk: None.
Target Draft: 6'   Course: 265 T   Speed: 16   Range: 3,190 yards (At firing)

Own Ship Data

Speed: 8   Course: 205–208 T   Depth: Surface   Angle: 0 (At firing)

Fire Control and Torpedo Data

Type Attack: Night Radar attack with final bearings by TBT.

Tubes Fired	No. 6	No. 5	No. 4
Track Angle	118 S	121 S	124 S
Gyro Angle	1 L	0	0
Depth Set	6'	6'	6'
Power	High	High	High
Hit or Miss	Miss	Miss	Miss
Erratic	No	No	No
Mark Torpedo	14-3A	14-3A	14-3A
Serial No	40777	40170	25794
Mark Exploder	6-4	6-4	6-4
Serial No.	17816	213	8685
Actuation Set	Contact	Contact	Contact
Actuation Actual	None	None	None
Mark Warhead	16-1	16-1	16-1
Serial No	12065	11311	12753
Explosive	TPX	TPX	TPX
Firing Interval	0 Sec.	8 Sec.	8 Sec.
Type Spread	-------------- Divergent --------------		
Sea Conditions	Calm	Calm	Calm
Overhaul Activity	Submarine Base, Midway		

Remarks: All torpedoes believed to have passed under target. Spread computed for 50 yards between torpedoes along target.

U.S.S. *Barb* (SS220) Torpedo Attack No. 4 Patrol No. 8

Time: 2334(K)   Date: 11 June 1944   Lat. 46-58.0 N., Long. 143-50.0 E.

Target Data – Damage Inflicted

Description: 1 Medium AK – (Unidentified) – Estimate 5,800 T. Based on estimated stack height and accurate measurement of length (410'). Tonnage average from tables.

Ship Sunk: None

Ship(s) Damaged: 1 Ak – 5,800 ton.

Damage Determined by: One hit observed aft.

Target Draft: 20'   Course: 160 T   Speed: 9 ¾   Range: 1,600 yards (At firing)

Own Ship Data

Speed: 4.4   Course: 070 T   Depth: Surface   Angle: 0 (At firing)

Fire Control and Torpedo Data

Type Attack: Night radar surface approach and attack. Final bearings by TBT.

	No. 1	No. 2	No. 3
Tubes Fired			
Track Angle	87 S	90 S	91½ S
Gyro Angle	4 L	1 L	1½ R
Depth Set	6'	6'	6'
Power	High	High	High
Hit or Miss	Miss	Miss	Hit
Erratic	No	No	No
Mark Torpedo	14-3A	14-3A	14-3A
Serial No.	26788	20310	26551
Mark Exploder	6-4	6-4	6-4
Serial No.	8611	4507	8623
Actuation Set	Contact	Contact	Contact
Actuation Actual	None	None	Contact
Mark Warhead	16-1	16-1	16-1
Serial No.	11449	3476	11897
Explosive	TPX	TPX	TPX
Firing Interval	0 Sec.	8 Sec.	8 Sec.
Type Spread	-------------- Divergent ---------------		
Sea Conditions	Calm	Calm	Calm
Overhaul Activity	Submarine Base, Midway		

Remarks: Spread computed for 50 yards between torpedoes along target.

U.S.S. *Barb* (SS220) 　　　Torpedo Attack No. 5　　　Patrol No. 8

Time: 2335(K)　　Date: 11 June 1944　　Lat. 46-58.0 N., Long. 143-50.0 E.

Target Data – Damage Inflicted

Description: 1 Large AK – (Unidentified) – Estimate 9,800 T. Based on estimated average stack height and accurate measurement of length (481'). Tonnage average from tables.

Ship Sunk: 1 AK – 9,800 T.

Damage Determined by: 2 hits observed. Sinking observed by CO, OOD, lookouts and quartermaster. Ship sank slowly by the stern.

Target Draft: 20'　　Course: 160 T　　Speed: 9 ¾　　Range: 1,900 yards (At firing)

Own Ship Data

Speed: 6　　Course: 058–059 T　　Depth: Surface　　Angle: 0 (At firing)

Fire Control and Torpedo Data

Type Attack: Night radar surface approach and attack. Final bearings by TBT.

Tubes Fired	No. 4	No. 5	No. 6
Track Angle	77 S	81½ S	84½ S
Gyro Angle	3 L	1½ R	4½ R
Depth Set	6'	6'	6'
Power	High	High	High
Hit or Miss	Miss	Hit	Hit
Erratic	No	No	No
Mark Torpedo	14-3A	14-3A	14-3A
Serial No.	24921	25429	40504
Mark Exploder	6-4	6-4	6-4
Serial No.	11655	8683	12904
Actuation Set	Contact	Contact	Contact
Actuation Actual	None	Contact	Contact
Mark Warhead	16-1	16-1	16-1
Serial No.	12352	11652	2894
Explosive	TPX	TPX	TPX
Firing Interval	0 Sec.	8 Sec.	8 Sec.
Type Spread	-------------- Divergent --------------		
Sea Conditions	Calm	Calm	Calm
Overhaul Activity	Submarine Base, Midway		

Remarks: Target increased speed as we fired. Spread computed for 50 yards between torpedoes along target. Continuation of torpedo attack No. 4.

U.S.S. *Barb* (SS220)   Torpedo Attack No. 6   Patrol No. 8

Time: 2349(K)   Date: 11 June 1944   Lat. 46-58.8 N., Long. 143-50.0 E.

Target Data – Damage Inflicted

Description: Same AK damaged in attack #4. Now practically dead in water.
Ship(s) Sunk: 1 AK – 5,800 T.
Damage Determined by: 3 hits observed. Sinking observed by CO, OOD, lookouts and quartermaster.
Target Draft: 20'   Course: 090 T   Speed: ½   Range: 1,900 yards (At firing)

Own Ship Data

Speed: 1½   Course: 179–176 T   Depth: Surface   Angle: 0 (At firing)

Fire Control and Torpedo Data

Type Attack: Night surface radar. Final bearings by TBT.

Tubes Fired	No. 7	No. 8	No. 9
Track Angle	85 S	88½ S	85 ¾ S
Gyro Angle	4 L	¾ R	2 ¾ R
Depth Set	6'	6'	6'
Power	High	High	High
Hit or Miss	Hit	Hit	Hit
Erratic	No	No	No
Mark Torpedo	14-3A	14-3A	14-3A
Serial No.	40640	40387	40516
Mark Exploder	6-4	6-4	6-4
Serial No.	6077	7842	8592
Actuation Set	Contact	Contact	Contact
Actuation Actual	Contact	Contact	Contact
Mark Warhead	16-1	16-1	16-1
Serial No.	11352	10608	12653
Explosive	TPX	TPX	TPX
Firing Interval	0 Sec.	8 Sec.	8 Sec.
Type Spread	-------------- Divergent --------------		
Sea Conditions	Calm	Calm	Calm
Overhaul Activity	Submarine Base, Midway		

Remarks: Several tremendous explosions occurred after torpedoes hit and the ship vanished below the surface. Evidently the magazines blew up. Spread computed for 50 yards between torpedoes along target.

U.S.S. *Barb* (SS220)   Torpedo Attack No. 7   Patrol No. 8

Time: 2231(K)   Date: 13 June 1944   Lat. 51-47.5 N., Long. 151-20.0 E.

Target Data – Damage Inflicted

Description: 1 AP – Similar *Husimi Maru* Class – Page 51, ONI 208-J. Length by binoculars formula 517' (minimum).

Ship(s) Sunk: 1 AP – Simlar *Husimi Maru*[12] Class.

Damage Determined by: 2 hits observed, one ½ way between stern and funnel and 1 in stern. Stern observed to break off and sink by all topside party. Target began settling by the stern, dead in the water. Lay off at 8,000 yards and target pip gradually became smaller and finally disappeared from radar 1 hour 45 after torpedoes hit. Passed within 1,000 yards of sinking and no target visible. Escort left area alone.

Target Draft: 29'   Course: 280 T   Speed: 14   Range: 1,770 yards (At firing)

Own Ship Data

Speed: 6.5   Course: 229–221½ T   Depth: Surface   Angle: 0 (At firing)

Fire Control and Torpedo Data

Type Attack: Night radar surface approach and attack. Final bearings by TBT.

	No. 9	No. 10
Tubes Fired		
Track Angle	53½ P	57¾ R
Gyro Angle	6½ R	¾ R
Depth Set	6'	6'
Power	High	High
Hit or Miss	Hit	Hit
Erratic	No	No
Mark Torpedo	14-3A	14-3A
Serial No.	40671	26226
Mark Exploder	6-4	6-4
Serial No.	40671	12340
Actuation Set	Contact	Contact
Actuation Actual	Contact	Contact
Mark Warhead	16-1	16-1
Serial No.	13090	12730
Explosive	TPX	TPX
Firing Interval	0 Sec.	8 Sec.
Type Spread	-----Divergent------	
Sea Conditions	2	2
Overhaul Activity	Submarine Base, Midway	

Remarks: Spread computed for 50 yards between torpedoes along target.

---

[12] Later determined to be the *Takashima Maru*, 5,633 tons, a passenger-cargo icebreaker.

U.S.S. *Barb* (SS220) Gun Attack No. 1 Patrol No. 8

Time: 1202(K)   Date: 11 June 1944   Lat. 48-13.0 N., Long. 144-21.1 E.
Target Data – Damage Inflicted
1 Fishing Trawler – Estimate 50 T. – Sunk
Damage Determined by: Target observed to settle slowly and finally sink. Took pictures.
Details of Action
Sighted trawler stopped in ice field. Closed to edge of ice field, range about 5,500 yards from trawler, and opened fire with 4"50 cal. gun. Trawler slowly got underway and started weaving in and out of ice floes, trying to keep a good sized berg between us. This proved to be a fatal move. 25 yard spots were crossing the target, but we did not observe any direct hits. Flying pieces of ice and shrapnel must have pierced his hull because he started settling slowly. Ceased firing when all that was visible was his mast at a rakish angle and his decks awash. Target disappeared from view as we sighted and headed to attack second trawler.

Ammunition Expended: 4"50 Cal. H.C.P.D. – 25 rounds.
                                4"50 Cal. Common – 6 rounds.

U.S.S. *Barb* (SS220) Gun Attack No. 2 Patrol No. 8

Time: 1259(K)   Date: 11 June 1944   Lat. 48-11.1 N., Long. 144-20.6 E.
Target Data – Damage Inflicted
1 Fishing Trawler – Estimated 50 T. – Sunk.
Damage Determined by: Target observed to sink. Took pictures.
Details of Action
Sighted trawler approaching ice field, range approximately 6,000 yards. Closed to about 2,500 yards and gave him a burst of 20 MM to see if he had anything with which to return fire. His only answer was to increase speed in the direction of the ice field. Closed to 500 yards and opened fire with 4 20 MMs and 2 .50 Cals. Completely sprayed him with automatic fire with no apparent effect. Opened fire with 4"50 Cal., range 850 yards, and systematically cut him apart. A large Jap flag painted on pilot house provided a nice point of aim until the third round carried away forward portion of pilot house. Remainder of ammunition put aft of pilot house and through hull. Target sank after third waterline hit.

Ammunition Expended: 4"50 Cal. H.C.P.D. – 16 rounds
                                20 MM 620 rounds.
                                .50 Cal. 700 rounds

Performance of guns was excellent, but ammunition performance left much to be desired. Estimate 300 rounds of 20 mm and .50 Cal. hit target but no fires were started. We could see 20 mm H.E., H.E.I.[13], and .50 Cal. incendiary explode and the spots which were hit glow for a few seconds, but no indication of fires. Numerous 4"50 Cal. H.C.P.D. rounds, set on "super-quick" passed through hull and superstructure and either did not explode at all, or exploded on far side after passing through, giving off clouds of yellow smoke.

Remarks: What do the aviators have that we lack? They continually report strafing attacks setting the building afire. We slap 1,320 rounds of incendiary into a diesel powered wooden tinder box at 500 yards without striking a light.

(H) Six foot depth setting was used for the following reasons:

1. May be kept set at all times, thus eliminating thought and communication on this subject during approach unless CO desires a different setting.

2. Definitely vents the target.

3. Causes consternation in a damage control party and prevents them shoring bulkhead below.

4. No change in setting required for escort, or surprise firing.

Unfortunately Captain Hensel's[14] remarks on the report of *Grouper* war patrol No. 8 concerning running of Mk. 18 torpedoes set at 5 feet were not read until after attack No. 5 on a *Chidori*. Upon identification of target, I was hesitant at using a depth setting less than 6 feet because of lack of knowledge of running characteristics. Had I read Captain Hensel's remarks prior to that time I would have fired the Mk. 14s set at 5 feet with, I believe, positive results. The range (3,190 yards) was excessive, but the setup was cold.

(I) MINES

P.O.W. information in a separate report.

(J) ANTI-SUBMARINE MEASURES AND EVASION TACTICS

Escort in attack #7 used radar jamming immediately after torpedoes struck target. This consisted of railings and had no effect on use of PPI or A-scope.

Depth charging and bombing were random. Evasions were doctrine. Enemy gunfire encountered on three occasions was disturbing, but lacked accuracy and did no damage. Being entangled in fishing nets and towing two red flags astern, while submerged off Paramushiru was humorous, later.

Nothing further to add to previous reports.

---

[13] H.E. and H.E.I.: High Explosive and High Explosive Incendiary.
[14] Captain Karl G. Hensel was the commander of Submarine Squadron 30.

(K) MAJOR DEFECTS

1. Serious grinding and squealing of starboard propeller shaft at speeds greater than 80 RPM. Re-wooding probably required. Port shaft is also noisy but to a lesser degree. These shaft noises could be heard through the hull without the aid of listening devices.

2. No. 1 and 2 I.C. Motor Generator Power Supply switches for starting panel burned out due to overload; jumpers were installed to maintain I.C. power. These sets operate under continuous overload when the radar is in operation. It is recommended that a new radar motor generator of sufficient capacity to supply the radar load be installed. Also, replacement of the above switches with fuses as an additional overload precaution is recommended.

3. Serious leakage of the hull regulator valves in the 600# MBT Blow system. These leaks caused flooding of the piping and manifold continuously.

4. Both periscopes fogged at sea. Gauging indicated nitrogen charge lost. Charged at sea. Leakage continues.

5. Loud rumbling noise occurs when starboard sound gear is trained at any but very slow speed.

(L) RADIO

Reception:

In spite of greatly intensified Japanese jamming after the invasion of the Mariannas, the Haiku Schedule got through and no serials were missed. 16.68 KCS was the best frequency and the only one on which the schedule could be heard during the hour 1900 G.C.T. while in the area. Reception of 14390 KCS and 17370 KCS was poor, and the intermediate frequencies were only fair.

Jamming was excessive at all times on the special aircraft frequency. Transmissions were weak, distorted, and very few words could be understood. It may have been that the aviators observed radio silence while in the target area, and the transmissions heard came from the Aleutians.

Transmissions:

The four transmissions made in the area were sent to NPM on 8470 KCS at approximately 1200 G.C.T. All call ups were answered immediately, and all transmissions were made quickly with no repeats. Both NPM's signal and our own were strength five in all instances. Transmissions were timed so that when DF'd, enemy traffic would be rerouted through the area to which we were shifting.

Occasional listening watches were kept on the various harmonics of 2435 KCS and stations in the Marshall Islands, Australia, New Zealand, Midway, and on both the East and West Coasts of the United States were heard—all with good signal strength.

Several attempts were made to raise *Herring*[15] on 450 KCS prior to rendezvous. These failed. At rendezvous both ships tested 450 KCS at 100 yards with better than 2 amp output. No reception either way. A light beat was noted, which was actually thought to be the key clicks being heard through the hull.

Casualties:

The antenna trunk flooded during a deep dive enroute station. Most of the leakage was stopped by tightening the insulators and inspection plates. Though it was not possible to rinse the insulators and antenna leads on the inside of the trunk with fresh water, the trunk was dried by placing a 200 watt light bulb in the lower end. This raised the reading from a zero ground to 150,000 ohms, and the antenna carried the full output of the transmitter on all transmissions.

(M) RADAR

Being DF conscious, SD equipment was used only prior to surfacing and in a few particular instances when it was keyed for 3 seconds at half hour intervals for information. During the third half hourly keying off Matsuwa interference was encountered and the SD was secured.

The SJ performed excellently. In this area land was normally picked up at 80,000 yards and ice at a maximum of 3,500 yards. The only major shut down was caused by a short to ground in the AC input selector switch (Radar M-G set or idle I.C. M-G set). The precision sweep was of no use to us for a while until C 28.1 and R 37 in the Range Indicator Unit were replaced. All other failures resolved themselves into routine maintenance repairs and replacements.

The Radar M-G set became a problem of low voltage early in the patrol. AC was supplied from the I.C. board thereafter. This unit will have to be replaced by one of the larger units.

In addition to the bearing repeater used by TDC and plot, a range Selsyn[16] transmitter is to be installed in the space provided in the Range Unit with range repeaters at both TDC and Plot.

SJ jamming from an escort was enountered night of June 13. Even at close range the pips were very weak, but appeared to be railings.

---

[15] This rendezvous was the last American contact with U.S.S. *Herring* (SS-233), which was sunk by a Japanese shore battery on 1 June 1944, two kilometers south of Point Tagan on Matsuwa Island. This followed an attack during which *Herring* was credited with sinking *Hiburi Maru* and *Iwaki Maru* at anchor in Matsuwa.

16 Selsyn: A type of three pole, single phase AC motor that can be connected to an identical unit located in another part of the ship. When power is applied, the motor does not rotate, but manually turning one Selsyn will cause any units connected to it to rotate an identical distance in the same direction. Most commonly used for transmitting angular or positional information, as with the Selsyn mounted in the Target Bearing Transmitter, which is connected to an indicator dial in the conning tower, or remotely sets the target bearing in later model TDCs.

Inter ship reception by means of coding the radar transmission worked very successfully. The best method of accomplishing this is by opening and closing the wave guide valve. Other methods upset the pulse repetition frequency, making recognition of code groups difficult.

(N) SOUND GEAR AND SOUND CONDITIONS

Sound conditions varied. The equipment was manned practically all hours of the day while cruising below ten knots. No contacts were made before radar contacts.

Very little time was spent submerged, but during this time a listening watch was maintained. Conditions were normal except as indicated below.

Contacts:

3-31-44 Sound good at 2,500 yards using the QB head. A single ping range at 1,600 yards checked against the TDC generated range within 10 yards. The SBT card showed an isotherm to 180'.

5-3-44 Contacted small fishing craft with both QB and JP at about 3,200 yards. Background noise was high in some parts of this area and low in others, a very noticeable change (44-41 N., 151-44 E.). SBT card showed a slight negative gradient (–2°/60 ft.) to 80 feet, then sharply negative.

6-8-44 JP contact at 18,000 yards. Very broad bearing covering forty degrees on bearing scale. Good turn count at 90 RPM. JK picked up same contact at 4,800 yards. With an increase in target speed and a decrease in range, there was a pronounced decrease in signal strength.

As this was a sudden change, operator attributed this to the target's power plant passing out of critical region of vibration. No ping range was obtainable. SBT card showed negative gradient (–2°/40 feet).

While the fathometer was in operation during our attack with the 4" gun, a receiver tube was shorted, probably by a shock.

During inoperation of the fathometer, satisfactory soundings were obtained with the QC equipment.

(O) DENSITY LAYERS

Negative gradients were encountered throughout the entire patrol. In the area, the sea condition was seldom greater than force 2. SBT records are tabulated below, the cards are being forwarded to the Hydrographic Office.

Depths noted are keel depths. Thermal element located at 25' above keel.

Time GCT Date	Lat. Long.	Surf. Temp.	Greatest Depth	Remarks
2030 (L) 23 May	35-17 N. 173-37 E.	55	140	Isothermal to 120', −2° to 140'.
2100 (K) 24 May	37-03 N. 164-16 E.	56	315	Isothermal to 120', −4° to 315'.
0022 (K) 25 May	37-26 N. 168-49 E.	52	300	−1° to 120', −2° to 170', −3° to 300'.
2100 (K) 25 May	39-46 N. 151-44 E.	48	310	Isothermal to 140', −2° to 170', −1 to 310'.
0215 (K) 28 May	44-41 N. 151-45 E.	38	65	−4° to 65'.
0700 (K) 31 May	47-53 N. 151-45 E.	3	300	Isothermal to 180', −2 to 240', isothermal to 300'.
2300 (K) 31 May	46-21 N. 148-01 E.	38	70	Isothermal to 60', −10 to 70'.
1703 (K) 1 June	43-47 N. 144-17 E.	40	300	−6° in stops to 100', −3° to 160', isothermal to 300'.
1200 (K) 2 June	46-12 N. 144-16 E.	40	130	−6° to 60', −4° to 130'.
2323 (K) 2 June	44-28 N. 144-06 E.	44	120	−2 to 60', isothermal to 80', −8° to 120'.
0010 (K) 3 June	44-23 N. 144-08 E.	43	110	−7° to 50', isothermal to 90', −4° to 100', +6 at 100', −2° coming up to 80', then relative even gradient back up to surface.
0915 (K) 7 June	48-53 N. 145-10 E.	42	65	−4° to 65'.
0210 (K) 3 June	44-12 N. 144-22 E.	43	85	−3° to 60', at 60' temp ranged from 35° to 51°.
0822 (K) 8 June	49-08 N. 145-35 E.	38	65	−2° to 65'.
0545 (K) 10 June	46-50 N. 141-54 E.	42	90	−1° to 60', −8 to 90'.
0600 (K) 11 June	47-45 N. 144-12 E.	44	60	−3° to 60', at 60' temp ranges from 35° to 41°.

0910 (K) 12 June	49-46 N. 148-02 E.	41	300	Isothermal to 60', −8 248 to 200', Isothermal to 300'.
2310 (K) 14 June	53-05 N. 155-55 E.	45	60	−7° to 69'.
0404 (K) 15 June	52-17 N. 156-06 E.	46	100	−9° to 75', isothermal to 100'.
2310 (K) 17 June	50-57 N. 156-04 E.	43	170	−8 248 to 170'.
1550 (K) 22 June	50-05 N. 156-18 E.	43	210	Isothermal to 60', temp ranged from 38°−44° at 60', temp drop fr. 40° at 60' to 34° at 210'.
2110 (K) 24 June	51-31 N. 156-26 E.	30	85	−11° to 85'.
2245 (K) 27 June	46-44 N. 144-02 E.	52	70	−1° to 60', −12° to 70'.

(P) HEALTH, FOOD AND HABITABILITY

Recreation period at Midway did much to put the ship's company in top physical shape, which was reflected at sea in general alertness and continued cheerfulness in spite of the discomfort of cold weather. W.E. Donnelly, PhM1c, deserves much credit for his prompt and effective treatment of one case of acute appendicitis, which was reduced by sulfadiazone with only 7 man days lost. Minor treatments were boils − 4, colds − 10, constipation − 15, conjunctivitis − 1, headaches − 15, indigestion − 1, ringworm − 1, sinusitis − 1, toothache − 1, dermatitis − 8, earaches − 2, gingivitis − 1.

Food was very good and well prepared. The following inferior items require correction, canned carrots, bologna, salami. More ice cream mix and vitamin capsules should be carried at advance bases for submarines.

Habitability was good. Injection temperature averaged 36°. We were submerged only one day. This dive was 19.3 hours. CO reached 3%, but air was not oppressive for smoking lamp was lighted for only 20 minutes during entire day.

(Q) PERSONNEL

A vigorous training program for officers and men was maintained during the patrol, which has enabled us to fleet up qualified reliefs while still at sea for those transferred upon arrival. Thus the maximum benefit will be derived from the training period following our refit, eliminating the confusion of adjustment which often marks the first day of post-overhaul operations.

The school of the boat qualified 14 men in submarines while each officer became qualified in some department other than his own.

The eager and earnest attitude of all new men towards learning their jobs and the ship was exceptional, while the cooperation of older hands, particularly the petty officer instructors, did much to maintain this spirit.

(a) Number of men on board during patrol   74
(b) Number of men qualified at start of patrol   55
(c) Number of men qualified at end of patrol   65
(d) Number of unqualified men making their first patrol   10
(e) Number of men advanced in rating during patrol   22

Morale is excellent. Esprit de corps is in keeping with the finest traditions of the submarine service.

(R) MILES STEAMED – FUEL USED

Midway to Area	1,842 miles.	20,825 gals.
In Area	8,701 miles.	68,260 gals.
Area to Midway	1,976 miles.	18,955 gals.
Midway to Pearl Harbor	1,400 miles.	18,500 gals.

(S) DURATION

Days enroute to area	6
Days in area	33
Days enroute to Midway	6
Days Midway to Pearl	5
Days submerged	1

(T) FACTORS OF ENDURANCE REMAINING

Torpedoes	Fuel Midway	Provisions	Personnel
4	6,250	30	30

Limiting factor this patrol – Operation Order.

(U) REMARKS

1. Under present system of identification of Russian ships, the situation is a real danger. Twice during low visibility, the first at night, the second in daylight, we attained firing position on Russians at 1,400 yards, final bearings were being

held in, and it was only a matter of seconds before we had to start shooting, when CO discovered they were Russians. The daytime target had been visible through the periscope from 8,000 yards in. Our attack periscope was slightly fogged, so other scope was being used. If attack scope had been used ship would have been sunk. The day Russian had made several course changes and was not on a listed Russian route. The night Russian made one 20° course change and one speed change of 3.5 knots, and was near a Russian route. Note also we used plenty of oil and time on every end around. In heavy fog after tracking for 9 hours we closed one Russian at night to 310 yards before identification, another to 525 and another to 1,300 yards. I believe this is exceedingly dangerous, but required by the situation. We have seen changes of visibility from 500 to 15,000 yards in less than a minute. Fortunately these did not occur while we were in such a tight spot. It is suggested that Russians be notified to burn their identification lights during day as well as night, that submarines in this area be notified of prospective Russian ship movements, that Russians stick to their tracks with as few course and speed changes as possible, and if they have sound gear to continuously send out the letters of their identification flags in certain areas of the Okhotsk Sea. As food for thought, many times when we were patrolling our assigned station for Jap ships we ended up in a Russian chase. One of these strongly resembled a Jap tanker, which we knew was being used on the Paramushiru run. Our P.O.W. says the Japs have never used Russian identification, but that they know our subs use Vladivostok[17]. Such tempers my suspicions.

    2. P.O.W., an armed guard petty officer of the regular Navy (on lookout watch) was taken from the second sinking. With due consideration of contents of U.S. Pacific Fleet Letter SL-44, I interrogated him. My objects in taking him was to get information on remainder of convoy and further information on this area.

    Intelligence Officers, probably to the contrary, it is my belief that more information can be obtained from a lone prisoner hauled out of a sure death in icy waters within a short time thereafter, while he is grateful to his rescuers for kind treatment, and a bit discouraged with his country, than if he were held incommunicado for weeks. Reason for this is, that after six daily periods of friendly interrogation he began to realize the traitorous things he had said and made me promise the information he had given would not get back to the Japanese or other prisoners, because after the war when he returned to Japan they would lop his head off. Two days later he decided he could never go back, so would remain in the U.S.

---

17   They did not. Russia followed neutrality rules in their Pacific regions, which included interning any belligerent ships and crews that entered their ports. This policy was primarily applied to American aviators who made emergency landings in Russians territory. The fliers were returned to U.S. jurisdiction via a clandestine route—officially they "escaped"—but the Russians kept the planes. The Russian Tu-4 bomber, an exact copy of the American B-29, was one result of this policy.

A Japanese dictionary would have been a tremendous help to us. The prisoner knew no English. Fortunately I had a short list of Japanese words torn from a Bureau of Personnel Bulletin in 1942. This was inadequate, but with it as a basis, supplemented by sign language and drawings, we made out fairly well.

As he gradually picked up some English he gave us a new version of his sinking—"Sighted sub, glub, glub."

3. Many submarines already have been forced to accept long night firing ranges to maintain the offensive. Improved maneuverability with increased ability to avoid escorts would improve this situation considerably. Radar equipped escorts will not only place a greater premium on our maneuverability, but will soon require the employment of offensive counter attack while evading. The use of a double rudder and a modified "mousetrap" projectile is suggested to accomplish these ends.

After observing a destroyer double rudder model at the Navy Model Basin (Carter Rock) the suggested use of double rudders on submarines was brought to the attention of the Submarine Design Section of the Bureau early in 1943. The idea was to be investigated, and practical objections were raised at the time, beyond the undesirability of departing from the standard design. Since then no discussion of projected plans in this direction has been heard in minor submarine circles.

A possible means of discouraging escorts from chasing down the torpedo track or the submarine wake, at night, is a floating mousetrap, to be thrown from a "W" gun (similar to a "Y" gun but a triple thrower) installed on the submarine stern and fitted with a standard flash eliminator. This gun would be loaded prior to night surface attack with three bundles of banded mousetraps. These projectiles must be made so that they will float, arming ½ minute after firing, have contact activation, and sink at a definite time (roughly 2 hours) after entering the water. In flight the mousetrap would be released in the same manner as the present bundles to give the desired pattern. An escort running into one of these, or wrapping a string of them alongside, would be sufficiently damaged to give up pursuit if not eliminated. Even a few submarines equipped with such gear might change Jap tactics from an offensive pursuit to a passive defense.

4. Further investigation should be made in use of SJ radar for identification and for transmission of messages. Our prearranged plan of private identification signals with the *Herring* worked perfectly at an unexpected rendezvous. Signals were received clearly by both ships. Signalling with the wave guide flapper proved best.

Enroute Midway to Pearl tests were conducted with *Gar* for transmission and reception of messages over SJ, both visually, and by listening over phone circuits rigged by the respective radar officers. While returning through Midway a lab demonstration of a keying and listening system, developed by a radar technician there, was witnessed. Apparently it is practicable and should prove an immediate must for all submarines.

5.   After spending the last half of our patrol rehashing, analyzing and double checking on attack data and fire control system in a determined effort to find the cause of our six torpedo misses, the following was uncovered. All misses were on night attack firing forward tubes on a starboard track. Of these, 3 misses in attack No. 3 were believed to have passed under. 2 misses in attack No. 4 were seen to pass aft, and 1 miss in attack No. 5 was seen to pass aft. When forward TBT was checked degree by degree we found a sudden transmission lag of 1½° between relative bearing 355° and 349°. Assuming our data to be correct this definitely accounts for 2 misses in attack No. 3, 1 miss in attack No. 4, and 1 miss in attack No. 5. Total loss to the war effort 4 torpedoes thrown away, 1 *Chidori* not sunk, 3 additional torpedoes expended to sink a damaged ship. The above has been added to this report to impress the necessity of a more thorough TBT check than the customary check on 8–10 miscellaneous bearings.

SUBMARINE DIVISION FORTY-FOUR

FB5-44/A16-3
Serial: (0-62)

Care of Fleet Post Office
San Francisco, California
11 July 1944

C-O-N-F-I-D-E-N-T-I-A-L

First Endorsement to
U.S.S. *Barb* Eighth
War Patrol Report.

From: The Commander Submarine Division Forty-Four.
To: The Commander-in-Chief, U.S. Fleet.
Via: The Commander Submarine Squadron Four.
                The Commander Submarine Force, Pacific Fleet.
                The Commander-in-Chief, Pacific Fleet.

Subject: U.S.S. *Barb* Eighth War Patrol – comments on.

    1. The eighth war patrol of the *Barb* and the first for the present commanding officer was conducted along the Kurile Island chain, the north coast of Hokkaido and in the Sea of Okhotsk from 21 May to 9 July.

    2. Of the twenty-seven ship contacts, thirteen were made on Russian ships; in several instances, it was extremely difficult to identify these ships because of foggy weather, dimmed navigational lights, failure of the ships to follow prescribed convoy routings.

    Numerous fishing boats were encountered.

    Fifteen aircraft were contacted. Because the SD was keyed only at half hourly intervals, but one plane was contacted by this method, while ten were picked up by lookouts or through the periscope. Two others were heard passing close to the ship during the period of dense fog. It is noted that one plane, identified through the periscope as Russian, made a pass at the exposed periscope, the *Barb* going promptly to one hundred feet.

    3. Torpedo attacks.

        (a) Attack number one was made on a ship similar to *Kasima Maru*. Three bow torpdoes were fired from a range of 1,400 yards and all hit. First contact was by radar; during the approach the fog lifted and remainder of approach was by periscope data. One air bomb was dropped during the approach. This ship, an Army transport in ballast, was carrying at least two Army type A landing craft, from which survivors fired machine guns at *Barb*. Ship was seen to sink.

(b) Attack number two was made on the *Koutou Maru*, a Navy transport, after an end-around; this ship had been in company with *Kasima Maru* and in a convoy which had been dispersed by attacks made by *Herring*. Three stern tube torpedoes were fired on 90° starboard tracks at range of 1,685 yards; all torpedoes hit and target sank. A prisoner of war was recovered, who later advised the commanding officer of probable mine fields and suggested that shore bombardment was inadvisable because of proximity of many air fields.

(c) Attack number three was an unsuccessful night radar attack on a *Chidori* class torpedo boat. Three bow torpedoes, set at six feet, were fired on 120° starboard track at range of 3,190 yards. This range was accepted because of uncertain submarine position and location of possible mine fields and patrol craft lanes. Torpedoes missed, apparently having run under target.

(d) Attack number four was made on an unidentified freighter, using radar on a black night. Of three bow tube torpedoes fired on a 90° starboard track at 1,600 yards, one torpedo hit the stern of the ship. This ship swung hard left and opened fire with amidships gun. *Barb* maneuvered to fire stern tubes and passed within 700 yards of damaged freighter. *Barb* fired three torpedoes on 90° starboard track, range 1,900 yards for about three hits and a sunk Jap ship. The excellent state of training of fire control party and the cool deliberate ship handling by the commanding officer accounted for this ship. Only a well organized and trained ship would have succeeded in this instance.

(e) Attack number five was made on a large unidentified freighter, which was following the ship attacked previously. After firing three bow tubes at first target, *Barb* swung ten degrees and fired the remaining bow torpedoes on an 80° starboard track at range of 1,900 yards. Two of these torpedoes hit and ship was seen to sink.

(f) On the last torpedo attack, a transport similar to *Husimi Maru*, escorted by torpedo boat, was attacked. Two stern torpedoes, both hits, were fired at range of 1,770 yards on a 55° port track. Transport broke up and sank.

Of twenty torpedoes fired, fourteen were hits and five ships were sunk.

4. Gun Attacks. In two gun attacks, two 50 ton fishing sampans were sunk from four inch gun fire. The comments of the commanding officer concerning poor ammunition performance are noted. The commanding officer is being directed to include the identifying data of this ammunition in a separate report.

5. Routine refit will be conducted by Submarine Base, Pearl Harbor in normal time. All items reported under material casualties will be investigated and rectified. In addition, the cause for the lag in the TBT will be determined. This equipment was made by Submarine Force personnel and was intended as a jury rig until receipt of the Mk 8 Mod 0 TBT is received as replacements. To date, only one of the new equipment has been received at Pearl, and that in a new construction submarine.

6. The commanding officer, officers and crew of the *Barb* are most heartily congratulated on the completion of a most aggressively conducted, successful patrol, which will aid materially in defeating the enemy.

                            E.R. Swinburne,
                            Acting.

SUBMARINE SQUADRON FOUR 11/jak

FC5-4/A16-3

Serial 0262

Fleet Post Office,
San Francisco, California,
14 July 1944.

C-O-N-F-I-D-E-N-T-I-A-L

Second Endorsement to:
U.S.S. *Barb* Report of
Eighth War Patrol.

From: The Commander Submarine Squadron Four.
To: The Commander-in-Chief, U.S. Fleet.
Via: (1) The Commander Submarine Force, Pacific Fleet.
           (2) The Commander-in-Chief, Pacific Fleet.

Subject: U.S.S. *Barb* Eighth War Patrol – Comments on.

1. Forwarded, concurring in the remarks of Commander Submarine Division Forty-Four.

2. It is noted with pleasure that the new Commanding Officer retained the initiative in all attacks. By so doing, he was able to attain 70% torpedo hits and in each case effect an expeditious retirement.

3. The use of the SJ wave guide flapper as a means of pulsing the outgoing signal is recommended to all submarines who are faced with recognition of radar interference on a like frequency. Considerable forethought was shown in prearranging recognition with the U.S.S. *Herring*.

4. The Commander Submarine Squadron Four concurs in the Commanding Officer's statements in paragraph 2 of section "U." It is felt that prisoners-of-War brought aboard a submarine on patrol are in an entirely different psychological status than those captured by other means. The Commanding Officer of the submarine is hardly in a position to accept or deny the validity of P.O.W. statements, but the P.O.W. probably will endeavor to save the submarine from destruction. Therefore, it is strongly recommended that all submarines be furnished a Japanese-American translating dictionary.

5. Investigation by the Submarine Base Repair Department has found that a lag in the flexible coupling of the forward TBT caused an error of one and one-half degrees in bearing throughout 360° of azimuth. This is being corrected.

6. The Commanding Officer, officers, and crew are warmly congratulated on this outstanding display of coordination, intelligent initiative, and seamanship.

C.F. Erck

SUBMARINE FORCE, PACIFIC FLEET   hch
FF12-10/A16-3(15)/(16)
                                       Care of Fleet Post Office,
Serial 01437   San Francisco, California,
                                       18 July 1944.

CONFIDENTIAL

Third Endorsement to   NOTE: THIS REPORT WILL BE
Barb Report of   DESTROYED PRIOR TO
Eighth War Patrol   ENTERING PATROL AREA

ComSubPac Patrol Report No. 472
U.S.S. *Barb* – Eighth War Patrol.

From: The Commander Submarine Force, Pacific Fleet.
To: The Commander-in-Chief, United States Fleet.
Via: The Commander-in-Chief, U.S. Pacific Fleet.

Subject: U.S.S. *Barb* (SS220) – Report of Eighth War Patrol.
           (21 May to 9 July 1944).

    1. The eighth war patrol of the *Barb* was the first for the new Commanding Officer, as such. The patrol was conducted in the Kurile Islands south of Okhotsk and the north coast of Hokkaido.
    2. This patrol was a fine example of outstanding determination, excellent initiative, aggressiveness, and splendid torpedo and gun attacks. The entire patrol was conducted under adverse conditions of fog and ice floes.
    3. Seven separate torpedo attacks were conducted, resulting in the sinking of five ships. In addition, two trawlers were sunk, one that was in an ice field and the other close aboard.
    4. The capture of the Japanese Naval rating from the ship sunk on 31 May and the subsequent examination of the prisoner aboard proved to be of help to the *Barb* during the remainder of her patrol.
    5. The Commanding Officer showed great care in identifying the many Russian ships encountered even though some of these ships were poorly marked for recognition.
    6. This patrol is designated as "Successful" for Combat Insignia Award.
    7. The Commander Submarine Force, Pacific Fleet, congratulates the Commanding Officer, officers, and crew for this extremely aggressive and successful war patrol of the *Barb*. The *Barb* is credited with having inflicted the following damage upon the enemy:

SUNK

1 – Transport (*Kasima Maru* class) –	9,900 tons	(Attack No. 1)
1 – Freighter (*Koto Maru*) –	1,100 tons	(Attack No. 2)
1 – Freighter (class unknown) –	9,800 tons	(Attack No. 5)
1 – Freighter (class unknown) –	5,800 tons	(Attack No. 6)
1 – Transport (*Husimi* class) –	10,800 tons	(Attack No. 7)
2 – Sampans –	100 tons	(Gun Attack No. 1)
Total	37,500 tons	

Distribution:
(Complete Reports)   C.A. Lockwood, Jr.
Cominch   (7)
CNO   (5)
CinCpac   (6)
Intel.Cen.Pac.Ocean Areas   (1)
Comservpac   (1)
CinClant   (1)
ComSubLant   (8)
S/M School, NL   (2)
ComSoPac   (2)
ComSoWesPac   (1)
ComSubSoWesPac   (2)
CTF 72   (2)
ComNorPac   (1)
ComSubsPac   (40)
SUBAD, MI   (2)
ComSubsPacSubOrdCom   (3)
All Squadron & Div
  Commanders, SubsPac   (2)
ComSubsTrainPac   (2)
All Submarines, SubsPac   (1)

E.L. Hynes, 2nd,
Flag Secretary.

Patrol Nine, 4 August 1944 – 3 October 1944

U.S.S. *Barb*

SS220/A16
Serial – 0013

Care of Fleet Post Office,
San Francisco, California.
3 October 1944.

CONFIDENTIAL

From:	The Commanding Officer, U.S.S. *Barb*.
To:	The Commander in Chief, United States Fleet.
Via:	(1) Commander Submarine Division 221.
	(2) Commander Submarine Squadron 22.
	(3) Commander Submarines, Pacific Fleet.
Subject:	U.S.S. *Barb*, Report of Ninth War Patrol
Enclosure:	(A) Subject Report.
	(B) Track Chart, ComSubPac only.

1. Enclosure (A) covering the ninth war patrol of this vessel conducted in the Luzon Straits Area during the period 4 August 1944 to 3 October 1944, is forwarded herewith.

E.B. Fluckey.

(A) PROLOGUE

Returned to Pearl Harbor from 8th war patrol on July 9, 1944. Completed normal refit under SubRon Four, four day training period and at readiness for sea date as August 2, 1944.

Transferred two officers. Received two new Sub School graduates.

(B) NARRATIVE

Assigned to Coordinated Attack Group consisting of *Tunny*, *Queenfish* and *Barb*. Commander E.R. Swinburne, U.S.N., ComTask Group 17.16 in Barb. ComTaskFor 17 Operation Order 265-44.

4 August
Departed Pearl in company with *Tunny* and *Queenfish*. Escorted by DE for 2 days. Exercised wolfpack tactics, communications and attack using DE as target.

5 August
Continued wolfpack exercises with DE.
1900(X) Escort Released.

6 – 8 August
Exercised group using each submarine in turn as target.

7 August
0915(Y) Arrived Midway. Topped off. Repaired bow planes. ComWolfPack held conference of Commanding Officers. Midway services were excellent.

10 August
0730(Y) Departed Midway. Formed scouting line. Interval 20 miles. Speed of advance 11 knots. Commenced training program for officers and men, daily dives and fire control party drills.
0900(Y) Exchanged calls with *Tautog*.

11 August
Omitted.

12 August
Crossed international date line.

13 August
1500(L) Encountered floating mine. Lat. 25-56.3 N., Long. 171-31 E. Opened

fire with automatic weapons. Numerous hits. A few holes, many dents. Mine did not sink.

1800(L) Rendezvoused with *Queenfish*.

14 August

Rendezvoused with *Tunny*.

16 August

1800(K) Radar rendezvous with *Tunny* and *Queenfish*. Changed speed of advance to 12 knots to take advantage of clement weather.

18 August

1905(K) (Ship Contact #1) Thirty minutes after dark radar contact at 3,500 yards, bearing 335° relative[1]. Lookouts reported object resembling submarine while OOD was turning away at flank speed. As we are in class D area notified *Tunny* and *Queenfish* to avoid. *Barb* trailed at 3,000 yards until radar interference from *Tunny* indicated she was clear. Target zigging between 80-100°T, speed 13.8 knots. No SJ interference from target. Believed to be *Puffer* with no radar on surfacing. Lat. 22-10.2 N., Long. 140-36.2 E. Night was extremely dark with heavy rain.

1953(K) Resumed base course 270°T.

2310(K) Left safety lane. c/c to 263°T.

20 August

2000(I) Had radar rendezvous with *Queenfish* and *Tunny*. Changed speed of advance to 10 knots, scouting line changed to 300-120°T. Interval 30 miles.

21 August

1214(I) (Aircraft Contact #1) Sighted plane at 10 miles. Dived.
1219(I) Surfaced.
1228(I) (Aircraft Contact #2) Sighted plane at 8 miles. Dived.
1244(I) Surfaced.
2010(I) SJ radar interference from vessel on opposite course. We are due to pass *Rasher*.

22 August

0200(I) Scouting line 270-090°T. Interval 20 miles. Base course 270°T.

---

[1] Bearings may be given as either relative or true. A true bearing is the actual compass bearing to the target, with north as 000°. A relative bearing is the bearing to the target relative to the submarine's course, and presumes that 000° is the sub's bow, regardless of the actual course. Relative bearings are normally used for reporting the position of any target or object sighted, though in most cases these were converted to true bearings in patrol reports.

23 August (All times How unless otherwise indicated).
    0523 (Aircraft Contact #3) Sighted plane at 7 miles. Dived.
    0548 Surfaced.
    1640 (Aircraft Contact #4) Sighted planes (4) at 11 miles. Did not dive.
    1643 Sighted Batan Island bearing 265°T, distant 35 miles.
    1803 Sighted smoke bomb on starboard beam.
    1804 *Queenfish* surfaced, distance 5,000 yards.
    2200 Passed between Batan and Itabayat Islands. See Radar report for interference.
    2215 (Ship Contact #2) Radar contact on two small patrol boats. Avoided. Notified *Tunny* astern of us by radar message.
    2250 Radar contact on patrol boat near Sabtang Island. Avoided. Completed passage of Luzon Straits.

August 24
    Proceeding through safety lane.
    1700 Entered Area Eleven Destroy.
    2200 Converted #4 fuel ballast tank.

August 25 (All patrol areas designated by Group Commander)
    Surface patrolling in area on Manila–Hong Kong route. Lying to after moonset to conserve fuel.

August 26
    Surface patrolling in area. Lying to after moonset. Notified *Queenfish* by radar of next area assignment.

August 27
    Surface patrolling in area on Manila–Hong Kong route. Lying to after moonset to conserve fuel.
    0819 (Aircraft Contact #5) Sighted Mavis at 7 miles. Dived.
    0827 Periscope depth. Plane still in sight slowly patrolling.
    0845 Plane eased over the horizon. Surfaced.
    1505 (Aircraft Contact #6) Sighted plane at 11 miles. Dived.
    1517 Surfaced.

August 28
    Surface patrolling in area. Lying to after moonset to conserve fuel.
    1601 (Aircraft Contact #7) Sighted plane at 7 miles. Dived.
    1614 Surfaced.

August 29
Surface patrolling in area. Lying to after moonset.
1617 (Aircraft Contact #8) Sighted plane at 10 miles. Dived.
1621 Watched plane through periscope.
1627 Surfaced.

August 30
Surface patrolling in area.
1215 Wolfpack headed for new station at 15 knots.
1330 (Aircraft Contact #9) Sighted plane at 10 miles. Dived.
1331 Distant bombs, believed to be on *Tunny*.
1335 More bombs distant. Watched plane circling over spot where *Tunny* dove. Attempted to contact her by sound to tell her to stay deep and we would inform her when plane departed. No luck.
1420 Plane headed west. Tried to raise *Tunny* by sound.
1427 Surfaced. Tried to raise *Tunny* again in vain.
2300 Picked up SJ interference from rest of pack. Sent all messages forming scouting line by radar, one of boats being 25 miles distant.

August 31
Surface patrolling on scouting line.
0120 (Ship Contact #3) Sighted smoke. Commenced tracking. Received report from *Queenfish*. Picked up three other sources of SJ radar interference. This area being unassigned is open hunting for any wolfpack. The Busters[2] must have arrived. Looks like a three ring circus is about to start with two wolfpacks and one convoy.
0130 Proceeded to position as starboard flanker.
0143 SJ radar contact on convoy at 18,000 yards. Also on a night flyer coming in fast. The show has started. Curtain time. Dived. (Aircraft Contact #10)
0150 Radar depth. No contacts.
0217 Sighted ships. Commenced approach. First act.
0223 Two torpedo explosions.
0225 Two more torpedo explosions.
0228 Sighted tanker on fire and sinking. Convoy has turned. We are losing contact. The villain is getting his early.
0229 (Aircraft Contact #11) Sighted plane between tanker and us. An inferno of fire on tanker and surrounding water. No other ships visible in light of fire, which lit up whole horizon. Other ship hit must have sunk.

---

[2] "Ben's Busters" consisted of *Growler* (Ben Oakley, wolfpack commander), *Pampanito* (Paul Summers), and *Sealion* (Eli Reich). *Barb*'s wolfpack, under Edward R. Swinburne, took the code name "Ed's Eradicators." Swinburne's only official duty aboard *Barb* was that of wolfpack commander, following the original system established by Swede Momsen. The "Busters" operated under the newer system, in which the senior commander in the group pulled double duty as wolfpack commander and CO of his own vessel.

0230 – 0238 About 25 assorted depth charges and bombs.

0240 Surfaced. Determined to introduce another character into the plot. End of Act I.

0242 (Aircraft Contact #12) Sighted plane 3 miles astern after another sub. Did not dive.

0245 Requested enemy position from *Tunny*, who was port flanker. Burning tanker had now sunk. Water surface still ablaze.

0305 (Aircraft Contact #13) SJ radar contact on plane at 8,650 yards. Slowed and turned away. Did not dive.

0341 Sighted gunfire at 040°T. Proceeding to position on starboard bow of convoy. Several subs near by.

0352 (Aircraft Contact #14) SJ radar contact on plane at 7,700 yards. Slowed and watched plane cross astern. Haven't time to dive now if we are to gain position ahead of convoy.

0409 During the intermission, the night flyers were using radar on 310 megacycles as picked up on APR. The APR gives a beautiful indication when they have you and are steady on.

0421 (Aircraft Contact #15) SJ contact at 9,000 yards opening. Did not dive.

0500 The first of morning twilight. Sighted subs everywhere. *Tunny* reported diving to attack east of *Barb*.

0501 Sighted smoke and commenced adjusting position.

0503 (Aircraft Contact #16) Sighted plane at 4 miles, heading down our throat. Dived. Act Two beginning.

0515 Echo ranging very weak.

0520 Sighted ships through scope. Commenced approach.

0523 Manned battle stations.

Convoy was in formation of 3 columns, with escort leading, using a zig plan 130-180-190-130-180-190, etc., speed 9 knots. Did not get very good check on log times. Starboard column consisted of a freighter followed by a tanker. Center column consisted of a large freighter of 6,500–7,000 tons, followed by a tanker and freighter. Port column consisted of a tanker followed by a small tanker and a tanker or freighter. About 8 ships exclusive of escorts, so *Queenfish* must have sunk two. None of the ships in the convoy were over 7,000 tons. The largest was the freighter leading the center column so made our approach on her. Echo ranging was heard. Convoy had air cover (Aircraft Contact #17), varying from 3 planes prior to attack to 8 planes after attack. We started out as a starboard flanker and quickly found we would be lucky to be a port flanker. Between observations went to 85 feet and pulled standard. Finally at

0624 we arrived at a position which has been my dream. Slightly ahead between the center and port columns. Made ready all tubes. A few more minutes and we would wipe out the center column and get the leading tanker in the port column. It seemed too good to be true. No chance at the escort, who was between starboard and center column and ahead. Then at

0625 saw signal flags going up on escort, probably indicating a submarine sighted on the starboard flank. Immediately thereafter sound reported torpedoes running, headed in our direction, and at

0626 Escort received two hits and blew up. One fish seemed to pick us out for a constant bearing, so lowered periscope to let it pass over if it came by. My castle crumbled. We weren't quite in position to fire and this would change the situation completely.

0627 – 0629 Two more explosions sounding like torpedoes. The whole formation was now swerving to the East.

0630 The leading ship in the starboard column was missing. Our primary target, the center column leader, now showed us a 10° starboard angle on the bow.

0634 Pulled out to the left to give him our stern tubes and at

0634:03 Introduced the character into the plot and fired tubes 7, 8, 9 on a 100 track to get the greatest course coverage,

0634:15 range about 1,000 yards. Medium tanker in ballast overlapping his stern about 500 yards beyond.

0635:16 First hit timed. Observed by CO near stern of freighter.

0635:22 Second hit timed. Observed by CO at after end of superstructure.

0635:45 Third hit timed. Hit in tanker. Torpedoes were spread from aft forward and first torpedo passed astern of freighter. Freighter began settling aft. Swung hard left at full speed to see if we couldn't catch something with our bow tubes. Depth charges, bombs, explosions all around. None close. After swinging to East nothing was left within Mk 18 range. Saw freighter sink stern first, also witnessed by Eradicators' Commander. Freighter was brand new with clean lines and new paint on topside and bottom. Tanker lost in the fray. Starboard flankers may have information as to whether it sank or not.

0645 Convoy now headed away to north after our strike from the south. If the starboard flankers will only strike now we can beat this gang around in an ever diminishing circle. No strikes from starboard flankers. Believed convoy might try heading west shortly and then ease around to the south, so headed west, at 150 feet. Secured the tubes and battle stations.

0650 Planes now began bombing our area. Some fairly close, but most astern.

0652 Assorted depth charges and bombs. Tempo rising. Sweet music. These continued throughout the remainder of the day, several hundred in all.

0735 Up for a look. Remains of convoy hull down now headed west with 8 planes covering (Aircraft Contact #18), a vicious circle for the Japs. The convoys bring gasoline and bombs for the planes to sink the subs, which sink the ships, which bring the gasoline and bombs for the planes, etc.

0820 (Aircraft Contact #19) Sighted plane searching, Mavis, through periscope.

0900 (Aircraft Contact #20) Sighted Nell[3] through periscope. Mavis still around.

0920 Convoy had now given up trying to make the Philippines and was now disappearing to the north towards Takao. Sighted a single column of smoke to the northwest, possibly a decoy dropped by planes to attract the submarines or make them speed up and show a wake. Regardless, held on to the west to establish contact. Explosions continuing. This smoke appeared and disappeared at about hourly intervals, no ship ever being sighted.

1250 No further smoke. Gave up high speed and set course to south west clearing area. End of Act II.

1300 During intermission air search became heavier (Aircraft Contact #21). Sighted 2 pontoon monoplanes, who joined the Mavis and Nells. All were dropping bombs at intervals and returning for reloads.

1349 Act III. Sighted smoke to the southwest. Commenced approach at high speed.

1522 Distant pinging. Several planes overhead continuously.

1655 Smoke developing. Sighted masts. Continued plugging along. Engineer worried about the battery turning to water. However another hour and we might get a shot.

1730 Target a small AK (MFM[4]) about 2,500 tons, with one or two sub chaser escorts on his quarter. He is heading west at 9 knots. Probably got lost in the morning merry-go-round.

Not sure of the number of escorts for we cannot waste time looking if we expect to be close enough to shoot. At this time, too, we encountered the latest fiendish anti-submarine weapon of the Japs. A bird which patrolled between 3–4,000 yards on the bow of the ship. As soon as he or she spotted a periscope he or she perched on it and draped his or her tail feathers over the exit window. This proved extremely confusing for the approach officer in the final stages of the approach. He banged on the scope, shook it, hooted and hollered at the blasted bird, swung the scope around quickly and raised and lowered it desperately, but the bird clung on tenaciously, hovering over the scope while it was ducked, then hopping back on when it was raised. As a last resort both scopes were raised for observation, one a few seconds ahead of the other as a feint, while the approach officer followed the other scope up. This completely baffled the bird and he was noted peering venomously down the other periscope as if saying, "Son of a Bishop, American ingenuity has won again, so solly."

Photographed bird for anti-submarine files and continued approach.

---

[3] Nell: Mitsubishi G3M, twin engine, long range land-based bomber employed by the Japanese Imperial Navy. A second-line bomber by 1944, Nells could carry torpedoes and depth charges and were employed as convoy escorts and anti-submarine patrols.

[4] Mast-Funnel-Mast.

1752 Made ready tubes 4, 5, 6. We've got him now.

1759 Fired tubes 4, 5, 6 at 1,300 yards on 130 starboard track. His last zig away and I mean last!

Three hits from midships forward. His guns forward and aft manned. About 15 lookouts dressed in white, which he had on a catwalk around the forward top part of the bridge, were unceremoniously dumped in the drink when the first fish hit under the bridge. Other two fish broke target in two forward, and he sank. Sinking observed by too many people in the conning tower for sub chaser spotted our scope and romped over with his crew greasing the racks. No time to turn for a down the throater, so assumed our evasive depth of 340 feet and had the yeoman break out the depth charge forms.

1804 Lightning and thunder. None too close. About 100—150 yards.

1824 Sound reported help arriving at high speed from the northwest and from the east, all pinging.

1825 Evaded to northwest on the assumption they wouldn't be looking where they had come from. Pinging screwing all around.

1900 Opposition became cautious and stingy with their depth charges.

1948 They finally made contact on something way astern of us. Distant depth charges.

1957 Periscope depth, getting dark except for full moon and no clouds. The team aft still giving the fish a drubbing. Hope it isn't another sub.

2010 Radar depth. Four contacts astern at about 9,000 yards. No aircraft in evidence.

2013 Surfaced with the villains still working us over about 5 miles astern. End of Act III. Depth charge expenditure – 58.

2025 Commenced clearing area to west at 17 knots with 2 engines on charge.

2032 (Aircraft Contact #22) Keyed SD radar, contact 10 miles. Secured it. First Curtain Call.

2038 Sighted patrol boat on starboard bow about 8,000 yards. Evaded to south. Second Curtain Call.

2045 Sighted patrol boat on port beam headed towards us. Evaded to southwest our last opening. Third Curtain Call.

2049 Sighted gunfire on port bow moving east. No other evasive courses left. Kept going. Fourth Curtain Call.

2050 Explosions astern, distant.

2130 Two small craft making about 15 knots sighted broad on starboard bow crossing our bow. SJ contacted at 4,000. Eased around at 20 knots outside of machine gun range. Fifth and last Curtain Call.

September 1

Surface patrolling in area.

0252 Transmitted Eradicators serial one.

0549 (Aircraft Contact #23) Sighted plane at 12 miles. Watched him working our way in his search.

0605 Dived. Watched plane through periscope.

0636 Surfaced.

0715 (Aircraft Contact #24) Sighted plane at 8 miles. Dived.

0730 Plane still in sight through periscope.

0750 Surfaced.

0755 Bow planes out of commission. Jammed in part rise position.

0800 (Aircraft Contact #25) Sighted plane at 8 miles. Dived and watched plane.

0838 Surfaced. Bow planes back in commission.

1010 (Aircraft Contact #26) Sighted plane at 10 miles. Dived.

1036 Surfaced.

1312 (Aircraft Contact #17) Sighted plane at 8 miles. Dived.

1328 Watched plane through periscope.

1358 Sighted rubber life raft. No survivors.

1407 (Aircraft Contact #28) Sighted plane at 8 miles. Dived.

1438 Lost sight of plane.

1453 Surfaced.

1459 (Aircraft Contact #29) Sighted plane at 15 miles. Did not dive. Plane passed on to northward.

1527 (Aircraft Contact #30) Sighted Mavis to southward. SJ radar range 14 miles. Did not dive. Trained all OODs in estimating distance to plane.

1601 Sighted *Tunny* at 6 miles.

1634 (Aircraft Contact #31) Sighted plane at 15 miles. Did not dive.

1725 Lookouts reported periscope on starboard beam. Turned away at flank speed. Probably a stick or he would have fired.

1841 Started up SJ radar. *Tunny* 9,000 yards.

1848 (Aircraft Contact #32) Dived. He is heading for *Tunny*.

1849 Saw planes drop bombs on *Tunny* as she was submerging.

1852 Another salvo of bombs on the *Tunny*.

Food for thought that no planes had detected us until shortly after the SJ was put into operation.

1914 Radar depth. APR indicating 310 megs. SJ contact at 8,300 yards from plane moving in.

1934 Trying again. SJ contact at 5,300 yards, same plane. *Tunny*'s position was marked by float lights and a string appeared to indicate her course on diving.

1945 Trying again. SJ contact at 8,000 yards on plane.

1946 Plane dropped a green parachute magnesium flare over *Tunny*'s position.

2035 Float lights went out.

2200 Surfaced.

2330 Enemy radar sweeping on 310 megs.

September 2

0000 APR indications on 310 megs after fading in and out now became much stronger.

0001 APR showing steady contact.

0002 (Aircraft Contact #33) Aircraft sighted us. Dived. Plane sighted close aboard on starboard beam. Passed 100 feet overhead while clearing bridge.

0003 Two bombs while passing 100 feet. Distance to bombs 50 feet maximum. Swinging hard left at the time. Plane must have dropped on second pass.

0005 Two bombs on starboard beam about 100 yards or less.

0008 One bomb on starboard quarter about 400 yards. Minor damage was sustained from first two bombs. Port antenna was carried away. SD antenna dipole supports were bent back and tuning wings detuned. Bridge repeater grounded out by leak. Several gauges and light bulbs broken. Pit log contactor arm shaft seal broken. Bow plane shafting now squealing. Some minor high pressure leaks.

0100 Periscope depth. Sighted float lights marking our position several miles astern.

0110 Commenced work on bow plane shaft slacking off on universal and regreasing.

0120 Bow planes back in commission.

0127 Enemy radar on 310 megs, picked up on APR sweep. Not steady on. Set continuous APR watch, hooked oscillograph to APR for visual strength observations.

0132 Surfaced. Distant sweeps of enemy radar at 310 megs on APR until dawn. Collected bomb fragments around conning tower and tail vanes of bomb from deck forward.

Shifted area for surface patrol. Tunny having left wolfpack due to bomb damage.

1833 Started SJ radar.

1915 Decided to use SD. Very difficult to spot a plane with sky as it is and surface still fairly bright.

1920 Enemy aircraft radar at 310 megs sweeping across us and getting steadily stronger—not fading in and out as per usual.

1928 (Aircraft Contact #34) SJ radar contact on plane coming in from ahead, range 5,200 yards. Dived. APR signal at 310 megs at diving was steady on.

1955 Radar depth. SJ contact on plane at 1,500 yards. That Jap evidently believes his radar.

2035 Surfaced. APR all clear. We will not use the SD again except on surfacing.

2230 APR at 310 megs indicating sweeps across us, the signal becoming stronger then fading out. This procedure kept up for a while then kept increasing in strength steadily over a period of time until at

2314 (Aircraft Contact #35) APR watch reported steady signal. Dived. While clearing bridge lookout reported plane ahead. SJ reported contact at 6,500 yards.

2316 Three bombs. Close and above to starboard while we were swinging left. No damage. These boys are varsity. Their christianizing influence is best brought out by a prayer one of our Scotsmen murmured at this time: "Oh, Lord, deliver us from the ghosties and ghoulies, and long legged beasties, and things that go boomp in the night." Aptly put.

September 3

0107 APR depth. Enemy planes sweeping across us on 310 megs every 1½ minutes, getting weaker. The oscillograph makes these strength observtions accurate and relative for the different watches. Set a certain indication height at which APR operator would give the bridge 4 buzzes as signal for OOD to dive.

0500 APR indicating plane working in.

0512 (Aircraft Contact #36) Plane sighted at 5 miles. 4 buzzes from APR. Dived.

0632 Surfaced. We are now becoming very suspicious of our SJ radar. From watching the APR it appears that Japs have a non-directional SJ detector on their planes. Our theory is that they work out and in on various directions until they find the approximate bearing of strongest detector signal, then work in steadily, make contact on their 310 meg radar and bomb on sight.

0811 (Aircraft Contact #37) Sighted plane at 8 miles. Dived. Routined torpedoes.

1100 Surfaced.

1215 (Aircraft Contact #38) Sighted Mavis at 14 miles. Dived.

1234 Lost sight of planes.

1238 Started SJ radar.

2100 Picked up 310 megs on APR. Same old stuff. He commenced working out and in then having found the bearing commenced working steadily in on us.

2134 (Aircraft Contact #39) Sighted plane at 4 miles. Dived. Decided to secure SJ. We are convinced it is being detected and menace on these moonlight nights.

2226 APR depth. All clear.

2235 Surfaced. SJ secured.

During the remainder of the night we had several instances of night fliers sweeping by at an APR strength from which they had previously worked in. However, with the SJ shut down all is quiet, they kept going on.

September 4

0458 (Ship Contact #4) Sighted object resembling submarine. Commenced closing.

0505 Submerged. Day breaking. Commenced tracking.

0600 Made it out to be a sampan with 4 auxiliary masts. Size undetermined. Closing at standard speed for sampan had no particular course. In view of the heavy plane coverage decided to battle surface using automatic weapons and having 4 inch gun crew stand by below.

0901 Battle surfaced at 1,000 yards and closed. 40 MM gun jammed after third shot with one hit. 6 Japs abandoned ship. Automatic weapons hitting continuously until range was so close the twin 20 MM could not depress sufficiently. No fires.

0911 (Aircraft Contact #40) Sighted Nell at 7 miles. Cleared topside. Dived.

0912 Watched plane coming in. Went to 160 feet and tracked sampan by sound, following him so he couldn't escape.

0922 Periscope depth. Plane shoving off. Sampan auxiliary engine, after going furiously, had now broken down. Some of our automatic hits must have taken effect. Decided to battle surface with 4 inch gun crew and one .30 cal. crew.

0941 Battle surfaced. Fired 10 rounds of 4 inch at ranges from 1,000 yards, closing. 6 hits and at

0945 Sampan sunk stern first. Secured battle stations.

1108 Test fired 40 MM gun.

1229 (Aircraft Contact #41) Plane sighted us. Sighted all silver colored Nell diving on us out of sun at ½ mile. Dived. Fortunately the course clock[5] had just given a big swing to the right so that plane missed his bombing position on first run passing about 100 feet up the port side. As the quartermaster was closing the hatch he made the classic remark, "Is there any use in closing it?" We kept swinging right and at

1230½ two close bombs on port beam.

1232 Two close bombs on port quarter.

This plane was exceptionally well camouflaged for day or night use. All others we had seen were brown. The OOD, quartermaster, and 2 after lookouts had covered this sector within 30 seconds of his sighting.

1428 Surfaced.

1605 Lookout reported periscope at 3,500 yards on starboard beam. Turned away at flank speed. Not sighted by OOD or CO.

1608 (Aircraft Contact #42) Sighted plane at 8 miles. Dived.

1625 Plane still in sight.

---

[5] Course Clock: A mechanical device designed to time and designate course changes for the ship's zigzag plan. After setting the base course, the clock would indicate when to zig, and onto what course, to keep the ship on a random course along the base course.

1650 Surfaced.
1735 (Aircraft Contact #43) Sighted plane at 10 miles. Dived.
1846 Surfaced.
1910 Distant APR indications on 310 megs. Swept by without working in. SJ secured. During night also encountered nearly continual sweeping indications of 250 megs radar. Probably shore based.

September 5
0105 Sighted Koto Sho.
0400 Passed through spot where *Queenfish* had reported torpedo being fired at her two hours earlier. Nothing in sight.
0501 Dived for submerged patrol east of Koto Sho, taking periscope observations at 48 feet.
1843 Surfaced and lay to. Greased topside.
2024 Enroute new area. APR readings at 250 megs.

September 6
Surface patrolling.
1300 APR showed steady contact on 150 megs. There were no prior sweeps and pips increased in strength until
1314 (Aircraft Contact #44) Sighted 3 fighter planes at 12 miles. Dived.
1336 Surfaced. All clear on APR.
1821 Started SJ radar for listening only.
1826 Distant APR at 310 megs.
1854 APR at 250 megs. Getting stronger.
2018 APR at 250 megs. Operator ordered bridge to dive. Submerged. As 250 megs is believed to be a shore station we will not dive on its indication from now on.
2035 Surfaced.
2111 Commenced SJ sweeps at intervals of 3, 7 and 10 minutes to find out what can't be detected.

September 7
Surface patrolling east of Bashi Channel.
1235 Sighted waterspout.

September 8
0511 Submerged off Yami Island patrolling Bashi Channel. Periscope observations at 48 feet and listening on pack frequency for 5 minutes each hour according to plan.
1902 Surfaced.
1924 Received contact report from *Queenfish*. She had lost contact at 1400 on convoy contacted at 1027. Guess we missed receiving earlier reports on our SD

antenna, which was raised 6 feet out of water from the hour to 5 minutes after the hour.

Commenced searching at full speed.

2040 *Queenfish* transmitted contact. We are proceeding to position as port flanker.

September 9

0115 (Ship Contact #5) Sighted port outer screen escort. SJ interference bearing 045° relative, must be *Queenfish*.

0112 *Queenfish* reported diving for attack. Bright moon and scattered clouds. Port flanker is a poor position tonight.

0119 SJ contact at 20,000 yards. Commenced tracking. We are now on beam of convoy. APR signals at 150 megs, strong.

0129 (Aircraft Contact #45) Sighted Nell flying about 300 feet above the water patrolling up port side of convoy. Range 3 miles. Sweeps at 150 megs on APR.

0130 Plane changed course to head across our bow. Dived. We are up moon. A tough one to take because we need 15 more minutes surface running to put us in position. Held standard in hopes we still might get in. Plane continued to circle around outer screen crossed about 6,000 yards astern of us. Now if only the *Queenfish* can sock them on their starboard flank we will have a good chance. Inner screen of spitkits is hanging close to the convoy. Can not make out the number of ships. Probably 9 or 10 assorted freighters and tankers.

0150 Radar depth. Plane circling overhead. APR very strong steady signals at 151 megs. No second harmonic could be obtained at 310 megs.

0213 Heard two explosions. *Queenfish* must be at work and convoy should soon head this way.

0217 One explosion.

0128 – 0226 Eleven explosions. Depth charges.

0227 One explosion.

0245 Several escorts blinking. Convoy proceeding nonchalantly along its way. Blast it all. Plane still circling. Plugged on.

0340 Convoy passed ahead. Nearest ship 4,350 yards. Mk 14s would do the trick. "If dog rabbit." A heart breaker to watch three large ones ease by just out of range, not to mention numerous smaller ones. Convoy on course 120°T. Changed course to 270°T to open out.

0432 Sighted sleeper escort astern of convoy. Looks like a *Chidori*. Set torpedoes at 4 feet. Scattered clouds, and being up moon, makes observations difficult.

0445 Dislike shooting at this target, really against my better judgment—if we hit they'll keep us down and the convoy will get away, if we miss the same results. However, once in every submariner's life there comes the urge to let three fish go, particularly after a convoy skids across his nose while his hands are tied. I dood it.

0446 Fired tubes 1, 2, 3 on 95 port track, zero gyro, range 3,000 yards.

0448 Sound reported torpedo coming up starboard side. Switched to loud speaker and heard one of fish circling us.

0449 Two others missed.

0453 Heard explosion. Probably end of run. Target turned towards.

0454 Two explosions. Probably end of run. Went deep.

0500 Several sets of screws and pingers around.

0800 Up for a look. One subchaser passing down our starboard side about 3,000 yards away. What long depth charge racks! Three anti-sub vessels, PCs or subchasers about 7,000 yards astern. Since we have never lost our original pinger, believe we may have fired at a subchaser. Planes all around. Too many to log.

0909 (Aircraft Contact #46) Sighted Nell at 2 miles.

0957 (Aircraft Contact #47) Sighted three Emilys at 4 miles.

1017 (Aircraft Contact #48) Sighted Nell at 3 miles.

1024 (Aircraft Contact #49) Sighted Mavis at 3 miles.

1101 Surfaced. No planes in sight. Commenced chasing convoy, 70 miles to go.

1124 (Aircraft Contact #50) Sighted Emily at 11 miles on starboard quarter with 90 starboard angle. Can't afford to lose any more ground, so staryed on surface and kept our tail at him. We must outrun him.

1127 Just as we thought we had escaped he headed towards us. Dived.

1131 One bomb. Fairly close.

1340 Surfaced. Commenced chasing again.

1430 (Aircraft Contact #51) Sighted Betty[6] at 11 miles. Dived.

1448 Plane departed.

1449 Surfaced. We try again.

1450 (Aircraft Contact #52) Sighted Hope at 9 miles. Dived.

1504 Plane still in sight shoving off.

1514 Surfaced. We try again. Convoy is now 100 miles away.

1519 (Aircraft Contact #53) Sighted Nell at 6 miles. Dived.

1620 Swinging left.

1621 One bomb. Very, very close on starboard side. The varsity and they always use the correct lead angle for original track.

Lots of cork flying. No damage.

1631 Another bomb on starboard quarter. Fairly close. The Japs seem determined to keep us away from the convoy. *Queenfish* must have made them mad.

1904 Surfaced. Chase abandoned. Impossible to reach convoy by dawn and it is deep in Sowespac area now.

2010 Proceeding to new convoy area.

2020 Exchanged recognition signals by radar with *Pampanito*. Using SJ radar at 5 minute intervals.

---

[6] Mitsubishi G6M1 twin-engine bomber.

2340 SJ contact on Calayan Island at 60,000 yards. APR indicting sweep frequency at 250 megs and 310 megs.

September 10
Patrolling off Calayan Island. APR indicating continued sweeps at 250 megs. Probably shore based. Many times he steadied on us. Several times while on us the operator commenced transmitting. This was picked up visually on the oscillograph and audibly. The transmissions were copied and will be enclosed in a separate report. This was the first and only time we have encountered keying of their radar and should serve as a warning to our subs not to transmitted in plain language when close to land.
0505 Dived for submerged morning patrol west of Calayan Island.
0807 – 0812 Heard 20 distant explosions. Could not determine direction. Sighted *Queenfish* on the surface patrolling, so remained down according to plan. She evidently couldn't determine direction either.
1140 Surfaced. Commenced surface patrol.
1311 (Aircraft Contact #54) Sighted 10 Bettys at 13 miles. Dived.
1347 Surfaced. Headed for new convoy lane.
2030 Patrolling south of Garahbi Light. APR signals at 250 and 310 megs. We now use SJ at 5 minute intervals, without being bombed.

September 11
0050 Sighted Koto Sho at 32 miles.
0300 Headed west for new patrol area.
0525 (Aircraft Contact #55) Sighted Nell at 13 miles. Did not dive.
0530 (Aircraft Contact #56) Sighted 3 Nells at 10 miles. Dived. Watched planes through periscope.
0559 Surfaced.
0601 (Aircraft Contact #57) Sighted 2 Nells at 8 miles.
0619 Surfaced.
0625 (Aircraft Contact #58) Sighted Nell at 18 miles. Did not dive.
All of the above Nells were silver or whitish colored. They were evidently night fliers returning from one sector. All were on same course headed towards the naval base at Pescadores Islands.
1048 (Aircraft Contact #59) Sighted plane at 9 miles. Dived.
1152 Surfaced. Decided to give the SD a try.
1240 (Aircraft Contact #60) Sighted plane at 8 miles. Dived.
1317 Surfaced.
1414 (Aircraft Contact #61) Sighted Rufe[7] at 9 miles. Dived.
1450 Surfaced. Secured SD so we could get some sleep.
2000 APR signals strong at 250 megs. Will now try using a sheet of metal held

---
[7] Nakajima A6M2-N. A float plane version of the Mitsubishi Zero fighter.

at various positions around APR antenna to see if we can determine approximate direction.

2100 No luck in making the APR directive after one hour. Signals are fairly weak.

September 12

Surface patrolling on station on convoy lane south of Pratas Reef.

1113 Sight U.S. submarine on the horizon. Not the *Queenfish*, must be the *Sea Lion*, since *Pampanito* and *Growler* are 40 miles further south along convoy lane. The set up looks good if a convoy comes along for a complete wipe out with 5 subs in the area. All we need is a contact.

1125 Submarine sighted at 1113 submerged. We are patrolling on surface all day so we can't possibly miss any contact report. Comsubpac has ordered all packs on the same frequency 2005 while patrolling this lane. *Queenfish* is patrolling on surface also.

1559 (Aircraft Contact #62) Sighted Mavis at 6 miles, coming out of clouds. Dived. Watched plane through periscope.

1624 Lost sight of plane.

1625 Surfaced.

2300 Commenced working northward along convoy lane.

September 13

Surface patrolling along convoy lane south of Pratas Reef.

0500 Headed east having covered this area from −24 hours to +18 hours. Now necessary to cover convoy lanes through Bashi Channel.

0541 (Aircraft Contact #63) Sighted Mavis at 5 miles. Dived.

0611 Surfaced.

0705 Received Comsubpac 122607 and heard of *Growler*'s good work. Later heard *Pampanito* had hit convoy with the *Growler*. Glad two of the five subs made contact, but it is very disappointing for the other three to have wasted two days on this lane. Have no idea when *Growler* made contact.

0817 (Aircraft Contact #64) Sighted Mavis at 8 miles. Dived. Watched plane through periscope.

0846 Surfaced.

0855 (Aircraft Contact #65) Sighted Mavis at 15 miles. Turned our tail toward him and slowed. Did not dive.

0905 Lost sight of plane.

1028 (Aircraft Contact #66) Sighted Mavis at 8 miles. Dived. Watched plane through periscope.

1055 Lost sight of plane which was on a steady course. Proof these planes are visible for long distances.

1056 Surfaced.

1648 (Aircraft Contact #67) Sighted Nell at 8 miles. A high flier. Dived.
1716 Surfaced.
2325 Exchanged calls by SJ with *Redfish*.

September 14

0003 (Ship Contact #6) Radar contact at 8,950 yards. Sent out contact report. Commenced tracking.

0018 Picked up another enemy contact about 6,000 yards on port quarter of first contact. Looks like 2 escorts. No convoy astern.

0023 Manned battle stations. Commenced night surface approach.

0121 At 4,000 yards made out enemy to be 2 *Chidori* Torpedo Boats. A killer group cleverly arranged. No definite zig plan and changing speed at intervals from 12.3 to 15.5 knots. Began working in on leading *Chidori* for a stern shot.

0133 (Torpedo Attack No. 4.) Fired stern tubes 8, 9, 10 on 65° port track, 25° left gyros, 1,580 yards torpedo run, depth set 3 feet, calm sea. This looked like a snap, but all torpedoes missed. Twenty seconds after torpedoes were due to hit, target commenced to reverse course. A miss we can't explain.

0140 Full speed clearing out ahead. Checked fire control system from top to bottom. Could find no errors so at

0225 Commenced second approach.

0300 Thin sliver of a moon now showing target is between us and the moon. *Queenfish* signalled she was attacking astern of us. Sent her reply that we were attacking from bow.

0316 *Chidori* sent us recognition signals. A "K" followed by a long dash. We are at 3,600 yards. Commenced to open out in case he really had us spotted.

0322 *Chidori* again challenged us. Our camouflage isn't working this time. Turned tail to him.

0326 *Chidori* turned on searchlight and opened fire with his forward gun. Dived. Perfect illumination and no trouble seeing the hatch. Set a new record for clearing the bridge.

0327 Shells landing about 1,000 yards ahead. Commenced swinging right for a down the throat shot watching his shooting through periscope.

0328 *Chidori* commenced shooting with his after gun at someone on his port flank. Possibly the *Redfish*. We had had another source of SJ interference from that bearing. *Chidori* turned off searchlight.

0330 Radar depth. Range 3,500 yards.

0345 Echo ranging. APR signals on 310 megs. He must have asked for air cover.

0349 Nearly in firing position when at

0350 Heard torpedoes running. Held up shooting. Torpedoes passed fairly close ahead, passing from 345° relative to 050° relative in less than a minute. No explosions. *Queenfish* must have fired.

0353 Depth charging commenced. *Chidori* reversed course.

0354 Another set of torpedoes running heading our way and passing down starboard side. These either came from the *Redfish* or the *Chidori*. All misses.

Depth charging continuing. Don't know who he's working over, but we are in a position to put a stop to it. *Chidori* was now steady on 002°T, speed 13½, range 1,500 yards. Took a few precious minutes to track him exactly by and radar and at

0400 Fired tubes 1, 2, 3 with 30° left gyros, 140° port track, range 1,500 yards, depth set at 3 feet. Depth charging ceased and *Chidori* swung for us as last torpedo was leaving the tube. We are in a poor position for down the throat so headed deep. All fish missed. He evidently had an excellent sound operator. Broke out depth charge forms.

0404 A string of 10 depth charges straddling and above us. First team.

0406 Another string of 10 depth charges close but high. He must be circling above us.

0408 Fairly distant depth charges. His teammate must be working on the *Queenfish*.

0410 Long scale pinging. Tried putting our tail towards it, but pinger worked around on our beam and slowed.

0413 Short scale pinging. Screws coming up astern and passing up port side. Real teamwork. Decided to hold course since dropper was to port.

0415 A string of 8 very close depth charges along port side and high. These were enough to jar your fillings loose, cork, light bulbs, etc. No damage.

0417 Came right and worked out from under the pair.

0652 Periscope depth. Sighted tops of *Chidori*'s astern. (Aircraft Contact #68) Sighted Mavis at 4 miles searching for us.

0700 Reloaded tubes.

1629 Surfaced, heading towards Bashi Channel for patrol.

1648 Sighted smoke. Looks like our *Chidori*'s again.

1707 Submerged, determined to avoid. Nine torpedoes and 9 misses at *Chidori*'s is enough for one run. Believe these babies have flat bottoms.

1807 *Chidori*'s passed at 3,000 yards, making 17 knots and turned towards Batan Island.

1909 Surfaced.

September 15

0037 Donk's Devils[8] patrolling Bashi Channel so shifted patrol station to point 4 miles east of Mabodis Island.

0501 Submerged for patrol. Periscope sweeps at 48 feet.

0759 (Aircraft Contact #69) Sighted plane at 5 miles. Land based, wheels down—probably landing on Itbayat Island.

---

[8] Donc's Devils consisted of *Picuda* (Donc Donoho), *Spadefish* (Gordon W. Underwood), and *Redfish* (Sandy McGregor).

1115 Sighted smoke on other side of island chain. Single column.
1852 Surfaced. Headed for Basco on Batan Island to search for convoy.
2130 Looked into Basco Harbor from 6,000 yards. No ships.
2135 Sighted small patrol boat patrolling around Sabtang Island. Commenced tour around Batan Island, looked into Sabtang Strait and around Iboros Island. No ships. Reported same to Donk's Devils. Headed for patrol station in Balintang Channel.

September 16
Surface patrolling south of Sabtang Island, searching for convoy.
0400 Received orders to proceed to Lat. 18-42 N., Long. 114-15 E. to pick up Australian and British survivors from Jap transport sunk by either *Pampanito* or *Growler* during night of Sept. 12–13. We now have over 450 miles to go to reach this point and must naturally give up the search on present convoy. The latter is not regretted, but the fact that the *Barb* and *Queenfish* were within 70 miles of the convoy on the night of 12–13, and are now 450 miles away is regretted.
0401 All ahead flank, making 19 knots.
0800 Made all torpedo skids into 3 bunks each and organized ship to take 100 survivors aboard, if they are still alive.
1234 (Aircraft Contact #70) Sighted Mavis at 12 miles. Dived.
1250 Lost sight of plane through periscope.
1251 Surfaced.
1311 Sighted U.S. sub on opposite course. This will be the *Sea Lion*.
2140 Received contact report from *Queenfish* concerning convoy of 5 ships and six escorts, course 040°T, speed 12.
2152 (Ship Contact #7) SJ contact on convoy at 30,000 yards. This is by far the best our radar has ever done! Must be something bigger than usual in the convoy. Commenced working ahead to position as starboard flanker. Convoy consisted of 5 ships, 2 in each outboard column, a destroyer leading, escorts on flanks and quarter and one large ship, giving the largest pip, in the middle between the after ship in each column.
2231 Eradicators sent contact report out in Devil's code.
2236 Saw flare sent up by escort.
2237 Heard explosion.
2243 Heard explosion.
2254 *Queenfish* reported attack completed. Directed her to trail. Commenced approach.
2305 Coming in on starboard bow could make out several very large, deeply laden tankers. Made ready all tubes. Columns had now squeezed closer together with 3 tankers in starboard column. One starboard bow escort had evidently gone around to port side where *Queenfish* had attacked. Am closing for attack on leading tankers. Will not be close enough to leading destroyer.

2323 Leading tankers now look like they're turning away. Am sure they haven't seen us. Can now see a subchaser escort just forward of their beams. They must be turning to original formation, after their squeeze from *Queenfish* attack. Looking aft for a better target and the largest pip at

2325 Ye Gods, a flat top! This was the large pip about 300 yards to port and just ahead of the very large after tanker in the starboard column. Range 4,900 yards. Went ahead standard to close for a good shot.

2328 Working for an overlap. Spotted a *Chidori*, whose bow we were crossing at 2,700 yards and another escort astern of her. This is undoubtedly the prettiest target I've ever seen. APR signals on 310 megs.

2331 At 2,000 yards slowed to 10 knots. *Chidori* is on our quarter showing us a 30° port angle on the bow. We have a perfect overlap of the tanker and just beyond the flat top. Binocular formula showing more than a full field. About 1,000 feet of target. *Chidori* is closing rapidly. APR steady signal on 310 megs. Night flier has contact.

2332-15 Commenced firing all bow tubes, point of aim bow of tanker, range 1,820 yards, zero gyros, 110-120 starboard track, depth setting 6 feet. First torpedo normal. As soon as all fish fired went ahead emergency with full right rudder to put the stern tubes into the carrier. Can't make it without being rammed by escort.

2333 *Chidori* at 750 yards. Dived. Rigged for depth charge, going deep. Gyro angle on 2 stern tubes too large to shoot.

2334:16 First hit in tanker.

2334:24 Second hit in tanker.

2334:53 First hit in carrier. *Chidori* passing overhead.

2335:01 Second hit in carrier.

2335:10 Third hit in carrier. No depth charges. *Chidori* must not have seen us.

2337–2345 Breaking up noises, very heavy underwater explosions, whistlings, cracklings. One ship sunk. Random depth charges started.

September 17

2357-0004 More depth charges. Another string of breaking up noises and very heavy underwater explosions. Second ship sunk. Hope the *Queenfish* is close enough to see these.

0004–0027 Miscellaneous depth charges. None close.

0031 Periscope depth, nothing in sight except possible mast of one escort well astern. No signs of burning oil.

0041 Radar depth. 2 small pips at 11,000 yards at position of our attack. Escorts must be picking up survivors

0055 Surfaced. While at Saipan the *Queenfish* furnished us the following information on our attack. Immediately after they fired, their OOD sighted a carrier in the formation. Concerning our attack directly at 2336 tanker exploded. A ball of flame about 500 feet in diameter shot up into the sky. The tanker then caught fire from stem to stern. No other ships in the convoy could be seen from their position about 12,000 yards on the port quarter of convoy. The flames went out and tanker disappeared at 2355. This checks with the time of our second set of breaking up noises, so carrier must have sunk first. *Queenfish* during period was tracking their cripple, which had stopped. Later they lost contact with remnants of convoy at 27,000 yards. They had initially obtained a range of 34,000 yards on the convoy.

With one torpedo remaining forward and two aft would like to chase the remains of this convoy to get rid of them. However, we would probably be held down during daylight when we must rescue survivors. The seas have been rising and if we don't reach the survivors today, their fifth day in the water, there will be none left alive. With a plan being dangled before my eyes, it is obvious after due consideration of all aspects, that our primary mission now is the search for survivors. We have already lost 5 hours by sidetracking to attack this convoy.

0100 Received orders from ComWolfPack to proceed to survivors area. I heartily agree. As an after thought inserted here, having seen the piteous plight of the 14 survivors we rescued, I can say that I would forego the pleasure of an attack on a Jap Task Force to rescue any one of them. There is little room for sentiment in Submarine warfare, but the measure of saving one allied life against sinking a Jap ship is one which leaves me no question, once experienced.

0105 Set course for survivor area at full speed. Lost radar contact on last escort at 14,000 yards.

0116 Sent BIMEK contact report to Donk's devils.

0122-0135 Enemy radar interference on SJ searching as a protection while picking up Jap survivors.

0530 Commenced search for Australian and British survivors along farthest west position they could possibly be considering tide and wind. Considered weather report as given by *Pampanito*, what we had encountered since then, and the present state of the weather. State of the sea now force 4, wind 20 knots. Both on the increase.

0930 Commenced passing through wreckage. Set course down wreckage.

1141 Sighted several floaters. Some Japs, some Allies.

1255 Sighted two rafts with 3 and 2 survivors aboard. All ahead full.

1303 Picked up three survivors. All ahead standard.

1317 Picked up two survivors.

1422 Sight raft with two survivors.

1429 Picked up 2 survivors. Sighted raft with 1 survivor. All ahead standard.

1435 Picked up 1 survivors.

1437 Sighted raft with 2 survivors. All ahead full.

1444 Picked up 2 survivors.

1509 Sighted raft with 2 survivors.
1519 Picked up 2 survivors. Sighted raft with one survivor.
1524 Sighted raft with 1 survivor.
1535 Picked up 1 survivor.

A word on the survivors. All were covered with a heavy coating of oil received when they drifted through an oil slick their second night on the rafts. This undoubtedly saved their lives. They were in the water or on their small wooden life rafts for a period of 5 days before being picked up. This in addition to 3 years of prison life under the Japs, which included bashings, beatings, starvation (all survivors were 25–30 pounds underweight), malaria, dysentery, pellagra, sores, ulcers, etc., left them in terribly poor physical condition. The at first dubious, then amazed, and finally hysterically thankful look on their faces, from the time they first sighted us approaching them, is one we shall never forget. Several of them were too weak to take the lines thrown to them. These men were rescued by the valiant efforts of Lt. Comdr. R.W. McNitt, USN, Lt. (D-V(G) J.G. Lanier, USNR, and Houston, C.S., MoMM2c, who dove in after them. Too much credit cannot be given to the crew for their superb performance and willing efforts in the production line we had formed from the deck party who picked them up, stripped them, and passed them on to the transportation gang to get them below, where they were received by the cleaners who removed the oil and grease, then on to the doctors and nurses for treatment, thence to the feeders, and finally to the sleepers, who carried them off and tucked them in their bunks.

The appreciation of the survivors was unbounded. Even those who couldn't talk expressed themselves tearfully through their glazed, oil soaked eyes. We regret there were no more, for we had found it possible, by taking over every square foot of space aboard ship, sleeping three to a torpedo rack, etc., to accommodate a hundred.

By separate correspondence a recommendation for commendation is being forwarded in the case of Donnelly, W.E., PhM1c. Through his untiring efforts working day and night those men were brought over the hump without the loss of a single life.

One the amusing side, the following remarks were recorded as the survivors were being carried to their bunks.

"I take back all I ever said about you Yanks."

"Three bloody years without a drink of brandy, please give me another."

"Turn me loose, I'll run to that bunk."

"Be sure to wake me up for chow."

"Matey, we're in safe hands at last."

"As soon as I can I'm going to write my wife to kick the Yankee out—I'm coming home!"

*As a matter of record I wish to express my appreciation to the officers and crew for their splendid contribution of over $300 as a stake for the survivors. After a refit in Pearl Harbor this included practically every cent aboard ship.

September 18

Surface patrolling searching for survivors. We are now in the tail end of a typhoon, the wind has picked up to 35 knots, and seas are very heavy. Believe it will be impossible for any survivors on rafts to last through this night.

0600 Commenced working up sea from maximum survivor position with Queenfish five miles to starboard. Sighted empty rafts and allied floaters throughout the day, but no survivors.

1900 Set course for Saipan.

September 19

Surface patrolling en route Saipan making turns for 8 knots in a typhoon. Wind 60 knots.

1800 Barometer commenced to rise and seas and wind to decrease. Increased speed to 10 knots.

September 20

Surface patrolling en route Saipan via Balintang Channel at full speed.

September 21

Surface patrolling en route Saipan at full speed.

0440 Passed Balintang Island abeam to starboard at 4 miles.

September 22

Surface patrolling en route Saipan at full speed.

September 23

Surface patrolling en route Saipan at full speed.

0130(J) SJ interference. Closed and challenged. Return signal unintelligible, unfortunately. Probably the *Cobia*. Had hoped to pot the Jap weather ship DF'd at this point.

1230(J) (Aircraft Contact #71) Sighted Mavis at 8 miles. Dived.

1249(J) Surfaced. Sent out contact report in view of present fleet operations.

1529(J) Sighted *Parche*. Exchanged calls.

September 24

Surface patrolling en route Saipan.

September 25

0600(K) Rendezvoused with escort U.S.S. *Case*, in company with *Snook* and *Queenfish*.

1134(K) Moored port side to *Queenfish* alongside U.S.S. *Fulton*. Received an excellent welcome with all facilities immediately available. Received one torpedo forward and 20,000 gallons fuel.

1913(K) Air raid alert.
1930(K) Secured from air raid alarm.

September 26
0745(K) Underway for Majuro in company with *Queenfish* and escort.
1400(K) Released escort. Entered northern safety lane.
1700(K) Passed between Sarigan and Anatanan Islands.
1812(K) Exchanged calls with U.S.S. *Cassin*. Neither of us had been notified of the other's presence in safety lane.

September 27
En route Majuro.

September 28
Several APR signals on 310 megs during night. Could not believe Japs had such a wide patrol even though signals were weak until at
   0943 (Aircraft Contact #72) Sighted a Mavis at 13 miles. Dived.
   1005 Surfaced.
   1233 (Aircraft Contact #73) Sighted biplane (?) at 5 miles. Dived.
   1242 Surfaced.
   1500 With ComWolfPack, determined to bombard Peale Island, Wake. *Queenfish* affirmed joint bombardment.
   1900 Notified Comsubspac of intention to bombard. Made all plans to bombard before moonset on morning of September 30.

September 28
1530 Comsubspac negated bombardment.

October 1
Exchanged calls with *Ronquil*.

October 5
Arrived Majuro Atoll.

(C) WEATHER

Typical late summer weather for this area. Water calm with slight ripples, no white caps. Typhoons were below average for this season. Atmosphere was hot and humid. Rain below average expected.

(D) TIDAL INFORMATION

Tide tables and pilots were not worth bothering with. Tides and currents were unpredictable. The Japan Stream moved sluggishly and we could always make headway at 2 knots.

(E) NAVIGATIONAL AIDS

Possible dimmed navigational lights on Caran Bi, Formosa.

(F) SHIP CONTACTS

No	Time Date	Lat. Long.	Type(s)	Initial Range	Est. C/S	How Contacted	Remarks
1	16 Aug 1905	22-01 N. 140-36 E.	US S/M	3,500	90°T 13.6	R	Probably USS *Puffer* with no radar.
2	23 Aug 2216	20-35 N. 121-55 E.	2 small patrol boats	6,000	070 4	R	Close to Batan Island. Avoided.
3	31 Aug 0120	21-18 N. 121-15 E.	Convoy	9 mi.	150 7	Sight	Moonlight. Smoke sighted.
4	4 Sept 0458	20-57 N. 119-38 E	Sampan	5 mi.	L.	Sight	Sunk. (Gun Attack No. 1)
5	9 Sept 0119	19-53 N. 120-57 E.	Convoy	11,000	135 8	R	Attack # 3.
6	14 Sept 0003	21-62 [*sic*] 121-12 E.	Two *Chidoris*	8,950	150 13	R	Attack # 4 & 5
7	16 Sept 2152	18-59 N. 116-18	Convoy	30,000	040 12	R	Attack # 6 & 7

(G) AIRCRAFT CONTACTS

	Contact Number	1	2	3	4	5	6	7
S U B M A R I N E	Date	Aug 21	Aug 21	Aug 23	Aug 23	Aug 27	Aug 27	Aug 28
	Time (Zone)	(I) 1214	(I) 1228	(H) 0523	(H) 1340	(H) 0319	(H) 1505	(H) 1601
	Position: Lat. N. Long. E.	21-05 132-25	21-05 132-23	20-46 125-02	20-33 122-52	19-22 116-20	19-20 117-18	19-00 118-56
	Speed	11	11	11	11	8	8	8
	Course	263	263	270	270	240	150°T	260
	Trim	Surf	Surf	Surf	Surf	Surf	Surf	Surf
	Minutes since last SD radar search.	1 min.	1½ min.	not used	not used	not used	6½ hrs.	not used
A I R C R A F T	Number	1	1	1	4	1	1	1
	Type	Unk.	Unk.	Unk.	Unk.	Mavis	Unk.	Unk.
	Probable Miss.	Unk.	Unk.	Unk.	Unk.	Unk.	Unk.	Unk.
	How Contacted	HiPer sight	Sight	Peris sight	Sight	Sight	Sight	Peris sight
	Initial Range	10 mi.	8 mi.	7 mi.	11 mi.	7 mi.	11 mi.	12 mi.
	Elevation Angle	5°	1½°	3°	3°	1°	1°	½°
	Range & relative bearing of plane when it detected S/M	ND	ND	ND	ND	ND	ND	ND
C O N D I T I O N S	Sea: (State (Beaufort)	2	2	1	0	0	2	0
	(Direction (rel)	160	160	090	—	—	340	—
	Visibility (Miles)	30	30	30	50	50	30	30
	Clouds: (Height in Ft.	6,000	6,000	5,000	5,000	5,000	2,000	2,000
	(Percent Overcast	40%	40%	10%	10%	40%	50%	30%
	Moon: (Bearing (rel) (Angle (Percent Illum.	— — —						
	Type of S/M Camouflage on this patrol: Light Gray.							

U.S.S. *Barb* (SS-220)

	Contact Number	8	9	10	11	12	13	14
S U B M A R I N E	Date	29 Aug	30 Aug	31 Aug	31 Aug	31 Aug	31 Aug	31 Aug
	Time (Zone)	(H) 1617	(H) 1330	(H) 0143	(H) 0229	(H) 0242	(H) 0305	(H) 0352
	Position: Lat. N. Long. E.	19-07 118-56	19-32 119-11	21-18 121-15	21-20 121-08	21-19 121-16	21-18 121-09	21-17 121-14
	Speed	8	15	5	2	5	15	15
	Course	180	049	160	160	160	090	070
	Trim	Surf	Surf	Surf	Surf	Surf Lt. T.	Surf	Surf
	Minutes since last SD radar search.	Not used	Not used	Not used	Not used	2 min.	25 min.	22 min.
A I R C R A F T	Number	1	1	1	1	1	1	1
	Type	Unk.	Unk.	Unk.	Unk.	Unk.	Unk.	Unk.
	Probable Miss.	Unk.	P	Unk.	Esc.	Unk.	Unk.	Unk.
	How Contacted	Sight	Sight	SJ radar	Per	Sight	SJ radar	SJ radar
	Initial Range	10 mi.	10 mi.	6 mi.	5 mi.	6 mi.	8,650 yd.	7,700 yd
	Elevation Angle	1°	4°	—	1°	1°	Unk.	Unk.
	Range & relative bearing of plane when it detected S/M	ND	ND	ND	ND	ND	ND	ND
C O N D I T I O N S	(State (Beaufort) Sea:(	2	2	1	1	1	1	1
	(Direction (rel)	350	080	025	225	225	295	315
	Visibility (Miles)	50	30	10	3	3	4	10
	(Height in Clouds: (Ft.	3,000	2,500	3,000	3,000	3,000	3,000	3,000
	(Percent Overcast	50%	70%	20%	40%	40%	20%	10%
	(Bearing (rel)	—	—	310	Set	Set	Set	Set
	Moon: (Angle	—	—	15 deg.	—	—	—	—
	(Percent Illum.	—	—	35	—	—	—	—
Type of S/M Camouflage on this patrol: Light Gray.								

Contact Number		15	16	17	18	19	20	21
S U B M A R I N E	Date	31 Aug	31 Aug	31 Aug	31 Aug	31 Aug	31 Aug	31 Aug
	Time (Zone)	(H) 0421	(H) 0506	(H) 0536	(H) 0735	(H) 0820	(H) 0900	(H) 1300
	Position: Lat. N. Long. E.	21-17 121-20	21-17 121-29	21-15 121-27	21-12 121-23	21-11 121-23	21-11 121-19	21-11 121-19
	Speed	18	18	2	4	2	2	2
	Course	080	270	225	220	264	264	240
	Trim	Surf	Surf	Per	Per	Per	Per	Per
	Minutes since last SD radar search.	Not used	Not used	Not used	Not used	Not used	Not used	Not used
A I R C R A F T	Number	1	1	3	8	1	1	2
	Type	Unk.	Unk.	Unk.	Unk.	Mavis	Nell	Unk.
	Probable Miss.	Unk.	Unk.	Esc.	Esc.	Esc.	Esc.	Pat.
	How Contacted	SJ radar	Sight	Sight	Sight	Sight	Sight	Sight
	Initial Range	9,000 yd	4 mi.	5 mi.	3 mi.	10 mi.	8 mi.	8 mi.
	Elevation Angle	Unk.	2°	1°	1°	1°	1°	1°
	Range & relative bearing of plane when it detected S/M	ND	ND	ND	ND	ND	ND	ND
C O N D I T I O N S	Sea: (State (Beaufort)	1	1	1	1	1	1	1
	(Direction (rel)	305	115	160	165	121	121	121
	Visibility (Miles)	10	15	30	40	50	50	50
	Clouds: (Height in Ft.	3,000	3,000	2,500	2,000	2,000	2,000	2,000
	(Percent Overcast	30%	20%	10%	10%	10%	10%	10%
	Moon: (Bearing (rel)	Set	Set	—	—	—	—	—
	(Angle	—	—	—	—	—	—	—
	(Percent Illum.	—	—	—	—	—	—	—
Type of S/M Camouflage on this patrol: Light Gray.								

U.S.S. *Barb* (SS-220)

	Contact Number	22	23	24	25	26	27	28
S U B M A R I N E	Date	31 Aug	1 Sept	1 Sept	1 Sept	1 Sept	1 Sept	1 Sept
	Time (Zone) "H"	2032	0549	0715	0800	1010	1312	1407
	Position: Lat. N. Long. E.	21-10 120-56	21-30 118-49	21-30 118-38	21-30 118-40	21-29 118-54	21-28 118-48	21-30 118-57
	Speed	16	15	10	8	8	8	8
	Course	180	279	279	092	090	092	092
	Trim	Surf	Surf	Surf	Surf	Surf	Surf	Surf
	Minutes since last SD radar search.	0	Not used	44 min.	10 min.	Not used	Not used	Not used
A I R C R A F T	Number	1	1	1	1	1	1	1
	Type	Unk.	Unk.	Unk.	Unk.	Unk.	Unk.	Unk.
	Probable Miss.	Pat	Pat	Pat	Pat	Pat	Pat	Pat
	How Contacted	SJ radar	Sight	Sight	Sight	Sight	Sight	Sight
	Initial Range	10 mi.	12 mi.	8 mi.	8 mi.	10 mi.	8 mi.	8 mi.
	Elevation Angle	Unk	1°	2°	1°	½°	1°	1°
	Range & relative bearing of plane when it detected S/M	ND	ND	ND	ND	ND	ND	ND
C O N D I T I O N S	Sea: (State (Beaufort)	1	1	1	1	1	1	1
	(Direction (rel)	205	101	101	238	290	292	290
	Visibility (Miles)	10	40	40	40	40	40	40
	Clouds: (Height in Ft.	2,500	2,500	2,000	2,000	2,000	2,000	2,000
	(Percent Overcast	10%	40%	40%	40%	30%	40%	40%
	(Bearing (rel)	270	—	—	—	—	—	—
	Moon: (Angle	30	—	—	—	—	—	—
	(Percent Illum.	95	—	—	—	—	—	—
Type of S/M Camouflage on this patrol: Light Gray.							

Contact Number		29	30	31	32	33	34	35
S U B M A R I N E	Date	1 Sept	1 Sept	1 Sept	1 Sept	2 Sept	2 Sept	2 Sept
	Time (Zone) "H"	1459	1527	1854	1848	0002	1929	2314
	Position: Lat. N. Long. E.	21-29 119-06	21-28 119-02	21-30 119-20	20-36 119-25	20-31 119-07	21-11 118-42	20-56 118-54
	Speed	8	8	8	8	10	8	8
	Course	090	080	080	300	265	130	130
	Trim	Surf	Surf	Surf	Surf	Surf	Surf	Surf
	Minutes since last SD radar search.	Not used	Not used	Not used	Not used	Not used	Not used	Not used
A I R C R A F T	Number	1	1	1	1	1	1	1
	Type	Unk.	Mavis	Unk.	Unk.	Unk.	Unk.	Unk.
	Probable Miss.	Pat	Pat	Pat	Pat	Pat	Pat	Pat
	How Contacted	Sight	SJ	Sight	Sight	Heard Sight	SJ radar	Sight
	Initial Range	15 mi.	14 mi.	16 mi.	6 mi.	2 mi.	5,200 yd	6,500 yd
	Elevation Angle	1°	1°	1°	½°	½°	Unk.	2°
	Range & relative bearing of plane when it detected S/M	ND	ND	ND	ND	180 1 mi.	ND	295 6,500 yd
C O N D I T I O N S	Sea: (State (Beaufort)	1	1	1	1	1	1	1
	(Direction (rel)	290	280	280	080	125	100	310
	Visibility (Miles)	40	40	40	20	10	10	10
	Clouds: (Height in Ft.	2,000	2,000	2,000	2,000	2,000	2,000	2,000
	(Percent Overcast	40%	40%	40%	40%	40%	40%	40%
	(Bearing (rel)	—	—	—	—	85	315	040
	Moon: (Angle	—	—	—	—	70	22	70
	(Percent Illum.	—	—	—	—	100	95	95
Type of S/M Camouflage on this patrol: Light Gray.								

U.S.S. *Barb* (SS-220) 211

	Contact Number	36	37	38	39	40	41	42
S U B M A R I N E	Date	3 Sept	3 Sept	3 Sept	3 Sept	4 Sept	4 Sept	4 Sept
	Time (Zone) "H"	0512	0811	1215	2134	0911	1229	1608
	Position: Lat. N. Long. E.	20-42 118-27	20-38 118-30	20-44 118-41	21-03 116-41	20-50 119-37	21-21 120-04	21-20 120-20
	Speed	8	8	8	8	10	15	18
	Course	130	130	310	100	Var	090	070
	Trim	Surf	Surf	Surf	Surf	Surf	Surf	Surf
	Minutes since last SD radar search.	Not used	Not used	Not used	Not used	Not used	Not used	Not used
A I R C R A F T	Number	1	1	1	1	1	1	1
	Type	Unk.	Unk.	Mavis	Unk.	Nell	Nell	Unk.
	Probable Miss.	Pat	Pat	Pat	Pat	Pat	Pat	Unk.
	How Contacted	Sight	Sight	Sight	Sight	Sight	Sight	Sight
	Initial Range	5 mi.	8 mi.	14 mi.	4 mi.	7 mi.	2 mi.	8 mi.
	Elevation Angle	1°	1°	1½°	1°	4°	1°	45°
	Range & relative bearing of plane when it detected S/M	ND	ND	ND	ND	150 5 mi.	180 2 mi.	ND
C O N D I T I O N S	Sea: (State (Beaufort)	1	1	1	1	1	1	1
	(Direction (rel)	300	300	140	330	Var	350	010
	Visibility (Miles)	10	40	40	10	40	40	40
	Clouds: (Height in Ft.	2,500	2,000	2,000	2,000	2,000	2,000	2,000
	(Percent Overcast	90%	60%	40%	40%	40%	40%	40%
	Moon: (Bearing (rel)	270	—	—	090	—	—	—
	(Angle	5	—	—	30	—	—	—
	(Percent Illum.	95	—	—	90	—	—	—
Type of S/M Camouflage on this patrol: Light Gray.								

	Contact Number	43	44	45	46	47	48	49
S U B M A R I N E	Date	4 Sept	6 Sept	9 Sept	9 Sept	9 Sept	9 Sept	9 Sept
	Time (Zone) "H"	1735	1314	0130	0909	0957	1017	1024
	Position: Lat. N. Long. E.	21-18 120-21	22-38 122-28	19-52 120-56	19-49 120-47	19-50 120-47	19-51 120-46	19-53 120-46
	Speed	15	8	18	2	2	2	2
	Course	090	260	150	300	300	300	300
	Trim	Surf	Surf	Surf	Per	Per	Per	Per
	Minutes since last SD radar search.	Not used	Not used	Not used	Not used	Not used	Not used	Not used
A I R C R A F T	Number	1	3	1	1	3	1	1
	Type	Unk.	Unk.	Nell	Nell	Emily	Nell	Mavis
	Probable Miss.	Unk.	Unk.	Esc.	Pat	Pat	Pat	Pat
	How Contacted	Sight	Sight	Sight	Per	Per	Per	Per
	Initial Range	10 mi.	12 mi.	3 mi.	2 mi.	4 mi.	3 mi.	3 mi.
	Elevation Angle	1°	½°	1°	3°	1°	1°	1°
	Range & relative bearing of plane when it detected S/M	ND	ND	ND	ND	ND	ND	ND
C O N D I T I O N S	Sea: (State (Beaufort)	1	1	0	1	1	1	1
	(Direction (rel)	010	180	—	340	340	340	340
	Visibility (Miles)	30	50	10	40	40	40	40
	Clouds: (Height in Ft.	2,000	2,000	1,600	2,000	2,000	2,000	2,000
	(Percent Overcast	40%	40%	10%	20%	20%	20%	20%
	(Bearing (rel)	—	—	140	—	—	—	—
	Moon: (Angle	—	—	45	—	—	—	—
	(Percent Illum.	—	—	80%	—	—	—	—
Type of S/M Camouflage on this patrol: Light Gray.							

	Contact Number	50	51	52	53	54	55	56
S U B M A R I N E	Date – Sept.	9	9	9	9	10	11	11
	Time (Zone) "H"	1125	1430	1450	1618	1311	0525	0530
	Position: Lat. N. Long. E.	19-58 120-44	20-01 120-32	20-00 120-32	19-47 120-33	19-44 120-32	21-07 120-27	21-07 120-26
	Speed	16	15	5	15	15	15	15
	Course	270	225	212	212	315	255	255
	Trim	Surf	Surf	Surf. Lt.	Surf	Surf	Surf	Surf
	Minutes since last SD radar search.	Not used	Not used	Not used	Not used	Not used	Not used	Not used
A I R C R A F T	Number	1	1	1	1	10	1	3
	Type	Emily	Betty	Rufe	Nell	Betty	Unk.	Nell
	Probable Miss.	Pat	Pat	Pat	Pat	Unk.	Unk.	Unk.
	How Contacted	Sight	Sight	Sight	Sight	Sight	Sight	Sight
	Initial Range	11 mi.	11 mi.	9 mi.	6 mi.	13 mi.	13 mi.	10 mi.
	Elevation Angle	1½°	4°	2°	4°	4°	2°	1½°
	Range & relative bearing of plane when it detected S/M	180 9 mi.	ND	ND	160 6 mi.	ND	ND	ND
C O N D I T I O N S	Sea: (State (Beaufort)	1	1	1	1	3	3	3
	(Direction (rel)	010	055	068	068	135	215	215
	Visibility (Miles)	40	40	40	40	40	50	50
	Clouds: (Height in Ft.	2,000	2,000	2,000	2,000	2,000	2,000	2,000
	(Percent Overcast	30%	30%	40%	40%	10%	10%	10%
	(Bearing (rel)	—	—	—	—	—	—	—
	Moon: (Angle	—	—	—	—	—	—	—
	(Percent Illum.	—	—	—	—	—	—	—
Type of S/M Camouflage on this patrol: Light Gray.								

Contact Number		57	58	59	60	61	62	63
S U B M A R I N E	Date – Sept	11	11	11	11	11	12	13
	Time (Zone) "H"	0601	0625	1048	1240	1414	1559	0541
	Position: Lat. N. Long. E.	21-07 120-25	21-07 120-24	20-51 119-25	20-47 119-13	20-53 119-03	19-44 116-00	20-07 117-39
	Speed	5	15	15	15	15	10	15
	Course	255	255	255	255	255	107	074
	Trim	Surf. Lt.	Surf	Surf	Surf	Surf	Surf	Surf
	Minutes since last SD radar search.	Not used	Not used	Not used	30 sec.	1 min.	Not used	Not used
A I R C R A F T	Number	2	1	1	1	1	1	1
	Type	Nell	Unk.	Unk.	Unk.	Rufe	Mavis	Mavis
	Probable Miss.	Unk.	Unk.	Unk.	Unk.	Unk.	Unk.	Unk.
	How Contacted	Sight	Sight	Sight	Sight	Sight	Sight	Sight
	Initial Range	8 mi.	10 mi.	9 mi.	8 mi.	9 mi.	8 mi.	6 mi.
	Elevation Angle	1½°	½°	2½°	1½°	2°	1°	½°
	Range & relative bearing of plane when it detected S/M	ND	ND	ND	ND	ND	ND	ND
C O N D I T I O N S	Sea: (State (Beaufort)	3	3	3	3	3	3	1
	(Direction (rel)	215	215	215	215	215	310	0
	Visibility (Miles)	50	50	50	50	50	20	15
	Clouds: (Height in Ft.	2,000	2,000	2,000	2,000	2,000	2,000	3,000
	(Percent Overcast	10%	10%	20%	40%	50%	60%	15%
	(Bearing (rel)	10	10	20	40	50	60	15
	Moon: (Angle	—	—	—	—	—	—	—
	(Percent Illum.	—	—	—	—	—	—	—
Type of S/M Camouflage on this patrol: Light Gray.								

Contact Number		64	65	66	67	68	69	70
S U B M A R I N E	Date – Sept	13	13	13	13	14	15	16
	Time (Zone) "H"	0817	0855	1028	1848	0652	0759	1234
	Position: Lat. N. Long. E.	20-17 118-08	20-18 118-10	20-26 118-29	20-45 119-51	20-53 121-12	20-49 122-03	19-31 119-25
	Speed	15	15	15	15	2	2	18
	Course	074	074	074	079	210	160	255
	Trim	Surf	Surf	Surf	Surf	Subm	Subm	Surf
	Minutes since last SD radar search.	Not used	Not used	Not used	Not used	Not used	Not used	Not used
A I R C R A F T	Number	1	1	1	1	1	1	1
	Type	Mavis	Mavis	Mavis	Nell	Mavis	Unk.	Mavis
	Probable Miss.	Unk.	Unk.	Unk.	Unk.	Anti-sub	Unk.	Unk.
	How Contacted	Sight	Sight	Sight	Sight	Per	Per	Sight
	Initial Range	8 mi.	15 mi.	8 mi.	8 mi.	4 mi.	5 mi.	12 mi.
	Elevation Angle	1°	1°	1½°	5°	2°	5°	1°
	Range & relative bearing of plane when it detected S/M	ND	ND	ND	ND	ND	ND	ND
C O N D I T I O N S	Sea: (State (Beaufort)	1	2	2	2	0	1	0
	(Direction (rel)	0	0	0	350	300	130	—
	Visibility (Miles)	30	40	50	50	25	30	25
	Clouds: (Height in Ft.	1,800	2,000	2,000	2,000	3,000	3,500	3,000
	(Percent Overcast	20%	10%	15%	20%	30%	20%	10%
	(Bearing (rel)	—	—	—	—	—	—	—
	Moon: (Angle	—	—	—	—	—	—	—
	(Percent Illum.	—	—	—	—	—	—	—
Type of S/M Camouflage on this patrol: Light Gray.								

Contact Number		71	72	73				
S U B M A R I N E	Date – Sept	23	28	28				
	Time (Zone)	1230	0909	1230				
	Position: Lat. N. Long. E.	16-27 154-35	18-59.5 156-05	19-06.2 156-34				
	Speed	18	14	15				
	Course	115	075	076				
	Trim	Surf	Surf	Surf				
	Minutes since last SD radar search.	Not used	Continuous	Continuous				
A I R C R A F T	Number	1	1	1				
	Type	Mavis	Unk.	Unk.				
	Probable Miss.	Unk.	Unk.	Unk.				
	How Contacted	Sight	SD Sight	Sight				
	Initial Range	7 mi.	13½ mi.	9 mi.				
	Elevation Angle	20°	20½°	3°				
	Range & relative bearing of plane when it detected S/M	ND	ND	ND				
C O N D I T I O N S	Sea: (State (Beaufort)	1	1	1				
	(Direction (rel)	0	076	076				
	Visibility (Miles)	50	30	30				
	Clouds: (Height in Ft.	1,600	1,500	1,500				
	(Percent Overcast	15%	45%	60%				
	Moon: (Bearing (rel)	—	—	—				
	(Angle	—	—	—				
	(Percent Illum.	—	—	—				
Type of S/M Camouflage on this patrol: Light Gray.								

(H) ATTACK DATA

U.S.S. *Barb* (SS-220) Gun Attack No. One Patrol No. 9
Time: 0903 Date: 9-4-44 Lat. 21-05 N. Long. 119-34 E

<u>Target Data – Damage Inflicted</u>

Sunk – One Sampan (50 tons) – 6 Japs

Damage Determined by: Six 4" 50 Cal. gun hits, numerous automatic weapon hits. Target observed to sink.

Details of Action

Battle surfaced at 1,000 yards range and opened fire with automatic weapons, observed hits from 20 MM and .50 cal guns. The 40 MM gun jammed after three rounds and prevented effective use of this weapon. Forced to dive by plane. Battle surfaced a second time and opened fire with 4" gun. Fired ten rounds for six hits at an opening range of 1,200 yards closing. Target was demolished and seen to sink.

U.S.S. *Barb*   Torpedo Attack No. 1   Patrol No. 9

Time: 0854   Date: 31 August 1944   Lat. 21-04.00 N., Long. 121-22.00 E.

Target Data – Damage Inflicted

Description: Large AK(EU) in convoy of 8 ships and unknown number of escorts—at least one *Chidori* escort. Convoy of 4 AK and 4 AO. Unable to identify ship from manual, MFM—composite superstructure—brand new. Visibility—excellent. Daytime contact by sight.

Ship Sunk;   Large AK(EU)

Ship Damaged: Medium AO(EU) in ballast.

Damage Determined by: Two hits timed and observed in AK by CO. Target seen to sink by CO, ComWolfPack and other conning tower personnel. One hit timed in AO, which overlapped AK. Unable to identify AO.

Target Draft: 15   Course: 110   Speed: 9   Range: 1,000 (at firing)

Own Ship Data

Speed: 2   Course: 192   Depth: 66   Angle: 0 (at firing)

Fire Control and Torpedo Data

Type Attack: Day submerged – periscope.

Tubes Fired – No.	No. 7	No. 8	No. 9
Track Angle	97½° S	100½° S	107½° S
Gyro Angle	15.5 R	18.25 R	25.5 R
Depth Set	6	6	6
Power	—	—	—
Hit or Miss	Hit	Hit	Hit
Erratic (Yes or No)	No	No	No
Mark Torpedo	18-1	18-1	18-1
Serial No.	55106	54964	55446
Mark Exploder	8-5	8-5	8-5
Serial No.	8063W	9085W	9387W
Actuation Set	Contact	Contact	Contact
Actuation Actual	Contact	Contact	Contact
Mark Warhead	18-2	18-2	18-2
Serial Number	1985	2424	2685
Explosive	TPX	TPX	TPX
Firing Interval	0	10 Sec.	10 Sec.
Type Spread	Divergent	Divergent	Divergent
Sea Conditions	1	1	1

Overhaul Activity: Mark 18 Shop, Pearl Harbor

Remarks: Spread computed for 50 yards between torpedoes along target. Target was in ballast.

U.S.S. *Barb*   Torpedo Attack No. 2   Patrol No. 9

Time: 1758   Date: 31 August 1944   Lat. 21-04.00 N., Long. 121-08.00 E.

Target Data – Damage Inflicted

Description: Small AK(EU), single ship with 2 subchaser escorts, believed to have scattered from original convoy of attack #1. Smoke contact—air cover. Visibility excellent.

Ship Sunk: Small AK(EU) – unable to identify from manual – MFM – 3 island – split superstructure.

Damage Determined by: Two hits observed by CO, three hits heard. Target observed to break in half and sink, by CO and other conning tower personnel.

Target Draft: 13   Course: 252   Speed: 9   Range: 1,300 (at firing)

Own Ship Data

Speed: 3   Course: 190   Depth: 65   Angle: 1° down (at firing)

Fire Control and Torpedo Data

Type Attack: Day submerged – periscope.

Tubes Fired – No.	No. 4	No. 5	No. 6
Track Angle	136 S	137 S	138 S
Gyro Angle	18 R	19 R	20 R
Depth Set	4	4	4
Power	—	—	—
Hit or Miss	Hit	Hit	Hit
Erratic (Yes or No)	No	No	No
Mark Torpedo	18-1	18-1	18-1
Serial No.	54982	54463	65891
Mark Exploder	8-5	8-5	8-5
Serial No.	—	—	—
Actuation Set	Contact	Contact	Contact
Actuation Actual	Contact	Contact	Contact
Mark Warhead	18-2	18-2	18-2
Serial Number	—	—	—
Explosive	TPX	TPX	TPX
Firing Interval	0	10 Sec.	10 Sec.
Type Spread	Divergent	Divergent	Divergent
Sea Conditions	1	1	1

Overhaul Activity: Mark 18 Shop, Sub Base, Pearl Harbor

Remarks: Spread computed for 30 yards between torpedoes along target.

U.S.S. *Barb*   Torpedo Attack No. 3   Patrol No. 9

Time: 0445   Date: 9 September 1944   Lat. 19-44 N., Long. 120-57 E.

Target Data – Damage Inflicted

Description: Escort vessel (UN). Contact by radar. Visibility fair.
Ship Sunk: None
Ship Damaged: None
Target Draft: 6' (E)   Course: 109½°   Speed: 9.5   Range: 3,000 (at firing)

Own Ship Data

Speed: 4   Course: 165.5   Depth: 63   Angle: 0 (at firing)

Fire Control and Torpedo Data

Type Attack: Night submerged – radar and periscope.

Tubes Fired – No.	No. 1	No. 3	No. 2
Track Angle	134	135	137
Gyro Angle	359	358	356
Depth Set	4	4	4
Power	—	—	—
Hit or Miss	Miss	Miss	Miss – Circular run.
Erratic (Yes or No)	No	No	Circular run.
Mark Torpedo	18-1	18-1	18-1
Serial No.	54462	54913	55013
Mark Exploder	8-5	8-5	8-5
Serial No.	—	—	—
Actuation Set	Contact	Contact	Contact
Actuation Actual	—	—	—
Mark Warhead	18-2	18-2	18-2
Serial Number	—	—	—
Explosive	TPX	TPX	TPX
Firing Interval	10 Sec.	10 Sec.	10 Sec.
Type Spread	Divergent	Divergent	Divergent
Sea Conditions	1	1	1

Overhaul Activity: Mark 18 Shop, Sub Base, Pearl Harbor

Remarks: Spread computed for for 50 yards between torpedoes along target. One torpedo was heard to make a circular run, cause undetermined. Reason for missing not known, but range now considered excessive.

U.S.S. *Barb*   Torpedo Attack No. 4   Patrol No. 9

Time: 0138   Date: 14 September 1944   Lat. 20-56 N., Long. 121-13 E.

Target Data – Damage Inflicted

Description: *Chidori* Class TB. One of hunter-killer group of 2 TB's. Contact – radar. Visibility – poor. Same group sighted following day.
Ship Sunk: None
Ship Damaged: None
Target Draft: 6'9"   Course: 150°   Speed: 13.5   Range: 2,100 (at firing)

Own Ship Data

Speed: 14.5   Course: 110   Depth: Surface   Angle: — (at firing)

Fire Control and Torpedo Data

Type Attack: Night surface – radar and TBT.

Tubes Fired – No.	No. 4	No. 5	No. 6
Track Angle	66.5	65.5	69.5
Gyro Angle	156.5	154.5	150.5
Depth Set	3	3	3
Power	—	—	—
Hit or Miss	Miss	Miss	Miss
Erratic (Yes or No)	No	No	No
Mark Torpedo	18-1	18-1	18-1
Serial No.	54918	55449	54358
Mark Exploder	8-5	8-5	8-5
Serial No.	8869W	9398W	—
Actuation Set	Contact	Contact	Contact
Actuation Actual	—	—	—
Mark Warhead	18-2	18-2	18-2
Serial Number	1912	2015	2850
Explosive	TPX	TPX	TPX
Firing Interval	10 Sec.	10 Sec.	10 Sec.
Type Spread	Divergent	Divergent	Divergent
Sea Conditions	1	1	1

Overhaul Activity: Mark 18 Shop, Sub Base, Pearl Harbor

Remarks: Spread computed for 50 yards between torpedoes along target. Reason for missing not known. Target did not change course until after torpedoes had crossed.

U.S.S. *Barb*   Torpedo Attack No. 5   Patrol No. 9

Time: 0400   Date: 14 September 1944   Lat. 20-56 N., Long. 121-14 E.

Target Data – Damage Inflicted

Description: *Chidori* Class TB. Same ship as Attack No. 4.
Ship Sunk: None
Ship Damaged: None
Target Draft: 6'9"   Course: 002   Speed: 13½   Range: 1,500 (at firing)

Own Ship Data

Speed: 4   Course: 068   Depth: 45   Angle: 0 (at firing)

Fire Control and Torpedo Data

Type Attack: Day submerged – periscope.

Tubes Fired – No.	No. 1	No. 2	No. 3
Track Angle	143	145	327
Gyro Angle	331	329	327
Depth Set	3	3	3
Power	—	—	—
Hit or Miss	Miss	Miss	Miss
Erratic (Yes or No)	No	No	No
Mark Torpedo	18-1	18-1	18-1
Serial No.	55010	54513	35513
Mark Exploder	8-5	8-5	8-5
Serial No.	8121	8887	8850
Actuation Set	Contact	Contact	Contact
Actuation Actual	—	—	—
Mark Warhead	18-2	18-2	18-2
Serial Number	2173	1029	2003
Explosive	TPX	TPX	TPX
Firing Interval	10 Sec.	10 Sec.	10 Sec.
Type Spread	Divergent	Divergent	Divergent
Sea Conditions	1	1	1

Overhaul Activity: Mark 18 Shop, Sub Base, Pearl Harbor

Remarks: Spread computed for 50 yards between torpedoes along target. Reason for missing – target heard torpedoes and turned sharply towards as third torpedo was fired.

U.S.S. *Barb*   Torpedo Attack No. 6   Patrol No. 9

Time: 2332   Date: 16 September 1944   Lat. 19-18.5 N., Long. 116-26 E.

Target Data – Damage Inflicted

Description: Large AO (*Itukusima* Class) (EC) MKMFK type. In convoy of 1 CVE and 4 AO's, 1-DD, 5 escorts. Contact – Radar. Visibility – Fair. Closest range 1,300 yards.

Ship Sunk: Large AO (*Itukusima* Class) (EC) – 10,020 tons

Damage Determined by: Two timed hits heard – breaking up noises heard – ship seen to explode and sink by *Queenfish*. Time of sinking – 2356.

Target Draft: 30' (E)   Course: 010   Speed: 11.8   Range: 1,820 (at firing)

Own Ship Data

Speed: 11.2   Course: 305   Depth: Surface   Angle: 0 (at firing)

Fire Control and Torpedo Data

Type Attack: Night surface – radar. Submerged upon completion of attack because we could not clear *Chidori*, 750 yards away.

Tubes Fired – No.	No. 4	No. 5	No. 6
Track Angle	109	113.8	004
Gyro Angle	354	358.5	004
Depth Set	6	6	6
Power	—	—	—
Hit or Miss	Miss	Hit	Hit
Erratic (Yes or No)	Broached badly.	No	No
Mark Torpedo	18-1	18-1	18-1
Serial No.	55019	54574	54888
Mark Exploder	8-5	8-5	8-5
Serial No.	—	—	—
Actuation Set	Contact	Contact	Contact
Actuation Actual	—	Contact	Contact
Mark Warhead	18-2	18-2	18-2
Serial Number	—	—	—
Explosive	TPX	TPX	TPX
Firing Interval	—	10 Sec.	10 Sec.
Type Spread	Divergent	Divergent	Divergent
Sea Conditions	2	2	2

Overhaul Activity: Mark 18 Shop, Sub Base, Pearl Harbor

Remarks: Spread computed for 50 yards between torpedoes along target.

U.S.S. *Barb*   Torpedo Attack No. 7   Patrol No. 9

Time: 2332   Date: 16 September 1944   Lat. 19-18.5 N., Long. 116-26 E.

Target Data – Damage Inflicted

Description: *Otaka* Class CVE (EC) from same convoy as attack No. 6. Australian and British survivors we picked up on special mission stated that they saw a converted merchantman carrier with a tanker convoy enter Singapore on 6 Sept 1944, while they were leaving. This carrier was noticed particularly because it had no funnels or superstructure above the flight deck. We believe this to be the the same convoy. OOD of *Queenfish* noticed carrier in convoy after their attack. Contact – radar at over 30,000 yards. Visibility – fair, closest range – 1,500 yards. Distinctive silhouette, as compared to other carriers.

Ship Sunk: *Otaka* Class CVE (EC), – 22,500 tons.

Damage Determined by: Three timed hits – breaking up noises heard 2337–2345. Two escorts picking up survivors when we surfaced to proceed on special mission.

Target Draft: 20' (E)   Course: 010   Speed: 11.8   Range: 2,120 (at firing)

Own Ship Data

Speed: 11.2   Course: 305   Depth: Surface   Angle: 0 (at firing)

Fire Control and Torpedo Data

Type Attack: Day submerged – periscope.

Tubes Fired – No.	No. 1	No. 2	No. 3
Track Angle	121	122	125
Gyro Angle	006	007	010
Depth Set	6	6	6
Power	—	—	—
Hit or Miss	Hit	Hit	Hit
Erratic (Yes or No)	No	No	No
Mark Torpedo	18-1	18-1	18-1
Serial No.	56179	66172	54944
Mark Exploder	8-5	8-5	8-5
Serial No.	9215	9541	9211
Actuation Set	Contact	Contact	Contact
Actuation Actual	Contact	Contact	Contact
Mark Warhead	18-2	18-2	18-2
Serial Number	1888	2006	2462
Explosive	TPX	TPX	TPX
Firing Interval	10 Sec.	10 Sec.	10 Sec.
Type Spread	Divergent	Divergent	Divergent
Sea Conditions	2	2	2

Overhaul Activity: Mark 18 Shop, Sub Base, Pearl Harbor

Remarks: Spread computed for 50 yards between torpedoes along target.

Mark 18-1 Torpedoes

No difficulty or serious inconvenience was experienced in charging and routining the full load of Mk. 18-1 torpedoes carried. A three day charging schedule was carried out in each room. Torpedoes were charged and routined, partially withdrawn from the tubes and secured by a securing device of *Barb* design. It consists of a hinged clamp ring, with canvas covering, and fitted with a bolt and butterfly nut for rapid installation or removal from the torpedo. A one half inch square steel rod is welded to the clamp ring at one end and secured to a tube door pad-eye, by means of a fork and locking bolt, at the other. This device can be installed or removed in one or two minutes and when not in use can be stowed out of the way. This device was in use, and held securely during numerous unexpected dives and bombings by aircraft.

No grounds or dead cells were encountered. It was not necessary to water batteries during the patrol, though one torpedo, fired on Sept. 16, would have required watering within a few days.

One torpedo fired from #2 tube, depth 63 feet, depth set 5 feet, gyro angle 356°, made a circular run. Rudder was free and of normal throw when last routined prior to firing.

One torpedo broached badly when fired from Tube #4 during surface attack with own speed 11.5 knots. Depth set 8 feet. All other torpedoes ran hot straight and normal.

40MM

It is recommended that the following alterations be made to the wet type 40MM gun installed on this vessel. Replace all steel axis pins in foot firing mechanism and linkage with CRS pins. Install a lubrication fitting to insure proper lubrication of the fire control rod passing through the automatic loader housing. At present there is no provision for lubrication of this part.

(I) MINES

Floating mine was encountered at Lat. 25-56.3 N., Long. 171-31.0 E. Mine was gunned with 20mm and .50 Cal. Several holes, creases and dents were obtained by a dozen or more hits. Mine did not sink.

(J) ANTI-SUBMARINE MEASURES AND EVASION TACTICS

Anti submarine measures were a bit terrific. Briefly these consisted of 75 enemy plane contacts, 5 bombings, 141 depth charges labeled *Barb*, 2-300 assorted depth charges and bombs aimed at submarines in general, gunfire from a *Chidori*, which illuminated us, and torpedoes from the *Chidori* or possibly the

Redfish. Some of *Sealion*'s torpedoes passed close aboard, but only required lowering of the periscope as a safety measure until torpedoes had passed by.

Air cover for convoys is heavy, never less that two planes and as high as eight or even more. The three convoys we encountered were at night. On two of these, the night flier evidently was called for after the *Queenfish* attack, for he came sweeping in and made his radar contact while we were inside the screens about a minute before we fired. We expected him to bomb, but evidently he didn't make sight contact.

Day air patrol was heavy throughout 11-Detroit, was encountered along the Manila-Hong Kong route and the Takao–Singapore route in 11-Destroy and was heavy on Formosa–Philippine routes in 11-Delete. The could generally be avoided by the customary up and down tactics of a submarine. We were caught with our pants down once in the daytime by a high flying all silver colored (beautiful camouflage) Nell, which dove on us out of the sun and bombed. The other two daytime bombings occurred because we were a bit over ambitious in chasing a convoy which had thumbed its nose at us. Several planes had forced us down, then we tried to outrun one on the surface and came in second best. Later, after a couple of hours surface running, we were caught in the bombsights of a plane emerging from a plane locker and were bashed again. This plane cover for the convoy extended at least 100 miles, but the *Queenfish* had excited them.

Night air patrol was particularly heavy in 11-Detect. That was our area during the full moon phase. All used radar. Only one with convoy was encountered using 150 megacycles. All other used 310 megs. Bright moonlight nights was their specialty. We were driven down by plane and watched *Tunny* being bombed. Her position was boxed by float lights, which burned for one hour. Float lights were also laid evidently marking the course on which she submerged. Later, a brilliant green magnesium parachute flare was dropped. We were bombed shortly after midnight the same night and later at periscope depth observed our submergence position marked by float lights.

One of these bombs left bomb fragments and tail vanes on deck, and minor damage was sustained. On both of the above occasions, APR had reported sweeps on 310 megs, fading out and in, then finally a steady contact just before sighting plane. As a defensive measure, we then hooked the oscillograph to the APR for visual strength observations so we would have a relative standard of measurement for the various personnel on watch. That evening, shortly after turning on the SJ and the SD, the 310 meg sweeps commenced, terminating in a steady contact when plane was picked up on SJ at 3,200 yards, just prior to diving. No bombs, but plane circled us for 40 minutes. We then secured the SD. Our defense, developing, now consisted of the APR watch giving the bridge 4 buzzes when steady contact was observed, which was an emergency order for the OOD to pull the plug. The ship was then dived with a 15° angle holding full speed to get to 150 feet as rapidly as possible inasmuch as bombs were apparently set for 50 feet. At

70 feet, full left rudder was put on to get off track quickly. Doing this we found we reached 150 feet in 70 seconds.

Three hours after the above contact the same procedure commenced again. OOD dived boat on buzzer signal from APR (indicating steady on) and while submerging the SJ picked up plane at 6,500 yards. Bombs again. Later that night the same procedure took place, but we were not sighted or bombed.

After starting the SJ the following evening the same old stuff commenced and down we went again. By now, from a careful observation of the APR, it became obvious to us that these night fliers must have a non-directional SJ detector. Their sweeps on 310 megs strengthened and weakened as if the plane was working out and in on different bearings until he found the bearing giving him the greatest strength increase. After this period his radar sweeps became stronger and stronger until he made contact. We know he did not bomb by radar for one plane passed 100 feet overhead after having contact, undoubtedly sighted us, then bombed on a second run over us. On surfacing from the above we left the SJ secured. The remainder of the night APR received many sweeps on 310 megs, some of a strength from which the plane had previously worked in on us, but the night remained calm and serene. The night flier swept by and kept on going. We were confident we now had the solution, but we also had no SJ.

Further experimenting was in order. We tried transmitting on the SJ at 10 minute intervals and got away with it, then gradually decreased this to 5 minute intervals successfully. We then tried using the SJ continually again, but the night fliers started working in again, so we had to secure it and they lost us. Our final solution, which kept us from being forced down at night for the remainder of the patrol, was to use the SJ as long as the APR was clear. On the first indication of 310 megs we would shift the SJ to listening only for 15 or 20 minutes, then start the SJ sweeping at 5 minute intervals, and if APR signals became stronger, shut the SJ down again until APR signals weakened, then start it on 5 minute intervals. We are convinced this works.

After receiving Comsubpac's query as to whether the 310 megacycle signal was the second harmonic of 150–155 megacycle radar, we made innumerable attempts to pick up a 150–155 signal when we had the 310 signals. Our APR showed nothing and as far as it is concerned 310 megacycles is a fundamental frequency.

On the convoy we missed getting in to, because of being forced down by a night flier, we received APR signals of 162 megacycles, the full height of the oscillograph, while at radar depth with the plane visible through the periscope circling our position, but the APR would show no signal at 310 megacycles.

At dawn one morning while southwest of Takao we observed 8 Nells returning to the Baku Naval Base in groups of 1, 2, 3s. All were camouflaged with light gray paint.

After our second attack (small AK sunk) about 5 anti-submarine vessels encircled us, sometimes pinging, sometimes listening. Evasion was accomplished at 340 feet by passing under them on a steady course at 100 RPM with a few zigs thrown in. Gradient, 5 degrees.

The *Chidori* killer group encountered were extremely capable of taking care of themselves once alerted. Their sound men must have been experts. On our second surface approach we were challenged at 3,800 yards. We turned tail. At 3,950 yards he illuminated us with search light and commenced firing simultaneously. We evaded by submergence. On the follow up approach at radar depth, while he was after someone else, three torpedoes came from his direction and passed fairly close down our starboard side. These may possibly have been from the *Redfish*, for the *Queenfish* had fired across our bow a short time before. If the *Redfish* did not fire, the *Chidori* did. *Chidori* then dropped a string of charges on someone. Shortly after the charges, we fired with him on a steady course at 1,500 yards. As our third torpedo was leaving the tube he practically spun on his heel and came for us. A nice pattern of depth charges bracketed us while at 340 feet. His sidekick then joined the *Barb* party. One stayed on our beam pinging with hand keying while the other came up from astern listening. Since the dropper was passing parallel to us and a bit to port we kept our course and set at 250–300 feet. In the turbulence following we took off and lost them.

After our last attack on the surface we could not clear a *Chidori* escort 750 yards away, closing rapidly, without being sighted and rammed in the force 4 sea, so submerged, turned in a circle to the right to avoid the sinking ships and then cut across the stern of the formation. Many depth charges were dropped, all well astern.

Three lifeboats from the brand new freighter we sank on 31 August were equipped with black and yellow vertically striped sails.

(K) MAJOR DEFECTS AND DAMAGE

1. Both high pressure air compressors were damaged due to overheating. It was found that the cooling water overboard discharge valve disk had worked loose from the valve stem. Thus, the discharge pressure kept this valve closed allowing no cooling water to flow and increasing the pressure on the system. The third stage cooler of No. 1 compressor had to be replaced and the piston rings of all four stages on No. 2 compressor had to be renewed because of this fault.

2. Gyro-compass follow-up system failed due to faulty follow-up motor. A bearing had to be replaced, which had been assembled incorrectly when the gyro compass was routined during refit.

3. Pit-Log control unit suffered damage due to aircraft bomb. The rubber shaft sleeve of contactor arm lever shaft was ruptured. This caused erratic operation due to salt water in the bearings. Rubber sleeve had to be renewed and unit re-adjusted.

4. The high pressure air piping to the main engine air starting flask developed slight leaks. The leaks were probably caused by a very close aircraft bomb.

5. With the increased radar and alternating current equipment the I.C. motor-generators are continually overloaded. The I.C. motor generators, besides supplying all the regular I.C. and F.C. power had to continually supply power for the SJ radar. This entailed running both I.C. motor-generators whenever the SJ radar was in use. It is recommended that an SJ Radar motor-generator of sufficient capacity be installed to replace the present *useless* one and/or divide the I.C. switchboard into F.C. and I.C. busses and install two F.C. motor-generators.

6. Main vent gaskets for F.B.T. 4A split and had to be replaced at sea with hatch gasket cut down due to the fact that ship had not been able to draw spare T shaped gaskets for vents.

7. Torpedo tube #3 vent gaskets blew out when tube was fired. Gasket was replaced.

8. Forward roller bearing on line shafting in bow plane gear box was ground up. Bearing could not be removed from shaft by boat at sea. This casualty was due either to misalignment or improper design for lubrication. Repairs accomplished by personnel at Midway.

(L) RADIO

General:

The original communication plan consisted of guarding Haiku continuously with one RAL, using 450 kcs CW as the daytime wolfpack frequency and 2006 kcs voice at night. It was soon discovered that 2006 kcs CW had to be used continuously to maintain satisfactory inter-boat communications. This left no high frequency receiver to copy China Air Force or Press. Haiku could not be copied on 16.68 kcs. The China frequency of 4155 kcs is outside the frequency range of the R.B.O. The problem was solved by copying China on the frequency meter, but it was not possible to obtain Press News. Another RAL receiver is necessary for wolfpack operations. The RAK was of no value in the area.

Reception:

The Japanese did the most skillful job of jamming on the Haiku frequency yet observed by this ship. At times they concentrated on the indicators. As usual reception was critical during the hours of 1900 and 2000 G.C.T. Reception on 2006 kcs CW was good. All China Air Force schedules were copied. It is interesting to note that training exercises on 2006 kcs voice in the Pearl Harbor area were heard intermittently at night as far out as the Mariannas.

Transmission:

All transmissions were made on 8470 kcs and 12705 kcs without difficulty.

(M) RADAR

SD – Used only upon surfacing. When tried once at night we had plane contact shortly thereafter so secured it.

SJ – With the new antenna, there has been no side lobe trouble. No major casualties were encountered during the patrol. Most of the troubles were traced to tube failures or faulty connections. The motor generator set had to be secured for lack of output. The SJ picked up a Mavis in daylight at 28,000 yards and numerous planes at night. It picked up one convoy at 30,000 yards.

IFF – The BH unit functioned properly with planes based at Pearl, but got no response from those based at Midway or Saipan. The ABK was secured after leaving Pearl Harbor.

APR – 123 MC recorded on 23 August 1944 while passing westward between Itbayat and Sabtang Islands. It appeared to be a sector search as it swept over us every two to five seconds as we went through the channel.

The pulses appeared on the oscilloscope as modulated CW with a P.R.F. of approximately 250 per second. The pulse duration was 200 to 500 micro-seconds. There is no directivity to our antenna, so position of station is not known.

150 MC picked up at 1300(H) 6 August 1944. Lat. 22-37 N., Long. 122-29 E. APR was searching from 80-320 megs every five minutes, otherwise steady on 310 MC. From the first, the note was loud and the pips large. The pips were steady on us, gradually growing stronger for seven minutes. Then began a series of sweeps every 2 or 3 seconds. After half a dozen of these, the pips became steady again until we dived six minutes later. We dived when the OOD sighted 3 aircraft (apparently fighters) bearing 350° relative, 20,000 yards, 80 starboard angle, flying under the clouds. APR was clear on surfacing.

PRF indefinite, approximately 1000–1300 cycles per second. The pulse duration appeared to exceed one tenth the period.

Our SJ and SD were secured at the time. It is possible that the aircraft had not picked us up when we dived, although the steady echoes alternated by occasional sweeps, tend to refute this.

At 0150(H) 9 Sept. 1944, during approach, APR picked up continuous enemy radar at 131 MC. We were submerged to 43 feet. The plane was observed to be a two engine bomber, screening the convoy. Probably due to his proximity, his radar was always visible on our screen, and as he flew close, it filled the screen. Due to the press of circumstances, no technical data was recorded. No second harmonic could be picked up at 310 megs.

250 MC. 6 September, 1944, 1845(H) Lat. 20-21 N., Long 122-39 E. APR was listening about 6 minutes on 310 MC and 6 minutes on 150 MC, making a band width (dial) search every 15 minutes. Nothing was picked up until 1845, when weak pips appeared at 250 MC. These were steady on for 25 seconds, off for about 3 seconds and on again for 35 seconds. At 1850 the response was steady on, but

too weak to give anything but occasional pips on the scope. At 1855 c/c from 180° to 090° and lost the response. At 1905 came back to 180°T. Began APR search, dividing time between 310, 150, and 250 MC.

At 1945(H) Lat. 22-22 N., Long. 122-43 E, contact was again made at 250 MC, being on for 45 seconds, then sweeps, which gradually died out.

All was quiet until 2019(H) when the station came on strongly for 20 seconds, made 3 quick sweeps, and stayed on for another 37 seconds, pips getting larger and larger until we dived.

From 2300(H) on, signals were rapidly growing weaker. The last one to be heard was at 2325.

During this time the SD was not on.

The SJ was started and made regular sweeps from 1909 to 1919, then was put on a listening watch from 1919 to 2325 with one sweep every 5 minutes.

The coincidence of APR and SJ at 2325 means little since the APR was gradually fading out at one sweep every 3 minutes, and the SJ was transmitting one sweep every five minutes. This procedure was adopted as a result of our analysis of the Nips' tactics. After watching the pips come and go on the APR, it seemed that the plane detected our SJ and flew first one way and then another, seeking a course that would bring our radar in stronger. They would then fly along that course, sweeping back and forth with their radar until they picked us up. We heard these sweeps on the APR at 310, getting louder and louder, then suddenly the sweep would center on us and the plane would "zoom" in. Once he actually flew over the bridge at 100 feet, but two other times the SJ picked him up at 6,600 and 6,800 yards and we submerged.

His dry run indicated that sight contact was needed for accurate bombing. This may be accounted for by the long pulse duration, measured on the APR – Oscillograph combination, which would indicate their radar was ineffective inside a thousand yards.

An APR log was started the evening of 7 September and the following are excerpts. The pulse repetition frequency was 1400–1500 per second.

Sept. 8 – 21-18 N., 122-16 E.
    0000–0500 Regular sweeps of 5 to 30 seconds duration 1–5 minutes apart. The pulses would be strong 10–15 minutes at a time, but the majority were weak.
    0510–1900 Submerged.
    1900–1918 Occasional weak sweeps.
    1918–2040 No sweeps.
    2040 Four light sweeps.
    2040–2200 All clear.
    2200–2345 Groups of 1, 2, or 3 sweeps every 1 to 8 minutes; some very weak, some rather strong.

2345 Clear for half an hour, then sweeps started again.
Sept. 8 – 19-41 N., 120-16 E.
    0150 See entry under 150 MC.
    1902 Surfaced.
    1902–2400 Groups of 1 to 5 sweeps, some weak and some strong, 3 to 5 seconds long, every 2 to 5 minutes.
Sept. 10 – 19-31 N., 121-02 E.
    0000–0130 Sweeps every 2 to 5 minutes, 5 to 20 seconds duration.
    0136 Following code came in, with apparent grouping. This is only the lattter portion of the transmission. (Our posit. 19-31 N., 121-02 E.)
UE UE UE IEK – EK IT – K TEKA A ET AS KV BT AUENPDTAGUAEETUABT – RWCW TSTIT LONG DASH
    0200 Started sending IEK over and over.
    0205 Signal and letters.
    0210 Commenced sweeps of 3 to 15 seconds duration, 1–2 minutes apart.
    0251 Sending signal and letters.
    0257 Returned to sweeps.
    0345–0500 No contact, all clear on APR.
    0500 Submerged.
    1530–1848 No contact on APR.
    1848 Usual irregular sweeps until
Sept. 12 – 19-44 N., 118-03 E.
    0545–1445 All clear, then at
    1512 Sweeps started again, etc.
Sept. 18 – 18-12 N., 113-44 E.
    Had sweeps off and on until noon, then none until 1500 of Sept. 19. Sweeps were very weak.
Sept. 21 – 20-35 N., 123-08 E.
    0300–1700 All clear on APR.
    1700–2400 Irregular, usual type sweeps.
Sept. 22 – 20-46 N., 130-07 E.
    0000–1205 Irregular, usual type sweeps.
    1205–1837 All clear.
    1837 One weak sweep.
    1852 Two weak sweeps.
    1900–2400 Irregular, usual type sweeps.
Sept. 23 – 18-27 N., 134-36 E.
    0000–0530 Usual type sweeps.
    0530–2120 No signal
    2122–2400 Usual signals, irregular strength.

310 MC.

This frequency was encountered only at night. Enemy radar was reported making occasional weak sweeps on 310 mc at 2200(H), 1 Sept. 1944, at 2300(H), APR operator reported a sweep every 75 seconds. The sweep was quite regular, of approximately one second duration, and was followed in two seconds by a weaker sweep. (Though non-conclusive, this last is the indication of lobe switching or two antennas. The absence of a leading weak sweep rules out side lobes.) In a few minutes, the sweep became medium strong and then faded, only to return 18 minutes later. It grew strong and in six or seven minutes had faded again. The third time the pips came in they were medium large to begin with and rapidly became larger. The radar was not sweeping, but was steady on.

By the time the phone was manned to warn the bridge, the diving alarm had been sounded, this latter occasioned by the visual observation of a twin motored bomber passing overhead at 100 feet elevation.

The sweeps were never evenly spaced. The PRF was 1500 per second with a pulse duration estimated between 100 and 150 micro-seconds.

Sept. 8 – 21-10.2 N., 121-50.2 E.
    1859(H)   Surfaced.
    2034   Reported strong sweeps, then none until
    2239   When two groups, a minute apart, of two sweeps each, duration of each sweep three seconds, were reported. Meanwhile APR had been guarding alternately 310 MC and 250 MC.
Sept. 9   Could get nothing on 310 MC during our approach nor the rest of the day, until 1900.
    1500–1600   APR watch reported no contacts.
    1900   Commenced nightly APR watch.
    2047   Two weak sweeps, three seconds each.
    Sept. 11
    2117   Only contact on 310 MC before 2400.
Sept. 12
    0000–0500   Four (4) widely spaced contacts on 310 MC. All clear the rest of the time. Signals very weak. All clear until
    1900   When APR picked up 310 MC very weakly. These became strong at
    2205   The sweeps coming in pairs, about 3 second each, a few seconds apart. Then they faded, the last one coming in at
    2257   Then all clear on 310 MC until
Sept. 13
    0145–0240 Occasional weak sweeps.
    0445 and 0522 Occasional sweeps.

Sept. 14   During approach on TB's there was considerable faint response on 310 MC. The sweeps would be steady for as long as two minutes at a time.

Sept. 15
- 1850   Medium strength sweeps on 310 mc.
- 1900–2150   All clear.
- 2150–0421   Sweeps in pairs or singly every few minutes.

Sept. 16, 17, 18   Clear most of the time. Occasional sweeps, but very weak.
Sept. 21   All clear from 0500–1800.

We have come to the following conclusions:

150 MC is definitely enemy air borne radar since planes were seen at times corresponding to the APR response.

310 MC is definitely enemy airborne. When this frequency was first noted the visual observation of plane movements corresponded to the size of the pips on the scope. Attempts were made to establish this as a harmonic by tuning to 155 mc, but without success.

250 MC. Here there is much room for doubt.

(1) Land based Jap station seems unlikely since the response came in with variations in strength while we were lying to at night.

(2) Jap airborne seems unlikely since the response came in at all times and in all kinds of weather.

(c) Jap ship borne is a possiblity (submarine).

(d) Possibility that we picked up a sub-harmonic of someone else's SJ. More evidence will be had if and when the intercepted message can be broken.

(N) SOUND CONDITIONS

August 26, 19-00 N., 116-50 E. Conditions very good for listening on JP-I sound equipment. Back ground noise low. SBT card showed sharp negative gradient below 130 feet.

August 31, 21°-06' N., 121°-04' E. During approach on target listening contact first made at 5,600 yards (QB sound equipment) during early daylight. Effective range decreased to 2,500 yards late in daylight hours.

Attack was made with other submarines.

Heard torpedoes running fired by one of the other submarines, their hits, and breaking up of their target as well as those of the *Barb*. SBT cards show 6°/260 foot negative gradient.

JP-I and QB had no trouble in tracking target and following torpedo runs.

8 Sept., 19-41.9 N., 121-00.2 E.

First listening contact (QB sound equipment) was on several escort vessels at 5,000 yards. No trouble in keeping track of their positions during our approach and their subsequent attack. SBT card showed negative gradient of 6° per 300 feet. During other attacks, conditions in general were similar to those above, except on 16 Sept., 19-17 N., 116-27 E., when a negative gradient of 20° per 310 feet was encountered.

Screws of the escort were heard, and these were very weak. Two sets of breaking up noises were heard and heavy underwater explosions.

Above 100 feet water conditions seemed noisy. Below this depth, background noise decreased.

In contrast to its excellent performance last patrol, the JP was a disappointment. It never outdistanced the QB.

(O) DENSITY LAYERS

Negative gradients were encountered throughout the patrol. SBT records are tabulated below, the cards are being forwarded to the hydrographic office.

The depths noted are those of the thermal unit, which is located 25' above the keel.

GCT	Position	Remarks
14 Aug. 2200	24-08 N. 163-30 E.	84° to 60', 83° at 110', 80° at 120'
16 Aug. 0330	22-50 N. 157-14 E.	84° to 160', 79° at 200', 76° at 300'
26 Aug. 1000	19-00 N. 116-30 E.	82° to 130', sharp break with convex curve to 65° at 320'
30 Aug. 1900	21-06 N. 121-04 E.	83° at surface, isoballast[9] to 100', isotherm[10] to 160', isoballast to 260'
8 Sept. 1730	19-58 N. 120-55 E.	85° at surface, isoballast to 81° at 120'
8 Sept. 2300	19-42 N. 121-00 E.	85° at surface, isoballast to 76° at 300', sharp break to 72°
9 Sept. 0300	19-42 N. 121-00 E.	82° at surface, isoballast to 74° at 300', sharp break to 70° at 310'

---

[9] Temperature dropping at an even rate.
[10] Isotherm[al]: Temperature unchanging.

10 Sept. 0515	19-47 N. 120-30 E.	83° to 60', 81° at 120'
11 Sept. 0600	20-54 N. 119-07 E.	84° isotherm to 120'
12 Sept. 0830	20-02 N. 118-09 E.	84° to 60', 81° at 90', 80° at 120'
14 Sept. 0800	20-32 N. 121-24 E.	84° at surface, isoballast to 76° at 350'
16 Sept. 1600	19-17 N. 116-27 E.	84° to 40', 81° at 110', 68° at 260', 65° at 315'

(P) HEALTH, FOOD AND HABITABILITY

Health was excellent. Survivors required full time attention.

Food was excellent. By diluting the ice cream mix to about half strength we were able to have ice cream nearly every day. The tea shortage at Pearl Harbor caused great inroads in our fruit juice supply early in the patrol and rationing during the latter part. The salami continues to remain of such inferior quality that an investigation at the source of its production should be made.

Habitability was fair considering the atmospheric heat and humidity. An additional air conditioning unit (not available at Pearl Harbor during last refit) is a must, for wardroom country, and the forward torpedo room for the officers and men to obtain the proper amount of beneficial rest and sleep.

(Q) PERSONNEL

The performance of officers and men left nothing to be desired. The Commanding Officer is proud to work with them. Their zeal for attack, unflagging spirit in the face of exceptionally heavy countermeasures, adaptability and heroically valiant efforts during duty is an unending source of inspiration.

(a) Number of men on board during patrol	75
(b) Number of men qualified at start of patrol	58
(c) Number of men qualified at end of patrol	73
(d) Number of men unqualified making their first patrol	14
(e) Number of men advanced in rating during patrol	8
(f) Number of men recommended to Squadron Commander for advancement – no vacancies on board	9

(R) MILES STEAMED – FUEL USED

	Miles.	Gals.
Pearl to Midway	1,650	16,565
Midway to 11-Dog	3,520	25,330
In Area	6,280	63,635
11-Dog to Saipan	1,210	18,435
Saipan to Majuro	2,400	28,974
Total	14,960	142,939

(S) DURATION

Days enroute to area	18
Days in area	30
Days enroute to base	12
Days submerged	6

(T) FACTORS OF ENDURANCE REMAINING AT SAIPAN

Torpedoes	Fuel	Provisions	Personnel Factor
3	18,500	30	30

Limiting factor this patrol – Rescue of survivors.

(U) REMARKS

1. It was a pleasure to be member of a well integrated wolf pack, under the command of Captain E.R. Swinburne. Unfortunately the *Tunny* was bombed out early, leaving the *Queenfish* and ourselves. The *Queenfish* proved a splendid partner, worked in harmony, and left nothing to be desired in cooperation. My appreciation is extended to Donk's Devils who cooperated closely during our short period with them.

2. Suggestions for Training.

(a) Submarine vs. submarine – In view of anticipated developments in submarines. Target submarine at periscope depth making approach. Other submarine on surface, upon sighting periscope, turns away, clears, then dives to 150 feet, searches for and tracks target using all means available until a firing position is obtained. Let's make it unprofitable for the Japs to employ midget or other submarines as an anti-submarine measure.

(b) Single targets – relegate to the attack teacher, unless CO expressly desires one.

(c) Screens – increase number of screens to four, preferably for day and night training. Utilize any type of spitkit for screens. PCs, retrievers, MTBs, etc.

(d) Air cover day attacks – at least three quarters of day targets should have one or two planes for close cover, preferably two engine planes.

(e) Air cover night attacks – at least one, two engine, plane on half of night attacks, acting as close cover for target, to familiarize personnel with night planes and estimates of their course. One night attack with air cover using radar of known frequency which can be picked up on APR.

(f) Multiple targets – an additional target in column, line, or echelon, but of different type than main target.

(g) Target tactics – more similar to those of the Japs as regards speed, zig zag courses, and length of zig legs.

I personally prefer fewer training approaches more nearly simulating actual conditions, than innumerable approaches which leave the personnel tired at the start of a patrol.

SUBMARINE DIVISION TWO HUNDRED TWENTY-ONE

FB5-221/A16-3

Serial (048)

Care of Fleet Post Office
San Francisco, California
4 October 1944

C-O-N-F-I-D-E-N-T-I-A-L

<u>First Endorsement</u> to
CO *Barb* Conf. ltr SS220/
A16, Serial 0015 of 10/3/44
Report of Ninth War Patrol

From:	The Commander Submarine Divison Two Hundred Twenty-One
To:	The Commander in Chief, United States Fleet.
Via:	(1) The Commander Submarine Squadron Twenty-Two.
	(2) The Commander Submarine Force, Pacific Fleet.
Subject:	U.S.S. *Barb*, Report of Ninth War Patrol.

1. The ninth patrol of the U.S.S. *Barb* was conducted in the general area of Luzon Straits and the South China Sea. The *Barb* was part of a coordinated attack group consisting of the *Barb*, *Tunny* and *Queenfish* under command of Captain E.R. Swinburne, U.S.N. The patrol was of 63 days duration, 30 days of which were spent in the area.

2. Excellent area coverage was rewarded with 5 contacts worthy of torpedo fire and 1 sampan gun target, all of which were attacked with the following results:

(a) In the early morning of 31 August after a five hour chase of a convoy, *Barb* fired three torpedoes at an overlapping target consisting of a large freighter and a medium tanker. Two hits were observed in the freighter which was observed to sink. One hit was timed in the tanker.

SUNK: 1 large AK (EU)   7,500 tons
DAMAGED: 1 medium AO (EU)   5,000 tons

(b) Later in the day of 31 August after a persistent submerged approach, *Barb* fired three torpedoes at a small freighter for three hits. Target was observed to break in two and sink.

SUNK: 1 small AK (EU)   2,000 tons

(c) On night of 9 September, *Barb*'s effort to attack a convoy was frustrated by persistent night flying planes. She fired 3 torpedoes at a *Chidori* class T.B. or a subchaser which was acting as a screen and missed.

(d) On 14 September two attacks were made on a hunter killer group of two *Chidori* class T.B. Three torpedoes were fired in each attack, all of which missed. In the last attack the target maneuvered to avoid.

(e) On 15 September, *Barb* fired six torpedoes at an overlapping target consisting of a large tanker and a auxiliary carrier of the *Otaka* class. Results were not observed due to counter measures but five hits were timed as follows: Two in the tanker and three in the carrier. Two distinct and unmistakable sets of breaking up noises were heard. The second set of these coincided closely with the extinguishing of the flames of the burning tanker observed by the *Queenfish*. It is believed that both ships sank.

SUNK: 1 large AO (*Itukusima* class) (EC)	10,000 tons
1 *Otaka* class CVE (EC)	22,500 tons

(f) On 4 September, *Barb* battle surfaced against a sampan using automatic weapons. Before the sampan was destroyed, a plane forced submergence. The Barb again surfaced 29 minutes later and completed the destruction of the sampan by six 4" hits. Sampan observed to sink.

SUNK: 1 Sampan (Mis)	100 tons
TOTAL SUNK:	42,100 tons
TOTAL DAMAGED:	5,000 tons

3. In addition to the above damage to the enemy the *Barb* is an extremely completely planned and executed maneuver in a force 4 sea rescued 14 Australians and Canadians[11] who had been Japanese prisoners of war and were on board a ship which had been sunk.

4. Strong anti submarine measures including many night flying planes were encountered.

5. The unremitting effort to solve the problem posed by night flying planes is noted and the results should prove valuable to the combat intelligence section.

6. The Barb was in fair material condition and all defects except the unsatisfactory I.C. motor generator condition will be remedied in a normal refit period. The SJ motor generator will be thoroughly overhauled and load tested in an attempt to make it perform its functions and thus partially relieve the I.C. motor generator problem.

7. The health and morale of the officers and men were excellent. The Commanding Officer, officers and crew are congratulated on this extremely aggressive and successful patrol.

Stanley P. Moseley

---

[11] Error in original endorsement. Rescued POWs were Australian and British.

SUBMARINE SQUADRON TWENTY-TWO

FC5-22/A16-3

Serial: 051

Fleet Post Office,
San Francisco, California,
5 October 1944.

<u>CONFIDENTIAL</u>

<u>Second Endorsement</u> to
U.S.S. *Barb* report of War Patrol
No. 9 dated 3 Oct. 1944.

From: Commander Submarine Squadron Twenty-Two.
To: Commander in Chief, United States Fleet.
Via: (1) Commander Submarine Force, Pacific Fleet.
(2) Commander in Chief, U.S. Pacific Fleet.

Subject: U.S.S. *Barb* (SS220) – Report of Ninth War Patrol
– comments on.

1. Forwarded, concurring in the remarks of Commander Submarine Division Two Hundred Twenty-One.

2. During this eventful patrol *Barb* watched *Tunny* being bombed twice and was herself bombed five times. The Japs are dropping them very close.

3. *Barb*'s reporting of night search plane tactics is excellent and the thorough and complete remarks under section (J) and (M) are considered to have great value. Section (U) contains some training suggestions which are worthy of development.

4. The reception in the Marianas of voice transmissions from the Pearl area as described on page 53 is of interest.

5. The Commanding Officer, officers and crew are heartily congratulated on another very aggressive and excellent patrol. The same hearty congratulations are extended to the commander of this Coordinated Attack Group, Captain E.R. Swinburne, on the damage inflicted on the enemy by the group.

W.J. Suits.

Copy to:
ComSubDiv 221.
CO *Barb*

FF12-10/A16-3(15) SUBMARINE FORCE, PACIFIC FLEET   mr

Serial   Care of Fleet Post Office,
                                          San Francisco, California,
CONFIDENTIAL   18 October 1944.

Third Endorsement to   NOTE: THIS REPORT WILL BE
Barb Report of   DESTROYED PRIOR TO
Ninth War Patrol.   ENTERING PATROL AREA

ComSubPac Patrol Report No. 548
U.S.S. *Barb* – Ninth War Patrol.

From: The Commander Submarine Force, Pacific Fleet.
To: The Commander-in-Chief, United States Fleet.
Via: The Commander-in-Chief, U.S. Pacific Fleet.

Subject: U.S.S. *Barb* (SS220) – Report on Ninth War Patrol.
          (4 August to 3 October 1944).

1. The ninth war patrol of the *Barb* was conducted in the Luzon Straits Area. The *Barb* along with the U.S.S. *Tunny* (SS282) and the U.S.S. *Queenfish* (SS393) formed an attack group with Captain E.R. Swinburne, U.S. Navy, as group commander.

2. This patrol is a continuation of the illustrious record of the *Barb*. In addition to the aggressive torpedo and gun attacks, which resulted in severe damage to the enemy, the *Barb* had the honor of rescuing fourteen Australian and British survivors from a Japanese ship which was sunk while transporting them from Singapore to the Empire.

3. The detailed and well considered comment on enemy anti-submarine measures and radar are noted, and will receive full consideration.

4. This patrol is designated as "Successful" for Combat Insignia Award.

5. The Commander Submarine Force, Pacific Fleet, congratulates the commanding officer, officers, and crew for this outstanding patrol. The spirit, determination, and coolness displayed, along with the tender care given the rescued nationals of our Allies, are in keeping with the splendid record already established by the *Barb*. The *Barb* is credited with having inflicted the following damage upon the enemy during this patrol:

SUNK

1 – Sampan	–	50 tons	(Gun Attack No. 1)
1 – Large AK (EU)	–	7,500 tons	(Attack No. 1)
1 – Small AK (EU)	–	2,000 tons	(Attack No. 2)

1 – Large AO (*Itukusima* Type) (EC) –   10,000 tons (Attack No. 6)
1 – CVE (*Otaka* Class) (EC)   –   <u>22,500</u> tons (Attack No. 7)

        Total Sunk   42,050 tons

DAMAGED
1 – Medium AO (EU)   –   5,000 tons (Attack No. 1)

    Total Sunk & Damaged   47,050 tons

                      C.A. Lockwood, Jr.

Distribution:
(Complete Copies)
Cominch	(7)
CNO	(5)
Cincpac	(6)
Intel.Cen.Pac.Ocean Areas	(1)
Comservpac	(1)
Cinclant	(1)
Comsubslant	(8)
S/M School, NL	(2)
Subase, PH	(1)
Comsopac	(1)
Comsowespac	(1)
Comsubsowespac	(2)
CTF 72	(2)
Comnorpac	(1)
Comsubspac	(40)
SUBAD, MI	(2)
ComsubspacSubordcom	(3)
All Squadron and Division Commanders, Pacific	(2)
Substrainpac	(2)
All Submarines, Pacific	(1)

E.J. Auer,
Flag Secretary.

Patrol Ten, 27 October 1944 – 25 November 1944

U.S.S. *Barb* (SS220)

File: SS220/A16
Serial: 016

Care of Fleet Post Office,
San Francisco, California,
25 November 1944

CLASSIFIED

From:	The Commanding Officer.
To:	The Commander in Chief, United States Fleet.
Via:	(1) Commander Submarine Division Sixty-Two
	(2) Commander Submarine Squadron Six.
	(3) Commander Submarine Force, Pacific Fleet.
Subject:	U.S.S. *Barb* – Report of Tenth War Patrol.
Enclosure:	(A) Subject Report.
	(B) Track Chart (ComSubPac only).

1. Enclosure (A) covering the tenth war patrol of this vessel conducted in the East China Sea off the west coast of Kyushu during the period 27 October 1944 to 25 November 1944, is forwarded herewith.

E.B. Fluckey

(A) PROLOGUE

Arrived Majuro on 3 October 1944 from Ninth War Patrol. Received an excellent refit from U.S.S. *Gilmore* and Submarine Division 221 relief crew. With the limited facilities available, training was thoroughly conducted, ably planned, and well coordinated. Convoy College was held on the beach, and night and day convoy exercises were held using everything that had a pair of oars. Readiness for sea October 27th. Transferred two officers. Received two new submarine school graduates.

(B) NARRATIVE

Oct. 27

0753(M) Departed Majuro enroute Saipan in company with *Queenfish, Picuda* and U.S.S. *Greiner* (Escort) in accordance with ComTaskFor 17 Operation Order No. 353-44, conducting daily dives, schools and drills. Group[1] commander, Commanding Officer *Queenfish*.

Nov. 1

0838(I) Arrived Saipan. Moored to U.S.S. *Holland*. Services were excellent.

Nov. 2

0821(I) Departed Saipan enroute area. Group Commander has divided area into three parts for individual submarine rotating patrol until suitable convoy is encountered, at which time coordinated attack group will form.

(All times Item[2] unless otherwise noted)

Nov. 4

1054 (Aircraft Contact #1) Sighted plane distant 10 miles. Dived.
1124 Surfaced.

Nov. 5

0617 (Aircraft Contact #2) Sighted plane at 15 miles. Did not dive.

Nov. 6

0716 (Aircraft Contact #3) Sighted Mavis at 12 miles, during training dive.

---

[1] This Coordinated Attack Group (Wolfpack) was styled "Loughlin's Loopers," and commanded by Charles E. Loughlin in *Queenfish. Picuda*, commanded by Evan T. Shepard, completed the group. On Barb's previous patrol, Captain E.R. Swinburne had commanded the group, riding *Barb*. On this patrol the group would be commanded by the senior of the three captains. As American wolfpack tactics developed, this became the more common system.

[2] Item: GMT +9 hours.

0751 Surfaced.
0935 (Aircraft Contact #4) Sighted plane at 10 miles. Dived.
0948 Surfaced.
1700 Sighted Yaku Shima.
1727 (Aircraft Contact #5) Sighted Mavis at 8 miles. Dived.
1739 (Aircraft Contact #6) SD contact at 31 miles.
1745 Surfaced. Entered area.
2000 Made passage of Tokara Strait. APR signals at 147 and 132 megacycles evidently from Yaku Shima and Kusakaki Shima. Using own SJ on 5 minute sweeps. Rounded Yaku Shima and Kuchinoyarabu at 4 miles.
2325 Avoided lighted sampan between Kuro Shima and Yu Ze.

Nov. 7
Patrolling down west coast of Koshiki Retto. No APR signals noted.
0613 Submerged at 100 fathom curve for patrol of traffic routes south of Nagasaki and Sasebo and routes through Koshiki Straits.
0920 Sighted crab trawler.
1126 Sighted sampan.
1421 Sighted motor whale boat.
1828 Surfaced. Commenced patrolling southwestern approaches to Nagasaki and Sasebo. Encountered an extended patrol line of about 60 small craft stationed about ¼ mile apart from a point 10 miles south of Nomo Saki to Kapa Shima. Believe their use precludes the possibility of any extensive minefields on the southeastern approaches.

Nov. 8
0015 Master gyro follow up system out of commission. An old headache.
0615 Submerged, 2 miles off the Naval Air Station harbor at Tomie on Fukae Shima for patrol. Covering harbor and coastal traffic routes between O Shima and Fukae Shima.
1532 Surfaced in a heavy rain squall off the lookout station on the point.
1545 Rainsquall lifted leaving us naked. Decided to remain on surface and if spotted in this position to accept it, inasmuch as this section seems devoid of traffic, no sizable patrol boat could reach us before dark, traffic might be shifted to northern approaches to Sasebo, and we plan to patrol the northern approaches for next two days. Headed south until dark.
1900 APR signals very strong at 94 megs with two distinct type pulses. Later we swung ship to determine position of Jap radar using the directivity of the APR antenna. Results showed the rectangular pulse signal to be from Danjo Gunto and the reverse sawtooth pulse signal to [be] from Ose Saki on Fukae Shima.

Nov. 9

Surface patrolling across western routes to northern approach to Sasebo.

0630 Sighted masts with small angle on the bow.

0852 Dived. Commenced approach.

0934 Identified craft as a 250 ton patrol trawler (#57) with radio antenna. Armament consisted of a 2 inch gun forward, a 20 mm on top of bridge and depth charges aft. Too rough for a quick battle surface sinking and did not want to give him a chance to disclose our position by an extended gun battle. Secured approach.

1030 Surfaced.

1035 (Aircraft Contact #7) Sighted 2 planes at 8 miles. Dived.

1100 (Aircraft Contact #8) Sighted 2 Rufes through periscope at three miles heading in same direction as previous planes.

1125 Surfaced.

1130 (Aircraft Contact #9) Sighted Kate[3] at 7 miles. Dived. Routined torpedoes.

1448 Surfaced.

1851 Observed searchlight drill on Hirado Shima. Commenced patrolling southern Tsushima Strait (Higashi Suido) and northern approach to Sasebo, jointly.

1945 Sighted Koshiki light at channel entrance. Characteristics normal.

Nov. 10

0245 (Ship Contact #1) SJ contact at 22,000 yards. A single large ship speeding along the coast towards the northern approach to Sasebo. Channel entrance lights, previously off, were now lighted. Went to full speed to catch him before he turned into channel. Manned battle stations. Visibility excellent in quarter moonlight. Picked up target visually at 17,000 yards. Target slowed to 12 knots as he approached entrance, zigzagging.

0327 Submerged at 4,700 yards for radar periscope attack.

0332 Set up for 60° port track when target turned away putting us on a 120° port track.

0334:30 Torpedo Attack #1(A) Fired tubes 4, 5, 6 with 20° left gyros, track 120° port, range 2,300 yards. Spread from aft forward.

0335 Target zigged 40° toward.

0337:10 One hit timed and observed midway between funnel and stern.

0337:20 Second hit timed and observed just aft of stack under passenger superstructure. Ship took a 30° list, commenced settling aft, and stopped. First torpedo must have missed astern indicating a higher target speed.

0339 Surfaced at 1,400 yards and turned away at emergency speed to clear area while watching ship sink.

---

[3] Kate: Nakajima B5N1 or B5N2. Carrier based attack bomber.

0342 Ship didn't sink as expected, but got underway at about 2 knots and slowly turned toward the beach. It appeared as if the skipper intended to beach her so at

0343 Slowed and swung left for the coup de grace.

To maintain control of the situation decided to attack on the surface since his large guns would be useless with the 30° list.

0353 Torpedo Attack #1(B). Fired tube #1 at 970 yards, on 150 port track, 3° left gyros, own ship speed 7 knots, target speed 1¾ knots. This torpedo took a jog to the left as it went out, before settling on its course, then at about 400 yards broached and veered sharply off to the left and ran off into the night. Erratic. A grotesque picture with the target lurching drunkenly on. A blinker gun on their bridge flashing AA[4] at us continually, and lifeboats being lowered on both high and low sides. Pandemonium. Some of the lookouts suggested we put our nose against the side and roll him over rather than waste any more torpedoes. However at

0354 Torpedo Attack #1(C). Fired tube #2 at 750 yards range on 170 port track with 4° left gyro. Torpedo took a jog to the left as it went out, before settling on its course and passing up the side of the target. Miss.

0355 Submerged at 500 yards to continue attack at radar depth, since we were now within automatic weapon range. The gunnery officer expressed our proximity perfectly by wanting to throw spuds using oranges as tracers. Swung left for stern tube shot on his beam. Target had stopped.

0409 Torpedo Attack #1(D) Fired tube #7 on a 90° port track, 1° right gyro, range 1,400 yards.

0410:30 Hit timed and observed. PCO[5] qualified at periscope by getting a hit 10 yards forward of MOT. Target rolled over and sank stern first. Sinking observed by CO, PCO, and other conning tower personnel.

0412 Sighted patrol boat heading our way.

0414 Surfaced and cleared area. Identified ship sunk as a large MKFKM transport of the *Aikoku* class[6].

As a matter of information to other submarines the above attacks were all no compass attacks. Our master gyro follow up system has been out of commission since entering the area. Fortunately we had had this trouble off and on for three patrols and particularly during our last training period. As a result we developed the "*Barb* No Compass Approach."

The follow up system of the master gyro is energized. One man calls off own ship's course from the auxiliary Mark 2 gyro every half degree. Another man in-

---

[4] "AA" is the universal maritime signal code for "who are you?"

[5] Lieutenant Commander Robert B. "Tex" Lander. Following his PCO cruise aboard *Barb*, Lander took command of U.S.S. *Ronquil* (SS-396) during her three final war patrols. His wartime credit in *Ronquil* was 2 ships for 14,000 tons, but JANAC disallowed both.

[6] Later confirmed as the auxiliary cruiser *Gokoku* (ex *Gokoku Maru*), 10,438 gross tons.

serts this course manually into the own course dial of the follow up head on the master gyro. Thus the TDC and all repeaters can be used during an approach. This method provides an accuracy of ¼° without the inherent confusion of the standard "no compass" approach.

08?? Submerged to patrol strait south of Tsushima. Distant depth charges commenced and continued throughout the day, many heavy salvos of 10– 15 charges being dropped. Depth charge expenditure—over 200. Face saving for the Hari Kari on the front doorstep.

1624 (Aircraft Contact #10) Sighted Mavis at 4 miles.

1726 Sighted several sampans.

1805 Distant depth charges ceased. To our knowledge this extensive depth charging was equalled only by that following the two wolfpack circus south of Formosa August 31, 1944.

1825 Surfaced. Proceeding to lifeguard station via round about route along the Korean coast.

1829 Avoided group of lighted sampans.

2005 Commenced passing through and avoiding a group of darkened sampans between Haku To and Shori To.

2213 Sighted Haku To light. Characteristics normal. Completed passage of sampan areas.

Nov. 11

0500 On lifeguard station.

0709 (Aircraft Contact #11) Sighted Kate at 7 miles. Dived.

0728 Surfaced.

0732 (Aircraft Contact #12) Sighted Rufe at 8 miles. Dived.

0744 Surfaced.

0755 (Aircraft Contact #13) Sighted plane at 10 miles. Slowed and kept stern towards. Did not dive.

0831 (Aircraft Contact #14) Sighted Rufe at 10 miles. Dived.

0839 Surfaced.

0917 Sighted group of black smoke columns on horizon. Not ships. Heard series of explosions. Somebody bombing what?

0923 (Aircraft Contact #15) Sighted Rufe at 8 miles. Kept bow at plane. Did not dive.

0924 (Aircraft Contact #16) Sighted 2 Kates at 7 miles. Did not dive.

0930 (Aircraft Contact #17) Sighted 4 Kates. Now have too many planes to keep track of. Dived.

0948 At 48 feet. Commenced using SD.

0950 (Aircraft Contact #18) SD contact at 13 miles, moving in.

0952 Sighted plane at 9 miles through periscope.

0955 Plane cleared area. SD depth.

0958 (Aircraft Contact #19) SD contact at 3 miles.
0959 (Aircraft Contact #20) SD contact on another plane at 10 miles.
1003 Surfaced. Using SD.
1011 (Aircraft Contact #21) SD contact at 18 miles. Did not dive.
1013 (Aircraft Contact #22) Sighted another plane (Rufe) at 7 miles.
1014 Rufe heading in. Dived.
1022 (Aircraft Contact #23) SD contact on plane at 4 miles.
1023 (Aircraft Contact #24) SD contact on another plane at 9 miles.
1024 (Aircraft Contact #25) SD contact on another plane at 10 miles.
1024 (Aircraft Contact #26) SD contact on another plane at 12 miles.
1024 (Aircraft Contact #27) SD contact on another plane at 3 miles.
1025 (Aircraft Contact #28) SD contact on another plane at 5 miles.
1025 (Aircraft Contact #29) SD contact on another plane at 9 miles.
1025 (Aircraft Contact #30) SD contact on another plane at 13 miles.
1025 (Aircraft Contact #31) SD contact on another plane at 17 miles. The SD screen now looked like a pin cushion. No planes answered IFF at IFF depth. All planes quickly passed off the screen. Evidently hot pursuit.
1036 (Aircraft Contact #32) SD contact. 6 miles. No IFF. Not sighted. Did not dive.
1038 (Aircraft Contact #33) Sighted Rufe at 7 miles. Did not dive in view of strike. These Japs must see us, but are more concerned with the strike.
1039 (Aircraft Contact #34) SD contact at 11 miles. No IFF.
1040 (Aircraft Contact #35) SD contact at 10 miles. No IFF.
1042 (Aircraft Contact #36) SD contact at 13 miles. No IFF.
1046 (Aircraft Contact #37) SD contact at 19 miles. No IFF.
1047 (Aircraft Contact #38) SD contact, 3 planes, at 17 miles. No IFF.
1048 (Aircraft Contact #39) SD contact at 15 miles. No IFF.
1049 (Aircraft Contact #40) SD contact at 13 miles. No IFF.
1050 (Aircraft Contact #41) SD contact at 8 miles. No IFF.
1051 (Aircraft Contact #42) SD contact at 14 miles. No IFF. SD a pin cushion again. Must be Jap fighters above the clouds.
1051 (Aircraft Contact #43) Sight and SD contact on B-29. Answered IFF.
1052 (Aircraft Contact #44) Sight and SD contact on B-29. IFF.
1053 (Aircraft Contact #45) Sight and SD contact on B-29. IFF.
1056 (Aircraft Contact #46) Sight and SD contact on B-29. IFF.
1059 (Aircraft Contact #48) Sight and SD contact on 3 B-29s at 9 miles. IFF. These B-29s were in lower edge of clouds.
1057 (Aircraft Contact #47) Sight and SD contact on B-29 at 10 miles.
1103 (Aircraft Contact #49) SD contact at 4 miles. No IFF.
1106 (Aircraft Contact #50) SD contact 8 miles. No IFF.
1107 (Aircraft Contact #51) SD contact at 16 miles. No IFF.
1108 (Aircraft Contact #52) SD contact at 14 miles. No IFF.

1109 (Aircraft Contact #53) SD contact at 17 miles. No IFF.

1112 (Aircraft Contact #54) SD contact at 13 miles. No IFF. Looks like the Jap fighters are above the clouds. No sightings. Nothing heard on life guard frequency.

1158 (Aircraft Contact #55) SD contact 7 miles. No IFF.

1409 (Aircraft Contact #56) Sighted Kate at 7 miles. Did not dive.

1413 (Aircraft Contact #57) SD contact at 14 miles. No IFF.

1500 Life guard duty completed. However kept frequencies manned till 1830 for possible downed planes.

1505 Received word of downed plane, 170 miles distant.

1506 Received word from *Queenfish* of convoy she contacted at 0900 forty miles south of us heading on course 260°, the same general direction as downed plane. Decided to combine mission of mercy with mission of murder. We are now 70 miles behind convoy. Bent on 4 engines and poured on the coal.

1507 (Aircraft Contact #58) Sighted Kate at 11 miles. Did not dive.

1539 (Aircraft Contact #59) Sighted Nell at 4 miles coming out of clouds. Dived. Turned left.

1542 One bomb, very close on starboard beam. A cork flier. Only damage was broken tube in SJ radar, and a few broken light bulbs. Went deep. Can't affort to stay down too long if we hope to catch convoy. Swept up cork[7] and at

1643 Surfaced.

1721 Passed a sampan at 4,000 yards. We haven't time to avoid and he does not have radio.

2255 (Ship Contact #2) SJ contact at 13,000 yards. Convoy of 11 ships and 4 escorts. Seas are now force 6. Commenced end around to starboard. Base course 195°T. This appears to be a different convoy from that of *Queenfish*. Sent contact report to all area submarines.

2352 Manned battle stations.

Nov. 12

Visibility poor. Sighted convoy at about 10,000 yards. Station keeping between columns and in columns very ragged. Convoy in three columns. Starboard column 3 ships. Center column 4 ships. Port column 4 ship, the last of which straggled between center and port columns. One escort was well ahead, one astern, one on port bow and one on starboard flank. Sea was from starboard with waves fifteen feet high.

0120 Commenced no compass approach. Ship surf boarding into convoy. Running down the mountainous seas we left a path of foam abreast us 100 yards to each side. Planned to attack on starboard bow, aft of lead escort and ahead of

---

[7] Cork was used as insulation on the interior of a fleet submarine's conning tower and pressure hull.

starboard flank escort firing 2 bow tubes at each of 3 ships and then swing right with the seas and fire 2 stern tubes at each of 2 ships.

0130 Commenced attack. Convoy formation keeping was so poor that targets were designated and redesignated twice before finally telling TBT operator to pick any suitable target. Escort on starboard quarter picked that time start easing up along the formation putting himself on a collision course with us, forcing us to accept larger ranges.

0140 Torpedo Attack #2(A) Fired tubes 5 and 6 at a large AK. Target speed 9 knots, track 82 starboard, range 2,700 yards, gyros 10° left. All torpedoes set on 8 feet, firing across the sea.

0141 Torpedo Attack #2(B) Fired tubes 3 and 4 at medium AK, track 90 starboard, range 3,240 yards, gyros 8° left.

0142 Torpedo Attack #2(C) Fired tubes 1 and 2 at a medium AK. Track 75 starboard, range 3,250 yards, gyros 25° left.

0143 One hit in large AK, observed. Swinging right for stern tubes.

0144 One hit in medium AK, observed.

0145 One hit in medium AK, observed.

Saw one medium AK with a 30° dive angle heading for the bottom. Large AK now had his bow nearly under with this stern high. Other medium AK not observed. Convoy now became melee. Lead escort dropped back alongside large AK leading center column. This AK zigged sharply right so crossed ahead of her and the escort at a range of 800 yards. Waited for completion of her zig, which was a 90° right zig and when she had steadied down at

0153 Torpedo Attack #2(D) Fired tubes 7 and 8. Range 2,300 yard, track 90° port, gyros 3 right.

0155 One hit observed in after hold. Radar operator and Executive Officer at PPI now reported pips disappearing from screen. Looked around for a suitable target for last 2 tubes, but scene was one of utter confusion. Could not find a target which had settled down. PCO suggested that it was high time for the remainder of the convoy to fall out and fall in again. Secured tubes 9 and 10 and hauled out on port bow of convoy for reload and observation.

Watched the last large AK which we had hit. She slowed down but did not sink. Convoy slowed to 7.5 knots. CO, PCO, and Executive Officer all took a careful radar check on the remainder of the convoy. There were definitely only 3 ships left. Three were sunk. This was substantiated by a visual count of 8 ships left in this convoy after moonrise. There were no cripples or stragglers left behind.

0300 Completed a difficult reload. Now about 15 minutes before moonrise, so took position on starboard bow of convoy for a night submerged periscope attack. Was positive we would be unable to control ship at radar depth. Consequently determined to get convoy speed prior to submergence and make attack using periscope bearings, estimated angle on bow and estimated range, firing with near zero gyro angles. Moon was less than a quarter on the wane, clear sky overhead, a low rim of clouds forming to the east.

0354 Submerged. Depth control was next to impossible. At 2/3 speed ship oscillated violently between 60 and 80 feet. Visibility, which had been fair on the surface after moonrise, was now very poor due to spindrift. A feature I had not counted on. Kept periscope up continually and even at 75 feet was able to see part of the time in the wave troughs.

0400 Commenced attack on a medium to large AK. We were cutting across convoy from starboard to port. Angle on bow zero. We would make stern tube attack on port track.

0406 Made ready tubes 8, 9 and 10.

0409 Target zigged to his right, swung periscope to another target, being unable to spot any slackening of her zig, and at

0410 Sighted a small AK, angle on bow 10 starboard, range estimated at 400 yards. Went to standard speed to cross ahead. She had not yet zigged to her right. This would be a very close shot, but am certain we can make it.

0411 Crossed ahead of target at estimated range of 200 yards. We are on a 120 port track. Target must zig. When angle on the bow was 20° port, target zigged 30° away. Could not see anything but the funnel in high power. In low power could not even see all of the target. Swung scope back and forth to obtain a retention of vision picture of the angle on the bow. In doing so noticed a medium AK overlapping ahead. Gave TDC an angle on the bow. Estimated range at 150 yards (actually 137 yards), but not to alarm or confuse the fire control party told TDC to use 300 yards, a range he could insert without running up against the stops. We are on a 150° port track, so torpedoes should have time to arm. Things are happening very fast now! The periscope is trained on the funnel continuously with the assistant approach officer calling out bearings as fast as he can. Can hear TDC operator muttering "she must be a lot closer." A whole of a lot closer, but we control the situation. An old headline flashed through my mind of an allied sub firing at the suicide range of 2,000 yards—what a joke. Gyros are racing towards zero. We can't miss. Sound operator unable to obtain a ping range. We couldn't use it anyway.

0412:00 Torpedo Attack #3. Fired tube #8.

0412:10 Fired tube #7.

0412:20 Fired tube #10.

0412:24 First torpedo hit in forward hold and target blew up in my face, literally disintegrating. This explosion was terrific. The engine room, not realizing that a torpedo could hit within 4 seconds of firing the third torpedo, immediately reported that a depth charge had blown off our after superstructure. The sound man reported the target was so close he could hear water rushing into her hull. Parts of the target commenced falling on top of us, drumming on the superstructure.

0413:09 Another hit. A lucky one undoubtedly in the medium AK overlapping from one of the two torpedoes which missed ahead. The first explosion had forced us down so that periscope was now ducked. Sound reported high speed screws approaching. Breaking up noises were heard throughout the hull from the close target, followed within a minute by a crunching thud believed to be the target hitting bottom. Depth of water 204 feet—ordered 120 feet.

0415 Breaking up noises from medium AK commenced. This was a separate and distinct set of noises. However inasmuch as we were held down by 2 escorts and unable to surface for a radar or visual check of ships remaining, this is classed as probably sunk.

0418 Rigged ship for depth charge and silent running.

0421 At 185 feet and sinking slowly unable to maintain depth at 100 RPM and a 3° up angle. Rigged in the sound head. An increase of up angle will cause our screws to hit. The bathythermograph shows isotherm. An increase of speed will surely bring the escorts. We must blow!

0422 By blowing caught her at 190 feet. The escorts also caught us. Slowed to 80 rpm to eliminate motor whine. Screws of one escort could be heard through the hull above us. A hush descended on all hands. Escort has shifted to short scale pinging[8]. Commenced evasive turns.

0424 Lowered sound head. The escorts have us sandwiched. We are making a doctrine evasion by slowly turning up sea and up wind. It is impossible to keep bow or stern at escorts when caught between. Ping are ringing off our sides.

0429 One escort is starting his run. Ordered full left rudder. He will pass to starboard.

0430 First depth charge. Could hear charge hit water. Estimate charge was set at 100–150 feet. Close.

0431 Depth charge. Close to starboard and at our depth. Several additional splashes were heard, but charges must have been set too deep and hit bottom without going off.

0432 Escorts stopped. Stand by!

0433 Long scale pinging. Escorts have lost us.

0443 Heard a pitter patter of splashes on the surface, followed by a close small explosion. Hedge hog? Sono Bomb?

0444 Another patter of splashing, followed by three close explosions. We are 18 feet off the bottom.

0450 Escorts apparently shoved off.

0540 Surfaced. Sky now overcast. Sea still force 6. Found one grating strip ripped out of deck aft. SJ interference, probably *Peto*. She had received our initial and amplifying contact reports. Convoy was now 17,000 yards. Dawn in half an

---

[8] Short scale pinging: Sonar pings less than two seconds apart are termed "short scale" and usually indicate that the sound operator has made contact and is attempting to localize it. Pinging at an interval greater than two seconds is called "long scale."

hour. An extended end around would be impractical for we are already deep in the Urchins[9] area and too little time for another surface attack.

Decided to leave rest of convoy to the Urchins. Saw a beautiful tower of an explosion from one ship when *Peto* attacked and felt one other hit.

0651 Submerged for the morning.

1400 Surfaced. Commenced search for downed aviator. Other subs will be searching to southwest, so searched southwest sector.

1740 Sighted *Peto* surfacing at 8,500 yards. She informed us that there were 7 ships and 1 escort remaining prior to her attack. Believe she may have mistaken at least one other escort for a ship in the poor visibility prior to dawn. The two escorts working us over had rejoined the convoy before she attacked.

2300 Radar rendezvous with *Queenfish*. Secured search for aviator and set course for area Shep, the western part of area 9.

Nov. 13

Surface patrolling southeast of Quelpart Island.

1004 (Aircraft Contact #60) Sighted Rufe at 10 miles. Dived.

1055 Surfaced.

1115 (Aircraft Contact #61) Sighted 2 Kates at 6 miles. Dived.

1145 Surfaced.

1151 (Aircraft Contact #62) SD contact at 6 miles. Dived. Decided to remain submerged for possibility of convoy coming through.

1435 (Aircraft Contact #63) Sighted Mavis at 8 miles.

1657 Surfaced. No evidence of traffic.

1900 Received word that convoy heading in this direction had returned to port.

Nov. 14

Surface patrolling northeast of Quelpart. Heavy overcast and drizzle. Looked like the morning would be ideal for a gun shoot, so headed north off Kako To towards Resui Wan where we had previously spotted a schooner route between there and Tsushima.

0700 (Ship Contact #3) Sighted 2 Jap schooners similar to ones pictured in ONI Bulletins. Estimate to be 100 ton vessels. Course westerly. Closed.

0741 Manned battle stations – guns.

0747 Lookout spotted a plane heading in. It just couldn't be, not at such a critical time. CO finally found reported plane and identified as a bird.

0751 Nearest schooner turned towards to ram us. Real courage. However his maneuver opened the way for a golden opportunity to make a simultaneous

---

[9] Underwood's Urchins, a three boat wolfpack commanded by Gordon Underwood in *Spadefish* (SS-411). The other two boats were *Sunfish* (SS-281), Edward Shelby, and *Peto* (SS-265), Robert H. Caldwell, Jr.

double attack firing port and starboard broadsides. Knew the crew would enjoy this, so easily slipped in between and at

0754 Gun Attack #1 (A, B) Commenced fire with 40 MM on target bearing 080 relative, range 1,000 yards. Commenced fire with four inch on target bearing 300 relative, range 1,800 yards. Fired 40 rounds of 40 MM for 22 hits and 15 rounds of 4" for 10 hits. Enemy personnel were quickly obliterated. One officer reported dummy wooden guns mounted aft in both schooners. A nice show with sails, masts and rigging toppling, and planking and siding flying through the air. Target B was completely destroyed, but 40 MM fire on target A did not effect complete destruction, so reversed course and commenced fire with 4 inch on target A bearing 270 relative, range 350 yards. Fired 7 rounds for 6 hits. Target A destroyed.

0806 Secured from battle stations.

0808 Sighted another schooner, distant 6 miles. Closed.

0821 Manned battle stations – guns.

0829 Gun Attack #1 (C) Commenced fire with 4 inch on target C bearing 290 relative, range 1,200 yards. Fired 9 rounds for 7 hits.

0332 Commenced fire with 40 MM on target C bearing 270 relative, range 800 yards. Fired 50 rounds for 32 hits.

0834 Target C destroyed. Secured from battle stations. With Kanjo Gan now 7,000 yards away, decided to clear area.

1651 Submerged on possible SD contact at 3 miles.

1728 Heard 6 distant explosions. Commenced high periscope searching.

1843 Surfaced.

Nov. 15

0027 Radar contact at 2,950 yards. Must be a spitkit. Avoided. Shortly thereafter noted peculiar interference from that bearing on our SJ scopes. This may have been a small enemy submarine. The night is black.

0632 Commenced surface patrol southeast of Quelpart Island.

0724 (Aircraft Contact #64) Sighted single engine plane at 7 miles. Dived.

0813 Surfaced.

0933 (Aircraft Contact #65) Sighted Rufe at 12 miles. Dived.

0956 Surfaced.

1021 (Aircraft Contact #66) Sighted Sally at 12 miles. Dived. Watched plane through scope.

1120 Surfaced.

1121 (Aircraft Contact #67) Sighted Kate at 10 miles. Dived.

1139 (Aircraft Contact #68) Sighted a fighter through periscope.

1155 (Aircraft Contact #69) Sighted a Nell at 4 miles. Aircraft activity indicates possibility of convoy. Decided to remain submerged.

1200 Heard distant series of depth charges – 15 total.

1214 (Aircraft Contact #70) Sighted plane at 9 miles.

1331 (Aircraft Contact #71) Sighted 2 Rufes at 7 miles.

1405 (Aircraft Contact #72) Sighted Mavis at 10 miles.

1511–1515 Twenty distant depth charges.

1543 Numerous distant explosions. No planes for almost 2 hours. Convoy may be re-routed due to an attack by *Queenfish*.

1600 Surfaced.

1813 (Aircraft Contact #73) Sighted plane at 25 miles. Did not dive.

1900 Received contact report from *Queenfish* on convoy which prior to her attack had been heading towards our position. Urchins were forming up beyond us on projected track. Since convoy had not reached our position at 1600 per speed of advance, decided it had been re-routed to the south.

1915 Commenced full speed chase along southern route.

1925 Transmitted our estimation and search intentions to *Queenfish* by radar. Received word of her two hits in escort carrier.

2151 Changed course to 250°T. Now in Urchins' area. Sea force 5.

2249 (Ship Contact #4) SJ radar contact at 19,000 yards, bearing 245°T. Believed we had outguessed convoy, but it soon became apparent that this contact was headed our way at high speed.

2256 Came right to 300°T at full speed to cross ahead and attack down sea from port bow. We are over 12,000 yards from the track. Sent out contact report to area subs.

2305 Slowed to standard. Pounding into the sea we are shooting columns of spray high in the air. If sighted we won't get in a shot. At standard, we are taking spray over the bridge.

Target is a *Shokaku* Class carrier with three and possibly four destroyer escorts. One escort is ahead, one on port beam, one on starboard quarter. Possibly a fourth escort is close alongside carrier. This may be a difference in pips on the carrier between the large island and the ship itself.

2309 Changed course to 330°T. Rough estimate of zig plan appears to be 000, 030, 000, 050, 000, etc., legs 5–7 minutes.

2314 Slowed to 2/3 to open outer doors.

2316 All ahead standard. Sent out contact report to area subs.

2322 Changed course to 340°T. Target has just zigged to 053°T.

2323 Torpedo Attack #4. All ahead 1/3. Fired tubes 5, 4, 3, 2, 1 on a 131 starboard track, range 2,580 yards, gyros 25° right. Torpedo run had steadied down at 3,500 yards its lowest point. All torpedoes set on 10 feet. We had closed our limit.

2324 Started swinging left towards escort 1,500 yards away, then opened out to track from astern. Not sighted.

2327:20 One hit timed from below and observed by lookout to be near stern of carrier. CO had his glasses riveted on near escort at the time. Evidently first torpedo hit and others passed to starboard and ahead as carrier started zig away 3 minutes after firing. Very disappointing, for if target had held course for another minute we would have had five hits.

2328 Starboard escort turned out to the right and commenced dropping depth charges.

2332 On base course of carrier, at emergency speed.

Commenced tracking and sending out contact reports to area subs at 15 minute intervals. Carrier had now slowed from 19 knots to 17.5 knots. Occasional depth charges were being dropped.

Nov. 16

0036 SJ interference from two different points forward of our port beam. These submarines will be unable to attack.

0105 Carrier slowed to 12.5 knots for 8 minutes then increased speed to 19 knots for the remainder of the night. We were attempting an end around to starboard at this time making turns for 20.5 knots and gaining slowly. Other subs were dropping astern and we had hope until this final increase in speed ruined our chances.

0113 Three more depth charges.

0200 Carrier changed base course to 060°T, heading for Tsushima.

0330 Other area subs reported unable to attack, so secured tracking. Full power run completed.

0345 Proceeding to assigned patrol station.

0646 Submerged for patrol during morning.

1359 Surfaced. Commenced patrolling near focal point.

1938 Proceeding to area Elliott in southeastern part of area. Decided to make submerged patrol off Noma Misaki for coastal traffic since we have only two torpedoes left and those in stern tubes.

Nov. 17

0711 Submerged 7 miles off Noma Misaki upon making out homes on the beach through morning mist. Closed the coast at 4 knots.

0820 Commenced patrol 3 miles offshore.

1052 (Ship Contact #5) Sighted smoke bearing 010°T.

1105 (Aircraft Contact #74) Sighted Dave[10] at 4 miles.

1110 Commenced closing coast, although smoke bearing was drawing the other way, in anticipation of ships rounding the cape and following coastline. Plane patrolling ahead.

1140 Sighted two ships. Estimated at 1,000 tons each. One an engine aft freighter, one an MFM freighter. Two escorts, one ahead, one on starboard quarter. Commenced approach.

1155 Targets rounding cape and headed down coast. Plane overhead.

---

10   Dave: Nakajima E8N1 reconnaissance seaplane.

1208 Now only 2,800 yards from the beach turned for stern tubes.

1213 Torpedo Attack #5. Fired tubes 9 and 10. Track 120 starboard, range 1,750 yards, gyros zero. One torpedo was fired at each ship. Both missed, due to an estimated 25% error in funnel height, with resulting speed error. Firing nearly parallel to coast.

1220 One explosion. End of run. Targets having been only 1,000 yards offshore, turned towards the coast, closing to approximately 500 yards before paralleling. Commenced clearing area.

1757 (Aircraft Contact #75) Sighted Pete at 10 miles.

1831 Surfaced. Sent departure report.

1849 (Aircraft Contact #76) Sighted plane in beam of searchlight during searchlight drill over Kagoshima.

2350 Passed through Tokara Strait. Departed area.

Nov. 18

0310 Transmitted another message concerning carrier action upon request.

0819 (Aircraft Contact #77) Sighted Mavis at 8 miles coming in. Dived.

0820 Going deep. Rigged ship for depth charge.

0822 Two bombs. Not close.

1034 Surfaced.

1035 (Aircraft Contact #78) Sighted float plane at 8 miles. Dived.

1117 Surfaced.

Nov. 19

Enroute Midway.

1318 (Aircraft Contact #79) SD contact at 4 miles. Dived. Bow planes out of commission. Remained submerged for electrical repairs.

1736 Surfaced. Repairs completed.

Nov. 20–25

Enroute Midway. Requested Midway refit upon learning of work overload at Pearl. We are a logical candidate.

Nov. 25

Added a second Nov. 25th upon crossing international date line.

1130(Y) Moored Midway. Received Midway's customary excellent welcome.

(C) WEATHER

Weather in general was excellent. Seas were calm north of Fukae Shima; and the northwest monsoon accompanied by a heavy ground swell was encountered south of Quelpart Island (Saishu To). Winds of about 30 knots were occasionally found in this same area, though wind and rainfall were below average expected. Clouds were broken and scattered and provided for better cover for aircraft than for the submarine. A persistent light surface haze frequently caused a mild mirage effect.

(D) TIDAL INFORMATION

Tide and currents conformed generally to tide tables and charts. A set of 1 knot to the north with flood tide was experienced in Lat. 32-15 to 32-20 and Long. 129-00 and 129-40.

(E) NAVIGATIONAL AIDS

The following aids to navigation were observed:
(Lights)
(Go) Kaku To – Lighted, normal characteristics.
Sori (Shori) To – Lighted, normal characteristics.
Gyu To – Lighted, normal characteristics.
Koshiki, Kuromo Se, (northern entrance to Sasebo) lighted temporarily for entering ships. Characteristics normal.
Fog horn on O Shima (southeast of Fukae Shima) – operating, normal characteristics.
Quelpart Island (Saishu To) was determined by celestial fixes, to be 4.5 miles off its position as charted. (H.O. Chart 5494).
Bono Misaki – Lighted, steady white light.

(F) SHIP CONTACTS

No.	Time Date	Lat. Long.	Type	Initial Range	Est. Course	How Contacted	Remarks
1.	0245 11-10-44	33-23.6 129-03.8	Large AP *Aikoku Maru*	22,000	103	Radar	Attack #1
2.	2255 11-11-44	31-39.0 125-36.0	Convoy, 11 ships, 4 escorts	18,000	195	Radar	Attack #2, A, B, C, D – #3
3.	0700 11-14-44	34-13.0 127-54.0	3 two mast schooners	14,000	270	Sight	Gun Attack # 1 A, B, C
4.	2249 11-15-44	32-15.7 128-38.5	*Shokaku* Class CV	19,000	050	Radar	Attack # 4
5.	1052 11-17-44	31-19.5 130-06.1	2 small AKs 2 Escorts	15,000	140	Sight	Attack #5

(G) AIRCRAFT CONTACTS

No.	Time Date	Lat. Long.	Type	Initial Range	How Contacted	Remarks
1.	1054 11-4	22-18.8 137-46.2	Unk.	10 mi.	Sight	Dived.
2.	0617 11-5	23-17.0 135-28.8	Unk.	13 mi.	Sight	
3.	0716 11-6	28-59.8 132-17.2	Unk.	12 mi.	Sight	During training dive
4.	0935 11-6	29-07.0 132-03.0	Unk.	10 mi.	Sight	Dived
5.	1727½ 11-6	29-52.0 130-48.8	Unk.	8 mi.	Sight	Dived
6.	1739½ 11-6	29-53.0 130-46.0	Unk.	31 mi.	SD	
7.	1035 11-9	33-22.2 128-29.0	Single Eng. Unk.	8 mi.	Sight	2 planes – Dived
8.	1100 11-9	33-23.2 128-29.3	Rufe	3 mi.	Sight	2 planes – Peris.
9.	1130 11-9	33-23.0 128-32.2	Unk	7 mi.	Sight	Dived
10.	1624 11-10	34-00.0 128-28.0	Mavis	4 mi.	Sight	Periscope
11.	0709 11-11	32-56.6 128-08.0	Kate	7 mi.	Sight	Dived
12.	0732 11-11	—	Rufe	8 mi.	Sight	Dived
13.	0756 11-11	—	Unk.	10 mi.	Sight	
14.	0831 11-11	—	Rufe	10 mi.	Sight	Dived
15.	0923 11-11	33-00.0 127-58.5	Rufe	8 mi.	Sight	
16.	0924 11-11	—	Kate	7 mi.	Sight	2 planes
17.	0930 11-11	—	Kate	6 mi.	Sight	4 planes, dived.
18.	0950 11-11	—	Unk.	13 mi.	SD	Radar Depth
19.	0958 11-11	33-02.0 128-00.0	Unk.	5 mi.	SD	Radar Depth

20.	0959 11-11	—	Unk.	10 mi.	SD	" "
21.	1011 11-11	—	Unk.	18 mi.	SD	On Surface
22.	1015 11-11	33-02.3 128-01.5	Rufe	7 mi.	Sight	Dived
23.	1022 11-11	—	Unk.	4 mi.	SD	Radar Depth
24.	1023 11-11		Unk.	9 mi.	SD	" "
25.	1024 11-11	—	Unk.	10 mi.	SD	" "
26.	1024 11-11	—	Unk.	12 mi.	SD	" "
27.	1024 11-11	—	Unk.	3 mi.	SD	" "
28.	1025 11-11	—	Unk.	5 mi.	SD	" "
29.	1025 11-11	—	Unk.	9 mi.	SD	" "
30.	1025 11-11	—	Unk.	13 mi.	SD	" "
31.	1025 11-11	—	Unk.	17 mi	SD	" "
32.	1036 11-11	—	Unk.	8 mi.	SD	Surface
33.	1038 11-11	33-01.3 128-00.6	Rufe	7 mi.	Sight	
34.	1039 11-11	—	Unk.	11 mi.	SD	
35.	1040 11-11	—	Unk.	10 mi.	SD	
36.	1042 11-11	—	Unk.	13 mi.	SD	
37.	1046 11-11	—	Unk.	19 mi.	SD	
38.	1047 11-11	—	Unk.	17 mi.	SD	3 planes
39.	1048 11-11	—	Unk.	15 mi.	SD	

40.	1049 11-11	—	Unk.	13 mi.	SD	
41.	1050 11-11	—	Unk.	8 mi.	SD	
42.	1051 11-11	—	Unk.	14 mi.	SD	
43.	1051½ 11-11	—	B-29	7 mi.	Sight SD	Answered IFF
44.	1052 11-11	33-01.3 128-00.6	B-29	5 mi	Sight SD	Answered IFF
45.	1053 11-11	—	B-29	2 mi.	Sight SD	Answered IFF
46.	1056 11-11	—	B-29	7 mi.	Sight SD	Answered IFF
47.	1057 11-11	—	B-29	10 mi.	Sight SD	
48.	1059 11-11	33-01.9 128-01.4	B-29	8 mi.	Sight SD	3 planes. Answered IFF
49.	1103 11-11	—	Unk.	4 mi.	SD	
50.	1106 11-11	—	Unk.	8 mi.	SD	
51.	1107 11-11	—	Unk.	16 mi.	SD	
52.	1108 11-11	—	Unk.	14 mi.	SD	
53.	1109 11-11	—	Unk.	17 mi.	SD	
54.	1112 11-11	—	Unk.	13 mi.	SD	
55.	1128 11-11	32-59.3 128-01.0	Unk.	7 mi.	SD	
56.	1409 11-11	—	Kate	7 mi.	Sight	
57.	1413 11-11	—	Unk.	14 mi.	SD	
58.	1507 11-11	—	Kate	11 mi.	Sight SD	
59.	1539 11-11	33-05.5 127-31.2	Nell	4 mi.	Sight	Bombed

60.	1004 11-13	33-01.0 127-19.4	Rufe	10 mi.	Sight	Dived
61.	1115 11-13	33-04.3 127-16.3	Kate	6 mi.	Sight	2 planes, dived.
62.	1151 11-13	33-05.3 127-17.8	Unk.	6 mi.	SD	Dived
63.	1433 11-13	33-05.3 127-16.5	Mavis	8 mi.	Sight	Periscope
64.	0724 11-15	32-53.2 127-17.0	Single Eng.	7 mi.	Sight	Dived
65.	0933 11-15	33-02.3 127-22.1	Rufe	12 mi.	Sight	Dived
66.	1021 11-15	33-06.0 127-28.3	Sally	12 mi.	Sight	Dived
67.	1121 11-15	33-08.0 127-29.2	Kate	10 mi.	Sight	Dived
68.	1139 11-15	—	Fighter	6 mi.	Sight	Periscope
69.	1155 11-15	—	Nell	4 mi.	Sight	Periscope
70.	1214 11-15	33-09.3 127-22.9	Unk.	9 mi.	Sight	Periscope
71.	1331 11-15	33-10.0 127-29.8	Rufe	7 mi.	Sight	2 planes – Periscope
72.	1405 11-15	33-09.2 127-29.6	Mavis	10 mi.	Sight	Periscope
73.	1613 11-15	31-19.8 127-32.4	Unk.	25 mi.	Sight	
74.	1105 11-17	31-20.7 130-04.3	Dave	4 mi.	Sight	Periscope
75.	1757 11-17	31-19.8 129-48.8	Pete	10 mi.	Sight	Periscope
76.	1849 11-17	31-16.5 129-48.3	Unk.		Sight	
77.	0819 11-18	29-41.2 131-31.5	Mavis	8 mi.	Sight	Dived, 2 bombs
78.	1035 11-18	29-41.2 131-47.9	Float Plane	8 mi.	Sight	Dived
79.	1318 11-19	29-43.4 138-45.7	Unk.	4 mi.	SD	Dived

(H) TORPEDO AND GUN ATTACKS

U.S.S. *Barb*   Torpedo Attack No. 1-A-B-C-D   Patrol No. 10
Time: 0334   Date: 10 Nov. 1944   Lat. 33-23.6 N., Long. 129-03.8 E

Target Data – Damage Inflicted

Description: Large AP (*Aikoku Maru* Class) MKFKM type. Target cruising singly. Contact radar. Visibility – excellent.
Ship Sunk: Large AP (*Aikoku Maru* Class)(EC) – 10,400 tons.
Damage Determined by: Target seen to sink by CO, PCO and other conning tower personnel.

Target Draft: 29'
           Course: B–039   Speed: B–1¾   Range: B–970
                      C–088   C–1¾   C– 750
                      D–075   D–0   D–1,455
                    A–105   A–12   A–2,560
                                                                             (At firing)

Own Ship Data
Speed: A–4   Course: A–179   Depth: A–45'   Angle: A–1° down
        B–7½   B–102   B–Surface   B–—
        C–5   C–102   C–Surface   C–—
        D–2½   D–348   D–63'   D–0°
                                                                                          (At firing)

Fire Control and Torpedo Data

Type Attack: A–Night submerged – Radar and periscope.
                 B–Night surface – Radar and periscope.
                 C–Night surface – Radar and periscope.
                 D–Night submerged – Periscope.

	A	A	A	B	C	D
Tubes Fired No.	4	5	6	1	2	7
Track Angle	124 P	126 P	128 P	149 P	169 P	86 P
Gyro Angle	342	340	338	356½	356	131½
Depth Set	6	6	6	6	6	6
Power	—	—	—	—	—	—
Hit or Miss	Miss	Hit	Hit	Miss	Miss	Hit
Erratic (Yes-No)	No	No	No	Yes – Broached and swung left.	No	No
Mark Torpedo	18-1	18-1	18-1	18-1	18-1	18-1
Serial No.	54441	54332	54367	54343	54685	54534
Mark Exploder	8-5	8-5	8-5	8-5	8-5	8-5
Serial No.	8952	8325	9145	9248	8235	8264
Actuation Set	Contact	Contact	Contact	Contact	Contact	Contact
Actuation Actual	—	Contact	Contact	—	—	Contact

Mark Warhead	18-2	18-2	18-2	18-1	18-2	18-2
Serial No.	2787	1729	1700	2157	2785	2020
Explosive	TPX	TPX	TPX	TPX	TPX	TPX
Firing Interval	0 s	10 s	10 s	0 s	0 s	0 s
Type Spread	Div.	Div.	Div.	None	None	None
Sea Conditions	2	2	2	2	2	2

Overhaul Activity: U.S.S. *Howard W. Gilmore*[11]

Remarks: Spread computed for 30 yards between torpedoes along target. Target turned 47° toward 1 minute and 20 seconds after firing first spread. Target turned away after second single was fired. No speed red. used.

---

[11] U.S.S. *Howard W. Gilmore* (AS-16) was originally ordered as *Neptune*, but renamed before launching. She was launched at Mare Island on 16 September 1943, sponsored by Mrs. Howard W. Gilmore. The tender was named for Commander Howard W. Gilmore. On the night of 7 February 1943 Gilmore was in command of U.S.S. *Growler* (SS-215), when she accidentally rammed the Japanese provision ship *Hayasaki*. The Japanese ship had, herself, been attempting to ram *Growler*, but a course change reversed the outcome. Following the collision, the Japanese ship's crew raked *Growler*'s bridge with automatic weapons fire. The JOOD and one lookout were killed instantly, and Gilmore was seriously wounded.

Gilmore ordered the bridge cleared, and the OOD, quartermaster and two lookouts dropped into the conning tower. Apparently too seriously wounded to get below, Gilmore ordered, "Take her down." After half a minute's hesitation, Gilmore's XO, Arnold F. Schade, complied. Gilmore received the Medal of Honor for his sacrifice, becoming the first submariner to receive that honor in World War II.

U.S.S. *Barb*   Torpedo Attack No. 2 A, B, C   Patrol No. 10
Time: 0140   Date: 12 Nov. 1944   Lat. 31-39.0 N., Long. 125-36.0 E.

Target Data – Damage Inflicted

Description: A–Large AK (EU)
               B–Medium AK (EU)
               C–Medium AK (EU)

       Convoy of four escorts and eleven large, medium, and small freighters. No air coverage. Visibility – poor. Contact – radar.

Ships Sunk: A–Large AK(EU). B–Medium AK(EU) C–Medium AK(EU)
Damage Determined by: Visual and radar observations.

	A–25'		A–171		A–9		A–2,700
Target Draft:	B–20'	Course:	B–171	Speed:	B–9	Range:	B–3,240
	C–20'		C–171		C–9		C–3,250
							(At firing)

Own Ship Data

	A–9		A–083				
Speed:	B–9	Course:	B–083	Depth: Surface	Angle: — (At firing)
	C–9		C–090		

Fire Control and Torpedo Data

Type Attack: Night surface – radar.

	A	A	B	B	C	C
Tubes Fired – No.	5	6	3	4	1	2
Track Angle	82 S	83 S	91 S	92 S	74 S	75 S
Gyro Angle	347	350	351	351½	334	335
Depth Set	8'	8'	8'	8'	8'	8'
Power	—	—	—	—	—	—
Hit or Miss	Hit	Miss	Hit	Miss	Hit	Miss
Erratic (Yes–No)	No	No	No	No	No	No
Mark Torpedo	18-1	18-1	18-1	18-1	18-1	18-1
Serial No.	54509	54751	54713	55031	54565	56444
Mark Exploder	8-5	8-5	8-5	8-5	8-5	8-5
Serial No.	8813	8117	8657	9439	8638	7980
Actuation Set	Contact	Contact	Contact	Contact	Contact	Contact
Actuation Actual	Contact	—	Contact	—	Contact	—
Mark Warhead	18-1	18-2	18-2	18-1	18-1	18-2
Serial No.	1411	2176	2406	1443	2692	2774
Explosive	TPX	TPX	TPX	TPX	TPX	TPX
Firing Interval	0 s	10 s	0 s	10 s	0 s	10 s
Type Spread	Div.	Div.	Div.	Div.	Div.	Div.
Sea Conditions	6	6	6	6	6	6

Overhaul Activity   U.S.S. *Howard W. Gilmore*

Remarks: Spread computed for 50 yards between torpedoes along target track. One half speed reduction used. Master gyro follow-up system out. Excessive range used because escort on collision course.

U.S.S. *Barb*   Torpedo Attack No. 2-D   Patrol No. 10
Time: 0153   Date: 12 Nov. 1944   Lat. 31-29.0 N., Long. 125-36.0 E.

Target Data – Damage Inflicted

Description: Large AK (EU). In same convoy as targets of attacks 2-A, B, C.
Ship Damaged: Large AK (EU)
Damage Determined by: Visual observation.
Target Draft: 25'   Course: 265   Speed: 9 knots   Range: 2,300 (At firing)

Own Ship Data

Speed: 12 knots   Course: 178   Depth: Surface   Angle: —

Fire Control and Torpedo Data

Type Attack: Night surface – radar, with TBT bearings

Tubes Fired No.	7	8
Track Angle	89 P	91 P
Gyro Angle	179	175½
Depth Set	8'	8'
Power	—	—
Hit or Miss	Hit	Miss
Mark Torpedo	18-1	18-1
Serial No.	54482	56411
Mark Exploder	8-5	8-5
Serial	9324	9958
Actuation Set	Contact	Contact
Actuation Actual	Contact	—
Mark Warhead	18-2	18-2
Serial No.	1611	2502
Explosive	TPX	TPX
Firing Interval	0 s	10 s
Type Spread	Div	Div
Sea conditions	6	6

Overhaul Activity: U.S.S. *Howard W. Gilmore*

Remarks: Spread computed for 50 yards between torpedoes along target track. One half speed reduction used. Master gyro follow-up system out.

U.S.S. *Barb*   Torpedo Attack No. 3   Patrol No. 10
Time: 0412   Date: 12 Nov. 1944   Lat. 31-29.0 N., Long. 125-19.0 E.

Target Data – Damage Inflicted

Description: Medium AK (EU)
                Small AK (EU)
                In same convoy as targets of attack, 2 targets overlapping.
Ship Sunk: Small AK (EU)
Ship Probably Sunk: Medium AK (EU)
Damage Determined by: Timed hits on both targets. Saw small AK blow up and sink. Heard distinct and separate sets of breaking up noises for both.
Target Draft: 25'   Course: 300   Speed: 7.7   Range: 300 yards (At firing)

Own Ship Data

Speed: 4   Course: 152   Depth: 65'   Angle: 0

Fire Control and Torpedo Data

Type Attack: Night periscope.

Tubes Fired No.	8	9	10
Track Angle	152 P	156 P	159 P
Depth Set	8'	8'	8'
Power	—	—	—
Hit or Miss	Hit	Miss	Hit
Erratic, Yes–No	No	No	No
Mark Torpedo	18-1	18-1	18-1
Serial No.	56445	56538	54593
Mark Exploder	8-5	8-5	8-5
Serial No.	8826	8611	9195
Actuation Set	Contact	Contact	Contact
Actuation Actual	Contact	—	Contact
Mark Warhead	18-2	18-1	18-2
Serial No.	2539	2393	1784
Explosive	TPX	TPX	TPX
Firing Interval	0 s	10 s	10 s
Type Spread	Div.	Div.	Div.
Sea Conditions	6	6	6
Overhaul Activity	U.S.S. *Howard W. Gilmore*		

Remarks: Spread computed for 50 yards between torpedoes along target track. One half speed reduction used. Master gyro follow-up system out.

U.S.S. *Barb*   Torpedo Attack No. 4   Patrol No. 10
Time: 2326   Date: 15 Nov. 1944   Lat. 32-15.7 N., Long. 126-38.5 E.

Target Data – Damage Inflicted

Description: Aircraft Carrier (*Shokaku* Class) (EC) Cruising with three or possibly four escorts. Contact – Radar. Visibility – Fair.
Ship Damaged: Aircraft Carrier (*Shokaku* Class) (EC) – 29,800 tons.
Damage Determined by: Visual observation and timed hit.
Target Draft: 21'   Course: 053   Speed: 19.4   Range: 2,680 (At firing)

Own Ship Data

Speed: 8.5   Course: 340   Depth: Surface   Angle: 0

Fire Control and Torpedo Data

Type Attack: Night surface radar.

Tubes Fired – No.	5	4	3	2	1
Track Angle	131 S	134 S	136 S	138 S	140 S
Gyro Angle	025	027½	030	032	034
Depth Set	10'	10'	10'	10'	10'
Power	—	—	—	—	—
Hit or Miss	Hit	Miss	Miss	Miss	Miss
Erratic – Yes–No	No	No	No	No	No
Mark Torpedo	18-1	18-1	18-1	18-1	18-1
Serial No.	54438	56402	55839	54443	56434
Mark Exploder	8-5	8-5	8-5	8-5	8-5
Serial No.	8962	8691	8973	8745	8673
Actuation Set	Contact	Contact	Contact	Contact	Contact
Actuation Actual	Contact	—	—	—	—
Mark Warhead	18-2	18-2	18-2	18-1	18-2
Serial No.	2530	2894	2776	1931	2684
Explosive	TPX	TPX	TPX	TPX	TPX
Firing Interval	0 s	10 s	10 s	10 s	10 s
Type Spread	Div.	Div.	Div.	Div.	Div.
Sea Conditions	5	5	5	5	5

Overhaul Activity: U.S.S. *Howard W. Gilmore*
Remarks: Spread computed for 50 yards between torpedoes along target. Target zigged away about three minutes after firing. No speed reduction used.

U.S.S. *Barb*   Torpedo Attack No. 5   Patrol No. 10
Time: 1213   Date: 17 Nov. 1944   Lat. 31-19.5 N., Long. 130-06.1 E.

Target Data – Damage Inflicted

Description: Two one thousand ton coastal freighters with two escorts. Smoke contact. Visibility – excellent.
Ships Sunk: None
Ships Damaged: None
Target Draft: 10'   Course: 140   Speed: 6   Range: 1,750 (At firing)

Own Ship Data

Speed: 4   Course: 262   Depth: 65'   Angle: 0°

Fire Control and Torpedo Data

Type Attack: Day submerged – periscope.

Tubes Fired – No.	9	10
Track Angle	123 S	116 S
Gyro Angle	180½	174½
Depth Set	3'	3'
Power	—	—
Hit or Miss	Miss	Miss
Erratic – Yes-No	No	No
Mark Torpedo	18-1	18-1
Serial No.	55636	54757
Mark Exploder	8-5	8-5
Serial No.	9132	9321
Actuation Set	Contact	Contact
Actuation Actual	—	—
Mark Warhead	18-2	18-2
Serial No.	2722	2886
Explosive	TPX	TPX
Firing Interval	0 s	35 s
Type Spread	None	None
Sea Conditions	2	2
Overhaul Activity	U.S.S. *Howard W. Gilmore*	

Remarks: Fired one torpedo at each ship. Misses due to fire control error. One half speed reduction used.

In attacks #2 and #3, nine torpedoes were fired across and two into a state six sea for six hits. The torpedoes were set on eight feet and there were no indications of erratic torpedo performance.

One torpedo (serial #54343) fired from #1 tube while on the surface in a calm sea, speed 7.5 knots, depth set 6 feet, gyro angle 356½, broached and swung left.

During the reload after attack #2, one torpedo could not be loaded into the tube due to a bulged section of the after body just aft of the joint ring. However, later the tube rollers were lowered, the torpedo loaded, and fired for a hit.

U.S.S. *Barb* (SS220)　　　Gun Attack No. 1–A, B, C　　　　　Patrol No. 10
Time: 0755　　Date: 14 Nov. 1944　　Lat. 34-15.0 N., Long. 127-54.0 E.
Target Data – Damage Inflicted
Destroyed: Three two masted schooners (300 tons)
Damage Determined by:　A – Six 4" hits and twenty-two 40 MM hits.
　　　　　　　　　　　　B – Ten 4" hits.
　　　　　　　　　　　　C – Seven 4" hits and thirty-two 40 MM hits.
Details of Action

Approached targets A and B on surface. Opened fire with 40 MM on A bearing 080 R, range 1,000 yards. Opened fire with 4" on B bearing 300 R, range 1,800 yards. Fired 40 rounds 40 MM for 22 hits and 15 rounds 4" for 10 hits. Target B destroyed. Reversed course and opened fire with 4" on A bearing 270 R, range 850 yards. Fired 7 rounds for 6 hits. Target A destroyed.

Half hour later approached target C on surface. Opened fire with 4" when target was bearing 290 R, range 1,200 yards and fired 9 rounds for 7 hits. Opened fire with 40 MM when target was bearing 270 R, range 600 yards and fired 50 rounds for 32 hits. Target C destroyed.

(I) MINES

No mines were encountered during this patrol

(J) ANTI-SUBMARINE MEASURES AND EVASIVE TACTICS

No night fliers were observed in the area. Seventy-nine day aircraft contacts were made. These resulted in two bombings, one while chasing a convoy at full speed, the other after having transmitted two messages to ComSubPac within a period of five hours. All bombs were avoided by using full rudder after passing 50 feet, going deep and maintaining high speed.

Evasion after the first attack consisted of immediately surfacing, although a patrol boat was approaching, and putting as much distance between us and the scene of attack as we could in the hour remaining before dawn. In view of the tremendous barrages throughout the day in the neighborhood of the attack, this was a fortunate move.

After the third attack in isothermal shallow water we were forced to blow to prevent bottoming. Two escorts immediately thereafter made contact and sandwiched us. Evasion was accomplished by slowly turning into a force 6 sea and upwind. Screws of escorts and the splashes of the depth charges were audible through the hull. Side throwers were used on two drops. Several charges apparently were set too deep and failed to explode. Twice, patterns of some bombs or hedgehogs, occurred. Of these the ones that exploded gave the impression of a small close charge.

Enemy radar stations were not approached closer than 10 miles when practicable and the SJ was not trained on them. The APR gave indications that several of these stations had contact on us. However no anti-submarine measures were taken, leading us to believe that most of these were either non directional or aircraft beacons.

An extensive lighted row of small craft effectively covered the southern approaches to Nagasaki and Sasebo.

No radar was in evidence during our attack on the *Shokaku* Class Carrier. Much to our surprise.

(K) MAJOR DEFECTS

H.P. Air Compressors.

Early in the patrol the 3rd stage pressures of both compressors became excessive, averaging 950# p.s.i. Several sets of 3rd and 4th stage suction and discharge valves were installed without beneficial results.

The condition was corrected by inserting an additional 1/32" gasket under each 3rd stage head and an extra copper ring under each 3rd and 4th stage suction and discharge valve. The additional gaskets increased the 3rd stage head clearances from .051 to .088 and reduced the operating pressure to 890# p.s.i.

Six days out of Midway the 4th stage pressure on the Port compressor dropped to 2000# and the 1st, 2nd, and 3rd stage pressures rose beyond the overload limit. All valves on 3rd and 4th stages were first reground, then renewed, and then reground again without correcting the condition. The 4th stage head was then lifted, six broken rings were discovered and replaced, and the head clearance was correctly adjusted. This resulted in no improvement in the operation of the compressor, and it was secured for the balance of the patrol.

Port Sound Head.

During the last patrol a hydraulic lock inside the port sound head flooded the upper part of the shaft with oil, saturating the rubber-coated electrical leads and causing a steady loss of hydraulic oil. The defect was corrected in dry dock and the head operated satisfactorily until the 22nd day of this patrol when the leak re-occurred and the hydraulic lines to the head had to be secured.

Main Hydraulic Plant

The main hydraulic plant failed to recharge at intermittent intervals throughout the patrol. It is believed that the pilot valve is worn, permitting the oil to pass between the piston and wall and find its way to the balance piston which operates the by-pass valve. When the plant reaches the stage in its cycle where the by-pass valve should close, the leakage past the piston counteracts the pressure of the spring, tending to close the by-pass valve and hold it just off its seat. The oil being delivered by the pump, which should all go to the accumulator, partially recirculates, and as a result the by-pass valve becomes stable in this position and the accumulator will not start downward.

Each time the plant failed to recharge the manual by-pass was opened to let the accumulator travel upward far enough to entirely trip the pilot valve piston. This procedure represented a remedy, not a cure.

Master Gyro.

The master gyro follow-up system was very erratic and sticky in operation. This is a re-occuring trouble, which had developed to a lesser degree on the two previous patrols. During each refit the trouble appeared to have been eliminated but reoccurred some time during each patrol. The defect showed up early in this patrol and was so bad that the input to the follow-up system had to be manually set in during every approach.

(L) RADIO

The frequency plan now employed for the Submarine Fox Schedule is very successful. Reception was possible at all hours, being made very difficult only occasionally due to enemy jamming, and not due to signal strength. The nine and sixteen thousand ranges were used during daylight, and the four or six thousand ranges at night, the choice depending on the effectiveness of enemy jamming. No lettered serials were missed. No difficulty was experienced in copying China Air Force traffic.

Wolf Pack Communications:

CW only was used for wolf pack communications, and frequency shifts were made in accordance with Wopaco 1. The pack frequencies seem to be becoming overloaded resulting in excessive jamming among ourselves, especially during periods of enemy contact. Circuit discipline exists only in the individual pack. One undesirable practice noted in communications of other packs was the calibration of transmitters and tuning of antenna circuits on station. This can be very simply avoided by having communications personnel calibrate transmitters, including tuning of antenna circuits, prior [to] departure on patrol. This would do away with so much tuning in the area, and, if frequencies are shocked with the frequency motor, there would be no need for exchange of signal strength. Excessive repetition necessary in use of Wopaco #1 presumes possibility of early compromise.

Ship to Shore:

Five transmissions were made on the ship to shore frequencies, 4235 kc for the first, third, fourth, and fifth, and 8470 for the second. Jamming was very bad and there was at least one hour delay in clearing each message. Jamming was strength 5 at both receiving and transmitting stations, except for the fourth message when jamming bothered only the receiving station.

Communications equipment has given no trouble at all and is in good operating condition. The RAK continues to have little value.

(M) RADAR

SD – The performance of the SD was a considerable improvement over previous patrols, but left much to be desired. A total of 49 aircraft contacts were made the day of the B-29 raid. Thirty one were SD only, eleven were sight only, and seven were picked up by SD and later seen. On this day, the sky was ninety percent overcast. Of the thirty contacts during the remainder of patrol, only three were picked up by the SD before sighting.

The SD was used to obtain ranges on land in sight but beyond the range of the SJ. The SD was keyed during daylight at irregular intervals, four times in five minutes, when over thirty miles from land.

The equipment was at no time out of commission.

SJ – The operation of the SJ was very dependable this patrol, although the ranges of initial contact were only average, e.g., ten thousand ton transport contacted at twenty-two thousand yards. Ranges on land were fair.

The only major material failure was the burning out of the motor feature of the time delay relay in the main control unit. Shorting across the contacts was slight risk because the operators were trained in the habit of waiting till the system was warmed up before turning on the high voltage.

Inside of fifteen thousand yards of land, especially land with known radio beacons and thus probable radar detectors, the SJ was limited to sector scanning. At other times the radar made continuous sweeps or stood a listening watch with one sweep every five minutes.

A close bomb knocked out a rectifier tube in the high voltage regulator.

IFF – This BN operated entirely satisfactorily throughout the patrol. Since drawing the OAP motor during our last refit, there has never been any doubt as to whether or not it was challenging and receiving. The best range we got on IFF was thirty-three miles. Several IFF contacts, with no accompanying SD contacts were made passing through the Marshall Islands and occasionally the SD would pick up a plane before we got its IFF response.

(E) SOUND GEAR AND SOUND CONDITIONS

The sound equipment is in good electrical condition and has given no trouble. Hydraulic failure in the JK/QC gear has again put it out of commission. In general sound conditions were poor, with background noise excessive.

First Attack: Sound not used (surface).

Second Attack: Sound conditions poor due to shallow water and exceptionally high background noises. During the depth charge attack the attacking ships did get return echoes and his screws could be heard through the hull. However it is believed that the listening range in this area is quite short, even without a temperature gradient.

Third Attack: Sound not used (surface).

Fourth Attack: Poor sound conditions again. Neither QB nor JP could give bearings accurately within six or seven degrees. Two single ping ranges were attempted but there was no return.

(O) DENSITY LAYERS

Iso thermals to 200 feet or deeper was the usual condition encountered on this patrol. No thermal gradients existed in water less than 200 feet deep. SBT records are tabulated below. The cards are being forwarded to the hydrographic office.

The depths indicated are those of the thermal unit, located 25 feet above the keel.

Oct:	Position:	Remarks
25 Oct. 2145	07-13 N. 171-08 E.	87° to 200', gradual curve, to 84° at 330'.
29 Oct. 0410	13-32 N. 159-31 E.	85° to 200', gradual curve to 83° at 300'.
30 Oct. 2310	15-43 N. 149-11 E.	86° to 230', break to 81° at 340'.
6 Nov. 2100	32-01 N. 130-42 E.	73° to 250', break to 71° at 310'.
9 Nov. 0230	33-25 N. 128-32 E.	72° to 260', curve to 70° at 290'.

(P) HEALTH, FOOD AND HABITABILITY

Health was excellent throughout the patrol. Food was excellent and the menus varied. Habitability was materially improved by the installation of an additional air-conditioning unit in the wardroom country.

(Q) PERSONNEL

The performance of officers and men, their never-say-die spirit when the enemy temporarily has the upper hand, and their eagerness for attack, continues to be an unending source of inspiration.

(a) Number of men on board during patrol — 75
(b) Number of men qualified at start of patrol — 64
(c) Number of men qualified at end of patrol — 65
(d) Number of unqualified men making their first patrol — 8
(e) Number of men advanced in rating during patrol _ 9
(f) Number of men recommended to Squadron for advancement – No vacancy on board. — 7

(R) MILES STEAMED AND FUEL USED

	Miles	Gals
Majuro to Saipan	1,870	23,295
Saipan to Area	1,626	16,030
In Area	2,301	21,385
Area to Midway	3,165	41,495

(S) DURATION

Days enroute from Majuro to Saipan	6
Days enroute from Saipan to Area	5
Days in Area	11
Days enroute to Midway from Area	9
Days submerged	5

(T) FACTORS OF ENDURANCE REMAINING AT MIDWAY

Torpedoes:	Fuel:	Provisions:	Personnel Factor:
0	38,800	60	60

Limiting factor this patrol – Expenditure of torpedoes.

(U) RADAR AND RADIO COUNTER MEASURES

Radar Countermeasures – APR-1 and SPA-1:
  This equipment was used throughout the patrol for detecting and determining the characteristics of enemy radar.
  In using the directivity characteristics of the APR antenna to determine the true bearing of the radar's source, the following difficulties were encountered:
    (a) The antenna being secured to the shears, necessitated swinging the ship's head to maximum signal on the APR. This maneuvering was very time consuming, and due to the slowness of the swing results were never certain.

(b) As maximum signal was determined by height of pip, one was never sure whether the maximum height at a certain bearing was due to a good bearing on the source or that the peak of a slow sweep had just passed over you.

(c) Some signals on APR come and go very irregularly, making it extremely difficult to swing the ship at the precise time it would do some good.

It is desired to install during the next refit an additional APR antenna on the radar mast just below the present one. The two antennas will be mounted to bear 315° R and 045° R respectively. The 90° angle between the antennas should overcome the poor directivity characteristics of a single antenna and insure a good bearing accuracy. The two coax cables would come down the present conduit through the pressure hull to a well shielded SPDT switch (similar to a telephone switchboard double throw switch) permitting a lobing action on the incoming signal. The ship could then be slowly swung and the bearing noted which produced two pips of equal size on the screen.

The following is from the APR log:

Local Date Time	Our Position	Freq. MC	Rate Pulse	Width Pulse	Sweep Rate
6 Nov. 1900	30-01 N. 130-24 E	152 147	440 490	25 25	None Apparent

Remarks: Course West. Picked up 152 MC, later 147 MC; as we passed through channel former failed, then the latter.

7 Nov. 0200	31-09 N 129-46 E	150	450	25	None Apparent

Remarks: Signal faded in and out as we passed Kusakaki Shima.

8 Nov. 1900	32-16 N 128-50 E	95 94	860 650	25 60	1 per 5½ min. 1 per 3 min.

Remarks: 95 MC possibly from Danjo Gunto. Other source bore 000°T from our position. 94 MC had very poor pulse shape (long trailing edge).

9 Nov. 1900	33-40 N 126-50 E	74	450	50	None Apparent

Remarks: Possible beacon for northern entrance to Sasebo.

13 Nov. 1900	33-20 N 127-30 E	164	500	7	Slow or None

Remarks: Double pulse (10 micro-sec apart). True bearing indicated Mara To as source.

| 14 Nov. | 32-28 N | 183 | 430 | 25 | Slow and |
| 2200 | 129-38 E | | | | Irregular |

Remarks: Several possible sources.

| 17 Nov. | 31-00 N | 75 | — | — | None |
| 2300 | 129-42 E | | | | |

Remarks: Apparent source Kusakaki Shima. It faded out as we proceeded south east. Then we picked up the following on

| 18 Nov. | 30-25 N | 75 | — | — | ? |
| 0100 | 130-00 E | | | | |

Remarks: Strongest while passing to south west of Yaku Shima. Appeared to fade at thirty to forty second intervals.

INTERCEPTION OF ENEMY RADAR TRANSMISSIONS

Date: 25 Nov. 1944   Report No. 1
1. Ship: U.S.S. *Barb* (SS220)
2. Area covered on this mission: East China Sea from 11-6 to 11-17.
3. Was enemy radar: Landborne, Yes (a) Enemy installations – Unk.
4. Intercept equipment: APR-1 and SPA-1
5. (a) Frequency: 147 – 153 mc   Dial Reading: 147, 150, 152, 153
   (b) PRF: 430 – 490   How measured: SPA-1
   (c) Pulse Width: 25 micro sec. How measured: SPA-1
   (d) Sketch Pulse:

   (e) Was lobe switching used: Rate: How Determined: No indication of lobe switching.
   (f) Polarization of enemy signal:
   (g) Sweep Rate: Did not sweep (see narrative).
6. (a) Was radar used for surface or air search, GL, SLC, OCL, or AL. Apparently surface search.
   (b) Evidence for this conclusion: Installation seemed to coincide with navigational aids.
7. ----------------------
8. Narrative: On entering the area, 6 Nov. at night, course west, south of Yaku Shima, one of the above stations was picked up, and as it began to fade, another was picked up. This latter was lost by the time we headed north west past Kuchinoyerabu. A few hours later that night we picked up a third installation when we passed to east of Kusanaki Shima, course north. This latter had a possible sweep rate of once in two minutes. On 17 Nov., 0500 (I) 31-25 N., 129-38 E, course 090 the fourth was picked up. This signal faded at four minute intervals.

INTERCEPTION OF ENEMY RADAR TRANSMISSIONS

Date: 25 Nov. 1944   Report No. 2

1. Ship: U.S.S. *Barb* (SS220)
2. Area covered on this mission: East China Sea from 6 Nov. to 17 Nov. 1944
3. Was enemy radar: Landborne. Yes.
4. Intercept equipment: APR-1 and SPA-1.
5. (a) Frequency: 95 mc and 94 mc. Dial readings: 94 – 95
   (b) PRF: 660 and 650   How measured: SPA-1
   (c) Pulse Width: 25 & 60 Micro Sec. How measured: SPA-1
   (d) Sketch Pulse:

   ```
         95 Mc              94 Mc
         660 PRF            650 PRF
         25 M.Sec.          60 Micro Sec.
   ```

   (e) Was lobe switching used: Rate: How determined: No indication.
   (f) Polarization of enemy signal: —
   (g) Sweep Rate: 5½ min/sweep & 3 min/sweep.
6. (a) Was radar used for surface or air search, GL, SLC, OCL, or AL. Apparently a Beacon or search radar of at least 50° beam width.
   (b) Evidence of this conclusion: We were 30,000 and 50,000 yards from any possible source (shore) and the signal was strong 20% or more of the sweep (not considering a sector scan)
7. ------------------------
8. Narrative: Our position 32-15 N, 128-30 E., course 000°T. The 95 mc, rectangular pulse seemed to have its source on the bearing 050° – 230°T (possibly Danjo Gunto). The other signal came from 000°T. Occasionally a strong pulsing note (similar to a beat note) would be heard at the same APR-1 dial setting. Its pulse rate was 176 per minute.

At times the trailing edge of the 94 mc pulse would change shape (be clipped a little shorter). This would be accompanied by a crackling noise in the APR-1 earphones.

INTERCEPTION OF ENEMY RADAR TRANSMISSIONS

Date: 25 Nov. 1944   Report No. 3
1. Ship: U.S.S. *Barb* (SS220)
2. Area covered on this mission: East China Sea from 6 Nov. to 17 Nov. 1944.
3. Was enemy radar: Landborne: Yes
4. Intercept equipment: APR-1 and SPA-1
5. (a) Frequency: 74 & 75 mc.   Dial readings: 75 – 75
   (b) PRF: 450   How measured: SPA-1
   (c) Pulse Width: 50–60 Micro Sec.   How measured: SPA-1
   (d) Sketch pulse:

   (e) Was lobe switching used: Rate: How determined:
       No indication of lobe switching.
   (f) Polarization of enemy signal:
   (g) Sweep rate: No sweep.
6. (a) Was radar used for surface or air search, GL, SLC, OCL, or AL.
       Appeared to be a beacon.
   (b) Evidence for this conclusion:
7. ----------------
8. Narrative: One with very irregular pulse rate (500 to 1,100) was noted near the northern entrance to Sasebo. The pulse rate would jump at irregular intervals from 500 to 800 or 950, etc. The pulse looked like one with a long, sloping trailing edge, the latter being clipped off abruptly at 55 or 60 micro seconds. Another source appeared possibly to be Kara To, a third on Kusakaki Shima, and a fourth was noted when we were at 30-10 N. and 13?-2- E.

INTERCEPTION OF ENEMY RADAR TRANSMISSIONS

1. Ship: U.S.S. Barb (SS220) Report No. 4
2. Area covered on this mission: East China Sea from 6 Nov. 1944 to 17 Nov. 1944.
3. Was enemy radar: Landborne: Yes.
4. Intercept equipment: APR-1 and SPA-1.
5. (a) Frequency: 164 MC   Dial Readings: 164
   (b) PRF: 500   How measured: APR-1
   (c) Pulse Width: 7 micro sec.   How measured: APR-1
   (d) Sketch pulse:

   ⌒⌒ (double pulse)

   (e) Was lobe switching used: Rate: How determined: No indication of lobe switching.
   (f) Polarization of enemy signal:
   (g) Sweep Rate: Irregular.
6. (a) Was radar used for surface or air search, GL, SLC, OCL, or AL. Apparently surface search.
   (b) Evidence of this conclusion:
7. --------------
8. Narrative: Appeared strongest on East-West bearing, probably Quelpart Island (25 miles).
The signal was a double pulse about 10 micro seconds apart.

(U) RADIO AND RADIO COUNTERMEASURES

RADIO

1. Ship: U.S.S. Barb (SS220)
2. Position when enemy radio signals were observed. On area and enroute to and from area.
3. Position of transmitting station: Shipboard (Jamming station unknown)
4. Date of jamming: All times in area.
5. Frequencies jammed: Ship to shore (4235 and 8470). Continuous jamming on Fox Schedule – most severe when BIMEK or FMMYH sent.
6. Describe signal jammed (Freq., type of modulation, etc.)
4235 kcs, 8470 kcs; Fox frequently.
7. Use of circuit (tactical, administrative). To receive submarine Fox; ship to shore; to receive China Air Force.
8. Was enemy jamming signal stable: Some were stable and others variable.
9. What was ratio of strength of own signal to enemy jamming signal. 5 by 5 at times. Enemy 5 compared to A strength. 2 signal at both receiving and transmitting station at time of jamming.

10. What was power output of own transmitter at time of jamming. 7 amps. Five amps when jamming not excessive.
11. Location of enemy jammer: Unknown (more than one at a time)
   Landbased   Y   Unknown   Y
12. Type of jamming signals:
   Bagpiper (musical tone).
   Saw (variable tone).
   CW-Random Keying.
   Voice Keying.
13. Effectiveness of jamming. Fox usable. Ship to shore strength 5.
14. Action taken to overcoming jamming: Sharp tuning.
15. Bandwidth covered by enemy jamming signals. 5 KCS either side of frequency used. Signal copied thru enemy zero beat at times.
16. Did jamming transmitter appear to be monitored by look-in receiver: Yes and by transmitting with variable oscillator.
17. If frequency was shifted, how long before enemy jammed new frequency: Control station did not order this, but reported jamming strength five.
18. Narrative: Jamming was in excess, especially on ship to shore frequencies. Wolf Pack frequencies were not effectively jammed. Submarine Fox was very well jammed, but intermittent traffic Repeater Rerun plan now in effect makes possible the interception of all transmitting station serial numbers.

(V) REMARKS

It is suggested that Area 9 be divided up into 3 or 4 areas for rotating patrol. In this way individual subs could be replaced without waiting for all members of pack to depart. The area itself is not suited for pack operations except for a known convoy. Coordinated attack for such within a rotating patrol can be easily attained using Wopacs.

SUBMARINE DIVISION SIXTY-ONE

FB5-61/A16-3

Serial: 0128

Care of Fleet Post Office,
San Francisco, California,
27 November 1944.

C-O-N-F-I-D-E-N-T-I-A-L

<u>First Endorsement</u> to
CO *Barb* Conf. Ltr.
SS220/A16, Serial 016
of 25 November 1944,
Report of Tenth War Patrol.

From:	The Commander Submarine Division Sixty-One.
To:	The Commander in Chief, U.S. Fleet.
Via:	(1) The Commander Task Group Seventeen Point Five.
	(2) The Commander Submarine Force, Pacific Fleet.
	(3) The Commander in Chief, U.S. Pacific Fleet.
Subject:	U.S.S. *Barb*, Report of Tenth War Patrol.

1. The tenth war patrol of the U.S.S. *Barb* was conducted in the East China Sea in the area to the westward of Kyushu and was of thirty days duration, covering the period October 27, 1944 to November 25, 1944. Eleven days were spent in the area. The *Barb* was a unit of a coordinated attack group; the *Queenfish* and *Pecuda*, with the group commander in the *Queenfish*, being the other units of the group. The patrol was terminated by the expenditure of all torpedoes.

2. Area coverage on this short and aggressive patrol was excellent and resulted in five contacts, all of which were developed into torpedo or gun attacks. A summary of these attacks follows:

<u>Attack No. 1</u> – On 10 November a large high speed unescorted AP, *Aikoku Maru* class, was intercepted off the northern approaches to Sasebo and a moonlight radar-periscope approach and attack resulted in two hits which slowed the target to 2 knots and gave it a 30° list. The *Barb* surfaced in pursuit and fired a single torpedo on two separate attacks at short ranges; both missed, one due to erratic run and the other took a jog to the left before settling down. A submerged approach was then made to point blank range and the single torpedo fired scored a hit, finally sinking this valuable ship. Ample opportunity was afforded to identify and witness the sinking of this target in the bright moonlight.

Attack No. 2 – Was on an eleven ship convoy with four escorts. A night surface attack with excellent fire control resulted in firing three two-torpedo salvos in two minutes at three targets (one large and two medium AKs) which netted one hit in each target. The *Barb* then swung and fired two stern tubes at another larger AK scoring one hit. The first three targets were sunk and the last damaged.

Attack No. 3 – Was a submerged periscope attack on the remainder of the same convoy. Three torpedoes were fired at extremely short range at a small AK being overlapped by a medium AK beyond. One hit blew up the small AK and the third torpedo hit the overlapping medium AK. While it is probable that this ship was also sunk, evidence is unfortunately inconclusive.

Attack No. 4 – on a *Shokaku* class CV with three or four escorts was an excellently conducted night surface radar attack. A zig away three minutes after firing caused all but one of a five torpedo spread to miss. This hit slowed the target temporarily. Chase had to be abandoned when it became evident that the damaged CV could not be closed prior to dawn.

Attack No. 5 – was made on two small coastal freighters discovered hugging the coast. The two remaining torpedoes were fired, one at each target. Both missed due to small size of targets and errors in fire control data.

Gun Attack No. 1 – was on three schooners. Divided fire, 40 mm and 4", was employed to sink a pair, and the third schooner was attacked and sunk a half hour later.

3. Numerous plane contacts were made, probably incident to B-29 strikes. Life guard duties were performed on one occasion and a search was conducted for downed aviators. Enemy counter measures were standard and gratifyingly light, probably due in no small part to the *Barb*'s aggressive tactics, severe damage inflicted, and smart evasive tactics. The *Barb* also noted the small bombs or hedge hogs being thrown as previously reported by other returning submarines.

4. The *Barb* returned from patrol in good material condition. All major defects will be corrected with particular attention to the master gyro compass and hydraulic plant. A normal refit is anticipated. This is the *Barb*'s fourth patrol since a navy yard overhaul.

5. The commanding officer, officers and crew are congratulated on this outstanding patrol, which carries on the tradition of this fighting ship. It is recommended that the *Barb* be credited with inflicting the following damage on the enemy:

SUNK

1 AP (*Aikoku Maru* class) (EC)	10,500 tons	(Attack #1A to D)
1 large AK (EU)	7,500 tons	(Attack #2A)
1 medium AK (EU)	4,000 tons	(Attack #2B)
1 medium AK (EU)	4,000 tons	(Attack #2C)

1 small AK (EU)	2,000 tons	(Attack #3)
3 miscellaneous schooners (EU)	300 tons	(Gun Attack #1A–C)
TOTAL	28,300 tons	

DAMAGED

1 large AK (EU)	7,500 tons	(Attack #2D)
1 medium AK (EU)	4,000 tons	(Attack #3)
1 CV (Shokaku Class) (EC)	29,800 tons	(Attack #4)
TOTAL	41,300 tons	
TOTAL SUNK AND DAMAGED	69,600 tons	

J.C. Broach.

cek.

COMMANDER SUBMARINE FORCE, PACIFIC FLEET
SUBORDINATE COMMAND, NAVY NO. 1504

A16-3

Serial: 0207

Care of Fleet Post Office,
San Francisco, California,
27 November 1944.

C-O-N-F-I-D-E-N-T-I-A-L

Second Endorsement to
U.S.S. *Barb* Report of
Tenth War Patrol dated
25 November 1944.

From: The Commander Submarine Force, Pacific Fleet,
        Subordinate Command, Navy No. 1504.
To: The Commander-in-Chief, United States Fleet.
Via: (1) The Commander Submarine Force, Pacific Fleet.
    (2) The Commander-in-Chief, U.S. Pacific Fleet.

Subject: U.S.S. *Barb* (SS220) – Report of War Patrol Number Ten.

    1. Forwarded, concurring in the remarks and recommendations of Commander Submarine Division Sixty-One.

    2. The Commander Submarine Force, Pacific Fleet, Subordinate Command, Navy No. 1504 wishes to add his congratulations to the Commanding Officer, officers and crew of the U.S.S. *Barb* for another very aggressive war patrol.

J.M. Will.

SUBMARINE FORCE, PACIFIC FLEET

FF12-10/A16-3/(15)

Serial 02764

CONFIDENTIAL

hch

Care of Fleet Post Office,
San Francisco, California,
8 December 1944.

Third Endorsement to
Barb Report of
Tenth War Patrol

NOTE: THIS REPORT WILL BE
DESTROYED PRIOR TO
ENTERING PATROL AREA.

ComSubPac Patrol Report No. 593
U.S.S. *Barb* – Tenth War Patrol.

From: The Commander Submarine Force, Pacific Fleet.
To: The Commander-in-Chief, United States Fleet.
Via: The Commander-in-Chief, U.S. Pacific Fleet.

Subject: U.S.S. *Barb* (SS220) – Report of Tenth War Patrol,
            (27 October to 25 November 1944).

1. The tenth war patrol of the *Barb* was conducted in the East China Sea Area off the west coat of Kyushu. The *Barb* was one of three submarines working together in the East China Sea Area in adjacent area for the purpose of cooperative attacks.

2. This was the third successive highly successful war patrol for the *Barb*. Within eight days the *Barb* fired all its torpedoes in a series of extremely aggressive torpedo attacks of all types. These excellent attacks resulted in the sinking of five enemy ships, the probable sinking of two more, and the damaging of a large enemy aircraft carrier. In addition the *Barb* sank three large enemy schooners by gun fire. The attacks made in the early morning runs of 12 November against a large convoy of eleven ships and four escorts demonstrated in a most brilliant manner how night radar and periscope attacks should be made. When the shooting was over at least four of the enemy ships had been sunk, and two more probably sunk or severely damaged. This convoy was hit later on by one of the other submarines of the group.

3. The attack on the large enemy carrier was also well conducted, but more hits on this target were lacking because of the carrier's zig just after firing.

4. Award of the submarine Combat Insignia for this patrol is authorized.

5. The Commander Submarine Force, Pacific Fleet, congratulates the commanding officer, officers, and crew of this fine fighting submarine for this third successive successful war patrol. He further congratulates the *Barb* for having sunk

14 ships, including one aircraft carrier, plus three sampans and three schooners, all totalling 108,450 tons; and for damaging four more ships including a large enemy carrier, totalling 46,300 tons. The *Barb* is credited with having inflicted the following damage upon the enemy:

SUNK

1 – Large AP (EC) (*Aikoku Maru* Class)	10,500 tons	(Attack No. 1)
1 – Large AK (EU)	7,500 tons	(Attack No. 2)
1 – Medium AK (EU)	4,000 tons	(Attack No. 2)
1 – Medium AK (EU)	4,000 tons	(Attack No. 2)
1 – Small AK (EU)	2,000 tons	(Attack No. 3)
1 – Schooner	300 tons	(Attack No. 1A)
1 – Schooner	300 tons	(Attack No. 1B)
1 – Schooner	300 tons	(Attack No. 1C)
Total Sunk	18,900 tons	

DAMAGED

1 – CV (*Shokaku* Class) (EC)	29,800 tons	(Attack No. 4)
1 – Large AK (EU)	7,500 tons	(Attack No. 2)
1 – Medium AK (EU)	4,000 tons	(Attack No. 2)
Total Damaged	41,300 tons	
Total Sunk and Damaged	70,200 tons	

Distribution:
(Complete Reports)

Cominch	(7)	C.A. Lockwood, Jr.	
CNO	(5)		
Cincpac	(6)		
Intel.Cen.Pac.Ocean Areas	(1)		
Comservpac	(1)		
Cinclant	(1)		
Comsublant	(8)		
S/M School, NL	(2)		
CO, S/M Base, PH	(1)		
Comsopac	(2)		
Comsowespac	(1)		
Comsubsowespac	(2)	Substrainpac	(2)
CTG 71.9	(2)	All submarines, Pacific	(1)
Comnorpac	(1)		
Comsubspac	(40)	E.L. Hynes, 2nd,	
SUBAD, MI	(2)	Flag Secretary.	
ComsubspacSubordcom	(3)		
All Squadron and Division Commanders, Pacific	(2)		

Patrol Eleven, 19 December 1944 – 15 February 1944

U.S.S. *Barb* (SS220)

File: SS220/A16
Serial: 02

Care of Fleet Post Office,
San Francisco, California,
15 February 1945.

CONFIDENTIAL

From:	The Commanding Officer.
To:	The Commander in Chief, United States Fleet.
Via:	(1) Commander Submarine Division
	(2) Commander Submarine Squadron
	(3) Commander Submarine Force, Pacific Fleet.
Subject:	U.S.S. *Barb* – Report of Eleventh War Patrol.
Enclosure:	(A) Subject Report.
	(B) Track Chart (ComSubPac only).
	(C) Information submitted to Hydrographic Office concerning East China Sea (copy to ComSubPac only).

1. Enclosure (A) covering the eleventh war patrol of this vessel conducted in the Formosa Straits and East China Sea off the east coast of China from Shanghai to Lam Yit during the period 19 December 1944 to 15 February 1945, is forwarded herewith.

E.B. Fluckey.

CONFIDENTIAL
U.S.S. *Barb* – Report of Eleventh War Patrol.

(A) PROLOGUE

Arrived Midway, from 10th War Patrol 25 November 1944, for second successive advanced base refit. Received an excellent refit from SubRon 6, SubDiv 61, Submarine Base, SubRon 24, SubDiv 242 and U.S.S. *Aegir* during squadron shift.

Transferred Executive Officer[1] to Kavela Hospital and one experienced officer[2] to new construction. Received a new Executive Officer[3] and a new sub school graduate.

Four day training period. Readiness for sea 19 December 1944. Training excellent considering facilities as available.

(B) NARRATIVE

Assigned to Coordinated Attack Group consisting of *Queenfish*, *Picuda* and *Barb*. Operation order to be picked up at Guam.

19 Dec.
1430(Y) Departed Midway. Commenced training program for officers and men, daily dives and fire control party drills.
Enroute Guam or Saipan.

20 Dec.
Omitted.

21 Dec.
Crossed international date line.

25 Dec.
Sank floating mine with twin 20 MM. Expended two magazines. Lat. 18-40.4 N., Long. 155-19.5 E. Celebrated Christmas with carols and festivities.

27 Dec.
Arrived Guam. Received an excellent welcome and voyage repair from *Sperry* and SubDiv 101.

---

[1] Lieutenant James G. Lanier, USNR, diagnosed with angina pectoris during Patrol Ten.
[2] Lieutenant Everett P. "Tuck" Weaver, USNR.
[3] Lieutenant James T. Webster, USNR.

29 Dec.
Underway in company with Loopers, *Queenfish* and *Picuda*. ComWolfPack, Commanding Officer *Queenfish*.

1 Jan.
0000(I) Celebrated the advent of what we hope is the final year of the war.
0947(I) Received patrol boat contact report from *Queenfish*. We will not be able to reach the contact prior to noon.
0938(I) Received message that *Queenfish* and *Picuda* were commencing gun attack.
1233(I) Sighted small thin column of white smoke.
1243(I) (Ship Contact #1) Lat. 25-09, Long. 135-15. Sighted patrol boat, lying to. Smoke had disappeared.
1305(I) Manned 4 inch and twin 20 MM guns. Requested information from *Queenfish*. *Queenfish* replied—sink target at discretion. Looked target over. She had been hit in bow by 4 inch shells. Automatic guns had sprayed her with the usual lack of effect. A good sized fire had evidently been started forward and a small fire on her port quarter. These had been brought under control. Her hull was in good shape, no flooding having taken place. Her bridge and engine room were unaffected. No personnel were in evidence. Probably hiding, since fires had been put out. Determined to board. Kept automatic weapons trained on all openings to eliminate any possible opposition.
1318(I) Away boarding party.
1328(I) Boarding party boarded patrol boat. Confiscated sextant, 7x50 German binoculars, compass, barometer, radio transmitter and receiver sets, charts, colors, rifles, professional looking books of undetermined value. Crews quarters were not searched because they were blacked out. Flashlights and crowbar proved to be the items lacking in our boarding party equipment.
1343(I) Boarding party returned with full bags. Patrol boat had been armed with a machine gun and rifles. Evidently being used as a weather ship. In view of the fact that she may have sent a message requesting assistance prior to *Queenfish* and *Picuda* attack, decided against sending party back to search for a prisoner. Backed clear.
1349(I) (Gun Attack #1) Commenced firing with 4 inch gun and 400 yard range. Fired 13 rounds for 13 hits. One hit lighted off the engine room fuel tanks. This made the midships section a blazing inferno. 8 or 9 Japs came scrambling out from below. The next shot landed in their midst. Took Kodachrome movies.
1352(I) Ceased firing. Secured the guns. Target was sinking. Cleared the area.
1405(I) Target sank.

2 Jan.
Entered Area 9.

3 Jan.

0400(I) Passed through Tokara Kaikyo. Encountered APR signals at 142, 148, 158 megs. Presumed to be shore based covering certain sectors of channel. Decided to run surface patrol through area nine, since we were astern of rest of pack who had submerged.

1135(I) Received China aircraft report of convoy near Danjo Gunto. Course 240°T, speed 12. Commenced search at full speed. Covered all speeds 7–12 knots and courses 230–260 in vain.

1420 (Aircraft Contact #1) Sight and SJ radar contact on Nell at 3 miles in drizzle. Dived.

1455 Nell departed.

1502 Surfaced.

4 Jan.

(All time How unless otherwise designated.)

0034 Sighted 2 lighted junks. 180 miles west of Shanghai. Avoided.

0400 Secured search for convoy in Area 12. Enroute Area 11 A & B.

1105 Sighted floating mine Lat. 30-48, Long. 125-08. Tried to sink it with 20 MM and .50 cal. Many hits, broke off horns, which erupted in a yellow vapor, but mine refused to sink. Entered Area 11A and B. Area has been divided into three sections of equal latitudes for independent rotating patrol until coordinated search is required. This to take care of the first traffic anticipated. Commenced patrol in Area Gene. Taking sounding at half hour intervals for hydrographic office.

5 Jan.

Surface patrolling ten miles off Yushan Liehtao.

1413 Dived and made approach on a junk.

1529 Surfaced. Went alongside to look him over. Typically Chinese.

1618 Encountered four junks.

6 Jan.

Surface patrolling ten miles off Yushan Liehtao.

1140 (Aircraft Contact #2) Sighted Betty at 9 miles. Dived.

1216 Surfaced. Commenced patrolling down China Coast along 20 fathom curve.

1514 Increased speed to 16 knots and commenced search for convoy reported by China aircraft in Formosa Straits heading towards Shanghai.

7 Jan.

Surface patrolling off Tongyong Tao, search secured.

0540 (Ship Contact #2) Radar contact at 20,000 yards. This contact was confused with the islands of TungYung Tao.

0601 Finally established contact as a definite convoy of seven ships. Sent out contact report. Commencing end around at full speed. Dawn has arrived. Sky is heavily overcast. Horizon hazy with about 12,000 yards visibility, varying. Ending around at 18,000 yards. Enemy appears to be enroute Keelong at 11 knots. Sea state 5.

0746 Ahead of convoy. Contact reports going out every 20 minutes. *Picuda* will be able to get in; *Queenfish* probably not.

0803 Submerged 14,000 yards ahead of convoy. Heading along base course to get a stable 60 foot trim in the heavy seas. Necessary to use 2/3 speed at all times.

0829 Commencing approach. Nothing in sight. Distant pinging. Visibility now estimated at 7,000 yards.

0843 JP picking up light and heavy screws intermittently. Using pinging bearing to conduct approach.

0845 Rain squall has reduced visibility to about 4,000 yards. Making continuous periscope exposure at 59 feet with over ten feet of scope out half the time. Cutting across convoy course, screws all over the dial, very loud pinging, and not a ship in sight.

0900 Swinging periscope wildly. Two sets of heavy screws crossing ahead, light screws astern and on port and starboard bows. Visibility is still apparently about 4,000 yards.

0902 Haze lifting. Sighted a large tanker broad on starboard bow[4], range 850 yards with 130 starboard angle on bow. Made ready bow tubes. Nearly whole formation is now in sight. A large freighter is about 1,500 yards beyond the tanker. Escorts are five destroyers, two stack, with white bands around stacks.

0905 Tubes are ready. Tanker is zigging away. Definitely a poor shot, which would not be worth the value of an alerted convoy to the *Picuda*. Withheld fire. Made a set up on a destroyer about 1,000 yards on port bow. An easy, provoking shot, but our torpedoes would never run up sea at 6 feet in this weather.

0907 Commenced taking periscope exposures at one minute intervals. Determined to surface when trailing destroyer has disappeared for another end around. Chalk this one off to visibility. Am amazed that no one spotted our scope, also that I have now developed enough self control to resist the temptation to let three fly at an escort unless conditions are right. The latter the result of twelve torpedoes I have wasted in the last three patrols.

0941 Surfaced. Convoy at 12,000 yards. Commenced end around at 10–14,000 yards depending on the visibility of the port screen. Base course 110°T.

1027 Two explosions.

1031 Four explosions.

1059 One explosion.

---

[4] Broad on starboard bow: Bearing 045° relative from submarine.

1115 Convoy changed base course to 150°T. Visibility increasing. Destroyers in sight. Secured end around. Impossible to beat them to Formosa now that haze has cleared. Heading back to China Coast. Some consolation with *Picuda* making the grade.

2126 Assumed coastal position of wolf pack scouting line patrolling along China coast northward searching for a convoy.

8 Jan.

Patrolling in wolf pack along convoy routes.

0441 Reversed course and headed southwest along China coast.

0500 Eased in towards coast in event convoy hugged coast.

1300 (Ship Contact #3) Sighted smoke of convoy towards the coast. Commenced closing. At least five ships.

1312 Sent out contact report to pack.

1330 Sent out contact report of convoy on southerly heading.

1350 Sent out contact report of convoy course 140. Seven or more large ships.

1415 Commencing end around on port flank of convoy at 22,000 yards. Visibility excellent. Sent out contact report of enemy base course 160, speed 12. The pack is closing. Heard occasional depth charges.

1442 Sent out contact report of enemy base course 170, speed 9.5.

1517 Sent out contact report of enemy base course 175, speed 9.5. Now have 6 ships. Possibly more, for some are straggling.

1549 In position ahead of convoy. We are now in the blind bombing zone. Sent out contact report giving enemy zig plan. Told pack to home on our SJ interference.

Have been ending around at 20–23,000 yards with funnels and masts of most ships clearly in view from bridge, some of escorts masts' tops barely visible. Using periscope for quick bearings, taking angles on bow from bridge and using radar ranges. If we had not been in wolf pack end around would have been made at greater range. However I estimate the situation as follows:

(a) Convoy is evidently heading for Takao, which will allow the pack only the early evening for attack at best, before getting too deep in blind bombing zone and too close to minefields.

(b) Our job is to bring pack into contact as expeditiously as possible, then make a daylight submerged attack from coastal flank and slow or turn the convoy into the *Queenfish* and *Picuda*.

(c) The above will require an accurate flow of information. This can only be obtained by close in tracking. Figured the *Barb* suitable for this as her old type sheers can easily be mistaken for a Chinese junk if seen by the merchantman (with no facilities for tracking), but not by the escorts.

(d) *Queenfish* and *Picuda* undoubtedly have been navigating by D.R. for past 36 hours, whereas *Barb*, being near coast, has accurate navigational positions. We can not attack until another boat has made contact.

1612 *Picuda* has contact.

1616 Informed pack we were diving to attack starboard flank. We are now well into blind bombing zone.

1618 Submerged. Sea force 5. Making attack at 60 feet.

1620 Distant depth charge.

1621 Distant depth charge.

1655 Echo ranging. A plump convoy of eight good sized ships. All better than 3,500 tons and many of these coal burners. Ships are in several echelon groups. The leading echelon to port consisting of a *Kaga Maru* Class MKFKM freighter with a destroyer about 1,500 yards ahead. About 500 yards on the starboard quarter of this freighter is a 4 goal poster transport surrounded by 4 spit kit escorts. A large MFM freighter straggles about 1,200 yards astern of the transport. The starboard echelon is about 1,000 yards on the starboard quarter of the above echelon. It consists of three brand new large engine aft freighters or tankers, possibly the type 45 MKKMF Standard A (Modified) Cargo Ships shown in the ONI Weekly of November 22, 1944. A small escort is close on each bow of the leading ship in the starboard echelon. Two escorts are about 3,000 yards out on the starboard flank. Between the two echelons and straggling about 3,500 yards astern are two more large freighters, probably MFM. There seems to be escorts everywhere. All ships are painted gray and are heavily laden.

It would be a snap to get in the center of this outfit. However it is imperative that we bend them to port, and prevent them from heading towards the shallow China Coast. Hold off on starboard bow. Plan to smack the 4 goal poster with the escorts in the port echelon since she is probably the most important ship, then use the other three bow tubes on the leading engines-aft job in the starboard echelon, following through with a stern tube attack on the second engines-aft ship.

1710 Coming in nicely. Made ready all tubes.

1725:30 Torpedo Attack #1(a). Fired tubes 1, 2, 3 at the large four goalposter transport on a 70 starboard track, range 2,700 yards, gyros zero. Can see *Kaga Maru* Class ship exposing itself from superstructure forward in a bow overlap. Shifted targets to engines aft ship.

1724:35 Torpedo Attack #1(b). Fired tubes 4, 5, 6 at the engines aft ship on an 80 starboard track, range 1,700 yards, gyros 5° left.

1725 Left full rudder. All ahead standard. Swinging for stern shot.

1726 Four torpedo hits close together, the third of which was a tremendous explosion. At the time, being intent on coming stern tube set up. I idly remarked, "Now that's what I call a good solid hit," when I heard someone mutter "golly, I'd hate to be around when he hears a loud explosion." This, accompanied by the tinkle of glass from a shattered light bulb in the conning tower, and the expressions on the faces of the fire control party, snapped me out of my fixation and the full force of the explosion dawned upon me. The ship had been forced sideways and down, personnel had grabbed the nearest support to keep from being thrown off their feet, cases of canned goods had burst open in the forward torpedo room. Later we found a section of deck grating ripped out of the superstructure aft. *Queenfish* later told us this last ship hit blew up and was obviously an AE.[5]

1728 Sound reporting high speed screws all around. Rig ship for depth charge. Steadying up and attempting to climb back to periscope depth at 2/3 speed. A look at our results is paramount. Breaking up noises.

1734 All screws going away on sound.

1737 Periscope depth. A smoke cloud where the engines aft had been. The stern of the transport sticking up at a 30° angle with two escorts close aboard. Her bow is evidently resting in the mud. Depth of water 30 fathoms.

A *Kaga Maru* class ship is on fire amidships just above the waterline. The whole formation has turned away and appears to be stopped. Amazingly, we appear to have leprosy. All escorts have scampered over to the unattacked side of the formation. The destroyer has reversed courses, and now has a 90 port angle on the bow.

1747 Can feel aggressiveness surging through my veins, since the escorts are more scared than us. Commenced reload forward. Heading towards convoy, with another engines after in our sights.

Destroyer suddenly turned towards us and shifted to short scale. Secured blowing down tubes.

1748 Maximum relative movement between destroyer and *Barb*. Nice spot for a down the throat shot, but no torpedoes forward.

1749 Aggressiveness evaporated. Resumed deep submergence of 140 feet, mud below. Breaking up noises continuing.

1815 Completed evasion. No depth charges. Reloaded forward.

1856 Surfaced with breaking up noises still being clearly heard. No contact.

1859 Heading down assumed enemy new base course.

1912 Jap radar interference. This interference was steady on us for the better part of the next five hours. Radar jamming was also encountered.

1914 *Queenfish* reported attacking.

1930 SJ contact at 20,000 yards on convoy. Queenfish attack completed.

1934 *Picuda* reported attacking. Reported 6 ships in convoy. That checks, unfortunately, with *Kaga Maru* still afloat.

1942 Gunfire from direction of convoy.

1945 Reported having contact and taking position on starboard flank.

1948 Explosion.

1956 Two explosions. *Picuda* has probably attacked. We are now about 8,000 yards abeam of last ship. Inasmuch as *Queenfish* would be anxiously awaiting com-

---

[5] AE: Ammunition ship.

pletion of our attack so she could get in again, decided to try our radical new system of continuous attack (see remarks). Commencing our normal screaming surface approach on last ship in the formation from the starboard flank. Another ship about 600 yards on his port bow overlapping. Two more ships about 3,000 yards ahead. Formation plot indicates five escorts around this tail group. One forward, one on starboard beam and two astern. Since we intend attack from starboard quarter these will not bother us (we pray).

Night is very dark and visibility poor. Sea state 4. Radar ranges and TBT bearings used.

2012 Torpedo Attack #2. Fired tubes 1, 2, 3 at trailing large AK on a 145 starboard track, range 2,100 yards, gyros zero, own ship speed 16.5 knots, torpedoes sounded like motor torpedo boats going out.

Overlapping ship is a large AO or AK. All ahead full, right rudder, swinging out to commence approach on the next ship up the line.

2015 Two hits observed and timed.

2016 One hit observed and timed in overlapping ship. First ship disappeared from view and radar—sunk. Second ship was engulfed in a cloud of smoke. Radar reported pip was half size when ordered to shift to new target ahead—probably sunk.

2018–2024 Explosions probably depth charges.

2025 Remaining two targets maintained formation but increased speed. These two ships were in column about 2,000 yards apart. Making approach on starboard flank of trailing ship. Formation plot showed 9 escorts within 5,000 yards. One about 1,000 yards on starboard beam, two close aboard, others scattered with apparent confusion. Having only eased out to 4,000 yards abeam for a setup this would be quick.

2032 One explosion.

2033 Torpedo Attack #3. Fired torpedoes 4, 5, 6 on a 127 starboard track, gyros 1 right, range 1,590 yards.

2034 Swinging right to ease out and then attack target ahead with stern tubes.

2035 Three hits timed and observed followed by a stupendous, earth shaking eruption. This far surpassed Hollywood and was one of the biggest explosions of the war. The rarefaction following the first pressure wave was breath taking. A high vacuum resulted in the boat. Personnel in the control room said they felt as if they were being sucked up the hatch. Personnel in the Conning Tower, wearing shortened shirts not tucked in at the belt, had their shirts pulled up over their heads. On the bridge as the air was wrenched from my lungs, somehow it formed the words "all ahead flank." The target now resembled a gigantic phosphorus bomb. In the first flash as the torpedoes hit all we could ascertain was that the target had a long superstructure and a funnel amidships. The volcanic spectacle was awe inspiring. Shrapnel flew all around us, splashing on the water in a splattering pattern as far as 4,000 yards ahead of us. Topside we alternately ducked and gawked. The horizon was lighted as bright as day. A quick binocular sweep showed only the one ship ahead remaining and a few scattered escorts. None of the escorts close to the ammunition ship could be seen. These were probably blown up and we would claim them as probably sunk except that I figure that 4 ships sunk, one probably sunk and one damaged is about all the traffic will bear for a twelve torpedo expenditure. In aftermath the forward torpedo room reported several missiles struck the hull, but no apparent damage was sustained.

At this point of the game I was ready to haul ashes. However the new TBT operator (the Engineer officer who had never seen a shot fired or ship sunk in five runs from his diving station) really had his guns out. Frantically, he pleaded that we couldn't let the last ship go, besides he loved to hear the thump, thump, thump of the torpedoes and to see millions of bucks going sky high.

Good sales talk. Commenced the approach for a stern tube attack on the ship ahead. No pip from our probably sunk ship on radar. From this and information from rest of pack her classification is now SUNK.

2055 *Queenfish* said she wanted to attack. *Picuda* said she would follow the *Queenfish*. The *Barb* could continue her attack as long as there were ships and torpedoes left. However we have our share, so gave them green light. Passed our new target abeam to port at 2,160 yards (what a temptation), and headed down towards pass between Formosa and minefield to make sure nothing escaped.

2110 Investigated a pip 10,000 yards ahead, which turned out to be two fair sized escorts high tailing it by themselves for Takao. Probably the destroyer. No other ships ahead.

2125 *Queenfish* requested enemy course and speed. Replied. Evidently she is distant, so recommended approach on the last merchant ship. Notified pack we were attacking single ship. This in view of the fact radar had spotted an escort on her starboard quarter approaching rapidly. This ship should be sunk before she obtained addition protection. One escort on her beam close aboard.

2150 Ahead of target 2,650 yards. Slowed to 1/3 speed. Stern tubes ready. Opening out slowly from the track and waiting a few minutes for target to close range before firing.

2153 Two torpedo explosions on target's starboard quarter. *Queenfish* must have attacked. Undoubtedly she is the escort we had picked up coming up on the starboard side. Close business for we had about 20 second to go before firing.

2156 Target stopped. *Barb* stopped. Would she sink? Range 2,600 yards.

2157 Target opened fire with automatic weapons, 40 MM and an estimated 3 inch gun in all directions.

2158 Believe *Queenfish* dived. Target's fire is high and erratic. Weird to be lying to, here, listening to the rattle of his 20 MM, the poomp-poomp-poomp of his 40 MM and the occasional blast from his 3 inch. The gunsmoke has a pungently foul odor, which hangs heavy throughout the ship. All fire is tracer. These are flying thick and fast from port to starboard then from starboard to port, with a 40 MM projectile sailing over us now and then. We are protected by the smoke from his guns.

2159 Range 3,000 yards. Radar reports no change in target pip. *Queenfish* can not attack submerged. All back 2/3. Intend to back in to 1,500 yards to make sure of a two torpedo *coup de grâce*.

2201 Target pip disappearing. Stopped. Pip now is a little more than half size. Evidently on her way down and not worth expenditure of more torpedoes. No more large ships can be found on the radar. Still several escorts left. Chalk off one convoy. Time to shove. All ahead full.

2202 Shore batteries joined the fray. Gunfire from about six points along the coast, 12,000 yards away. This is novel. Their shells are bursting when they strike the water about 7,000 yards west of us. Frankly, from all of this high shooting it now appears that the Japs believe they are being bombed instead of torpedoed.

2206 Gunfire ceased.

2219 Secured from Battle Stations. Searched area and then headed for lifeguard station, which is near scene of our submerged attack. Anticipate warm weather.

2356 *Picuda* reported attack completed with no hits on only remaining ship. The position given is near scene of our submerged attack. Wonder if she attacked an escort sent out to pick up survivors. Jap interference on SJ continues.

9 Jan.

0525–0350 Chased by a radar equipped patrol boat.

0500 On life guard station. Using SD radar. Sea state 6 again. Heavy overcast.

0750 SD contacts at 3, 5, 6, 9 miles. No IFF.

0755 SD contacts at 6, 7, 9 miles. No IFF.

0756 SD contacts at 7, 8, 9, 15 miles. No IFF.

0757 SD contacts at 11, 12, 18 miles. No IFF.

0758 SD contacts at 12, 13 miles. No IFF.

0759 SD contacts at 10, 12 miles. No IFF.

0800 SD contacts at 5, 7, 8, 9, 10, 11 miles. No IFF.

0801 SD contacts at 4, 6, 8 miles. No IFF.

0809–0817 Second wave appeared on SD screen.

0839–0905 SD contacts continually. One plane answered IFF.

0912 (Aircraft Contact #3) Sighted two Frances[6], distant 6 miles flying low and coming in fast. Dived to 100 feet.

0920 Surfaced.

1500 Secured from lifeguard duty, but kept lifeguard frequency manned because planes were reporting in.

---

[6] Yokosuka P1Y bomber.

1600 Asked China base if any planes were down. She checked and reported plane down 1 mile off east coast of Formosa. Out of our province, so notified pack commander on wolf pack frequency.

10 Jan.
Surface patrolling on 20 fathom curve, north along China coast.
0200 Made a short approach on an unnamed island off Tung Yung Tao, which insisted on making speeds of 6–15 knots. Hydrographic Office, by separate correspondence, is being requested to name this island Barb Island. TDC operator in the doghouse.
0800 Joined the Junk fleet for morning maneuvers.
1615 (Aircraft Contact #4) Sighted Nell at 9 miles. Dived.
1635 Surfaced.

11 Jan.
0042 *Queenfish* reported contact on one ship making 17 knots. Headed to intercept at maximum speed in prevailing seas.
0136 Encountered *Queenfish* instead of convoy. Ship had gone by. One of DRs must be out.
0933 (Aircraft Contact #5) Sighted Jake[7] at 7 miles. Dived.
1005 Surfaced. Commenced patrolling south along 20 fathom curve.
1112–1130 Junks around.
1532 (Aircraft Contact #6) Sighted Tess[8] at 10 miles. Dived.
1552 Surfaced.

12 Jan.
Surface patrolling off Foochow. Sea state 5. Visibility 7,000 yards in heavy haze. Sky overcast.
0800–1100 Investigated discolored water spot for hydrographic office. These are not shallows. Took soundings throughout spot. Believe these spots are due to subterranean streams. During a dive later at this spot we were 28,000 pounds heavy overall.
1500 *Queenfish* reported radar contact about 30 miles east of us. However we had her SJ interference bearing 160°T. Assumed her DR was in error and homed on her SJ.
1508 *Queenfish* dived.
1520 (Ship Contact #4) Radar contact on convoy at 18,400 yards. Commenced approach. We are well off the track.
1530 At standard speed on target's starboard bow. Rear escort at 8,000 yards, not visible in haze. Enemy course 315. Speed 14.5 knots. We are working ahead.

---

[7] Jake: Aichi E13A1 reconnaissance seaplane.
[8] Tess: Douglas DC-2 transport. Built under license in Japan by Nakajima.

1532 (Aircraft Contact #7) Sighted Zeke[9] carrying one bomb, at 2 miles heading in. Dived. This Jap doesn't realize he can't see anything in this poor flying weather.

1533 One bomb. Took normal approach course at high speed.

1544 Aircraft still in sight. Sighted one destroyer crossing ahead at about 5,000 yards.

1600 Whole formation in sight crossing about 6,000 yards ahead. Course 290. A heart breaker. Convoy consists of an unlisted escort carrier with a single funnel aft on starboard side and four poles along starboard side of flight deck, which goes all the way to the bow. It appears to have been converted. Possibly from a large tanker. One plane is circling it. The other ships are a four goal poster transport similar to the *Koku Maru* and a large MFM freighterr. Four destroyers act as escorts.

1625 Trailing formation, plane in sight frequently.

1759 Surfaced. Commencing the chase. Sent out contact reports to ComSubPac and Wolfpacks.

1803 (Aircraft Contact #8) SD radar contact 1 mile. APR signal at 153 steady on. We are heading into a heavy sea. It's very dark. From experience in Convoy College do not believe he can bomb without sight contact, which is impossible. We will not dive.

1806 Waiting breathlessly. Plane is circling at 3/4 to 1 mile.

1809 Plane shoved off. Our theory somewhat substantiated.

1901 Although making turns for 16 knots into heavy seas our pit log speed is less than 10 knots. Slowed and gave up chase.

13 Jan.

Surface patrolling north of Samsa Inlet off 20 fathom curve.

0800–0900 Junks.

1130 (Aircraft Contact #9) Sighted Betty 10 miles. Dived.

1203 Surfaced.

1205 (Aircraft Contact #10) Sighted Jake at 6 miles. Dived.

1230 Surfaced.

1322 (Aircraft Contact #11) Sighted Betty at 7 miles. Dive.

1422 Surfaced.

2200–2330 Junks.

14 Jan.

Surface patrolling off Seven Stars.

0500–0800 Junks.

0819 (Aircraft Contact #12) Sighted Mavis at 10 miles. Dived. Disassembled faulty torpedo for repairs.

---

[9] Zeke: Mitsubishi A6M Type 00 fighter. Zero.

1127 Surfaced.
1440 (Aircraft Contact #13) Sighted 2 Bettys at 7 miles. Dived.
1459 Surfaced.
1540 (Aircraft Contact #14) Sighted 3 Bettys at 3 miles. Dived.
1602 Surfaced. All planes bound for Formosa.

15 Jan.

Surface patrolling north of Formosa covering eastern approaches to Formosa Straits.

1459 (Aircraft Contact #15) Sighted Rufe at 3 miles. Dived. Plane type indicated possibility of fleet traffic. Remained submerged.

1822 Surfaced.

16 Jan.

Surface patrolling approaches to Formosa Straits.

0030 Made approach on a large junk.

0110 *Queenfish* reported contact on a single ship with 2 escorts over 100 miles away. She can handle it.

0526 *Queenfish* reported zero torpedoes and negative results. Commenced search for ship which was last heading for China coast.

0739 (Aircraft Contact #16) Sighted Betty at 3 miles. Dived.

0755 Surfaced. Commenced using SD at intervals.

0832 (Aircraft Contact #17) SD radar contact at 26 miles. No dive.

1020 Sighted *Queenfish* departing area.

1355–2400 Cruising among large junk fishing fleet closing coast for night traffic search.

2128 Received word from *Picuda* that *Barb* should search for aviator downed 3 miles off Shinchiku (Formosa) sometime on 15 January. A 3.5 knot current sets along here and we are 140 miles away. *Barb* at this time is having sufficient trouble of her own running down the coast north of Namkwan Harbor inside the 10 fathom curve. Searching for *Queenfish*'s ship and avoiding junks.

2359 Secured search for ship. No coast lights are burning. Covered all possible speeds and courses through western half of area. Assume ship stopped at Foochow or Samsa Inlet.

17 Jan.

Surface patrolling searching north of Formosa where current would have set aviator. Undoubtedly he was picked up by Japs.

2000 Commenced patrol 6 miles east of Haitan Island. Searching for convoy reported by China Air Group. Results negative.

18 Jan.
Surface patrolling Formosa Straits. *Picuda* and *Barb* decided to blockade the Straits. *Barb* covering to east, *Picuda* to west.

2117 Sighted Hakusha Ko (Formosa) light. Dimmed, shown at infrequent intervals, not visible outside of 6 miles.

2252 (Aircraft Contact #20) Strafed and bombed by night flier. Dived. Though particularly manning Jap aircraft frequencies 140–150 megs on APR, we had no indication. APR is operating properly. Night is very dark. Own speed eight knots. Wake is zero. Believe sighting of sub is impossible. First indication of plane was gunfire to starboard and high. While clearing bridge plane passed about 50 feet overhead (no exhaust visible) with more gunfire, possibly from tail gunner. Four bombs fell to port. Tactics excellent. No float lights were dropped. Since we are only ten miles north of blind bombing zone[10], will ask China Group if it is our own plane. China later replied that plane was not American. OOD involved intends to get flak suit before next patrol.

20 Jan.
0008 Surfaced.
China reported all traffic had holed up. However, continued surface patrol of Formosa Straits.

0901 (Aircraft Contact #21) Sighted Pete at 5 miles. Dived. Plane close to water. Remained submerged for possible traffic.

1017 Surfaced.

1030 (Aircraft Contact #22) SD contact at 8 miles. Dived.

1113 Surfaced. Several junks around.

1638 Sighted mine. Lat. 25-57.2, Long. 121-18.8. China reported more ships anchored in Lam Yit. Also another convoy from around there, apparently going through our area. Commenced searching again.

1738 (Aircraft Contact #23) Sighted Pete at 7 miles. Dived.

1802 Surfaced.

Have searched for all aircraft reported ships covering all possible speeds and courses. Since nearly all are reported from Lam Yit, and we are positive they do not pass Turnabout Light, those ships must go by an unknown route. Study of charts indicate that the passage of these ships could be effected without sighting by pack, if the Japs have dredged the long 1½ fathom stretch through Kaitan Straits. Requested China Air Group obtain information on Haitan Straits.

---

[10] Blind bombing zone: An area in which American aircraft were authorized to bomb any and all vessels on sight, without having to first confirm their identity. Usually these were areas where enemy mine fields or other hazards made it particularly dangerous for friendly ships to operate. American submarines sometimes operated inside these zones despite the added danger.

21 Jan.
Surface patrolling Formosa Straits searching for more ships which departed Lam Yit.
0633 (Aircraft Contact #24) Sighted Pete at 8 miles. Dived.
0658 Surfaced.
0757 (Aircraft Contact #25) Sighted Pete at 7 miles. Dived.
0841 Surfaced.
1900–2400 Junks around.
Received information from China that large ships are using Kaitan Straits. From Lam Yit to Formosa ships pass through blind bombing zone. This completes our analysis of shipping. While our own forces are hammering Formosa no shipping is moving around Keelung. All traffic is now running the inshore route along the China Coast. No lights have been observed burning along the coast. Consequently the Japs are running only in the day time, when it is impossible to make a submarine attack with their new close coast route. Anchorages being used are probably Shanghai, Wenchow, Samsa Inlet, Foochow, and Lam Yit, all of which are well mined and a day's run apart. Seas are continually state 5–7. In conclusion our prospectus appears poor, unless we can find a suitable opportunity at night to resort to torpedo boat tactics.

Basing the remainder of our patrol on the latter assumption, made a complete study of the China coast from Wenchow south to Lam Yit. Recent unknown mining has taken place north of Wenchow. If our assumptions are correct, the present convoy, for which we are searching, is anchored at Foochow tonight and will be enroute Wenchow tomorrow. To substantiate our conclusions, plan to mingle with the junk fleet north of Seven Stars tomorrow afternoon at a point 10 miles inside the 20 fathom curve and 15 miles from the coast where we can observe the passage of our convoy.

22 Jan.
Surface patrolling searching for convoy in accordance with plan. Seas have abated to state 3. Skies overcast.
0656 Sighted mine. Lat. 27-06, Long. 122-12. Have decided not to sink the drifting mines for they may possibly damage Jap traffic.
1203 Maneuvering among junk fleet. Crossed 20 fathom curve.
1421 (Ship Contact #5) Sighted smoke of 3 to 6 ships moving in column along the coast. Closed to 10,000 yards for accurate tracking and to determine types. Two ships are large AKs. Lost sight of other shortly. Their course is 225, speed 10 knots, their position, in 8 fathoms, several miles inside the 10 fathom curve. At 10 knots they could not make Samsa Inlet before 2100. If the overcast remains heavy enough to hide the moon we can tackle them in Siaoan Channel just north of Samsa Inlet.
Sent contact report to *Picuda*.

1512 Secured tracking. SJ radar lost target at 28,000 yards. Ended around Seven Stars, Tae Islands and Piseang Island, through junk fleets, outside of island visibility range.

1820 Dark. Commenced approach to coast south of Piseang Islands and north of Samsa Inlet.

1900 Passed edge of junk fleet. Approaching ten fathom curve. Sorry to clear the junks even though they provide an obstacle race, for we depend upon their routes to keep us clear of minefields.

1916 Quartermaster[11] tugged at my sleeve and confidentially said, "Don't look now, but we just passed a mine 10 yards abeam to port." Probably garbage.

1925 Picked up a junk 6,000 yards ahead. Joined him in 9 fathoms and commenced patrolling to seaward on his quarter using him for a mine sweeper.

2100 Still no coast light burning and no ships. Requested *Picuda* by radar to patrol off Tung Yung Island in event ships had departed coast north of Piseang Islands. Informed her that convoy had not passed our position.

2120 Have now covered route for convoy speeds 13–16 knots. Ships must have anchored. Decided to search coast. Lack of junks between coast and Piseang Islands may indicate a minefield. Instead of going directly up coast we will ease out around Piseang Islands and close coast north of them.

2257 *Picuda* reported negative contact.

2326 North of Piseang Island. Closing coast escorted by junk fleet, all constant helming. Visibility is lowering. Cannot see junks outside of 1,000 yards. Conning by PPI.

23 Jan.

Conducting inshore surface search for convoy anchorage. Maneuvering constantly to avoid collision with junks. Present entourage consists of several hundred darkened junks.

0030 Commenced taking PPI coast contour plots, for plexiglass matching with large scale chart of coast, to search for ships.

0112 Chart plot matching showed an uncharted smear northwest of Incog Light. Checked this on A-scope which showed saturation pips at 29,000 yards. Radar officer and operator said they were definite ships. Doubt existed, however, for our radar had never before had saturation pips on ships at such a range. Continuing to search up coast towards Incog Light.

0137 Moonset.

0240 Cleared junks. None ahead. Much prefer to have them, or know the reason for their absence.

0300 (Ship Contact #5) Rounded Incog Islands and had radar contact on a very large group of anchored ships in the lower reaches of Namkwan Harbor. Slowed to take stock of the situation.

---

[11] QM3c Paul D. Bluth, USNR.

Fully realize our critical position and the potential dangers involved. Estimate that situation as follows:

(a) Recent unknown mining in this vicinity is a known fact. Mines could be laid from Incog Island to Tae Island. However, a more effective minefield would be from Incog Island to Pingfong, the eastern entrance to Namkwan Harbor, which would provide a protected anchorage behind it. Since the position of the anchored convoys is too close to this line, assume the latter minefield does not exist. The former though doubtful, must remain a possibility, particularly in view of the absence of junks.

(b) Jap radar interference is showing up on the A-scope and PPI, sweeping. One escort appears to be patrolling several thousand yards northeast and a second escort to the east of the anchored ships covering the most logical position for entry and attack. A third escort is working close to Incog Light apparently more concerned with using his radar to keep himself off the rocks. Visibility is very poor.

(c) Assumed the closely anchored columns would be heading about 030°T heading into the wind and seas with a current of 1 knot. Plotted the navigational position from which we would attack, making our approach from the southeast. The attack would be made on approximately a 60° track so that our stern tubes would be fired with zero gyros on our selected retirement course.

(d) Elected to retire through an area marked "Unexplored" on our large scale chart, which contained sufficient "rocks awash" and "rocks, position doubtful" to make any over-ambitious escorts think twice before risking a chase. This course would also cross the mass of junks which would be a definite and final barrier to all pursuit. While retiring radar will only be used sweeping quickly from broad on one bow to broad on the other. All damage must be assessed without it.

(e) Countermeasures expected will be searchlights, gunfire, and hot pursuit. Against this we will have a stern tube salvo, 40 MM and automatic weapons.

(f) Inasmuch as our attack position will be 6 miles inside the 10 fathom curve and 19 miles inside the 20 fathom curve, we will require an hour's run before being forced down. Consequently our attack must be a complete surprise and the force of our attack must be sufficient to completely throw the enemy off balance. We have four torpedoes forward and eight aft. No time will be available for reload; for a speedy, darting, knife thrust attack will increase the probability of success.

0320 Figure the odds are 10 to 1 in our favor. Man Battle Stations Torpedoes.

0325 Fortunately we have a flexible control party and at this point we flexed it. CO secured the bridge and took over the conning tower; target plot was secured and the Assistant Approach Officer was shifted to PPI; and another officer was shifted to the bridge.

Seriously considered placing crew in life jackets, but the atmosphere through-

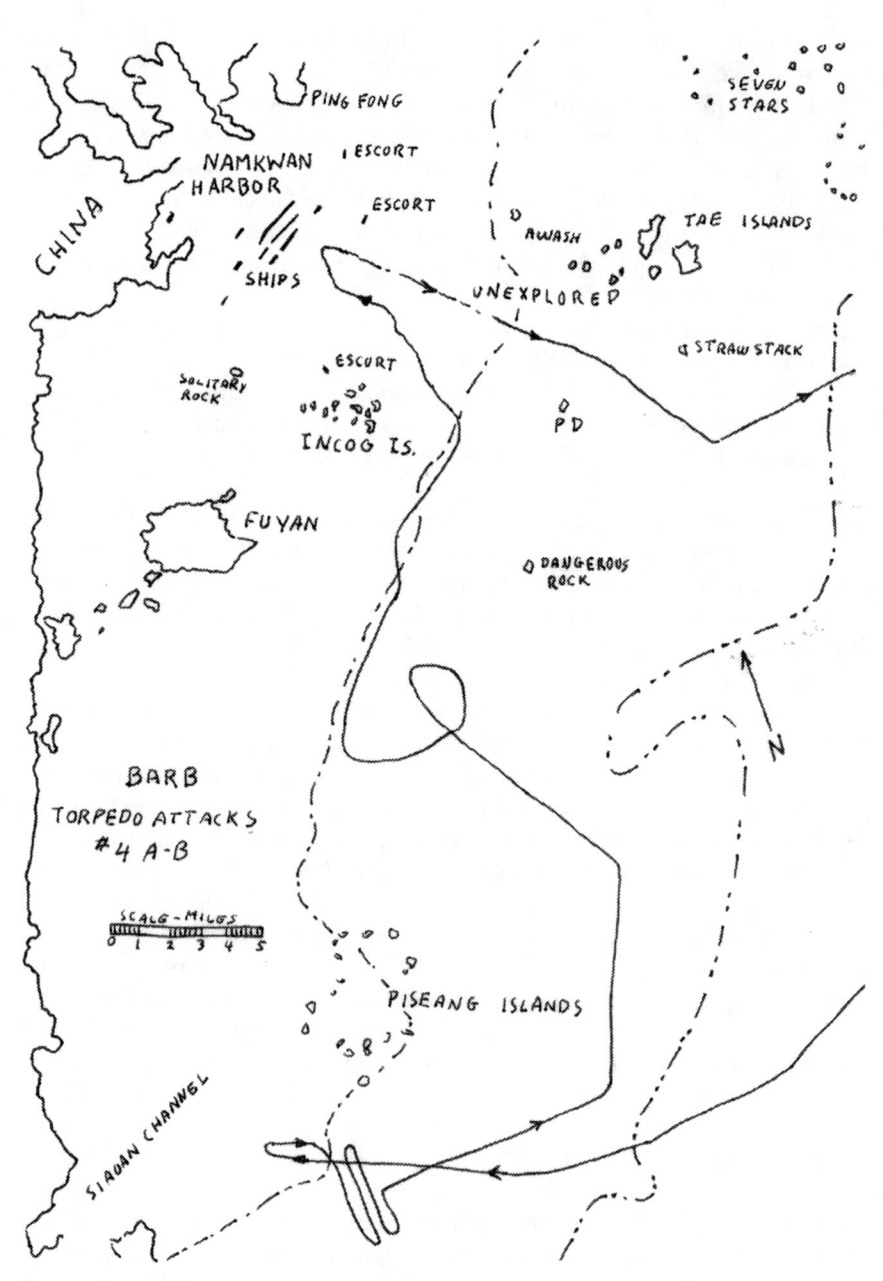

Chart of Namkwan Harbor and vicinity showing *Barb*'s track during approach and attack on the ships anchored there, and her escape following the attack. Commander Fluckey received the Medal of Honor for this attack.

out the boat is electric. The men are more tense that I've ever seen them. Save for an occasional report of "single ping sounding, 6 fathoms," the control room is so quiet the proverbial pin would have sounded like a depth charge. Discarded the idea of life jackets as definitely alarmist, with so many hearts doing flip flops.

Do not consider it advisable in our present precarious position to send a contact report to the *Picuda*. She could not possibly attack before dawn and get out. Will send one after the attack when our presence is known.

0352 Range 6,000 yards. Made ready all tubes. Ships are anchored in three columns about 500 yards apart with a few scattered ships farther inshore. This, frankly, must the most beautiful target of the war. Actual measurement of target length is 4,200 yards. Ships are banked three deep. Even an erratic torpedo can't miss. Radar officer counts twelve ships on one bearing. Estimate at least 30 ships present. Our biggest job will be to prevent too many torpedoes from hitting one ship. For purposes of set up chose one of the large ships to left of center of the near column as target. Using TBT bearings.

0402 Torpedo Attack #4A. Fired tubes 1, 2, 3, 4 with 150% spread, track 65 starboard, gyros 30 left, torpedo run 3,225 yards, depth set 6 feet, target speed 1½ knots, target course 040°T.

0402:16 Fired tube #1.
0402:26 Fired tube #2.
0402:36 Fired tube #3.
0402:46 Fired tube #4.

Right full rudder, all ahead standard. Sounding 5 fathoms. Shifted target to right for ships ahead in near column.

0404 Torpedo Attack #4B. Fired tubes 7, 8, 9, 10 with 300% spread, track 65 starboard, gyros 3 right, range 3,020 yards, depth set 6 feet.

0404:42 Fired tube #7.
0404:48 Fired tube #8.
0404:57 Fired tube #9.
0405:07 Fired tube #10.

All ahead flank!!! Commanding Officer manned bridge.

0406:02 Torpedo #2 hit on target. Timed and observed.
0406:09 Torpedo #3 hit on target. Timed and observed.
0407:27 Torpedo #1 hit in 2nd column. Timed and heard on bridge.
0408:16 Torpedo #4 hit in 3rd column. Timed and observed.
0408:31 Torpedo #6 hit in 1st column. Timed and observed.
0408:36 Torpedo #8 hit in 2nd column. Timed and observed.
0409:41 Torpedo #7 hit in 3rd column. Timed and observed.

Main target of attack 4A, large AK (EU), in first column was hit by torpedoes #2 and #3. Target observed to settle and undoubtedly sink.

Unidentified ship in second column was hit by torpedo #1. This was not observed since shielded by main target after turn to right. Damaged.

Large AK, in third column, hit by torpedo #4, shortly thereafter caught on fire. Fire later flared up 5 or 6 times then went out in a manner similar to a sinking ship. Probably sunk.

Torpedo #6 hit in the first column. Believed to have hit in main target of attack #4A or ship close to this target. Observation not sufficiently accurate enough to claim additional damage.

Large AK, in first column, to right of main target of attack #4A, hit by torpedo #8. Ship belched forth a huge cloud of smoke. Damaged.

Unidentified ship, in second column hit by torpedo #5. The whole side of this ship blew out in our direction in a manner similar to an AE or the magazine of a large warship. Ship sank.

Large AK, in third column hit by torpedo #7. Ship blew up with a tremendous explosion. Ship sank.

Tracers of all descriptions flew out from the two ships which exploded. At the same time several large calibre projectiles, estimated 8–12 inch, with tracers hurtled through the air. A moment after this searchlights were seen sweeping about for a short while.

0413 Smoke from the ships hit, on fire, and exploding completely obscured all ships and prevented any further observation of other damage.

The *Barb* is now high balling it for the 20 fathom curve at 21.6 knots, broken field running through the junk fleet, with the radar sweeping rapidly 30° either side of the bow—wildly maneuvering when some of the junks are inside the sea return. Expect to see a junk piled up on the bow at any second.

0436 Gun fire from well astern. Some poor junks getting it.

0438 Some form of navigational light lighted on Tae Island. Probably to aid the escorts' navigation.

0445 Sent contact report to *Picuda*.

0511 The Galloping Ghost of the China Coast crossed the 20 fathom curve with a sigh. Never realized how much water that was before. However, life begins at forty (fathoms). Kept going.

0512 Slowed to 19 knots.

0550 Dawn. Assume the Japs will expect us to submerge, so will stay on the surface.

0633 (Aircraft Contact #26) SJ radar picked up plane at 7 miles coming in fast. A CO's privilege to change mind. Dived. Range closed to 2½ miles.

1220 Surfaced. Retiring to east.

1621 Periscope sighted. Maneuvered closer. Doubtful sighting.

24 Jan.

Surface patrolling center of area.

1424 Sighted mine. Lat. 27-01, Long. 122-15.

1519 (Aircraft Contact #27) Sighted 3 Bettys at 6 miles. Dived. Worked on hydraulic plant.
1614 Surfaced.
2225 (Aircraft Contact #28) SJ contact on plane at 7 miles, closing. Dived.
2245 Surfaced.

25 Jan.

Surface patrolling off Samsa Inlet. Sea state 6.
1422 Received contact report from *Picuda* of 1 ship, unknown escorts, air coverage, sighted at 1200. Commenced search.
1900 Secured search. Ship probably went to Lam Yit.

27 Jan.

Surface patrolling Formosa Straits. Sea state 7. Attempted to investigate Lam Yit after dark, but seas piled up and we had enough to do to stay afloat.

28 Jan.

Surface patrolling off Lam Yit. Sea state 6.
1200 Invaded blind bombing zone during afternoon in hopes of picking up Amoy traffic.
2000 Investigating Lam Yit harbor. Empty.
2130 Sighted mine. Lat. 25-03, Long. 119-33.
2254 Sighted mine. Lat. 25-04, Long. 119-37.

29 Jan.

Surface patrolling along coast off Lam Yit.
0007 (Aircraft Contact #29) SJ contact on plane at 5 miles, closing. Dived. Plane closed to 1½ miles while submerging.
0030 Surfaced.
0345 China aircraft reported 1 AK, 1 AP, 1 escort leaving Amoy at 1750 headed northeast. They should be close to our position, and should pass through Lam Yit. Commenced search. As we will be in less than 20 fathoms it is imperative to find them and complete our attack prior [to] dawn.
0402 *Picuda* reported contact with 2 ships and 2 escorts on Formosa side of straits, distant 60 miles. Since she has 10 torpedoes, believe our present search is best gamble.
0450 (Ship Contact #6) SJ contact at 17,500 yards. Commenced approach. Convoy consists of 1 large AK, 1 medium transport in column with 1 escort on starboard flank of transport, which is leading. Heavy rain. Visibility is poor. Sea in Lam Yit about state 4. Targets on steady course 060°T, speed 7.8 knots. Sent contact report to *Picuda*.

0537 Range to large AK 1,800 yards. Swinging right for stern tube shot. TBT bearings inside 3,000 yards.

0540:10 Torpedo Attack #5. Fired tubes 7, 8, 9, 10 and 118 starboard track, gyros 2° right, range 2,010 yards, torpedoes set at 8 feet. Spread coverage 200%.

0543 Convoy no longer visible in rain squalls.

0544:10 One timed hit. Not observed.

0544:35 Second timed hit. Not observed.

Continued to track targets as we opened out. Target maintained steady course 060°T, speed 7.9 knots.

0555 CO in conning tower watching A-scope and PPI at 8,800 yards. At this time AP and escort pips were 4° to right of target.

Frankly assessment of damage in this attack from our standpoint can only be classed as unknown. The timed hits were over one minute late, which is incomprehensible unless these torpedoes run very slow in heavy sea. Tracking the target after the attack showed no apparent damage until the pip disappeared. Seas off the coast were state 7 and one hour after the attack we were forced to slow to 8 knots. Can not understand how we could possibly miss. The approach on a steady course, steady speed target was the simplest we've ever been offered. Even my conscience bothered me with the thought that I was practically jettisoning our last four torpedoes on such a simple set up, when I could have fired a split salvo of two torpedoes at the AK and two at the AP. Hit times, however, do not jibe and yet are much too early for end of run. Analysis is a mystery.

1000 Departing area in heavy seas. Making good 2 knots. Inductions closed.

30 Jan.

Surface patrolling enroute Midway, sea state 6, decreasing.

1108 Sighted mine. Lat. 27-14, Long. 121-47.

1420 Sighted mine. Lat. 25-35, Long. 122-07.

31 Jan.

Surface patrolling enroute Midway, sea state 4.

1424 Sighted mine. Lat. 30-10, Long. 125-28.

1630 Sighted mine. Lat. 30-15, Long. 125-35.

2130 Departed area 11, entered area 12.

1 Feb.

0200 Departed area 12, entered area 9.

0546 APR signal 96 megs. From Danjo Gunto.

0645 Sighted mine. Lat. 31-49, Long. 127-58.

1445 Sighted a U.S. submarine.

1459 Submarine fired identification flare. Range 12,000 yards.

1500 Answered with a flare. As colors changed at 1500 we fired a different color than she had fired. She then disappeared.

2000 Passing through Tokar Strait. APR contacts at 147, 154, 158, 139 and 160 megacycles. Several at 160 megs with different characteristics.

2100 SJ interference. Challenged but no answer.

2200 SJ contact on a U.S. Sub to south of us. Unable to raise on SJ. Probably Underwood's Urchins.

2 Feb.

0025 Exchanged messages with U.S.S. *Parche*.

3 Feb.

1420 Sighted Sofu Gan (Lot's Wife).

1426 Sighted possible periscope. Avoided.

9 Feb.

Repeated this day crossing date line.

Arrived Midway, channel closed. Patrolled south during night.

10 Feb.

Commenced search for Midway, which had moved northward at 4 knots during night.

1130 Finally overtook Midway and moored. Captain Crawford extended an exceptionally fine welcome in apologizing for the locking the barn door the 9th and because of Midway's current erratic movement when shrouded by darkness.

11 Feb.

Underway enroute Pearl.

15 Feb.

Arrived Pearl.

(C) WEATHER

Weather in general was very disagreeable. The seas were consistently rough, their average condition being state 4–5. The skies were completely overcast eighty percent of the time.

(D) TIDAL INFORMATION

Tides and currents encountered conformed generally with sailing directions, tables and charts.

(E) NAVIGATIONAL AIDS

The large rocks, islands and high peaks along the China coast in the East China Sea afforded excellent targets for radar navigation. The following light houses were observed and their conditions were as follows:
1. Yushen Lieh Tao – lighted, normal characteristics.
2. Siataechen Sahn – not lighted.
3. Chuanyuan (middle) Island – not lighted.
4. Tung Awe (shroud) Island – not lighted.
5. Incog Island – not lighted.
6. Spider Island – not lighted.
7. Tung Yung – not lighted.
8. Tung Koon – not lighted.
9. Turnabout Island – not lighted.
10. Ookseu Island – not lighted.
11. Nakusha Ko – lighted flashing white and red erratic period, and very dim.

(F) SHIP CONTACTS

No.	Time Date	Lat. Long.	Type	Initial Range	Est. CSC.	How Contacted	Remarks
1.	1243 H 1-1	25-18.0 135-21.0	300 tons.	17,000	Stopped	High Periscope	Gun Attack #1, Boarding party.
2.	0540 H 1-7	26-12.9 120-40.2	Conv of 2 ships & 5 DDs	15,450	150	Radar	Foiled by visibility.
3.	1256 H 1-8	25-37 120-30.7	Conv of 8 ships & 9 escorts	22,000	175	Sighted High Periscope	Attack #1-A, B. Attack #2-A. Attack #3.
4.	1541 H 1-12	25-31.5 120-10.5	Conv of 2 ships, 4 DDs & 1 CVE	17,000	310	Radar	Attacked by aircraft & forced to dive before reaching attack position.
*5A.	1421 H 1-22	27-14 120-42	Conv of 3 to 6 ships.	20,000	225	Sight	See note and contact #5B
*5B	0402 H 1-23	27-04 120-27	Conv of at least 30 anchored ships.	29,000	Anchored	Radar	Attack #4 -A-B including contact #5.
6.	0450 H 1-29	25-05.6 119-35.9	Conv of 2 ships & 1 escort	17,000	060	Radar	Attack #5

* Note the attacks listed in 5B were made on ships listed in 5A plus many other anchored ships.

(G) AIRCRAFT CONTACTS

No.	Time Date	Lat. Long.	Type	Initial Range	How Contacted	Remarks
1.	1420 I 1-3	31-16 128-14	Nell	3 mi.	Radar	Dived
2.	1140 H 1-6	29-04.6 122-31.7	Betty	9 mi.	Sighted	Dived
3.	0912 H 1-9	25-17.5 120-24.7	Frances	8 mi.	Sighted	Two planes, dived.
4.	1615 H 1-10	27-27.5 121-31.0	Nell	9 mi.	Sighted	Dived
5.	0933 H 1-11	28-32.5 122-17.1	Jake	7½ mi.	Sighted	Dived
6.	1552 H 1-11	27-34.1 122-00.0	Tess	10 mi.	Sighted	Dived
7.	1532 H 1-12	26-33.5 120-08	Zeke	2 mi.	Sighted	Dived – 1 bomb.
8.	1803 H 1-12	25-40.3 120-06.0	Unk.	1 mi.	SD radar	No dive.
9.	1130 H 1-13	26-43.9 120-49.0	Betty	10 mi.	Sighted	Dived
10.	1205 H 1-13	26-50.9 120-49.5	Jake	6 mi.	Sighted	Dived
11.	1322 H 1-13	26-43.5 120-53.3	Betty	7 mi.	Sighted	Dived
12.	0819 H 1-14	26-52.1 121-04.5	Mavis	10 mi.	Sighted	Dived
13.	1440 H 1-14	26-52.1 120-48.9	Betty	7 mi.	Sighted	Two planes, dived.
14.	1514 H 1-14	26-13.2 120-46.7	Betty	5 mi.	Sighted	Three planes, dived.
15.	1459 H 1-15	26-08.9 121-36.0	Rufe	8 mi.	Sighted	Dived
16.	0734 H 1-16	26-18.9 121-46.0	Betty	3 mi.	Sighted	Dived
17.	0832 H 1-16	26-14.5 121-35.0	Unk.	24 mi.	SD radar	No dive.

18.	1000 H 1-18	25-42.9 120-04.8	Zeke	3 mi.	Sighted	Two planes, dived.
19.	1249 H 1-18	25-38.0 120-19.2	Pete	5 mi.	Sighted	Dived
20.	2250 H 1-19	25-10.1 120-51.0	Unk.	Overhead	Heard Sighted	Bombed and strafed, dived.
21.	0901 H 1-20	25-57.0 121-09.8	Pete	5 mi.	Sighted	Dived
22.	1030 H 1-20	25-56.9 121-11.0	Unk.	8 mi.	SD radar	Dived
23.	1738 H 1-20	25-56.2 121-08.9	Pete	7 mi.	Sighted	Dived
24.	0658 H 1-21	25-55.1 121-00.5	Pete	6 mi.	Sighted	Dived
25.	0757 H 1-21	25-59.1 121-08.8	Pete	7 mi.	Sighted	Dived
26.	0633 H 1-23	26-55.0 12?-13.5	Unk.	7 mi.	SJ radar	Dived
27.	1519 H 1-24	26-56.8 122-11.6	Betty	5 mi.	Sighted	Three planes, dived.
28.	2225 H 1-24	26-47 124-29	Unk.	9 mi.	SJ radar	Dived
29.	0007 1-29	25-13.9 112-44.1	Unk.	4½ mi.	SJ radar	Dived

(H) ATTACK DATA

U.S.S. *Barb* (SS220)   Gun Attack No. 1   Patrol No. 11
Time: 1348:30 I   Date: 1 Jan. 1945   Lat. 25-15 N., Long. 135-20 E.

Target Data – Damage Inflicted

Sunk: 1 Mis. (Patrol Vessel, Armed) (EC) 300 tons.
(Previously attacked and damaged by *Queenfish* and *Picuda*)
Damage Determined by: Visual observation.

Details of Action

After boarding party returned to ship with loot, backed clear to 400 yards and fired 13 rounds of 4" H.C. for 13 hits. Seventh round exploded in the fuel tank, scattering fuel and flames over the superstructure. Eight or nine Japs scampered out of the hold just in time for the next round to explode in their midst. Several, though injured, jumped over the side. Target was seen to sink stern first at 1405.

U.S.S. *Barb*   Torpedo Attack No. 1A-B   Patrol No. 11
Time: 1724 H   Date: 8 Jan. 1945   Lat. 24-54.8 N., Long. 120-26.0 E.

Target Data – Damage Inflicted

Description: Attack 1A – Large AP (EU) – Large single stack, passenger superstructure, four king posts first and last of which supported masts, raked bow, cruiser stern. Overlapping forward 600 yards beyond was *Kaga Maru* Class (EC).

Attack 1B – Large AE (EU) – Brand new, engines aft. Above ships in convoy of eight large heavily loaded ships with one DD escort and at least eight smaller escorts. No air coverage. Visibility excellent. Contact – Smoke range 35,000 yards.

Ships Sunk: A – Large AP (EU) – 10,000 tons.
         B – Large AE (EU) – 7,500 tons.

Ship Damaged: A – *Kaga Maru* Class (EC) – 9,300 tons.

Damage Determined by: Large AP his forward by one and possibly two torpedoes. Ship last seen through periscope with stern sticking out with 30° angle, bow evidently sticking in mud.

Kaga Maru Class (EC) hit by one torpedo amidships. Ship seen through periscope with fire amidships just above waterline.

Large AE (EU) hit by two torpedoes. Ship seen to blow up and disintegrate. Breaking up noises heard for 1 hour and 30 minutes until surfacing.

Target Draft: A – 25'   Course: A – 143   Speed: A – 10   Range: A – 2,600
         B – 25'   B – 126   B – 10   B – 1,600
                                                           (At firing)

Own Ship Data

Course: A – 029   Speed: A – 3   Depth: A – 60 ft.   Angle: A – 1° Down.
     B – 031   B – 3   B – 60 ft.   B – 2° Down.

[Fire Control and Torpedo Data]

Type Attack: Day – Submerged.

Tubes Fired – No.	1.	2.	3	4.	5.	6.
Track Angle	69 S	70 S	72 S	76 S	80 S	84 S
Gyro Angle	001	003	005	360	354	358
Depth Set	8'	8'	8'	8'	8'	8'
Hit or Miss	?	Hit	Hit	Hit	Hit	Miss
Erratic	?	No	No	No	No	No
Mark Torpedo	18-1	18-1	18-1	18-1	18-1	18-1
Serial No.	55171	56400	55241	56433	55331	55798
Mark Exploder	8-5	8-5	8-5	8-5	8-5	8-5
Serial No.	9670	8415	9998	10210	10854	10175
Actuation Set	Contact	Contact	Contact	Contact	Contact	Contact
Actuation Actual	?	Contact	Contact	Contact	Contact	—
Mark Warhead	18-1	18-1	18-1	18-1	18-1	18-1

Serial No.	3383	2897	2529	2949	2725	2884
Explosive	TPX	TPX	TPX	TPX	TPX	TPX
Firing Interval	0 s	10 s	10 s	10 s	10 s	10 s
Type Spread	Divergent	Div.	Div.	Div.	Div.	Div.
Sea Conditions	5	5	5	5	5	5
Overhaul Activity	Submarine Base, Midway, T.H.					

Remarks: Spread from aft forward computed for 50 yards between torpedoes along target track. Speed reduction used. Made end around at 20–23,000 yards. Had zig plan and speed before diving, from visual observation of angle on bow from bridge, high periscope bearings and radar ranges during end around.

U.S.S. *Barb*   Torpedo Attack No. 2   Patrol No. 11
Time: 2011 H   Date: 1-8-45   Lat. 24-37.2 N., Long. 120-30.8 E.
                        Target Data – Damage Inflicted

Description: Large AK with large AK or AO overlapping. Same convoy as attack 1. Visibility – poor. Contact radar 20,000 yards.

Ships Sunk: Large AK (EU)   –   7,500 tons.
               Large AK or AO (EU) –   7,500 tons.

Damage Determined by: Large AK hit by first torpedo amidships and second torpedo forward. Large AK or AO hit by third torpedo amidships. Heavy cloud of smoke prevented further observation. Radar pips of primary target (large AK) disappeared immediately. Radar pip of overlapping target (large AK or AO) reduced to half size at range of 3,800 yards when radar was shifted to target of next attack. Upon completion of attack No. 3, 20 minutes later, there was no radar pip from this target. *Queenfish* also passed scene of this attack shortly thereafter without finding a target.

Target Draft: 25'   Course: 225   Speed: 10.3 knots   Range: 2,150 (at firing)
                             Own Ship Data
Course: 189   Speed: 16.5   Depth: Surface   Angle:
                       [Fire Control and Torpedo Data]

Type Attack: Night surface – Radar and TBT.

Tubes Fired – No.	1.	2.	3.
Track Angle	143 S	145 S	147 S
Gyro Angle	368	000	002
Depth Set	8'	8'	8'
Power	—	—	—
Hit or Miss	Hit	Hit	Hit
Erratic	No	No	No
Mark Torpedo	18-1	18-1	18-1
Serial No.	54820	56419	54640
Mark Exploder	8-5	8-5	8-5
Serial No.	9624	7942	9919
Actual Set	Contact	Contact	Contact
Actuation Actual	Contact	Contact	Contact
Mark Warhead	18-1	18-1	18-1
Serial No.	2891	2913	2978
Explosive	TPX	TPX	TPX
Firing Interval	0 s	10 s	10 s
Type Spread	Divergent	Div.	Div.
Sea Conditions	3	3	3
Overhaul Activity	Submarine Base, Midway, T.H.		

Remarks: Spread from aft forward computed for 50 yards along target track. Speed reduction used.

U.S.S. *Barb* Torpedo Attack No. 3 Patrol No. 11
Time: 2034 H   Date: 8 Jan. 1945   Lat. 24-31.5 E., Long. 120-28.8 E.
Target Data – Damage Inflicted
Description: Large AE (EU) – Large superstructure. Funnels amidships. Same convoy as attack No. 1 and 2. Visibility – poor. Contact – Radar.
Ship Sunk: Large AE (EU)   –   7,500 tons.
Damage Determined by: Target seen to blow up from bridge in a brilliant display and disintegrate. Three hits – aft, amidships and forward.
Target Draft: 25'   Course: 190   Speed: 11.5   Range: 1,590 (at firing)
Own Ship Data
Course: 134   Speed: 11.4   Depth: Surface   Angle:
[Fire Control and Torpedo Data]
Type Attack: Night Surface – Radar and TBT.

Tubes Fired – No.	4.	5.	6.
Track Angle	127 S	129 S	132 S
Gyro Angle	001	004½	007½
Depth Set	8'	8'	8'
Power	—	—	—
Hit or Miss	Hit	Hit	Hit
Erratic	No	No	No
Mark Torpedo	18-1	18-1	18-1
Serial No.	56691	55848	54862
Mark Exploder	8-5	8-5	8-5
Serial No.	9635	10339	10354
Actuation Set	Contact	Contact	Contact
Actuation Actual	Contact	Contact	Contact
Mark Warhead	18-1	18-1	18-1
Serial No.	2863	2948	2935
Explosive	TPX	TPX	TPX
Firing Interval	0 s	10 s	10 s
Type Spread	Divergent	Div.	Div.
Sea Conditions	3	3	3
Overhaul Activity	Submarine Base, Midway, T.H.		

Remarks: Spread from aft forward computed to 50 yards along target track. Speed reduction used.

U.S.S. *Barb*   Torpedo Attack No. 4A   Patrol No. 11
Time: 0406 H   Date: 23 Jan. 1945   Lat. 27-04 N., Long. 120-27 E.

Target Data – Damage Inflicted

Description: Convoy contacted in the afternoon plus other convoys – at least thirty ships. Anchored in three main columns 500 yards apart with other scattered ships. Twelve ships on firing bearing. Three radar equipped escorts patrolling. No air coverage. Contact – Radar – Full saturation pips at 29,000 yards. Visibility – Poor.

Ships Sunk: Large AK (EU) (Main target)   –   7,500 tons.
Ship Probably Sunk: Large AK (EU)   –   7,500 tons.
Ship Damaged: Unidentified.   –   4,000 tons.

Damage Determined by: Main target in first column hit by torpedoes 2 and 3 timed and observed. Target observed to sink.

Unidentified ship in second column hit by torpedo #1 – timed and heard on bridge – not observed since shielded by main target after turn to right.

Large AK, in third column, hit by torpedo #4 – timed and observed. Shortly thereafter caught on fire. Fire later flared up five or six times then went out in a manner similar to a sinking ship.

Target Draft: 25'   Course: 040   Speed: 1½ (tide)   Range: 3,400 (at firing)

Own Ship Data

Course: 320   Speed: 9½   Depth: Surface   Angle:

[Fire Control and Torpedo Data]

Type Attack: Night Surface – Radar and TBT.

Tubes Fired – No.	1.	2.	3.	4.
Track Angle	66 S	67 S	68 S	69 S
Gyro Angle	327	326	329½	329
Depth Set	6'	6'	6'	6'
Power	—	—	—	—
Hit or Miss	Hit	Hit	Hit	Hit
Erratic	No	No	No	No
Torpedo Run	3765	3250	3200	4225
Mark Torpedo	18-1	18-1	18-1	18-1
Serial No.	55869	55386	54925	56882
Mark Exploder	8-5	8-5	8-5	8-5
Serial No.	8660	9611	10558	9545
Actuation Set	Contact	Contact	Contact	Contact
Actuation Actual	Contact	Contact	Contact	Contact
Mark Warhead	18-1	18-1	18-1	18-1
Serial No.	1583	3444	1804	2207
Explosive	TPX	TPX	TPX	TPX
Firing Interval	0 s	10 s	10 s	10 s
Type Spread	Divergent	Div.	Div.	Div.

Sea Conditions 2 2 2 2
Overhaul Activity   Submarine Base, Midway, T.H.
Remarks: Torpedoes fired from aft forward. Spread covering 150%. Speed reduction used.

U.S.S. *Barb*   Torpedo Attack No. 4B   Patrol No. 11
Time: 0409 H   Date: 23 Jan. 1945   Lat. 27-04 N., Long. 120-27 E.

Target Data – Damage Inflicted

Description: Same target as attack 4A.
Ships Sunk: Unidentified (AE) (EU   –   4,000 tons.
               Large AE (EU)   –   7,500 tons.
Ship Damaged: Large AK (EU)   –   7,500 tons.

Damage Determined by: Unidentified in second column, hit by torpedo #5 – timed and observed. Whole side of ship blew out in our direction in a manner similar to an AE or the magazine of a large warship. Torpedo #6 hit in the first column. Believed to have hit in main target of attack #4A or ship close to this target. Observation not sufficiently accurate enough to claim additional damage. Large AE, in third column hit by torpedo #7 – timed and observed. Ship blew up with tremendous explosion. Large AK, in first column ahead of main target of attack 4A, hit by torpedo #8 – timed and observed. Ship belched forth a huge cloud of smoke. This smoke from fires and ships blowing up completely obscured all ships and prevented any further observation of other damage.

Target Draft: 25'   Course: 040   Speed: 1½ (tide)   Range: 3,020 (at firing)

Own Ship Data

Course: 100   Speed: 9½   Depth: Surface   Angle: —

[Fire Control and Torpedo Data]

Type Attack: Night surface – Radar and TBT.

Tubes Fired – No.	7.	8.	9.	10.
Track Angle	60 S	62 S	64 S	66 S
Gyro Angle	181½	183½	185½	187½
Depth Set	6'	6'	6'	6'
Power	—	—	—	—
Hit or Miss	Hit	Hit	Hit	Hit
Erratic	No	No	No	No
Torpedo Run	3515	3060	4190	3160
Mark Torpedo	18-1	18-1	18-1	18-1
Serial No.	55572	58544	57059	53808
Mark Exploder	8-5	8-5	8-5	8-5
Serial No.	9639	10167	10343	9868
Actuation Set	Contact	Contact	Contact	Contact
Actuation Actual	Contact	Contact	Contact	Contact
Mark Warhead	18-1	18-1	18-1	18-1
Serial No.	2962	3644	2420	1641
Firing Interval	0 s	10 s	10 s	10 s
Type Spread	Divergent	Div.	Div.	Div.
Sea Conditions	2	2	2	2

Overhaul Activity   Submarine Base, Midway, T.H.

Remarks: Spread from aft forward. Spread coverage 300%. Speed reduction used.

U.S.S. *Barb*   Torpedo Attack No. 5   Patrol No. 11
Time: 0540 H   Date: 29 Jan. 1945   Lat. 25-08 N., Long. 119-39 E.

Target Data – Damage Inflicted

Description: 1 Medium AP (EU) with 1 large AK (EU) nearly in column with one escort on starboard flank of AP. No air coverage. Visibility – very poor (rain). Contact – Radar, 17,000 yards. Target approaching Haitan Straits.
Ship Sunk: Unknown.
Ship Damaged: Unknown.
Damage Determined by: Two timed hits 1½ minutes late. Tracked target (AK) after firing, no change in course or speed. Target not visible after firing. Target pip suddenly disappeared from radar screen at 8,800 yards.
Target Draft: 25'   Course: 060   Speed: 7.8   Range: 2,010 (at firing)

Own Ship Data

Course: 175   Speed: 8.5   Depth: Surface   Angle: —

[Fire Control and Torpedo Data]

Type Attack; Night Surface – Radar and TBT.

Tubes Fired – No.	7.	8.	9.	10.
Track Angle	118 S	121 S	124 S	127 S
Gyro Angle	182½	185½	188½	192
Depth Set	8'	8'	8'	8'
Power	—	—	—	—
Hit or Miss	Miss	Miss	Prob. Hit	Prob. Hit
Erratic	No	No	No	No
Torpedo	2180	2240	2320	2410
Mark Torpedo	18-1	18-1	18-1	18-1
Serial No.	54483	56689	55861	55202
Mark Exploder	8-5	8-5	8-5	8-5
Serial No.	9859	10059	8452	9655
Actuation Set	Contact	Contact	Contact	Contact
Actuation Actual	—	—	?	?
Mark Warhead	18-1	18-1	18-1	18-1
Serial No.	2279	3413	2912	3603
Explosive	TPX	TPX	TPX	TPX
Firing Interval	0 s	10 s	10 s	10 s
Type Spread	Divergent	Div.	Div.	Div.
Sea Conditions	4	4	4	4

Overhaul Activity   Submarine Base, Midway, T.H.

Remarks: Target on steady course at steady speed. Spread coverage – 200%. Approach elementary. Speed reduction used.

Mark 18-1 Torpedoes

The *Barb* carried a full load of Mk. 18-1 torpedoes.

In torpedo attack #2, three torpedoes were fired from the bow tubes down a state 3 sea when the ship's speed was 18.5 knots. Three hits were observed. Torpedoes were set on 8 feet.

On January 12 the afterbody of one torpedo (Serial #55869) was flooded due to a faulty handhole gasket when the tube was made ready. Later the afterbody was detached from the battery compartment and the motor fields were found to be completely grounded out. The armature insulation resistance was still up to the required meghms. The motor was disassembled and the field coils were washed and baked. Baking was done with three 100 watt light bulbs in an improvised oven consisting of blankets and winter clothing. In this manner the insulation resistance of the entire motor circuit was brought up to 6 megohms. The gyro pot was also flooded, so the gyro was withdrawn, cleaned, and a light coat of oil applied. The torpedo was reassembled and later fired for a hit.

In torpedo attack #5, four torpedoes were fired into a state 4 sea with an eight foot depth setting. Two explosions were timed one minute late. Radar ranges and TBT bearings were used and the solution was cold. Target was on a steady course. Unable to offer explanation other than the possibility of a reduced torpedo speed due to the sea.

(I) MINES

Floating mines in the area are a hazard. However, since there is the remote possibility that they might damage a Jap, the expenditure of ammunition on them was not considered justifiable.

(1) Lat. 18-40 N., Long. 155-19.5 E.   – Sunk by gunfire.
(2) Lat. 30-48 N., Long. 125-07.8 E.   – Damaged, horns erupted with yellow vapor.
(3) Lat. 25-57.2 N., Long. 121-18.8 E.   – Avoided.
(4) Lat. 27-05.6 N., Long. 122-12 E.   – "
(5) Lat. 27-01 N., Long. 122-15 E.   – "
(6) Lat. 25-02.8 N., Long. 119-32.5 E.   – "
(7) Lat. 25-03 N., Long. 119-37 E.   – "
(8) Lat. 25-04 N., Long. 119-37 E.   – "
(9) Lat. 25-35 N., Long. 122-07 E.   – "
(10) Lat. 27-14 N., Long. 121-47 E.   – "
(11) Lat. 30-10 N., Long. 125-28 E.   – "
(12) Lat. 30-15 N., Long. 125-35 E.   – "
(13) Lat. 31-49 N., Long. 127-58 E.   – "

(J) ANTI-SUBMARINE MEASURES AND EVASIVE TACTICS

Aircraft: Only 29 enemy aircraft contacts were made.

Many aircraft skimmed the surface. These are a nuisance. Convoy air cover from escort carrier persisted even when visibility was less than 7,000 yards. One Jap carrier owes its present existence to one of these pilots who surprised and bombed us. Night aircraft were few. One plane, with steady radar contact on APR at 153 megs, circled us at 3/4 to 1 mile by SD on a dark night, while chasing carrier convoy, and then departed without bombing. During another dark night we were strafed and bombed by an expert. He gave no APR signal in the 140–160 band and no exhaust was seen. First indication was his strafing to starboard and high. While clearing bridge he passed about 50 feet overhead. Four bombs fell to port. This was new and unnerving. He must have used a radar frequency outside of the 140–160 meg band, which we watch continuously. He could not have sighted the *Barb*.

Convoys Underway: Convoys were heavily escorted. The most effective evasive tactic we know is to blow up an ammunition ship. This clears the area so fast the escorts forget to drop depth charges. After Torpedo Attack #1, blowing the tubes dry during reload immediately brought a destroyer back to the scene. Evasion was accomplished by heading up sea and retiring tactically and tacitly to deep submergence of 140 feet.

Escorts were bewildered during night attack. Their gunfire and depth charging was pure face saving. The use of shore batteries was novel, but all firing was evidently ranged to fall well clear on seaward side of convoy. All types of Jap radar were in evidence.

Convoys Anchored: Definitely asleep at the switch. Only three radar equipped escorts were under way. All were dozing, apparently satisfied that the water was sufficiently shallow and obstacles sufficiently great to afford complete protection. Unfortunately, this situation will, in all probability, never occur again.

Evasion was accomplished through an area of navigational hazards with the junk fleet as a final impassable barrier.

Depths during patrol seldom exceeded 30 fathoms. Normal soundings were taken at half hour intervals while in area. Single ping soundings were taken during attacks.

Mines: Thirteen floating mines had to be avoided. Known or suspected minefields were given a 5 mile berth. All water in the area is mineable.

(K) MAJOR DEFECTS AND DAMAGE

Only known damage is minor superstructure damage incurred when an ammunition ship exploded.

The major defects which have prevailed throughout several patrols are not worthy of mentioning as they will be corrected during the navy yard overhaul at the conclusion of this patrol.

Engineering: The main engines showed the definite need of a major overhaul. The engines required constant repair and minor replacement during the whole patrol. Numerous oil and water leaks had to be repaired, gaskets and grommets renewed, and injectors had to be overhauled continually. All four engines have over 3,000 hours since last major overhaul.

The reoccurring trouble of exhaust piping and mufflers leaking and wearing through will necessitate having new mufflers and piping installed at the end of this patrol. They were repaired during the last refit and at Guam before departing for the area but were leaking again before two weeks had passed.

The breaking down of the shaft seal of one compressor of the vapor compression still necessitated putting one evaporator out of commission for repairs. The water shows a trace of oil when this still is used. The stills were given a very poor overhaul during last refit.

Mechanical: We were troubled again this patrol with elusive battery grounds in the ventilation[12]. The grounds finally became so excessive, 120 volts, that all the ducts in the battery wells were pulled out and washed with soda water. The grounds were reduced to 30 volts. All the ducts will have to be reparafined at the end of the patrol. This trouble has occurred before but the highest the ground ever became was 90 volts. We hope this will be corrected during the navy yard overhaul by removing all soft rubber joints, completely cleaning and reparafining all hard rubber ducts and standpipes, and painting with acid resisting paint the blowers, housings and discharge casing.

Early in the patrol the pit-log gave trouble. The pump motor and gearing were replaced and the unit gave satisfactory performance thereafter.

The follow-up system of the master gyro failed again this patrol, but was put back in satisfactory operation by the ship's electrician. The collector rings were cleaned and the brushes reseated on the spider assembly and the follow-up motor replaced. The bridge pelorus grounded out during the first deep dive out of Guam but was satisfactorily repaired by ship's electrician.

The slip-rings on the #1 I.C. motor generator became deeply scored necessitating decommissioning for about four hours for repairs. This is more serious than is readily apparent. The lack of AC power on this vessel requires that both I.C. motor generators be run when using fire-control equipment during attacks and for the radar about 50% of the time. This somewhat overloads the lighting motor generator and makes it impossible to go into an attack with only one I.C. motor generator. This must be corrected in the Navy Yard.

---

12 Fleet type submarines had an extensive ventilation system in the battery wells designed to safely remove the explosive hydrogen gas produced by the battery cells during charging.

HULL:

Periscopes: Both periscopes have given constant trouble throughout this patrol and have required constant attention. #1 periscope[13] has steadily leaked and fogged up. #1 is packed with flax packing and trained with much greater ease than #2, which has the new Garlock "Chevron" packing. Two days out from Midway #2 periscope began to leak like a faucet and developed a loud grind in the lower bearing. Upon reaching Guam, #2 was pulled, its lower bearing cleaned and smoothed up, and another ring of the Garlock packing added, making a total of four rings. At the suggestion of the periscope experts a ring of flax packing was also added to permit the packing gland to be taken up ¼ inch in case of further excessive leaking. An adequate grease seal could not be obtained and both periscopes were thereupon packed with torpedo tail-packing grease. All these measures were in vain, for we had been in area only one day when all the troubles reappeared.

It is the opinion of the C&R officer that the bearing clearances of the lower bearing and the bearings in the shears are too great and beyond the limiting value for both periscopes.

Hydraulic Plant: The hydraulic plant cycles too frequently and its charging interval is not within allowed limits. The present packing on the hydraulic ram is of the old type and does not allow sufficient lubrication. This necessitates a special watch just to keep the ram lubricated and prevent the accumulator from hammering excessively.

The new type of packing, a "U" shaped fibre material (unavailable at Midway and Guam) with metal inserts will allow a film of oil for lubrication and should therefore eliminate this defect.

The plant has been repaired at Pearl, Majuro, and Midway, and it appears that the work required is beyond the capacities of these bases.

Rudder: The noise level from the rams, follow-up system, and rudder carrier bearings is excessive—beyond maximum allowed. This was proven during sound tests after completion of refit at Midway. The noise in the follow-up system has increased since the time of the tests as a result of a scored piston and cylinder wall.

Hull Regulator Valves: These valves have leaked constantly, flooding all main ballast tank blow piping and the 600# manifold. The hull regulator valves on Safety tank are in the same condition.

---

13 Periscopes were numbered starting with the forwardmost on older American submarines. Periscope #1 was normally the "search" periscope, with a larger head and greater light gathering capability. Later models had ST radar, which was used for range finding, built into the head. Number 2 was the "attack" periscope, with the smallest practical head and upper shaft to reduce the likelihood of its being sighted during daylight approaches. Fleet submarines had two periscopes. Some earlier types had three.

Conning Tower Drain: The conning tower drain now installed proved to be inadequate and of faulty design when water was taken down the hatch. It is recommended that a larger draining system be installed.

(L) RADIO

In general communications were successfully carried out and performance of equipment was satisfactory. Enemy counter-measures (jamming) were more effective during this patrol, in regard to reception of SubFox, than encountered on previous patrols, due either to location of patrol area or to increased enemy activity. On one occasion during daylight hours a jamming station (XCE) completely blanked out Fox on all frequencies. This was also reported by U.S.S. *Queenfish*.

Submarine Fox from Guam was heard for the first time on 9090 kilocycles 31 January at 1700 GCT, resulting in greatly improved signal strength and good transmitter note. Throughout the patrol 3045, 9090, and 16730 kilocycles were used for Sub Fox reception, 4515 being unusable due to jamming.

China Air Force: Traffic was, in general, of very good signal strength. Only once did it fade out so as to be unreadable. On a few occasions jamming was heavy, but jamming was never effective enough so that it could not be copied. In accordance with information received in despatches from China, 7365 KCS was guarded from time to time for contact reports, but nothing was ever heard except Japs.

Life Guard: When assigned lifeguard duty, communication was established on 4475 kcs voice with raiding planes. Jamming was very bad, but not impossible, and all information on ditches was heard, most of the transmissions in this case apparently coming from an airbase. VHF was also guarded during lifeguard duty but nothing was heard.

Wolf Pack Communications: The only delay in delivery of wolf pack traffic was due to subs being submerged. Communication in general was carried out with no delay and proper circuit discipline. It is recommended that the possibilities of an underwater antenna suitable for wolf pack frequencies be investigated.

Ship to Shore: Two transmissions were made to ComSubPac. (1) on 8470 KCS, relayed by VHJ, with some delay due to jamming. (2) on 12,705 KCS at 1120 GCT, relayed by NPN, Guam. No delay.

Four transmissions were made to ComNavGroup China, only one of which was cleared direct to NKN on 8470 KCS at 1229 GCT, after a few minutes delay due to jamming. Two of the transmissionss were relayed by radio Guam, one of them taking forty-five minutes and shift from 8470 to 12705 KCS in order to clear. The other transmission was relayed by VHC, with no delay.

(M) RADAR

SJ: The last refit at Midway left the SJ radar in excellent condition. Weekly check-up on the tuning maintained this performance throughout the patrol. A 325 foot light house was picked up at 34,000 yards.

On three occasions, the SJ picked up and tracked aircraft, however, the first indication of the plane that strafed us was latter's gun fire.

The outstanding radar view of the patrol on both the A-scope and the PPI was the anchored convoy. It appeared as an island on the PPI at 29,000 yards, and at 5,000 yards the A-scope had twelve pips on one bearing.

The SJ suffered no major material failure during the patrol.

APR/SPA: These units were in operation day and night. When the gain fell off; the first IF tube in the APR was replaced. After leaving the area, the SPA power transformer burned out.

IFF: The BN and ABK were used only enroute and during life guard duty. Both units operated satisfactorily.

(N) SOUND GEAR AND SOUND CONDITIONS

There were no equipment failures, and the results obtained with sonic and super-sonic gear closely paralleled each other. Sound conditions were very poor, with background noise high and variable. Most of our operating was in shallow water, often near river mouths, and fairly close to the shore, a combination of circumstances readily accounting for poor results, in spite of isothermal conditions.

Only one attack was made submerged. Screws were not heard until range was below 3,000 yards, and then they were intermittent, broad, and the bearings were not dependable. When screws could be heard they covered the bearing dial, and this, combined with much echo ranging by escorts, made it very difficult to get information on a single target. Breaking up noises were heard loud and clear. It was observed the escorts were unable to detect us even at close ranges.

(O) DENSITY LAYERS

No thermal gradients were encountered in the area.

Variations in water temperature to the extent of several degrees per hour were encountered while cruising surfaced and submerged. It becomes necessary while on the surface to make hourly compensations for changes in injection temperature.

Salinity variations were very noticeable in the vicinity of rivers and inlets along the China coast.

During one dive in muddy water the salinity change was such that we submerged 26,000 pounds heavy overall.

(P) HEALTH, FOOD AND HABITABILITY

Excellent. The patrol was completely on the surface which inherently decreases the amount of sleep obtained but increases the general well being.

(Q) PERSONNEL

Even after a second advanced base refit and in spite of a long siege of shallow water operations, Officers and men put everything they had into this patrol with determination and an inspired zeal for action, knowing that it would be followed by a period of recuperation during Navy Yard overhaul in the States.

(a) Number of men on board during patrol	75
(b) Number of men qualified at start of patrol	58
(c) Number of men qualified at end of patrol	70
(d) Number of men unqualified making their first patrol	5
(e) Number of men advanced in rating during patrol	6
(f) Number of men recommended to Squadron for advancement – no vacancy on board.	13

(R) MILES STEAMED AND FUEL USED

	Miles	Gals.
Midway to Guam	2,707	29,545
Guam to Area	1,619	16,510
In Area	7,507	54,640
Area to Midway	3,376	57,245
Midway to Pearl	1,300	17,000
Total –	16,509	154,940

(S) DURATION

Days enroute Midway to area via Guam	14
In Area 11 A, B, C, 9, 12	30
Days enroute Area to Midway	10
Days enroute Midway to Pearl	5
Days submerged	Zero

(T) FACTORS OF ENDURANCE REMAINING AT MIDWAY

Torpedoes	Fuel	Provisions	Personnel Factor
0	5,000	30	30

Limiting factor this patrol – Expenditure of torpedoes.

(U) RADIO AND RADAR COUNTER-MEASURES

RADIO COMMUNICATIONS – JAMMING BY THE ENEMY

1. Ship or Station – U.S.S. *Barb* (SS220).
2. Position, bearing and altitude when enemy radio signals were observed – entire period in patrol area 11 A & B. Also enroute to and from area.
3. Position of Transmitting Station – Unknown. Several stations most effectively jamming (station XGE) believed to be near Shanghai.
4. Date of jamming – All times.
5. Frequencies jammed – All frequencies used except VHF. Most effective on Sub Fox and ship to shore frequencies.
6. Describe signal jammed (Freq. Type of modulation, etc.) – 4515, 6045, 9090, 4235, 8470. CW note.
7. Use of circuit (tactical, administrative) – Fox for intercept, Ship-to-Shore for administrative and tactical.
8. Was enemy jamming signal stable? Both encountered – stable and variable.
9. What was ratio of strength of own signal to enemy jamming signal – At night usually stronger (enemy QSA5, own QSA2, 3, 4). During daylight our signal is usually stronger.
10. What was power output of own transmitter at time of jamming? – Medium 200 watt, installation aboard. Wolf pack jamming, negligible.
11. Location of enemy jammer – Unknown.
12. Type of jamming signals:

Bagpipe (musical tone)	X	Voice	X
Saw (variable tone)	X	Noise modulation	X
CW – random keying	X	MCW	X

13. Effectiveness of jamming – Critical to communication both intercept and ship to shore.
14. Action taken to overcome jamming – Usually received three zero beat of jammer. Used broad sharp switch.
15. Bandwidth covered by enemy jamming signals – 4 to 5 kilocycles.
16. Did jamming transmitter appear to be monitored by a look-in receiver – On some occasions.
17. If frequency was shifted, how long before enemy jammed new frequency? – Always present on 4235 and 8470 on one occasion shifted from 8470 to 12705 and had no jamming.
18. Narrative: On one occasion, station XGE so effectively jammed all Sub Fox frequencies that recognition was completely impossible on 12 January 1945, from 0600 to 0640 GCT.

Date: 3 Jan. 1945   Report No. 1

Enemy radar appeared to be – Land Based.

Frequency – 148 MC

PRF – 300

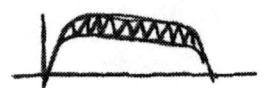

Pulse Width – 10 Micro-sec.

Sweep Rate – not sweeping.

Detection equipment – APR/SPA

Narrative: If this set was sweeping, it was a very slow sweep and the beam width was very broad. Otherwise this was a possible beacon. Possible location – either side of Tokara Kaikyo.

Date: 3 Jan. 1945   Report No. 2.

Enemy radar appeared to be – Land Based.

Frequency – 158 MC

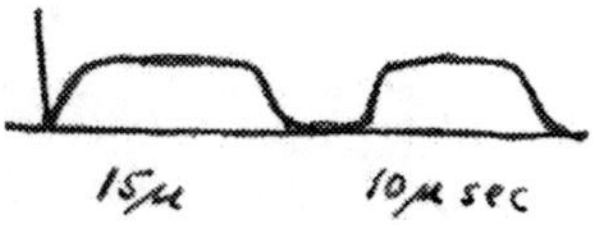

PRF – 500

Pulse width – 15–10 Micro-sec.

Sweep Rate – erratic.

Detection equipment – APR/SPA

Narrative: This was detected only occasionally and then very weakly, as we entered channel from east Tokara Kaikyo.

Date: 5 Jan. 1945 			Report No. 3

Enemy radar appeared to be – Land based or air borne.

Frequency – 153 MC 			SKETCH

PRF – 500

Pulse Width - 15 micro-sec.

Sweep Rate – irregular.

Detection equipment – APR/SPA

Narrative: This was picked up as we passed S/W of Kaku Shima. It was stronger when we has [sic] a plane contact on SJ radar 12 miles dead ahead. Plane (radar-equipped) also reported by submarine ahead.

Date: 8 Jan. 1945 			Report No. 4

Enemy radar appeared to be – Land based: 24-30 N., 120-30 E.

Frequency – 153 MC 			SKETCH

PRF – 550

Pulse Width – 8 micro-sec.

Sweep Rate – not sweeping.

Detection equipment – APR/SPA

Narrative: This was encountered during attack #2 and #3. No evidence that we were picked up. Possible beacon.

Date: 8 Jan. 1945   Report No. 5

Enemy radar appeared to be – Land based: 24-30 N., 120-30 E.

Frequency – 97 MC   SKETCH

PRF – 550

Pulse Width – 28 micro-sec.

Sweep Rate –

Detection equipment – APR/SPA

Narrative: This was noted during heat of battle so no accurate sweep data was noted. At time the signal was very strong, other times it couldn't be picked up at all.

Date: 19 Jan. 1945   Report No. 6

Enemy radar appeared to be – near Hakusha Ko – 24° N., 121° E.

Frequency – 98 MC   SKETCH

PRF – 125

Pulse Width – 20 Micro-sec.

Sweep Rate: 4 to 2½ min per sweep.

Detection equipment – APR/SPA

Narrative: Third harmonic noted at 292 MC. Very loud (close) signal appeared to have side lobes. This night we were strafed so possibly air borne.

Date: 19 Jan. 1945   Report No. 7

Enemy radar appeared to be – near – 24° N., 121° E.

Frequency – 161 MC   SKETCH

PRF – 150

Pulse Width – 5 micro-sec.

Sweep Rate – Steady or 5 min/sweep.

Detection equipment – APR/SPA

Narrative: This was encountered the same night we were strafed. Did not appear to be sweeping.

Date: 19 Jan. 1945   Report No. 8

Enemy radar appeared to be near, 24° N., 121° E.

Frequency – 163 MC   SKETCH

PRF – 150

Pulse Width – 8 Micro-sec.

Sweep rate – Same as #7 above.

Detection equipment – APR/SPA

Narrative: Also encountered night of strafing. Very slow sweep, if any. There was no indication that this was land based or air borne.

Date: 19 Jan. 1945   Report No. 9

Enemy radar appeared to be on Danjo Gunto.

Frequency – 98 MC   SKETCH

PRF – 750

Pulse Width – 10 micro-sec.

Sweep rate – not sweeping.

Detection equipment – APR/SPA

Narrative: This is the same signal picked up on our tenth patrol when cruising near 32° N., 122° 30' E. Appears to be navigational beacon.

Date: 1 Feb. 1945   Report No. 10

As we passed eastward through Tokara Kaikyo, numerous frequencies were picked up, noted for a while, then lost. Not being in the position or frame of mind to maneuver the ship and take advantage of the directivity of the APR antenna, it is not known which side of the strait the stations were located, but everything indicated that there were installations on Kuchina Yerabu, Yaku Shima, and Tanega Shima.
The following frequencies were noted.
(a) 147 MC and 144 mc (too weak to get any data on their characteristics)
(b) 159 MC, PRF 500, Pulse width 7 micro-sec.
(c) 154 MC, PRF 500, Pulse width 9 micro-sec.
(d) 158 MC, PRF 500, Pulse width 4 micro-sec.
(e) 160 MC, 3 stations. One possibly on Yaku Shima, 500 PRF, and 6 micro-sec each pulse.
The stations of d and e above had rapid, well defined, sweeps, of apparently narrow beam width.
There was no definite sweeps rate. At times there would be two or more strong sweeps a minute, including simultaneous sweeps of two stations (superposition of wave forms on SPA). Then there would be lapses of five or ten minutes between sweeps. At times, the indication so resembled patrolling aircraft that the SD radar was keyed but no contact was made.

(V) REMARKS

To stimulate discussion of new methods of approach and attack, the following is offered, of possible interest, from our meagre experience, for what it is worth. It is a special situation of a dark night, poor visibility convoy attack.

Fault was found with the standard off bow attack in that an end around was required; usually only two targets presented themselves at the optimum torpedo accuracy range, which were readily taken care of by the bow tubes; shifting nests for low parallax stern tube salvo resulted in no suitable target for the stern salvo at a satisfactory range of 1,800–3,000 yards; escorts were passed close aboard; another end around was required for next attack; and the formation turned, or was so fouled up, another lengthy tracking period was required.

To obviate this second end around on our last patrol, we changed our off bow attack tactics so that our nest shift would be a high parallax stern tube set up, though contrary to doctrine, and we would emerge ahead of the convoy, ready for a reload and another attack. Again no stern tube target was immediately available at hitting ranges and, while pulling out ahead, we had to cross in front of the convoy to fire the stern tubes at the leader of another column. Per usual the formation became disorganized. It was two hours before targets and escorts were sufficiently settled for another attack even then it was poor. Disorganization of the formation with the targets wandering about, continually changing position, course and speed was a distinct disadvantage.

Realizing the advantage of maintaining convoy organization new tactics were developed and tried which we label the "Barbarian Attack."

Briefly it consists of a quarter attack firing three bow torpedoes at the trailing ship of an outboard column. The sub then turns out at a 60° angle from the convoy course and opens out on the flank to 4,000 yards. Paralleling the formation at this range, fifteen minutes is utilized in tracking and reload while moving up on the next ship. This ship is then attacked from the flank or quarter with a three torpedo bow tube salvo and the sub again opens out and reloads while tracking the next ship ahead. If this ship is not the leading ship of the column the procedure is repeated. Assuming it is the leader, a stern tube off bow salvo is fired and the sub pulls out ahead of formation ready to reload that stern tubes and proceed with any type of attack desired.

The above method was tested on this patrol with such ease and lack of expected difficulties, that attack was only secured to give the rest of the pack a chance. The convoy was contacted at 20,000 yards with the *Barb* broad on its starboard quarter. 42 minutes later the trailing ship was attacked.

The convoy remained organized, used same zig plan and increased speed slightly. 21 minutes after the 1st attack, the second attack was made on the next ship up the line. 20 minutes after the second attack was made the *Barb* passed the next ship ahead at 2,160 yards foregoing an attack in deference to the rest of the pack. Thus in less than 1½ hours after contact, we found ourselves ahead of the convoy, without making an end around, with all tubes reloaded and with two concentrated attacks under our belts. Trouble from escorts, which were still stationed astern, on the flank and off the bow was nil. As we had anticipated, not seeing us, they turned towards the stricken ship to drop depth charges, maintained course and speed to hold gunnery practice, or, in the case of the exploding AE, were intent upon saving their own necks. If they had turned out to chase us we had the advantage of a head start on our departure course and at full speed before the torpedoes hit.

Consequently, to us, the tactics of this attack appear ideal in its particular sphere; no end around, the accuracy of concentrated fire, requires only one third of the time normally used, automatically takes care of reload, minimum escort trouble, maximum convoy organization, and best possible position of sub upon completion of first wave of attacks. Obviously it is flexible and easily adaptable to special circumstances.

2. Analysis of Japanese shipping lanes and suggested operations is being forwarded by separate correspondence.

3. It is with regret that the *Barb* detaches herself, temporarily for overhaul, from the Loopers under the excellent leadership of Commander C.E. Loughlin. To have had the privilege of fighting alongside such splendid packmates as the *Queenfish* and *Picuda* is a source of inspiration and pride to we in the *Barb*. It is hoped that, after our sojourn in the States, the Loopers may again be formed for a deeper invasion of enemy waters.

SUBMARINE DIVISION FORTY-FOUR

FB5-44/A16-3

Serial (023)

Care of Fleet Post Office,
San Francisco, California,
20 February 1945.

C-O-N-F-I-D-E-N-T-I-A-L

First Endorsement to
U.S.S. *Barb* Eleventh War
Patrol.

From: The Commander Submarine Division Forty-Four.
To: The Commander-in-Chief, United States Fleet.
Via: (1) The Commander Submarine Squadron Four.
                (2) The Commander Submarine Force, Pacific Fleet.
                (3) The Commander-in-Chief, U.S. Pacific Fleet.

Subject: U.S.S. *Barb* (SS 220) Eleventh War Patrol – Comments on.

1. The eleventh War Patrol of the *Barb* was conducted in the East China Sea off the East Coast of China from Shanghai to Lam Yit. The *Barb* was one of three submarines forming a coordinated attack group. The Patrol was of 59 days duration.

2. The attacks made on this patrol and the results obtained were most spectacular and outstanding. The Commanding Officer, making his fourth patrol on the *Barb* as such, displayed not only outstanding aggression but also unusual tactical ability. His outstanding courage and aggression were best displayed in his attacks made in the very restricted waters of the China Coast. This patrol, which ends a sequence of four highly successful ones for the Commanding Officer, indicates that the *Barb* is one of the finest fighting submarines this war has ever known.

3. The attacks were aggressively conducted, characterized by outstanding skill and tenacity. A summary of these attacks follows:

4. <u>Torpedo Attack No. 1 – 8 January 1945</u> – A convoy of eight large ships and many escorts were contacted at 1300 and tracked for five hours while the *Picuda* was coached on to the targets. The Commanding Officer gallantly adjusted his position so that he could force the convoy away from the coast and towards the other submarines of the group. Finally at 1724, the *Barb*, making a day periscope attack, fired three torpedoes at a large transport and one minute later fired three more at a large engines-aft freighter. Four hits were obtained; the engines-aft freighter was demolished and the transport was left sinking. In addition another

freighter-transport, which happened to be overlapping the tanker was also hit and set on fire amidships.

Torpedo Attack No. 2 – 8 January 1945 – After the attack above the other two submarines of the pack managed to get in attacks also. Then the *Barb* began another attack on the same convoy. Coming up from the quarter in an outstanding display of tactical command, the *Barb* fired three torpedoes in a night surface attack on the trailing ship of the convoy, which was a large freighter. Two of these torpedoes hit and sank this freighter and the third hit an overlapping tanker whose pip was seen to disappear from the radar screen twenty minutes later.

Torpedo Attack No. 3 – 8 January 1945 – Twenty-one minutes after attack No. 2 the three remaining bow tubes were fired at a large ammunition ship. This ship followed the usual reaction of the *Barb*'s treatment, absorbing three hits and exploding with one of the largest explosions ever seen by the Commanding Officer. The disintegration of the target and the tremendous explosion made by the ship may have also sunk two escorts, which had been close aboard it and were never seen again, but the Commanding Officer made no claim to them. The one remaining target of the convoy was turned over to the *Queenfish* for attack. The *Barb*, however, stayed in the vicinity in order to make sure that this target did not get away. Note:—It is of note that only 4½ hours elapsed from the time of the *Barb*'s first attack on the eight-ship convoy until its complete elimination was made.

Torpedo Attack No. 4 – 23 January 1945 – This outstanding one–ship battle will be one of the great stories to come out of this war when it can be told. For over two weeks the *Barb* had been unable to find any targets in submarine waters. The *Barb*, assuming the role of a motor torpedo boat, launched an eight-torpedo attack on a large anchored convoy, after running 19 miles inshore from the 20-fathom curve. The whole passage was made through an unexplored area, dodging junks and patrolling escorts. About thirty ships were estimated in the anchored convoy and three radar escorts were patrolling on its outer edge. The *Barb* maintained complete tactical command of the situation throughout. Picking the targets such that each torpedo would account for a separate ship, the *Barb* fired its four remaining bow tubes first and then turned to fire its four stern tubes; eight hits were obtained. A large freighter was observed to settle and sink; another caught fire and probably sunk; a large ammunition ship blew up with a huge explosion and sunk; an unidentified ship, which either may have been an ammunition ship or a combatant ship, had its whole side blown out before sinking; another unidentified ship was hit but the results of this could not be seen as it was shielded by the near ship; and another large freighter was hit and was left in a cloud of smoke. The tremendous damage done on this single attack inflicted by the eight torpedoes is a fitting tribute to the entire *Barb* organization.

Torpedo Attack No. 5 – 29 January 1945 – A large freighter and a medium transport with one escort were contacted by radar. After obtaining position the last four stern tube torpedoes were fired at the large freighter. Two hits were heard but not seen because of a rain squall. Ten minutes later the target disappeared from the radar screen at a range of 8,800 yards while the initial contact had been 17,500 yards; at the same time the pip of the transport and escort still remained on the screen. Although the Commanding Officer claims no damage on this attack because the timed hits did not agree with the range, the Division Commander feels that this target was at least damaged.

5. In addition to the damage inflicted on the enemy above, the *Barb* also finished off a 300-ton patrol vessel, which had been previously damaged by the *Queenfish* and *Picuda*. After a boarding party succeeded in obtaining gear from this vessel, the *Barb* sank it with 13 rounds of 4-inch ammunition.

6. The *Barb* returned from patrol in a high state of cleanliness. Morale of this vessel is, of course, high. The *Barb* is now returning to the West Coast for Navy Yard overhaul.

7. The Commander Submarine Division-44 takes great pleasure in congratulating the Commanding Officer, Officers and crew for this extremely aggressive and highly successful war patrol.

E.W. Grenfell

SUBMARINE SQUADRON FOUR
Fleet Post Office
San Francisco, California

ll/wft

FC5-4/A16-3
Serial: 0166

21 February 1945

CONFIDENTIAL

<u>Second Endorsement</u> to
U.S.S. *Barb* (SS220) – Report
of Eleventh War Patrol.

From:	The Commander Submarine Squadron Four.
To:	The Commander-in-Chief, United States Fleet
Via:	(1) The Commander Submarine Force, Pacific Fleet, Administration.
	(2) The Commander-in-Chief, U.S. Pacific Fleet.
Subject:	U.S.S. *Barb* (SS220) – Report of Eleventh War Patrol.

    1. Forwarded, concurring in the remarks of Commander Submarine Division Forty-Four.

    2. The Commanding Submarine Squadron Four heartily congratulates the Commanding Officer, officers, and crew of the U.S.S. *Barb* upon completion of one of the most outstanding patrols of the war. The extreme aggressiveness combined with skill and daring, resulted in devastating losses to the enemy. The percentage of hits, around 80%, is evidence of the superb quality of this fighting ship.

    3. It is recommended that the *Barb* be credited with the following:

SUNK		PROBABLY SUNK	
1 AK (EU)	10,000 tons	1 AK (EU)	7,500 tons
1 AE (EU)	7,500 tons		
1 AK (EU)	7,500 tons	DAMAGED	
1 AK or AO (EU)	7,500 tons	1 AK (EU)	9,300 tons
1 AK (EU)	7,500 tons	1 UN	4,000 tons
1 AE (EU)	4,000 tons	1 AK (EU)	7,500 tons
1 AE (EU)	7,500 tons	1 UN	<u>4,000 tons</u>
*1/3 Misc. (Patrol boat) (EU)	<u>100 tons</u>		24,800 tons
	59,100 tons		

    Total sunk, Probably Sunk, or Damaged – 91,000 tons

    *300 tons patrol vessel with credit for sinking divided among *Picuda*, *Barb* and *Queenfish*.

                                      W.V. O'Regan

FF12-10(A)/A16-3(18)　　SUBMARINE FORCE, PACIFIC FLEET　　Ga
　　　　　　　　　　　　　　　　　　　　　Care of Fleet Post Office,
Serial 0390　　　　　　　　　　　　　　　San Francisco, California,
　　　　　　　　　　　　　　　　　　　　　1 March 1945.
Third endorsement to
Barb Report of Eleventh　　　　NOTE: THIS REPORT WILL BE
War Patrol　　　　　　　　　　　　DESTROYED PRIOR TO
　　　　　　　　　　　　　　　　　ENTERING PATROL AREA.
CONFIDENTIAL

ComSubPac Patrol Report No. 675
U.S.S. *Barb* – Eleventh War Patrol

From:　　　　The Commander Submarine Force, Pacific Fleet.
To:　　　　　The Commander in Chief, United States Fleet.
Via:　　　　　The Commander in Chief, U.S. Pacific Fleet.

Subject:　　　U.S.S. *Barb* (SS220) – Report of Eleventh War Patrol
　　　　　　　(19 December 1944 to 15 February 1945).

　　1.　The eleventh war patrol of the *Barb* under the command of Commander E.B. Fluckey, U.S. Navy, was conducted in the Formosa Straits and East China Sea off the coast of China from Shanghai to Yam Lit. The *Barb*, along with the *Picuda* and the *Queenfish*, formed a coordinated attack group with the commanding officer of the *Queenfish* as the group commander.
　　2.　The same fighting spirit and group cooperation displayed by these three submarines on the last patrol were evident throughout this one. The *Barb*, continuing her illustrious record, turned in a performance during this patrol which is probably an all time record. The patrol started by the three submarines sinking a small craft by gunfire. The *Barb*'s next action against the enemy was in the form of three aggressive attacks delivered upon a large convoy on 8 January. The *Barb* sank four ships and shared honors with the *Picuda* for sinking two more out of this convoy. The *Queenfish* accounted for a large tanker. On 22–23 January the *Barb*, displaying the ultimate in skill and daring, penetrated Namkwan Harbor on the China Coast to wreak havoc upon a convoy of some thirty ships at anchor. The Barb proceeded some six miles inside the ten-fathom curve, nineteen miles inside the twenty-fathom curve, to fire first her bow tubes, then her stern tubes into this choice group of targets. The expert handling of the *Barb*, both in delivering her attacks and in making good her evasion, was a remarkable accomplishment. The *Barb* had one other contact on 29 January, which resulted in two timed hits. These hits were a little late for a proper time interval for normal running Mark 18 torpedoes, which was probably due to the low temperatures existing. This patrol

should be studied in detail by submarine personnel. The remarks concerning a new method of successive attacks from rear to leading ship in lieu of end around, paragraph (V), are of particular interest to the Commander Training Command, Submarine Force, Pacific Fleet.

    3. Award of Submarine Combat Insignia for this patrol is authorized.

    4. The Commander Submarine Force, Pacific Fleet, congratulates the commanding officer, officers, and crew of the *Barb* for this history-making fighting performance. The *Barb* is credited with having inflicted the following damage upon the enemy during this patrol:

SUNK

*1/3 MIS (Armed Patrol Vessel) (EC)	– 100 tons	(Gun Attack No. 1)
1 Large AP (EU)	– 10,000 tons	(Attack No. 1A)
**½ Large AK (*Kaga Maru* Type) (EC)	– 4,650 tons	(Attack No. 1A)
1 Large AE (EU)	– 7,500 tons	(Attack No. 1B)
1 Large AK (EU)	– 7,500 tons	(Attack No. 2)
***½ Large AK (Possibly AO) (EU)	– 3,750 tons	(Attack No. 2)
1 Large AE (EU)	– 7,500 tons	(Attack No. 3)
1 Large AK (EU)	– 7,500 tons	(Attack No. 4A)
1 Medium AE (EU)	– 4,000 tons	(Attack No. 4B)
1 Large AE (EU)	– 7,500 tons	(Attack No. 4B)
TOTAL SUNK	– 60,000 tons	

DAMAGED

1 Large AK (EU)	– 7,500 tons	(Attack No. 4A)
1 UN	4,000 tons	(Attack No. 4A)
1 Large AK (EU)	– 7,500 tons	(Attack No. 4B)
1 Large AK (EU)	– 7,500 tons	(Attack No. 5)
TOTAL DAMAGED	– 26,500 tons	
TOTAL SUNK AND DAMAGED	– 86,500 tons	

    * –1/3 credit to each: *Barb*, *Picuda*, and *Queenfish*.

    ** –Estimate this same ship hit later by *Picuda* in Attack No. 2 – ½ credit for sinking to each: *Picuda* and *Barb*.

    *** –Estimate this same ship hit previously by *Picuda* in Attack No. 2 – ½ credit for sinking to each *Picuda* and *Barb*.

                                                Merrill Comstock,
                                                Chief of Staff.

DISTRIBUTION:
(Complete Reports)
Cominch   (7)
CNO   (5)

Cincpac	(6)
JICPOA	(1)
AITGPOA	(1)
Comservpac	(1)
Cinclant	(1)
Comsublant	(8)
S/M School, NL	(2)
CO, S/M Base, PH	(1)
Comsopac	(2)
Comsowespac	(1)
Comsubsowespac	(2)
CTG 71.9	(2)
Comnorpac	(1)
Comsubspac	(3)
ComsubspacAD	(40)
SUBAD, MI	(2)
ComsubspacSubordcom	(3)
All Squadron and Div. Commanders, Pacific	(2)
Substrainpac	(2)
All Submarines, Pacific	(1)

E.L. Hynes, 2nd,
Flag Secretary.

Editor's Note: On 23 March 1945, Commander Eugene B. Fluckey was presented the Medal of Honor by Secretary of the Navy James Forrestal. The citation follows:

Citation: "For conspicuous gallantry and intrepidity at the risk of his life above and beyond the call of duty as commanding officer of the U.S.S. *Barb* during her 11th war patrol along the east coast of China from 19 December 1944 to 15 February 1945. After sinking a large enemy ammunition ship and damaging additional tonnage during a running 2-hour night battle on 8 January, Comdr. Fluckey, in an exceptional feat of brilliant deduction and bold tracking on 25 January, located a concentration of more than 30 enemy ships in the lower reaches of Nankuan Chiang (Mamkwan Harbor). Fully aware that a safe retirement would necessitate an hour's run at full speed through the uncharted, mined, and rock-obstructed waters, he bravely ordered, "Battle station—torpedoes!" In a daring penetration of the heavy enemy screen, and riding in 5 fathoms of water, he launched the *Barb*'s last forward torpedoes at 3,000 yard range. Quickly bringing the ship's stern tubes to bear, he turned loose 4 more torpedoes into the enemy, obtaining 8 direct hits on 6 of the main targets to explode a large ammunitions ship and cause inestimable damage by resultant flying shells and other pyrotechnics. Clearing the treacherous area at high speed, he brought the *Barb* through to safety and 4 days later sank a large Japanese freighter to complete a record of heroic combat achievement, reflecting the highest credit upon Comdr. Fluckey, his gallant officer and men, and the U.S. Naval Service."

In addition to Fluckey's Medal of Honor, *Barb* received a Presidential Unit Citation for her eighth, ninth, tenth, and eleventh war patrols.

Policy at that time called for a commanding officer to be relieved after the completion of four war patrols, and would normally have resulted in Commander Fluckey going to a shore assignment, or new construction, following *Barb*'s eleventh war patrol. In addition, there was a policy which dictated that Medal of Honor recipients should be kept away from dangerous areas. The majority of Medals of Honor were presented posthumously, so there was a strong incentive to keep any living recipients around.

Fluckey had wangled an agreement from Admiral Lockwood that, should Patrol Eleven be successful, he would be able to take *Barb* on a "graduation" patrol, on which he would select his own area and be permitted to experiment with some new ideas. Lockwood, at the time he agreed to this, obviously had no idea that Fluckey was going to receive a Medal of Honor for the eleventh patrol, but held up his side of the agreement after that happened.

Patrol Twelve, 8 June 1945 – 2 August 1945

File: SS220/A16-3
Serial: 043

U.S.S. *Barb* (SS220)
c/o Fleet Post Office,
San Francisco, California,
2 August 1945.

CONFIDENTIAL

From:	The Commanding Officer, U.S.S. *Barb*.
To:	The Commander-in-Chief, United States Fleet.
Via:	(1) The Commander Submarine Division 322.
	(2) The Commander Submarine Squadron 32.
	(3) The Commander Submarine Force, Pacific Fleet.
	(4) The Commander-in-Chief, U.S. Pacific Fleet.
Subject:	U.S.S. *Barb* (SS220), Report of Twelfth War Patrol.
Enclosures:	(A) Subject Report.
	(B) Track Chart (ComSubPac).
	(C) Special Report (Separate Cover).

1. Enclosure (A), covering the Twelfth War Patrol of this vessel conducted along the North Coast Hokkaido, in Aniwa Wan, Taraika Wan (Patience Bay) and East Coast Karafuto during the period 8 June 1945 to 2 August 1945 is forwarded herewith.

E.B. Fluckey

U.S.S. *Barb* – Report of Twelfth War Patrol.

(A) PROLOGUE

On 27 February 1945 arrived Navy Yard, Mare Island from Eleventh War Patrol for yard overhaul. All outstanding important alterations were completed with the exception of JT, FM, TDM, SV, Sound Dome, 15KVA I.C. motor generators and directional APR for which material was lacking. Schools at Mare Island were excellent and well coordinated. Overhaul was average. On 16 May 1945 departed Navy Yard for Pearl Harbor. Voyage repairs at Pearl Harbor accomplished by SubRon 18 and U.S.S. *Euryale*, very cooperative and very good.

An underway training period of 8 days was started 28 May 1945, with Captain C.C. Burlingame, U.S.N. as Training Officer. Eight steam torpedoes were fired. Three days were devoted to special exercises. Training Curriculum under ComSubsTrainPac was excellent.

Two Officers were transferred and two received.

Transferred 15 men.

Readiness for sea date 8 June 1945. Installed rocker launcher. Comdr. H. Hull cosuggested. Admire his elimination of red tape to procure it.

(B) NARRATIVE

Officers and Chief Petty Officers		Number of War Patrols
Comdr. Eugene B. Fluckey, U.S.N.		Prior 10
Lieut. James T. Webster, U.S.N.R.		Prior 5
Lieut. Max C. Duncan, U.S.N.		Prior 3
Lieut. William M. Walker, U.S.N.R.		Prior 1
Lt(jg) David R. Teeters, U.S.N.R.		Prior 4
Lt(jg) Charles W. Hill, U.S.N.R.		Prior 0
Lt(jg) Thomas M. King Jr., U.S.N.R.		Prior 2
Lt(jg) Lawrence J. Sheffield, U.S.N.R.		Prior 2
Ensign William (n) Masek, U.S.N.R.		Prior 0
Saunders, Paul G.	CGM, U.S.N.	Prior 11
Wade, Gordon L.	CEM, U.S.N.	Prior 10
Williams, Franklin A.	CMoMM, U.S.N.	Prior 5
Gierhart, Frank W.	CRM, U.S.N.	Prior 4
Noll, Thomas J.	CMoMM, U.S.N.R.	Prior 7

8 June 1945

1400(VW) Departed Pearl Harbor, T.H. enroute Midway in accordance with ComSubPacAd Comd Operation Order No. 121-45. Conducting daily dives, schools, and drills.

9 June 1945
   1200(W) Position: Lat. 24-47 N., Long. 161-34 W.

10 June 1945
   1200(W) Position: Lat. 26-48 N., Long. 167-26 W.

11 June 1945
   1200(X) Position: Lat. 28-26 N., Long. 172-53 W.

12 June 1945
   0820(Y) Moored Midway. Received Midway's customary excellent welcome and services.

13 June 1945
   0900(Y) Underway for patrol area consisting of North Coast Hokkaido, Aniwa Wan and Taraika Wan, (Patience Bay) in Karafuto.

14 June 1945
   Skipped this day. Crossed international date line.

15 June 1945
   1200(M) Position: Lat. 29-44 N., Long. 176-23 E.

16 June 1945
   1200(L) Position: Lat. 31-38 N., Long. 170-56 E.

17 June 1945
   1200(L) Position: Lat. 34-35 N., Long. 166-08 E.

18 June 1945
   1200(L) Position: Lat. 37-40 N., Long. 161-21 E.

19 June 1945
   1200(K) Position: Lat. 41-05 N., Long. 155-06 E.

20 June 1945 (All times King unless noted otherwise)
   1200 Position: Lat. 43-25 N., Long. 149-22 E.
   2138 Sighted Etorofu Island.
   2200 Transited Kunashiri Suido.

21 June 1945
   Entered Area. Surface patrolling along northwest coast of Kunashiri.

0015 (Contact #1) Radar contact on two small craft at 4,800 yards. Closed but unable to see them at 1,000 yards clearly enough to determine whether luggers or motor torpedo boats. Decided on dawn gun attack, so took position to westward information. Course 070(T), speed 8 knots.

0230 Closed to 1,000 yards awaiting first streaks of dawn.

0300 Manned battle stations – gun.

0318 Made out targets to be standard 100 ton luggers in early dawn. Range to forward lugger 850 yards broad on starboard bow. Range to after lugger 1,200 yards on starboard beam. 40 MM to take on forward target, 5 inch[1] on after target.

0319 Gun Attack #1. Commenced firing. Fired one round of 5 inch for one hit in after target. Fired seven rounds of 40 mm for four hits in forward target. Forward target commencing firing to his starboard with a 37 mm (approximately) gun, only 180 degrees out of phase. Shifted 5 inch to forward lugger and fired 4 rounds for 3 hits. Forward lugger sank. Reversed course to finish off after lugger, which was sporadically firing a 37 mm splashing well astern of us. At 200 yards fired 3 rounds of 5 inch for 2 hits and 9 rounds of 40 mm for 6 hits. Target filled with water and settled, a shambles, as we left the area it sank. Did not desire a prisoner from this vicinity, since we plan to take prisoners from the Karafuto area.

Attack position: Lat. 44-39 N., Long. 146-43 E.

0336 Secured. Headed towards Kehuro Kaikyo.

0426 APR contact 76/500/7.

1150 APR contact 81/500/40.

1155 APR contact 78/500/24.

1200 Position: Lat. 44-32 N., Long. 145-44 E.

1321 Dived for a periscope. Probably a seal. Now patrolling off Shiretoko Misaki, Hokkaido.

1436 Surfaced.

1454 Sighted aircraft Hap[2] at 6 miles. Dived. We are using SD keying at 1 minute intervals in accordance with latest SORG information.

1517 Surfaced.

1520 Sighted aircraft – a different plane at 10 miles. Slowed to 2/3 speed.

1522 Dived.

---

[1] *Barb*'s old 4" gun was removed during the Mare Island overhaul and replaced by a new 5"/25 Caliber gun. Based on a 5" anti-aircraft weapon, the 5"/25 was specially designed for submarine use, and built of corrosion resistant steel, making it the most immersion tolerant of all submarine deck guns. This was the last deck gun designed for submarines, and the development of a new deck gun this late in the war was a testament to the effectiveness of American submarine operations in the Pacific. During the same period, German U-boats, faced with far more effective anti-submarine forces, removed their deck guns as essentially useless appendages whose only contribution was additional drag and underwater noise.

[2] Hap: Mitsubishi A6M3, a clipped-wing version of the Zero fighter. "Hap" was the original code name for this plane, but later lists changed that to "Hamp."

1533 Surfaced.

1537 Sighted some aircraft patrolling Abashiri Wan. Commenced easing out from coast. Not worried about being sighted because we have been asked to raise a rumpus.

1604 Dived. Aircraft heading towards. SD range 10 miles.

1608 One bomb.

1610 Second bomb. Astern, port, below by indicator[3]. We are at 140 feet.

2010 Surfaced, sun still up. Decided to repay the compliment by making this initial submarine rocket assault tonight on Shari, a city of about 20,000 population on the North Coast of Hokkaido.

2309 Sighted Hotoro Misaki light, characteristics normal.

22 June 1945

0150 Manned battle stations–rockets. Set up rocket launcher and loaded twelve five inch rockets. Set rocket range 5,250 yards. Cleared decks.

0233 Rocket Assault #1. In position 4,700 yards off the beach. Visibility – fair. Range to center of town 5,250 yards. Depth 20 fathoms.

0234 Rockets Away!!!

An inspiring sight. CO wore polarized goggles at darkest setting for launching to maintain night adaptation. All rockets left in 5 seconds and their trail disappeared about 20 feet above the deck. Rockets observed to fall in an area estimated at 500 yards in diameter in the center of the town. Explosions were seen, heard and felt. No fires were started.

Reversed course and withdrew at high speed as dawn was breaking. Each rocket carries a 9.6 pound explosive charge and the effect is similar to plane bombing on a small scale.

0250 APR contact 79/500/7. Shore based air search radar was turned on. Evidently the Japs did think they were being bombed.

0400 APR contact 195/1000/32.

0811 Sighted plane at 12 miles. Dived.

0835 Surfaced.

1045 Sighted Karafuto.

1200 Position: Lat. 45-53 N., Long. 143-59 E.

1735 APR contact 153/500/24. Steady. Swung ship but could obtain no definite bearing.

2200 Commenced search of coast line on Taraika Wan (Patience Bay).

23 June 1945

Surface patrolling along coast of Patience Bay.

---

3   Indicator: Depth Charge Direction Indicator (DCDI). A system of microphones placed fore, aft, port and starboard on the conning tower fairwater and superstructure, in the periscope shears, and on the keel. When depth charges (or, in this case, bombs) exploded, lights on a panel in the conning tower would indicate the relative direction of the detonation.

0346 (Contact #2) Sighted trawler to seaward. Closed.

0413 Man battle stations—guns.

0423 Gun Attack #2. Range 2,000 yards. Commenced firing 40 MM at large two decked, two masted diesel wooden trawler similar to 150 ton class in identification manual. This to determine extent of answering fire. First shot over, second short, third a hit. What a beautiful weapon this 40 MM is now we have telescopic sights and sight bar. Once the range is determined, we hit consistently. Expended 3 more rounds of 40 MM for 3 hits, then checked fire. Seven Japs ran forward. Trawler was still going ahead at eight knots, so fired three round of 5 inch for 3 hits at 700 yards to stop it. No answering fire. Called away boarding party. Fired 13 more round of 40 MM for 11 hits to quell any opposition from possible machine guns. Unfortunately a fire now broke out below his decks and quickly spread through the superstructure. This prevented boarding. The Japs, forward, seemed content to be fried, rather than come out of hiding and risk survival in the icy water. Consequently, since we now wanted a prisoner and did not want to leave a blazing mark of our presence, determined to sink trawler by a high speed sweep close aboard in order to wash sufficient water through a large 5 inch hole near the waterline. Opened out, speeded up to 16 knots and swept by about 10 yards off his port beam. Target filled and sank.

0504 Took aboard one prisoner. Five others volunteered and another committed Hari-Kari [*sic*] by slitting his throat.

0700 After an hour returned to wreckage to see if the survivors had possibly made a raft. All had joined their ancestors.

1200 Position: Lat. 47-59 N., Long. 142-38 E.

Continued coastal sweep on the surface.

24 June 1945

Surface patrolling coast of Karafuto – Patience Bay.

0126 Closed Shikuka to 5 fathom curve because of bogeys. This being an air base it is believed some form of radar balloon or decoy exists along shoreline. Definitely no ships were present though pips resembled ships.

0452 Passed through field of drift ice in northern end of bay.

1200 Position: Lat. 48-34 N., Long. 144-48 E.

1520 APR contact 78/750/28.

25 June 1945

Surface patrolling along east coast of Karafuto and Russian Sakhalin going as far north as Urkt. Possibly Japs may be buying oil at Urkt.

1200 Position: Lat. 52-04 N., Long. 144-13 E.

Toured as far north as Lat. 53-34 N., then turned south swinging well out from coast and following 100 fathom curve down, which we believe Japs use from Paramushiru. Passed one field of drift ice east of Urkt.

26 June 1945

Surface patrolling south along Sakhalin.

1200 Position: Lat. 51-04 N., Long. 144-13 E.

1655 (Contact #3) Through a remarkable atmospheric lens sighted a convoy at a range later determined to be 40–45,000 yards. With the lens effect, the convoy appeared to be viewed from about a 5 degree elevation, all ships being on this side of the horizon in minature with bow waves visible and no parts of the ships sticking up above the normal horizon. Thermal waves were apparent throughout this sector. Commenced end around.

1720 APR contact 79/500/30.

1746 Lens persisting. Sighted aircraft apparently leaving convoy.

1850 APR contact 75/500/24.

1910 Ahead of convoy. In view of no darkness tonight—late sunset, long twilight, full moon and after previous days of fog, a sparkling clear, cold day—decided on a submerged attack now.

1920 Submerged. Range unknown. However, enemy may have spotted us as easily as we have him. Closing at high speed. Convoy consists of 2 medium and 1 small freighter escorted by 1 DD (*Terutsuki*), 2 DEs and 2 PCs. Plane cover has now gone. Probably en route to La Pérouse from Paramushiru. Looks like Japs are determined to get through.

2028 ST range 11,000 yards. Angle on the bow zero.

2037 Convoy turned towards beach sharply, giving large port angle on the bow. Commenced approach on far seaward escort, a *Terutsuki*, since we have now been cut out by base course change.

See special report. [Not available. Ed.]

2200 Surfaced under a cloudless sky and full moon. Closed coast.

2219 Picked up target group near Anaiwa Misaki well inside 10 fathoms.

2234 One or more escorts, probably that d— *Terutsuki*, gave us several broadsides at 12,000 yards. Gunfire was seen and heard in and pointed in our direction. No splashes were observed by CO or OOD. All others had been cleared from the bridge. We are brightly silhouetted by moon. Headed for Netonu Misaki forty miles south along the coast where we might get in a submerged attack in 15 fathoms.

27 June 1945

0200 Circling off Netonu Misaki. Convoy evidently anchored at twilight at Anaiwa Misaki, and escorts patrolling off anchorage had fired at us.

0749 Contact with convoy coming down coast deep inside ten fathom curve. Dived and commenced closing coast, sea an oily calm.

0810 Surface haze lifted near coast. Visibility excellent.

0822 Two bombs. Close. Just as periscope was being raised for first time in 12 minutes. Evidently our hull is visible against the bottom in such shallow water with a calm sea above us. Raised periscope anyhow to observe formation. *Terutsuki* is leaving formation and giving us a zero angle on the bow at about 7,500 yards. Plane overhead. This looks like a nice place to take departure from. Secured attack and commenced evasion.

0825 Two bombs. Close.
0832 Depth charge distant.
0833 Depth charge distant.
0852 Made ready all tubes.
0855 Two depth charges to port. Fairly close.
0900 Twenty-six fathoms.
0900 Two depth charges to port and ahead. Depth charge indicator doing a nice job.
0904 Two depth charges to port. Decided to open coast, surface and end around to a point south of Kaihyo To where we should have 30 to 40 fathoms to attack in.

Less than 20 fathoms is evidently too little with a calm sea and an alert plane cover. Undoubtedly he is spotting our silhouette against the sand bottom.

1039 Surfaced. Smoke of target in sight. Plane out ahead. Commenced end around at 30,000 yards.
1148 Dived for plane. Wilson, R.(n), 671 69 24, RM2c received laceration on forehead and nose requiring sutures while clearing bridge[4].
1200 Position: Lat. 48-38 N., Long. 145-08 E.
1215 Surfaced. Figured the convoy would head for Airo Misaki so opened out to an estimated 40,000 yards to avoid plane sighting during end around.
1319 Dived for plane.
1336 Surfaced. Opened out to an estimated 50,000 yards. No contact with convoy. Headed for position ahead.
1640 APR contact 79/500/30.
1733 Ahead of convoy's estimated position. Commenced search.
1800 APR contact 78/500/7 and 82/500/10.
1835 APR contact 98/500/24.
1956 Dived for plane at 8 miles.
2025 Surfaced. Resumed search.

Searched coast from Airo Misaki to Sakayehana during night, then patrolled off Airo Misaki, which convoy must round.

2307 APR contact 79/500/20.

28 June 1945

Patrolling submerged off Airo Misaki.

---

[4] Normal procedure on clearing the bridge was for the lookouts to tuck their binocular inside their shirts or jackets so that they wouldn't catch on a ladder rung and smack their owner in the face as he slid down the handrails. Wilson, who was not a regular lookout, forgot this and sustained a bloody nose and a gash in his forehead requiring several stitches.

0024 APR contact 79/500/20.

0338 Dived for submerged patrol.

0712 Sighted DE, who commenced patrol about 8,000 yards to seaward of us. Thought he was trying to draw us out so we remained close in along coast.

0900 DE shoved off to southward.

0946 Sighted plane patrolling our position.

1200 Position: Lat. 46-48 N., Long. 143-30 E.

2134 Surfaced. Am sure convoy has not gone by. Commenced search up the coast of Patience Bay.

29 June 1945

Searching for convoy along coast of Patience Bay.

0512 Submerged for patrol along north coast of Motomari.

1200 Position: Lat. 48-22 N., Long. 142-45 E. Off Kashiho.

1217 CO raised periscope to find himself looking at the buck teeth of a Jap pilot in a Rufe about 200 yards away. This single pontoon plane was flying about 50 feet off the water. Angle on the bow 90 port. Went to 90 feet. Water is an oily calm. Depth 20 fathoms. Visibility excellent.

1242 Periscope depth.

1245 Sighted same convoy coming down coast at 1,500 yards inside 10 fathom curve with a DE and two PCs patrolling on their beam along the 10 fathom curve. The *Terutsuki* in acting as an outer screen about 1,500 yards outside the 10 fathom curve. A clever set up with plane patrolling ahead of *Terutsuki*. Manned battle stations torpedoes and headed in.

1255 *Terutsuki* is swinging out from formation giving us a zero angle on the bow at about 9,000 yards. Plane about halfway between us. Heading on in, hoping we haven't been spotted.

1305 Angle on bow still zero with plane weaving across his bow. This boy looks menacing. Coming left to give him a down the throat with stern tubes. Depth 18 fathoms. Using ST scope for ranges.

1307–1309 *Five* bombs. Dust and cork flying. Periscope acting like a whip antenna.

1316 Having difficulty separating plane and DD on ST radar. Plane is doing figure eights across the bow of the DD.

1317 Target speed 10 knots – pinging. Range 1,700 yards, angle on bow 5 starboard.

See special report. [Not available. Ed.]

1318 Depth charge.

1319:30 Explosion or depth charge.

1320 Torpedo Attack #1A. Range 960 yards, speed 10 knots, angle on bow 3 degrees starboard. Fired tubes #7, #8, #9 down the throat gyro angles 20 degrees right. Went ahead full to create a ping target. DD has now shifted to short scale.

After about 20 seconds slowed to 1/3. All torpedoes missed.

1324 Terutsuki passing overhead. Screws clearly audible.

1325 Eight depth charges. Ahead, above and below mostly to port. Raised scope to see a continuous stream of depth charges coming out of his side throwers. A thrilling sight with the ship doing a St. Vitus' Dance and the ST picking up the geysers from the depth charge explosions.

1326 Range 800 yards. Angle on the bow 175 starboard. Speed 10 knots. See special report. [Not available. Ed.]

1327 Six or more depth charges. Terrible *Terutsuki* now turning and coming back with plane doing figure eights just forward of his bridge.

1331 Torpedo Attack #1B. Range 620 yards. Speed 12 knots. Angle on bow 10 starboard. Fired tubes #1, #2, #3 down throat. All misses. Turned away at full speed and went to deep submergence 80 feet. I am positive this boy draws at least 10 feet, at 620 yards he looks like a battleship.

1333–34 Ten or more depth charges to starboard and astern, above and below. Released 5 NAC beacons[5] set on 3 minutes delay at about one minute intervals. Threw a couple of full speed knuckles[6] then slowed to 70 RPM and withdrew tactically and tacitly from the coast. Several escorts made sweeps around us occasionally but never picked us up again.

Consider ourselves extremely unfortunate to only get a draw in this beautiful fight after all the punches we threw.

1450 Periscope depth. DD and a DE still searching well astern of us.

1615 Bomb – distant.

1950 All clear. Sun still up. Surfaced, plotting all kinds of foul deeds. The convoy has now gone by. It is probable that they will spend the 4 hours of darkness at Airo Wan, then on through La Pérouse. Much to our disgust we lack two hours of being able to hop in the ring with the *Terutsuki* for a fifth round. Set course for Anaiwa Misaki, certain now that this is the principal convoy departure point for Paramushiru. Possible, also, that surface force bombardment of that island several days ago may drive some ships out.

20 June 1945

Surface patrolling off Anaiwa Misaki.

0925 APR contact 79/500/10.

---

[5] Mechanical decoys designed to "swim" out of a submarine's torpedo tubes. They are equipped with a noise maker that, upon activation, creates the sound of a submarine taking evasive action. The idea is to trick the escorts into chasing the decoy while the submarine slips away. During this action, *Barb* also released a large number of "pillenwurfer" decoys, essentially a giant bicarbonate tablet, which makes a lot of noise and sends up a cloud of bubbles that reflect active sonar.

[6] Making a sudden sharp course change at high speed creates a "knuckle," or cavitation disturbance, in the water. As this will reflect the beam of active sonar, it can fool an operator into thinking the knuckle is the target—at least, until he realizes that it isn't moving.

0945 APR contact 50/600/40.
1010 APR contact 68/1260/40 and 72/500/40.
Swung ship but unable to determine direction.
1200 Position: Lat. 49-29 N., Long. 144-39 E.
1715 APR contact 117/1250/12.

1 July 1945

Surface patrolling off Anaiwa Misaki. Our first fog in the area.

1200 Position: Lat. 49-24 N., Long. 144-39 E.

1330 Tested out both rubber boats with four, 200 pounds plus, Officers in view of anticipated future operations.

2030 Set course for Kaihyo To for morning bombardment. This island contains a large government operated seal rookery on the eastern side. Buildings and warehouses are located on the western side. We plan to land and take it. A prisoner will be valuable to check routing and frequency of Kurile convoys.

2 July 1945

Surface patrolling off Kaihyo To.

0500 Sighted Kaihyo To. Visibility about 10,000 yards. Large stockades of the seal rookery were in evidence on the eastern side. Two beacons, radio antenna and an observation post were on the flat top of the island. Eased around south of island, on edge of visibility circle, trusting to our camouflage for non detection before the bombardment. Reefs and shoals extend off the island, with the best and most sheltered approach from the west.

0625 Headed in for bombardment. Was a bit surprised to find 20 or more large barracks, warehouses and buildings on the western side. Looks like business has expanded beyond our expectations and those of the pilot and charts.

0638 Commenced continuous keying of fathometer.

0641 Manned battle stations – gun. Noticed people madly running around the island. Our presence is known. The 10 fathom curve extends 2,000 yards off shore.

0650 Sounding 7 fathoms. Range 1,100 yards. Visibility – excellent. Fog has cleared. Skies overcast.

0651 Shore Bombardment #1. Commenced firing 40 MM. Simultaneously island personnel opened up on us with machine guns, which walked across us without hitting. Immediately returned their fire with our twin 20 MM, 2-.50 calibre and 2-.30 calibres, concentrating 40 MM on an exposed .50 calibre mount, which the enemy had mounted on top of the 50 foot cliff overhanging the buildings on this side of the island. Opposition ceased. Range 900 yards. Commenced firing 5 inch gun, systematically destroying all buildings. Spotted a 75 MM field piece unmanned on the cliff. Turned the 40 MM gun on it, and their fourth shot hit it, knocking a wheel off – leaving it lying on its side.

0704 Reversed course to remain in close. Sounding 6 fathoms. At range 800 yards stopped and let the guns literally tear the place to pieces. The 40 MM destroyed the observation post, three sampans close to the beach and an oil dump of about thirty drums. These drums must have contained seal oil, for the automatic fire striking the oil pouring down the beach gave off large flashes, but never set it on fire. A fire broke out in one of the large buildings near the center of the concentration and quickly spread to other buildings. Really a wonderful sight and the ideal submarine bombardment—huge fires burning, sections of building flying up in the air, sampans destroyed, oil drums tumbled and split, a field piece overturned and a machine gun hanging loose, unattended. Too much praise cannot be given the gun crews. We have emphasized thrifty use of our limited ammunition, almost to the danger point, and not a bullet or shell was wasted. The 5 inch shifted targets methodically, as quickly as previous target was destroyed. The 40 MM, with its new telescopic sights and sight bar, proved its worth as an accurate weapon. The automatic weapons outdid themselves by firing properly in short bursts. To really appreciate this bombardment one must see the results obtained by our photographer.

0724 Ceased fire. Opened out to observe results. Secured guns. Island in shambles with fires spreading. Stopped and lay to at 3,500 yards to observe results and give the planes a couple of hours to arrive in case a transmission had been sent before we silenced their transmitters. This as a precaution preparatory to our projected landing.

1030 No planes yet. We had heard nothing on 500 KCS so assume bombardment is still a private matter. Flooded down forward and inflated rubber boats. Called away assault force and briefed them. Plan to land on northwest side of island with 40 MM laying a barrage 200 yards ahead of party.

1045 Manned battle stations – guns, working back in toward beach, heaving the lead to check fathometer. Stopped 650 yards from beach in 5 fathoms. Looked every bit of island over for possible unknown fortifications. Fires burning merrily—about 1/3 of buildings having now been consumed.

1102 To our amazement CO and OOD spotted 4 pillboxes along the top of this barren island protecting this side.

1103 Commenced firing 40 mm at one large pillbox from which an antenna led. Fire was immediately returned by machine gun and rifles. Opened up with all automatic guns, which silenced the opposition. After 18 shots, the 40 MM put one in the slit of the pillbox and blew open part of the front side. Real accuracy. Gave up the idea of landing as too risky with the results to be obtained other than project No. 3 and withdrew. At about 4,000 yards the Japs again opened up with machine guns in a face saving attempt. On losing sight of the island now rechristened Little Iwo, fires were still burning.

As an interesting sidelight members of the Assault Force had refused offers of $200 to swap with other members of the crew prior to discovery of the pillbox.

Afterwards, the price was best expressed by one of our Commandos—"You can buy me for a nickel."

1200 Position: Lat. 48-24 N., Long. 144-25 E.

Set course to investigate town of Shiritori.

1640 APR contact 135/1500/12.

1752 Dived. Closed beach until we had only 3 fathoms under keel. Shiritori is a greatly enlarged thriving town with numerous factories. Spotted trains shuttling back and forth for future reference.

2126 Surfaced. Set course for Shikuka. Our presence in Patience Bay will be a sore subject for the Japs by tomorrow so decided to give Shikuka a rocket massage. Shikuka is another large town in the northwestern part of Patience Bay which has really grown up. It has many factories and land and seaplane air bases. 10 fathom curve is 5 miles off the beach.

3 July 1945

0100 Sighted range lights of Shikuka harbor. Heavy overcast and a light drizzle. Perfect for rocketeering. Set up rocket launcher and checked circuits.

0210 Manned battle stations – rockets. Loaded 12 rockets. Set rocket range at 5,250 yards. Target to be center of town with drift going into factories.

0239 Rocket Assault #2. In position, 4,900 yards off the beach. Sounding 5 fathoms. Put on polaroid goggles to watch the fun.

0240 *Rockets Away!!!*

Nothing happened. After a few frantic minutes found a loose connection in the circuit. Backed down and regained firing position.

0247 *Rockets Away!!!* This time the system worked and the 5 inch rockets went swishing out.

0247:31 Rockets landed with their usual thunder and explosions amongst a mass of buildings. Scampered for deep water. No fires were started. Lights blinked on and off in town for a few minutes then darkness. This area will need cooling off. Fog set in with visibility variable.

0943 (Contact #4) Sighted a small coastal freighter (KMFK), 1,000 tons, coal burner in the haze, en route Shikuka, zig zagging. Radar made contact at 13,000 yards. Commenced end around.

1010 APR contact 59/500/40.

1200 Position: Lat. 48-24 N., Long. 143-56 E.

1206 Submerged in position ahead, speed and zigzag plan determined.

1227 Angle on bow zero. The lifeboats are swung out and half lowered. Range 1,800 yards. Went deep.

See special report[7]. [Not available. Ed.]

1249 Surfaced. Picked up a total of 17 charts. All Japs committed Hari-Kari [*sic*]. Eliminated as much evidence as possible. International signal flags and col-

---

7   At 1233 a Mark 27 homing torpedo was fired at the target from a depth of 135 feet.

ors floating in tightly wrapped individual bundles were numerous, but heavy swell washed them away when scavenging was attempted. Moral – bring a dip net.

Set course for Aniwa Wan and Otomari.

4 July 1945

0535 APR contact 155/500/20. Swung ship without success.

1200 Position: Lat. 45-48 N., Long. 143-37 E.

1604 (Contact #5) Sighted frigate. Dived. Commenced approach. Frigate did a figure 8 in our direction and then opened out, closest range 8,000 yards before frigate returned to his patrol down a possible mine line, which is charted.

1846 Sighted *Russian* destroyer, which we made a successful approach on, until he was identified by his merchant ship markings at 3,500 yards. A two stacker, which had passed east through La Pérouse. A surprise for we have not expected Russian Men-of-War. Fortunate that we weren't planning on special weapons for outer doors on bow tubes had been opened before he was identified.

2023 Surfaced. Radar contact on another ship. Used flank speed to get ahead.

2038 Submerged. Commenced approach.

2046 Sighted another Russian, a liberty ship heading for La Pérouse.

2050 Surfaced 6,000 yards from him. Our position between two mine lines without a check on our DR for over 12 hours is not good.

During night searched west coast of Aniwa Wan from La Pérouse to Otonari via the 10 fathom curve.

2330 APR contact 95/500/40.

5 July 1945

0450 Submerged for day patrol off Takana Se just south of Venkochi Point and north of La Pérouse minefields. After close study of this coast and the traffic routes we anticipate, particularly, the daily train ferries. This appears to be the only point where an attack is possible. Here we can get to within 3,000 yards of the beach. Unfortunately it is an uneasy position close to the minefields with a maximum of 15 fathoms of water, and the surface is a mirror like calm. The boys are now getting pretty good at diving with a maximum of 2 degree dive angle. Would we could encounter some fog.

0730 Sighted a trawler working close in to the beach.

0820 Another trawler passing close.

0829 Sighted a lugger heading towards La Pérouse.

0846 Two more trawlers.

0910 (Contact #6) Sighted a frigate coming down the coast outboard of us. Went to full speed commencing approach. Target pinging.

0922 During an observation sighted two train ferries swinging down the coast. These were almost invisible against the land background. The leader of these was a beautiful job, more or less of a combination of the *Seinan Maru #2* and the *Tugara Maru*. A two stacker, stacks athwartship, with three decks of superstructure under a large bridge—estimated tonnage 4,000. Close behind it was a medium AK, which had been converted to a train ferry, judging from its stepped fantail. Turned around again and commenced approach on train ferry at high speed.

Approach ended up with *Barb* in the middle. Closest range to after ferry 3,400 yards. Frigate 3,000 yards outboard of us. Target speed 15 knots. Both ferries passed within two hundred yards of the rocks. Kicked myself for being drawn out from the coast by the escort.

0953 (Contact #7) Sighted smoke coming north through La Pérouse.

1000 Made out two ships under the smoke heading our way. One is very large resembling a Liberty Ship. Had a good comparison between it and the large train ferry as they passed. The big ship eased out from the coast to let the ferries pass inboard. The small ship identified as a small engines aft coastal AK passed inshore of the ferries. Had a few bad moments when a large rust patch on the side of the large AK resembled the Red Russian markings—angle on the bow is small. A nice picture presented itself of the coastal AK using the Russian to screen it. Could practically hear the howls if we fired fish across the bow of a Russian at a coastal AK.

1038 Raised the periscope nearly clipping off the pontoons of a Jap seaplane. This plane was a twin floater doing figure eights across the bow of the large AK. This is no Russian. Eased out a bit and large AK eased in towards coast.

1047 Torpedo Attack #2B. Fired tubes #7, #9. Dropped target speed to 8 knots. Track angle 135 degrees starboard, range 1,670, gyros 25 degrees left, depth 6 feet.

Another explosion—probably bomb.

1054 One hit. Raised periscope. Target had heavy clouds of white smoke under stack and was listing to starboard. Tops of screws were visible and screws were stopped. Coastal AK was stopped on his port bow, but being in ballast with the bow part of his keel showing, not suitable for torpedoes.

1057 Breaking up noises commenced. Lowered scope and hauled ashes for twenty fathom curve.

1106 Took a final periscope check on target. Three lifeboats were in the water. Ship now listing to port about 10 degrees, her anchor down—evidently the torpedo explosion had anchored her. Breaking up noises continued loudly, but target did not appear to be settling. Much as I disliked the idea it was imperative to reverse course and deliver the *coup de grâce*.

1114 Made ready tube #1. Could not sight plane, but pinging was heard with an up doppler. Decided to use ST and some exact dope on these Mk 18-2 fish. Found our funnel height was off to the extent that target speed was 9¼ knots. Our first spread should have caught him easily.

1123 Range 1,400 yards. Standby—hold everything, target is sagging amidships. Secure tube #1.

1124 Target broke amidship and sank in a "V" for victory witnessed by CO and Exec. Breaking up noises lasted about 5 more minutes.

1130 Having spotted escorts coming in from north and south, dropped down to 80 feet and buried our heads, hopefully.

1136 Distant bomb or depth charge. Pinging now loud.

1200 Position: Lat. 46-05 N., Long. 142-19 E.

A concentrated sweep was now made of this area by at least two pairs of escorts. We avoided by running east silently, using 100 RPM when escorts were distant and 40 RPM when they were close. This course was a necessity because an undetermined current sets southerly on to the minefield and the bay shoals to the north.

2116 Surfaced. Still daylight, but even the escorts seem to be leery of hanging around a submarine after dark. Set course for Hokkaido to cool this off and to give personnel a chance to relax. In spite of the fact that this attack was consummated without any close depth charges or bombs, it has affected personnel more than any other. Frankly Anaiwa Wan seems to permeate most with an electric, nerve wracking claustrophobia. No one likes it. Believe this is due to shallow water, proximity of minefield and the obvious fact that our fish are not hittng even with the best of set ups.

2133 APR contact 210 meg.

6 July 1945

Surface patrolling along north coast of Hokkaido from Esashi Ko to Abashiri.

0030 APR contact 95/500/40.

0545 Variable fog and rain. Adjusted courses so that breakers on beach would be visible without getting ourselves sighted by land. Area empty.

0900 APR contact 79/500/40.

1152 Dived and closed Shimoyusetsu to 12 fathom curve for observation. Many small factories.

1200 Position: Lat. 46-04 N., Long. 142-20 E.

1403 Surfaced.

1805 APR contact 79/250/20.

2109 APR contact 135/250/20.

2330 Set course for Anaiwa Wan to take advantage of foggy weather.

7 July 1945

Surface patrolling east of la Pérouse en route Anaiwa Wan. Weather deserted us after dawn. Visibility 20,000 yards.

1127 (Contact #8) Sighted a frigate at 15,000 yards.

1129 Dived. Commenced approach. Frigate was patrolling southwest, perhaps coincidentally, from Haka Shiretoko Misaki along possible mine line.

1159 Target reversed course at about 8,000 yards and escaped.
1200 Position: Lat. 45-45 N., Long. 142-55 E.
1223 Sighted Russian freighter.
1241 Surfaced.
1253 (Contact #9) Dived. Sighted another frigate patrolling northeast, perhaps coincidentally, along possible mine line from Hokkaido northeast. At about 12,000 yards target reversed course.
1359 Surfaced. Further approach on these targets is out of the question. We have not had a fix for 16 hours.
1700 Obtained fix. Recorrecting our track shows that were within 500 yards of eastern possible mine line during our approach on the first frigate of the day.
1715 APR 75/500/40.
1802 (Contact #10) Dived. Sighted two frigates patrolling slowly down the coast out from position of our attack. Regret they won't join us in thirty fathoms, but they appear to like 20 fathom water.
1930 Last sight of frigates.
2016 Surfaced. Sun still up. Looks like the heat is still on. Set course for Patience Bay.
2100 APR contact 80/750/24.

8 July 1945

Surface patrolling along east coast of Karafuto and Patience Bay.
1200 Position: Lat. 46-56 N., Long. 143-17 E.
Haze set in. Visibility 12,000 yards.
1625 APR contact 77/500/28.
1833 (Contact #11) Sighted a lugger making 9 knots heading south along 10 fathom curve. Decided to follow on edge of visibility until light fog thickens or twilight, for if lugger sights us he can beach himself before we get a shot off.
2010 Sunset. Commenced closing. Eased inside the 10 fathom curve.
2050 Fathometer showing 2½ fathoms beneath keel. Rigged in sound heads. Target evidently heading for Sakamehara, 2½ miles south of us.
2055 Gun Attack #3. All stop. Range 1,100 yards commenced firing 40 MM. Gun crew for 5 inch standing by below decks. Fired 32 rounds for 20 hits. Lugger destroyed and sinking by the stern.
2038 Reliable lookout spotted large 2 engine plane rising from field near the beach. Cleared the decks and went to emergency speed heading for 10 fathom of deep water, zigzagging wildly. Raised periscope to watch plane.
2101 Reached the 10 fathom curve, but plane had not been picked up again. These three intervening minutes seemed like hours of being an ostrich, and everyone in the control room was urgently beseeching the fathometer to show us 10 fathoms. Mentally booted myself a hundred times for not fighting the plane off with guns, but my snap decision had been to clear everybody off topside and

close the hatch, so that no second would be wasted in getting the gun crews below when we had sufficient water beneath us to dive. As a post-mortem the snap decision was correct.

2102 With no plane on SD or periscope, decided it was evidently a transport plane on a routine takeoff which hadn't seen us, so returned to the bridge.

2103 CO, OOD, Quartermaster and periscope spotted two medium calibre guns firing at us from Sakayahara. The opposition had broken out the village guns and were pumping out shots every five seconds. All were well astern in the vicinity of the sinking lugger. Shifted my horseshoe to another pocket and set course for Nemuro Kaikyo en route lifeguard station for carrier strike.

9 July 1945
Surface patrolling across Okhotsk Sea en route Nemuro Kaikyo.
0900 APR contact 74/500/25.
1200 Position: Lat. 46-06 N., Long. 144-54 E.

10 July 1945
0040 APR contact 79/500/70.
0045 APR contact 198/1150/24.
0545 APR contact 198/900/25.
Surface patrolling along west coast of Kunashiri in Nemuro Kaikyo.
Visibility excellent.
0918 (Contact #12) Sighted smoke coming up through Nemuro Strait. Probably coastal AKs, which would pass close to Shiretoko, so commenced high speed dash across the straits to obtain close inshore attack position.

1000 Submerged 7 miles off Shiretoko with fishing shacks in clear view without binoculars. We must accept being sighted by people on shore and trust they have no telephone or signal communication to warn approaching ships. Continued closing coast at full speed.

1015 Manned battle stations–torpedoes. Commenced ST approach. Targets–two Coast AKs (800 tons est.). Smokey Joes MFM. No escorts. Course and speed steady. One target 2,000 yards astern of other. Decided to fire from close position so Mk 18s couldn't miss. Estimated draft of target 8–10 feet. Set torpedoes on 3 feet.

1117 At firing position, range 600 yards, but periscope is ducked.

1118 Torpedo Attack #3. Fired tubes #1, #2, #3. Range 540 yards, track 145 starboard, gyros 43 degrees right, target speed 8 knots. No hits. Torpedoes tracked towards target and then were lost. Target maintained course and speed. Commenced turning left for attack on second target.

1125:30 One torpedo explosion on the beach. Went to 150 feet dead ahead of second target. JP unable to pick up screws of second target until after it had passed overhead.

1128 Secured from battle stations. Disappointed. Watched targets go over the hill and turn [toward] Shiretoko Misaki en route Abashiri. Considered a battle surface action, but targets were alerted, armed with 40 MM and I expected the Hokkaido Coastal Air Patrol to arrive momentarily.
1200 Position: Lat. 44-04 N., Long. 146-15 E.
1307 Sighted aircraft, which searched area.
1340 Sighted aircraft, which searched area.
1636 Surfaced and set course for Kunashiri Suido.

Of possible interest concerning these coastal AKs is the fact that both were dragging a rope net astern similar to the type used in the old "Cast" recovery on our BBs. At first this was considered a possible anti-submarine drag, until I watched three sampans work close aboard the AKs and hook on to the net with a grapnel for a free ride.
1808 APR contact 75/500/50.
2100 APR contact 80/600/50.
2200 Converted #4 fuel ballast tank.

11 July 1945

Surface patrolling between Kunashiri and Shinotan.
0200 Transmitted Kunashiri Strait.
0445 APR contact 79/500/50.
0755 (Contact #13) Sighted a large diesel sampan. Visibility excellent.
0850 Manned battle stations—gun. Since we are 15 miles from air bases on Shikotan, maneuvered into firing position so that guns would fire on a line between Shikotan and Kunashiri thus lessening the noise.
0902 Gun Attack #4. Commenced firing 40 MM at range of 900 yards. Target speed 7 knots. Fired 40 rounds of 40 MM for 35 hits. Target stopped, but refused to sink.
0908 Ceased firing. Circled and made a high speed sweep close aboard target, but she stayed afloat.
0927 Fired two rounds of 5 inch at 350 yards. Target opened all seams and sank. Continued patrol.
1200(I) Position: Lat. 44-04 N., Long. 146-19 E.
2200(I) Transited Shikotan Strait. Fairly shallow, 15 fathoms. En route lifeguard station.

12 July 1945

Surface patrolling Suisho Shoto to Akkeshi Wan, light fog, visibility 10,000 yards. Patrolling with beach visible.
0055(I) APR contact 79/500/60.
1040(I) APR contact 153/500/22.
1200(I) Position: Lat. 43-05 N., Long. 145-30 E.

1210–1320(I) APR contact 153/500/22.
1700(I) APR contact 102/500/22. Lasted while in this area.
1832–2400(I) APR contact 152/500/22.

13 July 1945
Surface patrolling on lifeguard station south of Akkeshi.
Strike was cancelled, so closed coast for patrol. Low visibility.
1200(I) Position: Lat. 42-39 N., Long. 144-59 E.

14 July 1945
Surface patrolling on lifeguard station.
0000(I) APR contacts 78/300/60; 102/500/22; 305/500/17 and 206/500/22.
0410(I) Dived. SJ contact at 18,000 yards closing fast.
0516(I) Surfaced. All clear.
0524(I) Fighter cap 4 planes arrived. Strike commenced. During day large fires were started at Kushiro and Makeshi, which burned all night.
1200(I) Position: Lat. 42-39 N., Long. 145-04 E.
1720(I) Air cap departed.
1910(I) Dived. Plane sighted at 4 miles, flying low, zero angle.
2000(I) Surfaced. Set course for new lifeguard station south of Nemuro. No APR contacts.

15 July 1945
Surface patrolling on lifeguard station.
0450(I) Fighter cap of four planes arrived.

Closed the beach to watch the fun. The first wave quickly set Nemuro afire and knocked out all important targets. Then a search began for something to strike. About 50 fighters scoured the area. We spotted a few radio stations, which they immediately set ablaze. This section of Hokkaido appears very soft. Thought we might join in the sport by a shore bombardment, but neither our cover nor ourselves could find anything worth wasting a 40 mm on after scouting along the shore. There were only a few impoverished small villages left. The high point of the strike came when the following VHF conversation was overheard: Ambitious Pilot to Section Leader, "There's a horse, I'm going after him." Stern Section Leader, "You leave that poor horse alone."

We noticed 5 or 6 horses grazing in a field. The last of the opposition.
1200(I) Position: Lat. 43-11 N., Long. 145-46 E.
1600(I) Cover departed. Secured from lifeguard. Requested a week's extension to cover area time we had absorbed in lifeguard and en route. Extension granted.
2200(I) Transited Shikotan Strait.

16 July 1945 (All times King unless otherwise designated.)
Surface patrolling en route Aniwa Wan.
0400 Transited Kunashiri Strait.
1200 Position: Lat. 45-07 N., Long. 145-23 E.
2140 APR contact 95/500/22.
2330 Entered Aniwa Wan.

17 July 1945
Patrolling Aniwa Wan near La Pérouse.
0550 Dived north of minefields off Chishiya Saki.
0603 Sighted lugger going up coast. Followed by 3 sampans.
0915 Visibility decreased to 4,000 yards.
0922 Surfaced.
1100 (Contact #14) Sighted *Shimushu* class frigate 150 degrees true. Small angle on the bow. Range 10,000 yards.
1102 Dived. Commenced approach.
1117 Manned battle stations torpedoes.
1150 Frigate definitely identified as *Shimushu* Class Frigate. Target has no set zig plan, patrolling at 7 knots with zigs as large as 90 degrees. Masthead height 57 feet—for future reference. At 6,000 yards target turned away and headed towards minefields lazily patrolling. Secured approach.
1200 Position: Lat. 46-03 N., Long. 142-18 E.
1216 Headed back towards our shore position. This approach had drawn us out 3,000 yards. Visibility lowering along coast.
1222 (Contact #15) Sighted another frigate and small AK hugging the coast. Commenced approach, but closest range obtained was 2,700 yards on the frigate, which is too great for our torpedoes. We only have 5 left, their performance so far has been very poor. Consequently they will be expended only on close shots.
1300 Noted the Japs have placed a spar buoy at position where we sank the large AK. This menace to navigation forces traffic out into 13 fathoms of water and accounts for our being able to get as close as we did on our last approach, when we had been drawn out of position by the frigate.
1449 Sighted lugger hugging the beach.
2005 Sighted lugger hugging the beach.
2138 Surfaced. Set course south to investigate night patrol activity La Pérouse minefields.
2215 APR contact 95/450/40. Probably Nishi Notoro Misaki.
2221 (Contact #15) Radar contact, 12,000 yards, 2 frigates patrolling along minelines. One of these frigates using 10 CM radar.

18 July 1945
0145 Radar contact at 17,000 yards. Closed to discover another Russian.

0331 Radar contact at 20,000 yards. Russian lights.

0416 (Contact #17) Sighted one of the minefield frigates at 17,000 yards.

0425 Dived off Vennochi Point to take a crack at the daily traffic, which must pass outside our spar buoy, thus allowing us to be off the coast in 20 fathoms.

1000 Our train ferries, which we have pointed for since the start of the patrol failed to appear for the second consecutive day. News broadcast stated that the recent fighter strikes on Japan had eliminated 3 train ferries at Hakodate. Thus our two must have been sent south to replace them.

1047 Our minefield frigate again put in a distant brief appearance. We are staying put today for some real traffic.

1127 (Contact #18) Sighted a large AK escorted by the customary *Shimushu* class frigate coming down the coast. Manned battle stations and commenced approach in a calm sea. Using only attack scope and taking observations on the frigate only, since we have his masthead height cold. Frigate about 1,500 yards broad on port bow of large AK (KFK), passenger superstructure. Decided to fire 2 torpedoes at frigate and 3 at AK. Set up checking exactly.

Paralleled frigate to present small target. He is pinging and we have an isotherm.

Took a quick peek as frigate passed 3–400 yards abeam, staring into the ends of half a dozen binoculars with with their lookouts were sweeping, noticed Jap OOD berating one port lookout and man fiddling around the depth charge racks. Target now on steady course 196 degrees true, speed 12 knots. To complicate matters the elevation handle[8] of the periscope picked this opportune moment to come off, much to my surprise. Couldn't resist exclaiming "See—no hands," however soon returned to the serious business of consummating a one-armed approach.

1158:25 Torpedo Attack #4A. Fired tubes #4 and #6 at the frigate. Range 1,240 yards, track 160 degrees port, gyros 10 degrees right.

Swung right and at

1159:18 Torpedo Attack #4B. Fired tubes #2, #3, #5 at large AK. Range 1,510 yards, track 120 degrees port, gyros 43 degrees right. All torpedoes set on 4 feet, since we believe torpedoes are running deep.

1200 Position: Lat. 46-04 N., Long. 142-29 E.

1200:28 One hit in stern of frigate. This set off his depth charges and blew his stern off in a tremendous explosion. Noticed his rising sun man-of-war flag sinking properly. The bow end quickly assumed a 90 degree rise angle. Took pictures. Forward end of ship sank until it hit bottom leaving about 20 feet of bow sticking up vertically. this will provide a much better marker than a spar buoy. Sinking witnessed by entire conning tower party. There were no survivors.

---

[8] Elevation Handle: The outer section of the left handle controls elevation of the periscope optics. The optics in a Type II attack periscope can be elevated to 74° above the horizontal and depressed to 10° below. The right handle controls magnification, which varies from 1.5 power in the "low" setting to 6 power in the "high" setting.

1205 Large AK made a 90 degree turn toward, then 180 degree away, then right 90 degrees to go back up the coast followed by a 180 degree turn to resume course for his original destination. Seems to have a difficult time making up his mind, which would be eased, if he only knew we were out of torpedoes. Unaccountably we missed him.

1213 Secured from battle stations and opened coast.

1536 Surfaced. Visibility 12,000 yards. We now feel very dangerous with a full forty fathoms of deep water beneath us, and we have a few bitter pills for the other three frigates in this area, if they care to play on our ground.

1545 APR contact 95/450/40.

1601 (Contact #19) Sighted 2 frigates astern of us about 11,000 yards in 20 fathoms of water. Their decks and superstructure were completely visible. Remained surfaced, hoping to draw them out. Their angle on the bow 20 degrees port. Frigates declined the invitation and, apparently on sighting us, quickly changed their angle on the bow to 90 degrees port and made tracks for the minefield.

1743 Sighted a Russian ship south of us.

1807 Radar contact at 9 miles closing fast. Dived. Oh well, plane opposition has been light since the fighter strike.

2121 (Contact #20) End of twilight, bright moonlight. While making SJ sweep, prior to surfacing, made radar contact on 3 frigates, two together and one several thousand yards astern. All searching for us, and equipped with 10 CM radar. Commenced approach, but unable to gain position ahead. Frigates passed at 2,000 yards plainly visible in night periscope. Unfortunately we have no shooting fish.

2220 Surfaced. Did not consider it good policy to tackle this whole group, with what we have, with the possibility of being held down all night by moonlight. Hope to be able to handle these singly at a later date. Avoided. Set course for Patience Bay and a backlog of unfinished business.

2225 APR contact 95/450/40.

2337 Another Russian ship contact.

19 July 1945

Surface patrolling Patience Bay. Our plan is to locate a suitable coastal position of the railways, land our saboteur force and plant a 55 pound demolition charge under the tracks. Then this charge will be exploded by a train passing over and closing the micro switch.

1022 APR contact 76/500.

1130 APR contact 79/500/60.

1200 Position: Lat. 47-03 N., Long. 143-44 E.

1837 Dived and closed coast for observation.

1932 Sighted the regular northbound train. Located a fairly good position. We had previously located two good landing spots north of Shireturi.

2201 Surfaced. Bright moonlight and no clouds. Operation off tonight.

20 July 1945

Surface patrolling across Patience Bay in hopes of finding a sampan to assist our project. We are remaining undetected until this is completed. Cloudless skies.

1200 Position: Lat. 48-03 N., Long. 143-06 E.

A close study of the Japanese charts of Karafuto recovered from the sinking of the coastal AK has revealed more accurate sounding information than our own charts.

Selected a more suitable position for the sabotage.

1517 Dived and closed coast for observation.

1648 Sighted train.

1947 Sighted regular train. Previous observations have given us their time tables now. Selected optimum position for landing while we coasted with 2 fathoms beneath the keel. Sandy beach, no houses within 700 yards of spot and our submarine could approach to 1,000 yards from beach without grounding. Our plans have been laid for three long weeks, every detail checked, the waterproof firing system made up—now, all we await is 4 hours of darkness with the moon covered and a calm sea.

2132 Surfaced. Sea calm, but we are fouled up by a perfect lovers' night, bright moon. Cloudless.

21 July 1945

Surface patrolling diagonally across Patience Bay towards Ohire, obtaining sounding information of uncharted sections for the Hydrographic Office and praying for clouds.

1200 Position: Lat. 48-52 N., Long. 143-23 E.

Southerly breezes brought a stratus. At last the weather is right. Passed word that saboteurs will land tonight. After days of patiently waiting and observing, the undercurrent of expected action that ran through the boat made one's spine tingle. Even our prisoner "Kamikaze" was swept away with it and asked to be permitted to join the party. Not an escapist, he supplied information on dogs and beach patrols when questioned. Briefly, the outline of our project is as follows:

General Plan

To blow up a train at a vital point in the Karafuto east coast railway system. Under overcast submarine to approach beach on batteries at slack water, flooded down, until two fathoms of water remained under the keel, as checked by leadsman. Here, approximately 1,000 yards offshore, the two rubber boats, containing eight men and equipment, would be launched. Navigation in to be by radar. Hoped for landing point to be 800 yards from nearest houses. Upon beaching signalman and guard would remain with boats. Other six men would proceed across highway to track. At suitable position for planting charge party would divide. One guard proceeding 50 yards up the track near the road. Another 50 yards down track and a third 20 yards inland. The remaining three would dig under the tracks, plant the battery and charge, test and adjust the firing circuit, recall the men, make final hookups and return to the ship. All men carried red flashlights, matches, knives, two "D" rations, lifejacket, cigarette lighter and pistol. Other equipment in the boats consisted of radar corners, carbines, tommy guns, hand grenades, Mk 108 (55 pound) demolition charge, electrical equipment, home manufactured shovels and pick, signal gun, Very pistol, binoculars, line and wedges. Party should land at 2330 and return prior to 0230. Twilight commences about 0245.

Communications are to be simple:

(1) Alert – 2 Bob White whistles.

(2) Assemble – Whippoorwill whistles.

(3) Mechanical whistle – emergency dash for the boats.

(4) Two Very star – we are in trouble – lay a barrage in direction indicated.

(5) One Very star from submarine – we are in trouble, will return every night.

(6) "W" on blinker gun – party is returning to boat.

(7) One Very star at 15 minute intervals – unable to locate submarine after 30 minutes paddling from beach.

The party will be comprised of the following personnel:
Lieut. William M. Walker, U.S.N.R., File No. 120037.
Sever, Francis N., 621 82 53, SM2c, U.S.N.R.
Richard, James E., 564 85 40, MoMM2c, U.S.N.R.
Markuson, John (n), 234 39 38, MoMM1c, U.S.N.
Saunders, Paul G., 265 72 19, CGM, U.S.N. (Chief of the Boat).
Hatfield, Billy R., 828 15 66, EM3c, U.S.N.R.
Newland, Lawrence W., 279 79 21, SC1c, U.S.N.
Klinglesmith, Edward W., 877 88 49, TM3c, U.S.N.-I

Trains at this point have varied from 7 to 32 cars. The average train consists of twelve freight cars, three passenger cars, and one mail or baggage car. Though narrow gauge, the engines are large and of the European type rather than the Oahu type.

2145 Trim dive.

2155 Surface, flooded down.

2200 Briefed Saboteur party. Headed in.

The atmosphere is charged with excitement. Rubber boats are being inflated, equipment is being gathered, and last minute joshing is well in progress. The night is perfect with a moderate overcast hiding a 3/4 moon, so that we have just enough light, the sea is calm and the tide is slack.

2230 SJ contact at 4,500 yards on two spitkits coming down the coast. Probably luggers or sampans. Lay to and tracked them across our bow at 5 knots.

2255 Man battle stations–guns. Raised sound heads. Opened out as spitkits zigged our way.

2318 Losing valuable time with these spitkits. They are by, now. Commenced closing beach, wiggling back and forth adjusting position. Planned for landmarks indefinite.

23 July 1945

0000 Saboteur Attack #1. In position at last. Two fathoms under the keel. Shore line 950 yards. We can do no better. Launched rubber boats.

0005 As boats shoved off had planned to say something apropos to such an operation such as "Synchronize your watches," however all I could think of was, "Boys, if you get stuck, head for Siberia 130 miles north—follow the mountain ranges, good luck."

Watched the boats all the way in, and radar easily tracked them by their radar corners. I imagine the Barb is easily sighted from the beach but, I hope, hard to identify.

0035 Party landed on the beach. Seconds are dragging by. Feel positive that once initial landing is made, unopposed, the rest will go off smoothly. Momentarily expecting shots, flares and a general clamor, but the blackness of the night has engulfed all in a challenging silence.

0047 An unscheduled north bound train coming up the tracks. No lights except from the firebox, white smoke swirling back. The boys ashore must be in the middle of their job now. Crossed my fingers and held my breath. Imagination running rampant.

0052 Train passed by successfully. Heaved a sigh of relief and shifted that horseshoe around again.

0132 At last, the boats are leaving the beach. Muffled cheers from our side. They are blinking their signal—holding off our answer. Surely they can see us. Their blinking becoming insistent—perhaps they mistake us for a patrol vessel. Gave them a short dash and darkness settled.

0145 Ye Gods! another northbound train coming up the tracks. Broke the silence to yell to the boats, "Paddle like the devil." Entirely wasted, the boats have spotted the train and the paddles are churning like eggbeaters. The train is getting closer and closer. Any second now. What a moment! Even the boats have stopped to look. Everyone is awe stricken with the expectancy of momentary destruction.

0147 *Wham!!* What a thrill! What a beautiful sight! The charge made a much greater explosion than we expected, the engine boilers blew, wreckage flew two hundred feet in the air in a flash of flame and smoke, cars piled up and rolled off the track in a writhing, twisting mass of wreckage. Cheers!

0151 Hauled the boats aboard and backed clear.

0202 Kicked ahead and hauled out to deep water. A small fire flickered alongside the tracks and, shortly, lights of a car came dashing along the road. Feel more proud and happy over what my lads have done than I would in sinking a hundred ships. Their stories are priceless. Bear with me while I give you the highlights briefly as heard over the medicinal libation.

Our navigation, though close for such a coastline, was about 500 yards off to the north. Haze covered the two close peaks the party was to work in on, and the boat compass was erratic. Consequently when the party landed they found themselves in somebody's back yard, fifty yards from a house. Fortunately no dog put in an appearance, though dog tracks with human barefoot print alongside were noticed on the beach. After a short period of huddled reconnaissance, the main party left the boat guards and proceeded cautiously inland skirting the houses. At this point what had appeared to be grass, from our offshore view, turned out to be waist high bullrushes, which crunched and crackled with every move, shrieking out their presence. All shapes took on human forms. About two hundred yards inland they came to the highway. Another huddled reconnaissance. All clear, so Lt. Walker arose starting a dash across the road and immediately fell head first into a four foot ditch. Picking himself up, he cautioned the rest to watch out for the ditch, then made a dash across the highway and immediately fell head first into the ditch on the other side.

A hundred yards further and they arrived at the track, reconnoitered, and selected their spot. Having notice a peculiarly shaped object a short way down the tracks, Markuson, a guard, was told to check on it and the guards were sent out. Digging commenced, but soon stopped when someone came running up the track. It was Markuson, who reported, "Jeepers, that thing is a lookout tower." When queried as to why he didn't give the alert to warn of his approach, he replied, "I tried to whistle, but when I saw that tower my mouth dried up." Quiet continuing, he was again sent out. Digging recommenced, but the picks and shovels shattered the night with loud ringing sounds. They were laid aside and excavation continued dog fashion. A flickering light was spotted down the tracks. A train? Work ceased. In proper frontier fashion all ears were pinned to the rails. No sound. Turn to again.

Suddenly, at an estimated range of 75–100 yards, a train loomed up, roaring down upon them. Nearly the entire party made a dive for the nearest foxhole, the few remaining squeezed themselves into hiding behind bushes six inches high and two inches wide. The train blared past with the engineer hanging far out of his cab looking each of the party over personally.

When the initial foxhole crash dive was made, Hatfield, the electrician, landed in such a fashion that both carbon dioxide cartridges attached to his life jacket went off. He was sure he was shot, yet soon found that he was merely approaching maternity as his Mae West inflated.

The train went by, the project hurried along with no untoward occurrence, other than the boys decreasing the micro switch clearance to the rail well below what had been assigned—just to be sure it would work. Circuits were checked, the charge was hooked up, the digging disguised and then the night filled with whippoorwills. A little difficulty was encountered in launching the boats through the light surf with everyone getting a bit soaked. About two thirds of the way back they sighted the train, and thoroughly enjoyed watching the fruits of their effort being explosively plucked.

1200 Position: Lat. 48-16 N., Long. 143-41 E.
1611 APR contact 99/375/20.
1722 Submerged off Shiritori for reconnaissance.
2001 Surfaced. Reconnaissance a failure due to haze.
2016 APR contact 74/500/40.

24 July 1945

Surface patrolling off Shiritori.
0718 APR contact.
0810 Exchanged recognition signals with *Kingfish*. Attempted to send her a message giving her most of our area but interference faded. Tried VHF and wolf-pack frequencies in vain.
1200 Position: Lat. 48-52 N., Long. 143-17 E.
1210 APR contact 99/500/30.
1215 APR contact 68/1000/25.
1219 Submerged for reconnaissance of coast, from Niitoi to Shiritori. Close work with 3 to 4 fathoms below the keel. However, planning a rocket massage tonight, it is necessary to locate targets. This is a large factory town, one chimney, disappearing in the clouds, measured at better than 400 feet high. Checked its ST pip and decided to use it in conjunction with TDC for our attack. Shiritori looks so promising that we plan a triple rocket massage, two on the factory district, one on the town.
1934 Surfaced. Received message from ComSubPac telling us to depart area. it now becomes necessary to speed up our unfinished business.
2117 Man battle stations–rockets. Poor visibility, but we have a nice radar picture. For this job one of the Jap charts recovered from a sinking is proving invaluable. It has an enlarged insert of Shiritori, including the plan of the factory districts.
2235 Rocket Assault #3. In position 5,100 yards from high chimney.
2236 *Rockets Away!!!* Our first batch of 12 went swishing on their way towards the factory district.
2236:05 Reload.
2236:30 First batch landed with their customary heavy explosion.
2239 *Rockets Away!!!* Second batch of 8 headed for the factories. Reload. Twisted ship to get the town in our sights.

2239:30 Second batch landed.

2242 *Rockets Away!!!* Third batch off for the town.

2242:30 Third batch landed.

2244 Secured from battle stations–rockets. Set course for town of Kashiho, fifteen miles south, to give its factories our final rocket massage as a reminder that no town can sit and laugh at the depth charges while the *Barb* is getting her ears pinned back by a *Terutsuki* offshore.

2310 Two large fires broke out at Shiritori, followed by muffled explosions. Reversed course.

2311 Another fire started. Many explosions shooting the flames up into the heavy overcast. Crew came topside to enjoy the unexpected effect of our rockets. Circled while fires spread amid continuing explosions.

2350 Headed south for Kashiho with fires and explosions increasing.

25 July 1945

Surface patrolling en route Kashiho.

0024 Man battle stations–rockets.

0309 Rocket Assault #4. In position 5,200 yards from target center.

0310 Rockets Away!!! Twelve heading for the factories as our repayment.

0310:30 Rockets exploded in target area. No fires. Set course for Shiritori to review our damage.

0400 Heavy fog. Visibility 100 yards. Can smell smoke strongly.

0424 Assorted light and heavy explosions. Smoke thicker. We are 5 miles south of the town. These explosions continued sporadically. Definitely not gunfire. Passed 6,000 yards from factories and since visibility has blocked us, set course for Chiri on northeast coast of Patience Bay, for canneries bombardment and sampan sweep.

0449 Very loud rumblings explosion which drove personnel out of their bunks.

0600 APR contact 99/375.

0912 (Contact #21) Sighted mast of sampan.

0946 Man battle stations–guns.

0959 Gun Attack #5. Commenced firing 40 mm. Range 1,400 yards, closing. Fired 20 rounds for 18 hits.

1009 Away boarding party! Led by Lt(jg) King boarding party boarded, captured one prisoner from the crew, and collected three anchors and a steering wheel.

1024 Boarding party returned. Backed clear.

1030 Fired one round of 5 inch. Hit at waterline. Sampan sank.

1200 Position: Lat. 49-09 N., Long. 143-56 E.

1203 (Contact #22) Sighted mast of sampan towards Chiri, our anticipated bombardment target, and another sampan down the coast. One of prisoners picked up informed us that 15 seaplanes are based at lake close inland from Chiri. Doubt this, however, we will remain outside of 15 fathoms for bombardment.

1226 Manned battle stations–guns.

1233 Gun Attack #6. Commenced firing 40 MM at sampan. Range 1,100 yards, closing. Fired 20 rounds for 16 hits.

1234 Fired one round of 5 inch. Hit at waterline. Sampan sank. Shifted 5 inch to canneries at Chiri.

1235 Shore Bombardment #2. Commenced firing 5 inch. Range 5,700 yards. fired 43 rounds for 20 hits. No fires. Visually damage consisted of large holes and sections of buildings blown up. Incendiary ammunition is a necessity.

1250 Secured gun stations.

1254 Other sampan coming up the coast.

1308 Man battle stations–guns.

1314 Gun Attack #7. Commenced firing 40 MM, range 1,450 yards, closing. fired 20 rounds for 15 hits.

1315 Fired one round 5 inch. Waterline hit. Sampan sank. Secured gun stations.

1334 (Contact #23) Sighted sampan. Sighted 2 more sampans. One towing the other. Decided to attack these first, as they were closer to beach. Other was outboard of us.

1350 Manned battle stations–guns.

1355 Gun Attack #8. Commenced firing 40 MM at towing vessel. Range 900 yards, closing. Fired 13 rounds for 11 hits.

1356 Fired one round 5 inch. Waterline hit. Leading sampan sank.

1357 Shifted 5 inch to towed sampan. Fired one starshell and three rounds of high capacity. One waterline hit. Target sank. All high capacity now expended. A few starshells left.

1410 Gun Attack #9. Commenced firing 40 mm. Range 1,000 yards, closing. Fired 25 rounds for 21 hits.

1413 Fired two 5 inch starshells set on 10 seconds. Two hits passing on through near waterline. No explosions, though we had considered them a poor possibility. Sampan sank.

1415 Secured gun stations.

1630 Passed by Kaihyo To for observation of reconstruction work since our bombardment on 2 July. Only two buildings had possibly been patched. The place still in ruins. The fires we left burning had wiped out half the buildings.

Set course south to depart area via minefields and north coast Hokkaido, hoping we might entice a single frigate out in deep water by use of the Buck Rogers gun and radar balloon.

2340 Heavy fog set in. Our plans foiled. Set course for Kunashiri Strait. We will arrive there during daylight. If clear intend to sweep northwest coast of Kunashiri for canneries and sampans.

26 July 1945

Surface patrolling en route Kunashiri Strait.

0825 APR contact 79/500/50.

1130 Fog lifted. Visibility excellent. Kunashiri ahead.

1200 Position: Lat. 44-38 N., Long. 146-38 E.

1230 Being nearly certain there would be no aircraft left in this vicinity and believing the Japs would have no reason for having coastal defenses on the northwest coast of the island, started a surface sweep 2–3,000 yards offshore, using fathometer continuously. Passed several small villages and pipsqueak fishing stations. Anticipate some sampans around Shibetoro.

1435 Sighted Shibetoro. Looks good. One lumber mill with single tall black stack. Three large main buildings and many smaller houses and shacks. To the right and toward the beach we have a sampan building yard with sixteen rectangular, box like cradles, resting on some form of tracks, which run down into the water. To the left of the cradles, clear of the water's edge, are neat rows of brand new sampans. We can count twenty-six and there are probably more behind them. To the right of the cradles are three more neat rows of sampans, that we can see, counting seventeen more, with three buildings behind them and lumber piles to the right. Evidently the sampans are built in the cradles and the cradles run down to the water to launch the sampans. Then the sampans are hauled back up on the beach by rollers. All buildings, cradles and sampans have large fir tree branches scattered over them for camouflage from aircraft.

Made a sweep by to draw any opposing fire. None encountered.

1502 Shore Bombardment #3. Commenced firing 40 MM and 20 MM at 2,100 yards. A lucky hit in an oil tank started a large fire behind the mill, which quickly spread and turned the mill into a blazing inferno. this spread among all the sampans to the left of the cradles and destroyed them completely during the afternoon.

Throughout the afternoon and evening peppered area with 20 MM, .50 cal. and .30 cal. guns to prevent any attempts to put fires out. Expending a total of 157 rounds of 40 MM, 2,400 rounds of 20 MM, 1,000 round of .50 cal. and 500 rounds of .30 cal. ammunition.

1630 (Contact #24) Sighted a trawler on the horizon. Closed.

1656 Gun Attack #10. range 400 yards. Commenced firing 20 MM, .50 cal. and .30 cal. machine guns while passing close aboard. Turned and swept back and forth across his stern attempting to sink target with rifle grenades. His hull is very heavy and tough, our rifle grenades for the most part failed to penetrate. This amazed me, for when our boarding party was trained by the Marines at Midway, this same type grenade had ripped through large timbers and even gone through eight inches of reinforced concrete. Here, only three grenades, out of eighteen, penetrated. These only made holes one to three inches in diameter. Fired a total of 720 rounds of 20 mm, 1,000 rounds of .50 cal., 1,000 rounds .30 cal., and 15 rifle grenades. Trawler caught fire and stopped.

1740 Selected two prisoners who appeared to be in fair shape.
Returned to lumber mill and building yard.
1800 APR contact 99/500/18.
1815 The fires have done a good job. All buildings are nearly leveled, leaving the tall stack standing alone and red hot. Sampans to the left are completely destroyed. A fire has broken out to the right of the cradles in the lumber piles and is spreading towards the remaining seventeen sampans and cradles. Commenced firing with 20 MM to force personnel back under cover. A few Japs were noticed working with something on the beach. They soon cleared the beach. Then trained the twin 20 MM on the remaining sampans and cradles.
1825 APR contact 79/500/50.
1846 Headed out, to see how our trawler was coming along.
1920 Trawler burning nicely, yet it looks like a long process before it will sink. Several oil explosions had occurred on our way out, but this is the most rugged hull we've encountered. Tried more 20 MM and rifle grenades, in vain.
1945 This trawler will burn all night. Some spots in the hull look weakened by the fire. Decided to ram.
1953 Rammed target at slow speed. Target rolled towards us as her side caved in, sinking stern first with her foremast snapping across the bow.

Extra loud cheers from the CO and groans from the first lieutenant. This because CO had wagered the First Luff, before the start of the patrol, 32 ounces of the best Midway had to offer that we would sink 15 vessels. The First Luff had refused to count those destroyed by shore bombardment as sunk. This made the fifteenth vessel. Mission accomplished.

Backed clear and investigated bow. No apparent damage to bow or shutters other than paint scraped off.

Returned to shore target.

2030 Lying to off shore. Seems to take ages for the fires to spread to the sampans, our principal interest. Fair breeze blowing, about 10 knots., but for the most part in the wrong direction. As darkness fell quite a picture was presented with the flames licking hungrily throughout the area. Finally they made their way through the lumber piles and reached the last group of sampans. With the right breeze these all would go up together, but with this perverse wind the fire nearly burns one before the adjacent one catches fire.

2100 The moon rose like a moldy lemon through the heat waves.

2200 Time to shove. The fire has eaten its way through an estimated nine of the seventeen sampans in this group and should soon attack the cradles. This makes a total of 35 sampans in this haul, which is sufficient a bag, that we need not claim the remaining eight. As no engines had been installed, from what we observed after burnng, tonnage estimate will be difficult.

Set course for the Strait.

27 July 1945
　0047 Transited Kunashiri Strait.
　En route Midway.
　0050 APR contact 78/500/60.
　1200 Position: Lat. 44-11 N., Long. 149-43 E.

28 July 1945
　1200(L) Position: Lat. 43382-38242 N., Long. 157-43 E.

29 July 1945
　1200(L) Position: 41-44 N., Long. 161-41 E.

30 July 1945
　1200(L) Position: Lat. 38-10 N., Long. 165-13 E.

31 July 1945
　POW, taken near Chiri, informed us that he had read in the local Japanese paper that our train was destroyed by a bomb and that 150 men had been killed.
　1200(L) Position: Lat. 33-51.1 N., Long. 168-52.0 E.

1 August 1945
　1200 Position: Lat. 31-23.0 N., Long. 173-42.3 E.

2 August 1945
　1200 Position: Lat. 29-34.3 N., Long. 177-56.2 E.
　Crossed International Date Line.

2 August 1945
　1000 Arrived Midway. An excellent welcome.

(C) WEATHER

　The weather in general was very agreeable. The seas were calm and very little of the expected fog was encountered. Although there was a high overcast which completely covered the sky eighty-five percent of the time.

(D) TIDAL INFORMATION

　Tides and currents conformed generally with sailing directions, tables and charts.

(E) NAVIGATIONAL AIDS

No difficulty was experienced in navigating by radar in the area.
The following light houses were observed and their conditions were as follows:
1. Haka Siretoka Misaki – Latitude 46-02   Longitude 143-24
   lighted normal characteristics.
2. Motomari – Latitude 48-16   Longitude 142-38
   lighted normal characteristics.
3. Shikuka Hakuchi – Latitude 49-13   Longitude 143-07
   lighted normal characteristics.
4. Otomari Hakuchi – Latitude 46-39   Longitude 142-45
   lighted normal characteristics.
5. Nishi Hatoro Misaki – Latitude 45-54   Longitude 142-05
   lighted normal characteristics.
6. Atoiya Misaki – Latitude 44-27   Longitude 146-34
   lighted with period as follows: 60 second light 12 eclipse 48 sec.

(F) SHIP CONTACTS

No.	Time Date	Lat. Long.	Type	Initial Range	Est. Course Speed	How Contacted	Remarks
1.	0015 21 June	44-32.5 146-15.6	Lugger	2¼ miles	C–070 S–7 kts.	R	Two 100 ton armed luggers. One sunk, one destroyed.
2.	0346 23 June	47-33.1 142-58.5	Trawler	8 miles	C–310 S–8 kts.	Sight	Sunk One prisoner.
3.	1655 26 June	50-17.6 144-15.2	Convoy	15 miles	C–190 S–8 kts.	Sight	Three freighters and five escorts. Attack. Missed.
4.	0943 3 July	48-20 144-11	Small coastal AK	6 miles	C–340 S–8.1	Sight	Sunk
5.	1604 4 July	45-53 143-47.1	Frigate	10 miles	Patrolling	Sight	Approach
6.	0320 5 July	46-05.0 142-14.1	Train Ferry	5 miles	C–210 S–14	Periscope	Two train ferries and one frigate escort. Approach
7.	1000 5 July	46-04.0 142-14.0	Large AK	5½ miles	C–014 S–9	Periscope	Two AKs one large and one small. Sunk large AK.
8.	1127 7 July	45-45.0 142-56.7	Frigate	8 miles	Patrolling	Sight	Approach

No.	Time Date	Lat. Long.	Type	Initial Range	Est. Course Speed	How Contact	Remarks
9.	1253 7 July	45-46.5 142-53.7	Frigate	8 miles	Patrolling	Sight	Dived Approach
10.	1755 7 July	46-13.2 142-37.0	2 Frigates	10 miles	Patrolling	Sight	Dived
11.	1833 8 July	47-38.0 142-42.0	Lugger	3 miles	C-130 S-9	Sight	Sunk gunfire.
12.	0918 10 July	44-12.6 145-42.2	Two small AKs	12 miles	C-020 S-8	Sight	Two small coastal AKs. Attack. Missed.
13.	0755 11 July	44-05.4 146-14.0	Sampan	9 miles	C-120 S-7	Sight	Sunk gunfire.
14.	1100 17 July	46-08.5 142-19.0	Frigate	5 miles	Patrolling	Periscope	Patrol craft
15.	1222 17 July	46-04.1 142-17.5	Small AK & one frigate	5 miles	C-187 S-9	Periscope	Approach
16.	2221 17 July		Two frigates	6 miles	Patrolling	SJ radar	Frigates patrolling near minefield
17.	0416 18 July	46-02.5 142-26.8	Frigate	10 miles	C-350 S-8	Sight	Approach
18.	1127 18 July	46-03.2 142-15.5	Large AK & one frigate	4½ miles	C-196 S-12	Periscope	Sunk frigate missed AK
19.	1601 18 July	46-03.2 142-27.8	Two frigates	10 miles	Searching	Sight	Frigates avoided
20.	2121 18 July	46-04 142-46	Three frigates	3 miles	Searching	Radar	Approach
21.	0912 25 July	48-59.0 144-52.9	Sampan	5 miles		Sight	Sunk
22.	1208 25 July	49-09.8 144-00.0	Two Sampans	5 miles		Sight	Sunk
23.	1334 25 July	48-57.4 144-19.0	Three Sampans	6 miles		Sight	Sunk
24.	1630 26 July	44-18.4 145-52.3	Trawler	6 miles	C-070 S-9	Sight	Sunk

Contacts No. 5, 8, 9, 10, 14, 16, 17, 19, 20 are on one or more of same group of 4 frigates.

RUSSIAN SHIP CONTACTS

No.	Time Date	Lat. Long.	Type	Initial Range	Est. Course Speed	How Contact	Remarks
1.	1850 4 July	45-55.4 143-40.0	Large DD	5 miles	C-080 S-10	Periscope	Russian
2.	2023 4 July	45-47.5 142-38.0	AK	9 miles	C-275 S-10	Sight	Russian

3.	0445 5 July	45-51.7 142-30.2	AK	15 miles	C-275 S-10	Sight	Russian
4.	1223 5 July	45-46.2 142-54.0	AK	8 miles	C-100 S-9	Sight	Russian
5.	0145 18 July	45-55.0 142-30.0	AK	8 miles	C-270 S-8	Radar	Russian
6.	0331 18 July	45-55.9 142-38.9	AK	10 miles	C-100 S-6	Radar	Russian
7.	1743 18 July	45-48.0 142-37.8	AK	15 miles	C-270 S-8	Sight	Russian
8.	2327 18 July	45-42 143-48	AK	8 miles	C-100 S-8	Sight	Russian

(G) AIRCRAFT CONTACTS

Fifteen enemy aircraft contacts were made in the area. All but two of these occurred prior to the carrier strike on Hokkaido. These planes were engaged in escort work, coastal patrol and anti-submarine patrol. Although Karafuto was not included in the strikes it is probable that all planes have left that area, with the exception of Otomari. This, an observation, resulting from the impunity with which we could make coastal sweeps and shore bombardments during excellent visibility where communication facilities by telephone and radio are known to exist.

We were bombed on three occasions—twice well bombed.

(H) ATTACK DATA

U.S.S. *Barb*   Torpedo Attack No. 1A   Patrol No. 12
Date: 29 June 1945   Time: 1320 (K)   Lat. 48-25 N., Long. 142-47 E.

Target Data – Damage Inflicted

Description: Target was DD escort of a convoy of three merchantmen and five escorts. Convoy had air cover, which sighted periscope and directed attack of DD. Contact – Periscope. Visibility – excellent.
Ship Sunk: None.
Ship Damaged: None.
Target Draft: 10'   Course: 233   Speed: 10 knots   Range: 960 (at firing)

Own Ship Data

Speed: 3 knots   Course: 218   Depth: 61'   Angle: 0 (at firing)

[Fire Control and Torpedo Data]

Type Attack: ST Periscope

Tubes Fired	No. 7	No. 8	No. 9
Track Angle	4 S	5 S	5 S
Gyro Angle	20½ R	20 R	19½ R
Depth Set	6 feet	6 feet	6 feet
Power	27.2 knots	27.2 knots	27.2 knots
Hit or Miss	Miss	Miss	Miss
Erratic (yes/no)	No	No	No
Mark Torpedo	18-2	18-2	18-2
Serial No.	100255	58116	99975
Mark Exploder	8-7	8-7	8-7
Serial No.	16643	16193	16375
Actuation Set	Contact	Contact	Contact
Actuation Actual	—	—	—
Mark Warhead	18-2	18-2	18-2
Serial No.	6102	6219	6200
Explosive	TPX	TPX	TPX
Firing Interval	0 s	10 s	10 s
Type Spread	¼° R.	0	¼° L.
Sea Conditions	0	0	0

Overhaul Activity   U.S.S. *Euryale* (AS-22)
Remarks: Electrolyte – 48°
               Injection – 35°

Reason for misses undetermined. Target did not maneuver to avoid.

U.S.S. *Barb*   Torpedo Attack No. 1B   Patrol No. 12
Date: 29 June 1945   Time: 1331 (K)   Lat. 48-24 N., Long. 142-47 E.

Target Data – Damage Inflicted

Description: Same as attack No. 1A.
Ship Sunk: None.
Ship Damaged: None.
Target Draft: 10'   Course: 012°T   Speed: 12 knots   Range: 620 (at firing)

Own Ship Data

Speed: 3.6 knots   Course: 162°T.   Depth: 61'   Angle: 0 (at firing)

[Fire Control and Torpedo Data]

Type Attack: ST Periscope.

	No. 1	No. 2	No. 3
Tubes Fired			
Track Angle	10 S	14 S	20 S
Gyro Angle	042	045	051
Depth Set	6'	6'	6'
Power	27.2 kts.	27.2 kts.	27.2 kts.
Hit or Miss	Miss	Miss	Miss
Erratic (yes/no)	No	No	No
Mark Torpedo	18-2	18-2	18-2
Serial No.	99405	100141	100277
Mark Exploder	8-7	8-7	8-7
Serial No.	16641	16635	16120
Actuation Set	Contact	Contact	Contact
Actuation Actual	—	—	—
Mark Warhead	18-2	18-2	18-2
Serial No.	5206	6283	4990
Explosive	TPX	TPX	TPX
Firing Interval	0 s	10 s	10 s
Type Spread	¼° R.	0	¼° R.
Sea Conditions	0	0	0
Overhaul Activity		U.S.S. *Euryale* (AS-22)	
Remarks:	Electrolyte – 48°		
	Injection – 35°		

Reason for misses undetermined. Target did not maneuver to avoid.

U.S.S. *Barb*   Torpedo Attack No. 2A   Patrol No. 12
Date: 5 July 1945   Time: 1047 (K)   Lat. 46-04 N., Long. 142-14 E.

Target Data – Damage Inflicted

Description: Large AK with plane escort hugging the coast. Contact – Periscope. Visibility – Good.
Ship Sunk: None
Ship(s) Damaged: None
Damage Determined by: None
Target Draft: 25'   Course: 003   Speed: 11.5 kts.   Range: 1,570 (at firing)

Own Ship Data

Course: 260   Speed: 2.15 kts.   Depth: 65'   Angle: 0 (at firing)

[Fire Control and Torpedo Data]

Tubes Fired	No. 4	No. 5	No. 6
Track Angle	90 S	95 S	99 S
Gyro Angle	015	018½	022½
Depth Set	6'	6'	6'
Power	27.6 kts.	27.6 kts.	27.6 kts.
Hit or Miss	Miss	Miss	Miss
Erratic (yes/no)	No	No	No
Mark Torpedo	18-2	18-2	18-2
Serial No.	58255	58085	100294
Mark Exploder	8-7	8-7	8-7
Serial No.	16524	16570	16699
Actuation Set	Contact	Contact	Contact
Actuation Actual	—	—	—
Mark Warhead	18-2	18-2	18-2
Serial No.	6171	6151	5966
Explosive	TPX	TPX	TPX
Firing Interval	0 S	10 S	10 S
Type Spread	2° L.	0	2° R.
Sea Conditions	1	1	1

Overhaul Activity   U.S.S. *Euryale* (AS-22)
Remarks: Injection – 49
                      Electrolyte Temp. – 54
                      Torpedoes hit beach and exploded 4m 30s and 4m 45s after No. 4 was fired.

Two misses due to speed error. One torpedo should have hit, possibly two.

U.S.S. *Barb*   Torpedo Attack No. 2B   Patrol No. 12
Date: 5 July 1945   Time: 1052 (K)   Lat. 46-04 N., Long. 142-14 E.

Target Data – Damage Inflicted

Description: Same as Attack No. 2A
Ship(s) Sunk: Large AK (EU)
Damage determined by: Timed hit. Sinking witnessed by Commanding Officer, Executive Officer and TDC Operator.
Target Draft: 25'   Course: 024   Speed: 8 kts.   Range: 1,680 (at firing)

Own Ship Data

Course: 182   Speed: 2.2   Depth: 65'   Angle: 0 (at firing)

[Fire Control and Torpedo Data]

Type attack: Periscope.

Tubes Fired	No. 7	No. 9
Track Angle	133 S	135 S
Gyro Angle	153½	157½
Depth Set	6'	6'
Power	27.6 kts.	27.6 kts.
Hit or Miss	Miss	Hit
Erratic (yes/no)	No	No
Mark Torpedo	18-2	18-2
Serial No.	100013	100055
Mark Exploder	8-7	8-7
Serial No.	16791	16553
Actuation Set	Contact	Contact
Actuation Actual	—	Contact
Mark Warhead	18-2	18-2
Serial No.	5278	6153
Explosive	TPX	TPX
Firing Interval	0	10 s.
Type Spread	1° L.	1° R.

Overhaul Activity   U.S.S. *Euryale* (AS-22)
Remarks: Injection: 49
                      Electrolyte Temp: 54
                      Torpedo run #9 – 2,070 yards timed hit 2m 15s
                      Miss due to speed error.

U.S.S. *Barb*   Torpedo Attack No. 3   Patrol No. 12
Date: 10 July 1945   Time: 1118 (K)   Lat. 44-13 N., Long. 145-23.5 E.

Target Data – Damage Inflicted

Description: Two coastal AKs hugging coast. 2,500 yards between ships. No air cover. Visibility – Excellent. Contact – Smoke (30,000) yards.

Ship Sunk: None.

Ship Damaged: None.

Target Draft: 8'   Course: 012   Speed: 8 kts.   Range: 540 (at firing)

Own Ship Data

Course: 293   Speed: 2.1   Depth: 65'   Angle: 0 (at firing)

[Fire Control and Torpedo Data]

Type Attack: Periscope – Occasional ST range. Check bearing between No. 1 and 2.

	No. 1	No. 2	No. 3
Tubes Fired			
Track Angle	143 S	145 S	145 S
Gyro Angle	042	044	044
Depth Set	3'	3'	3'
Power	27.7 kts.	27.7 kts.	27.7 kts.
Hit or Miss	Miss	Miss	Miss
Erratic (yes/no)	No	No	No
Serial No.	99408	100103	100070
Mark Exploder	8-7	8-7	8-7
Serial No.	16623	16363	16847
Actuation Set	Contact	Contact	Contact
Actuation Actual	—	—	—
Mark Warhead	18-2	18-2	18-2
Serial No.	6064	6169	6241
Explosive	TPX	TPX	TPX
Firing Interval	0 s.	18 s.	10 s.
Type Spread	4° R.	0	4° L.
Sea Conditions	0	0	0

Overhaul Activity   U.S.S. *Euryale* (AS-22)

Remarks: Injection – 51; Battery Temp – 60

Reason for misses undetermined. Target did not maneuver to avoid.

U.S.S. *Barb*   Torpedo Attack No. 4A   Patrol No. 12
Date: 18 July 1945   Time: 1158:25 (K)   Lat. 46-03.8 N., Long. 142-16.2 E.

Target Data – Damage Inflicted

Description: A large AK with frigate escort hugging coast. Frigate abeam 1,500 yards to seaward. Contact – Periscope. Visibility good. No air cover.
Ship sunk: *Shimushu* class frigate (EC) 1,000 tons.
Damage Determined by: Target observed by ten Conning Tower personnel to be perpendicular to the bottom. Photograph obtained.
Target Draft: 8'   Course: 196   Speed: 12 kts.   Range: 1,240 (at firing)

Own Ship Data

Course: 200   Speed: 2 kts.   Depth: 65'   Angle: 0 (at firing)

[Fire Control and Torpedo Data]

Type Attack: Periscope, having determined masthead height by ST range.

Tubes Fired	No. 4	No. 6
Track Angle	160 P	164 P
Gyro Angle	015½	010½
Depth Set	4'	4'
Power	27.7 kts.	27.7 kts.
Hit or Miss	Hit	Miss
Mark Torpedo	18-2	18-2
Serial No.	99212	53246
Mark Exploder	8-7	8-7
Serial No.	16720	16563
Actuation Set	Contact	Contact
Actuation Actual	Contact	—
Mark Warhead	18-2	18-2
Serial No.	6321	6164
Explosive	Torpex	TPX
Firing Interval	0	10 s
Type Spread	1° R.	1° L.
Sea Conditions	2	2
Overhaul Activity	U.S.S. Euryale (AS-22)	
Remarks:	Injection – 49	
	Battery Temp – 60	
	Torp. run #4 – 2,000	
	Timed hit #4 – 2 min. 3 sec.	

Reason for miss – Target blew up.

U.S.S. *Barb*   Torpedo Attack No. 4B   Patrol No. 12
Date: 18 July 1945   Time: 1159 (K)   Lat. 46-03.8 N., Long. 142-16.2 E.

Target Data – Damage Inflicted

Description: Same as attack 4A. Fired at large AK.
Ship Sunk: None.
Ship Damaged: None.
Target Draft: 25'   Course: 200   Speed: 12 kts.   Range: 1,510 (at firing)

Own Ship Data

Course: 214   Speed: 2 kts.   Depth: 65'   Angle: 0 (at firing)

[Fire Control and Torpedo Data]

Type Attack: Periscope Attack. ST information obtained exact target speed.

Tubes Fired	No. 2	No. 3	No. 5
Track Angle	047½	043½	039½
Depth Set	4'	4'	4'
Power	27.7 kts.	27.7 kts.	27.7 kts.
Hit or Miss	Miss	Miss	Miss
Erratic (yes/no)	No	No	No
Mark Torpedo	18-2	18-2	18-2
Serial No.	100289	99419	99254
Mark Exploder	8-7	8-7	8-7
Serial No.	16717	16926	16571
Actuation Set	Contact	Contact	Contact
Actuation Actual	—	—	—
Mark Warhead	18-2	18-2	18-2
Serial No.	6218	6165	6166
Explosive	TPX	TPX	TPX
Firing Interval	0 s	10 s	10 s
Type Spread	2° R	0	2° L
Sea Conditions	2		2

Overhaul Activity   U.S.S. Euryale (AS-22)
Remarks: Injection – 49
                    Battery Temp. – 60
                    Two end of runs – 5 min. 42 sec., 6 min. 2 sec.
No maneuvers for four minutes after firing. Reason for misses undetermined.

U.S.S. *Barb* (SS220) Gun Attack No. 1 Patrol No. 12
Date 21 June 1945 Time: 0319 (K) Lat. 44-39 N., Long. 146-42.5 E.
Target Data – Damage Inflicted
Description: Two luggers (100 tons each) approximately in column on course 075T, speed 7 knots. Contact radar – 4,800 yards, visibility poor.
Sunk: 1 lugger 100 tons
 1 lugger 100 tons
Damage Determined by: First lugger observed to sink after 3 5-inch and 4 40 mm hits. Second lugger sank after 3 5-inch and 7 40 mm hits.
Details of Action

Picked up targets at 0015 and kept position abeam until 0230, 45 minutes before dawn. Then closed in on formation and when after lugger was 1,200 yards abeam to starboard and the forward lugger 850 yards broad on the starboard bow, opened fire with 5 inch on after target and with 40 mm on forward target. Fired one round 5 inch for one hit and seven rounds 40 mm for four hits. Forward target returned fire but bearing was 180 degrees out. Overhauled forward target and at 1,000 yards fired four rounds 5 inch for three hits. Target observed to sink. Reversed course to finish off other lugger. At 800 yards fired three rounds 5 inch for two hits and nine rounds 40 mm for six hits. Target returned fire, splashes astern, until gun was hit. Target sank. Guns on the targets are believed to have been approximately 37 mm.

U.S.S. *Barb* (SS220) Gun Attack No. 2 Patrol No. 12
Date: 23 June 1945 Time: 0423 (K) Lat. 47-41 N., Long. 145-06 E.
Target Data – Damage Inflicted
Description: Radio equipped diesel trawler (150 tons) on northwesterly course, speed 5 knots. Contact – visual. Visibility – good.
Sunk: 1 diesel trawler 150 tons.
Damage Determined by: Trawler observed to sink.
Details of Action

Sighted large trawler at dawn at about 12,000 yards. Closed target and gained radar contact at 8,600 yards. When target was 2,000 yards broad on the starboard bow, opened fire with 40 mm. First shot over, spotted down. Second shot short, spotted up. Third shot hit. 40 mm hit consistently once the sight bar range was determined. When target was abeam, at 700 yards, fired three rounds 5 inch for 3 hits. Fired a total of 20 rounds 40 mm for 15 hits. Fire broke out below decks and quickly spread to the superstructure. Fuel oil caught fire later and burned until target sunk. Target finally sunk by high speed sweep close aboard, which filled hull with water through shell holes. Took one prisoner—six others perished.

U.S.S. *Barb* (SS220)   Gun Attack No. 3   Patrol No. 12
Date: 8 July 1945   Time: 2055 (K)   Lat. 47-26.8 N., Long. 142-46.9 E.

Target Data – Damage Inflicted

Description: Lugger hugging coast in 3½ fathoms of water. Visibility – poor. Contact – visual.

Sunk: Lugger 75 tons.

Damage Determined by: Target destroyed and sinking by the stern when forced to leave the scene by aircraft.

Details of Action

Sighted target in the haze while patrolling 10,000 yards from the beach in a light fog. Forced to trail target until visibility decreased enough permit closing target without being sighted. Closed target to 1,100 yards and opened fire with 40 MM gun. Range to beach 2,800 yards. Depth of water 3½ fathoms. Fired 32 rounds 40 MM for 20 hits. Engine knocked out and several hits along waterline. Aircraft sighted over land so turned away with full rudder, emergency speed, and headed for deep water—10 fathoms, then 1 mile distant. Two village guns at Sakayehama, 2½ miles distant, opened up and shoveled out 30 rounds in record time. No splashes observed. Reached 10 fathom curve and aircraft had not attacked, so guess he didn't see us.

U.S.S. *Barb* (SS220)   Gun Attack No. 4   Patrol No. 12
Date: 11 July 1945   Time: 0902 (K)   Lat. 44-03.2 N., Long. 146-30.0 E.

Target Data – Damage Inflicted

Description: Diesel sampan (50 tons) enroute home after a successful day's work. Visibility – Excellent. Contact – Visual.

Sunk: Diesel Sampan 50 tons.

Damage Determined by: Target observed to sink.

Details of Action

Sighted mast of target on the horizon and commenced closing for the attack. Target homeward bound at 5 knots. Opened fire with 40 MM at 900 yards. Target poured on coal and increased speed to 7 knots. Fired 40 rounds 40 MM for 35 hits. Target was stopped and in shambles but refused to sink. Secured 40 MM and manned 5 inch. Fired two rounds five inch for two hits. Target sunk.

U.S.S. *Barb* (SS220)   Gun Attack No. 5   Patrol No. 12
Date: 25 July 1945   Time: 0959 (K)   Lat. 49-03.8 N., Long. 143-49.5 E.
Target Data – Damage Inflicted
Target Description: Diesel sampan on easterly course, speed 5 knots. Contact – visual. Visibility – good.
Sunk: 1 Diesel Sampan. 50 tons.
Damage Determined by: Sampan observed to sink.
Detail of Action
    Sighted mast of sampan on the horizon. Speeded up and closed range at two engine speed. At 1,400 yards opened fire with 40 mm and fired 20 rounds for 18 hits. Target stopped. Came alongside target and put over boarding party. Took one prisoner. Hauled out 500 yards and fired one round of 5 inch. Target sunk.

U.S.S. *Barb* (SS220)   Gun Attack No. 6   Patrol No. 12
Date 25 July 1945   Time: 1233 (K)   Lat. 49-06 N., Long. 144-10 E.
Target Data – Damage Inflicted
Target Description: Diesel sampan on southwesterly course, speed 5 knots. Contact – Visual. Visibility – good.
Sunk: 1 Diesel Sampan. 50 tons.
Damage Determined by: Sampan observed to sink.
Details of Action
    Sighted mast of target on horizon and closed range at two engine speed. Target was about 4,000 yards off beach. At 1,100 yards opened fire with 40 mm and fired 20 rounds for 16 hits. Then fired 1 round 5 inch and target sunk.

U.S.S. *Barb* (SS220)   Gun Attack No. 7   Patrol No. 12
Date: 25 July 1945   Time: 1314 (K)   Lat. 49-01 N., Long. 144-19.2 E.
Target Data – Damage Inflicted
Description: Diesel sampan on southerly course, speed 5 knots. Contact – Visual. Visibility – good.
Sunk: 1 Diesel Sampan. 50 tons.
Damage Determinted by: Target observed to sink.
Details of Action
    While retiring from Shore Bombardment No. 2, sighted target on horizon. Closed target and at 1,450 yards opened fire with 40 mm. Fired 20 rounds 40 mm for 15 hits. Target stopped. Fired one round 5 inch. Target sunk.

U.S.S. *Barb* (SS220)　　　　Gun Attack No. 8　　　　　Patrol No. 12
Date: 25 July 1945　　Time: 1355 (K)　　Lat. 48-52.2 N., Long. 144-21.2 E.
Target Data – Damage Inflicted
Description: One Diesel sampan with another in tow on northerly course, speed 4 knots. Contact – Visual. Visibility – good.
Sunk: Two diesel sampans. 100 tons..
Damage Determined by: Targets observed to sink.
Details of Action
　　Sighted targets on horizon and closed at two engine speed. At 900 yards opened fire on towing vessel with 40 MM and fired 13 rounds for 11 hits. Fired one round 5 inch. Target sunk. Shifted 5 inch to towed vessel and fired 3 High Capacity and one Starshell for one hit. Target sunk. Used starshell because all High Capacity now expended.

U.S.S. *Barb* (SS220)　　　　Gun Attack No. 9　　　　　Patrol No. 12
Date: 25 July 1945　　Time: 1410 (K)　　Lat. 48-52.8 N., Long. 144-19 E.
Target Data – Damage Inflicted
Description: Diesel sampan on easterly course, speed 4 knots. Contact – Visual. Visibility – good.
Details of Action
　　Sighted target before targets of Gun Attack No. 8, but went after two sampans together first because we were between single target and land and knew he couldn't get away. After sinking two sampans, turned on original contact and at 1,000 yards fired 25 rounds 40 MM for 21 hits. Target stopped. Fired two 5 inch starshells set on 10 seconds for two hits. Had hoped stars would explode on contact but no luck. Didn't really expect them to explode but they were the only kind of 5 inch we had left. Stars went right through target at waterline. Target sunk.

U.S.S. *Barb* (SS220)　　　　Gun Attack No. 10　　　　Patrol No. 12
Date: 26 July 1945　　Time: 1656 (K)　　Lat. 44-20.7 N., Long. 145-52 E.
Target Data – Damage Inflicted
Description: Large Diesel Trawler approaching the coast of Kunashiri from the direction of Hokkaido. Contact – Visual. Visibility – good.
Sunk: 1 Large Diesel Trawler. 100 tons.
Damage Determined by: Observed target to sink

Details of Action

Sighted target while circling off target of Shore Bombardment No. 3. Closed target and at 400 yards opened up with 20 MM, .50 Cal. and .30 Cal. machine guns. A couple of rounds more of 5 inch sure would come in handy here. Passed target close aboard and fired rifle grenades as well as machine guns. Fired 720 rounds of 20 MM, 1,000 rounds of .50 Cal., 1,000 rounds of .30 Cal. and 18 rifle grenades. Target burning internally. Target stopped. Took two prisoners. Hauled out and took a short trip to take another look at fires on beach. Fires on trawler spread until fuel oil tanks caught on fire. Three beautiful explosions. Target completely gutted but refused to sink. No ammunition left large enough to do the job. Final sinking accomplished by ramming.

U.S.S. *Barb* (SS220)　　　Shore Bombardment No. 1　　　Patrol No. 12
Date: 2 July 1945　　Time: 0651 (K)　　Lat. 48-30 N., Long. 144-37.8 E.

Target Data – Damage Inflicted

Island of Kaihyo To located off the southeastern tip of Patience Bay. Destroyed twenty warehouses and barracks and three sampans. Visibility – Fair.

Damage Determined by: Observed all hits by large and small calibre ammunition, leaving island in a shambles with large spreading fires.

Details of Action

Approaching the western side of the island on course 054(T) at 0651 commenced firing 40 MM, 1,100 yards range on course 020(T) placing island on our starboard beam. Island returning fire with small calibre weapons, which was immediately returned with our 40 MM, 20 MM and small arms (Opposition ceased). Continued firing small calibre and commenced firing 5 inch. Changed course to 180(T) placing island on our port beam, and continued destruction of all buildings. Fire broke out in a large building in the center of the island quickly spreading to the surrounding buildings. Three sampans close to shore were also destroyed by 40 MM and small calibre fire. At 0724 ceased fire as all buildings were destroyed and some of them being consumed by fire. Opened range to 3,500 yards and observed the effects of our bombardment. At 1103 closed range to 700 yards (5 fathoms) for closer observation and discovered four pill boxes. Opened fire with 40 MM and destroyed one of them. Ceased fire and left the island to its misery. A word of praise is due the 40 MM gun crew for their accuracy of fire. Total ammunition expended: 35 rounds 5 inch, 232 rounds 40 MM, 780 rounds 20 MM, and 2,100 rounds of .50 & .30 cal.

U.S.S. *Barb* (SS220)　　　Shore Bombardment No. 2　　　Patrol No. 12
Date: 25 July 1945　　Time: 1235 (K)　　Lat. 49-05 N., Long. 144-17.5 E.
Target Data – Damage Inflicted
Description: Target was large Canneries in town of Chiri
Damaged: Large Canneries.
Damage Determined by: Twenty rounds seen to land in target area. Several large holes in roof of main buildings and smaller buildings immediately surrounding.
Details of Action
Sighted canneries while making approach on target of Gun Attack No. 6. Immediately after trawler sunk, shifted fire to factory. Target consisted of large building with two tall stacks and accompanying buildings. Average range 5,700 yards. Fired a total of 43 rounds of 5 inch high capacity.

U.S.S. *Barb* (SS220)　　　Shore Bombardment No. 3　　　Patrol No. 3
Date: 26 July 1945　　Time: 1500 (K)　　Lat. 44-20 N., Long. 146-01 E.
Target Data – Damage Inflicted
Air camouflaged lumber mill and Sampan building yards at Shibetoro on west coast of Kunashiri. Visibility – good.
Damage: 1 Lumber Mill.
　　35 Sampans (destroyed by fire). Completely destroyed 700 tons.
Damage Determined by: Observed hits by 40 MM and 20 MM ammunition in lumber mill, sampans and oil tank. An oil fire started, which quickly spread to lumber mill. Sampans begin burning, leaving the industry in ashes.
Details of Action
Closed range to 2,100 yards and opened fire with 40 MM and 20 MM. A lucky hit in an oil storage tank started a large fire behind the lumber mill, which quickly spread to the mill and surrounding buildings. Sampans and building cradles were destroyed by gun fire, which resulted in a large fire sometime later. Several large spreading fires were still visible as night settled over the area, which reminded one of a large steel company with its characteristic glow. Fired a total of 157 rounds 40 mm, 2,400 round 20 mm, 1,000 round .50 Cal., and 500 rounds .30 Cal.

U.S.S *Barb* (SS220)　　　Rocket Assault No. 1　　　Patrol No. 12
Date: 22 June 1945　　Time: 0234 (K)　　Lat. 43-45 N., Long. 144-40 E.
Target Data – Damage Inflicted
Town of Shari on the north coast of Hokkaido with a population of about 20,000. Visibility – Fair.

Damage Determined by: Observed all rockets to fall and explode approximately in the center of town. The rockets erupted with a shower of sparks. No fires were observed.

Details of Action

Maneuvered into position 4,700 yards off the beach and 5,250 yards from the center of town using radar and line of bearing on a distant peak for navigation. Launched 12 Mk 10 5-inch rockets from Mk 51 rocket launcher, which is located on 5 inch gun foundation forward and is secured trained dead ahead. Reversed course and withdrew at high speed as dawn was breaking. Rockets observed to fall in an area about 500 yards in diameter in the center of town as well as can be estimated. Explosions were seen, heard, and felt.

U.S.S. *Barb* (SS220)　　　Rocket Assault No. 2　　　Patrol No. 12
Date: 3 July 1945　　Time: 0246 (K)　　Lat. 49-13.5 N., Long. 143-07.4 E.

Target Data – Damage Inflicted

Town of Shikuka located on the east coast of Karafuto at the northern tip of Patience Bay with a population of about 20,000. Visibility – poor.
Damage Determined by: Observed all rockets to fall and explode in the center of the town. Damage undetermined. No visible fires.

Details of Action

Maneuvered into position 4,930 yards off shore navigating by radar, which placed the ship approximately 5,250 yards from the center of the town. 0246:30 launched 12 Mk 10 5-inch rockets from Mk 51 rocket launcher located on the forward 5 inch gun platform. Reversed course and headed for deep water. The rockets exploded in the center of the town but the damage was undeterminable. The explosion brought forth several lights in the town, but they were quickly turned off.

U.S.S. *Barb* (SS220)　　　Rocket Assault No. 3　　　Patrol No. 12
Date: 24 July 1945　　Time: 2236 (K)　　Lat. 48-37 N., Long. 142-51 E.

Target Data – Damage Inflicted

Town of Shiritori located on the east coast of Karafuto. Visibility – poor.
Damage Determined by: Observed all rockets to fall and explode on the target; namely, on a large factory and in the center of the town. Large, spreading fires were observed accompanied with a series of explosions of an undetermined nature. Returned to target seven hours later. Small and large explosions were heard, although visibility prevented any further observations. Smoke hung throughout the area.

Details of Action

On several occasions observed target area from periscope depth to find any outstanding landmarks which would give us navigational aid for the night attack. A large factory with a 400 foot chimney gave an excellent landmark for radar navigation.

Maneuvered into position 5,250 yards from the first target, the large factory, using radar navigation. 2237 launched 12 Mk 10 5-inch rockets from the Mk 51 rocket launcher. 2238 launched 8 more rockets on the same target. Maneuvered the ship to the left using the smokestack as a reference point to gain a firing position on the center of the town. 2242 launched 12 rockets and then changed course to 180(T). Fifteen minutes after rockets hit fires became visible, so reversed course to observe the spreading fires. The factory was burning along with buildings in the center of the town. Explosions were also seen and heard. Visibility was very poor, but the fires were of such a magnitude that the burning structures were visible.

Left this area and proceeded to our second victim. Returned seven hours later approximately 7,700 yards off land and heard several series of rapid, small and large explosions followed sometime later by a very large explosion, which made the whole ship vibrate. Visibility was too poor to observe what was happening. The odor of burnt wood was heavy in the air.

U.S.S. *Barb* (SS220)   Rocket Assault No. 4   Patrol No. 1
Date: 25 July 1945   Time: 0310 (K)   Lat. 48-21 N., Long. 142-43 E.

Target Data – Damage Inflicted

Town of Kashiho located on the east coast of Karafuto. Visibility – poor.
Damage Determined by: Observed all rockets to fall and explode approximately in the center of the town. No visible fires.

Details of Action

Maneuvered into position 5,000 yards off the beach using radar navigation. 0310 launched 12 Mk 10 5-inch rockets from a Mk 51 rocket launcher. All rockets hit in the center of the town as best could be estimated with no visible fires resulting from the attack.

U.S.S. Barb (SS220)   Saboteur Attack No. 1   Patrol No. 12
Date: 22 July 1945   Time: 0147   Lat. 47-42.8 N., Long. 142-32.6 E.

Target Data – Damage Inflicted

Description: Northbound train of 12 freight cars, 3 passenger cars, and one mail car.

Destroyed: 1 Train.
Damage Determined by: Observed explosion when charge was set off

Details of Action

Observed trains running up and down coast during early period of patrol. Decided on operation and selected spot. Waited for calm sea and overcast night. Proceeded to selected spot, 950 yards off the beach, using radar navigation – flooded down and on the batteries. Put ashore Saboteur Party of seven men and Lt. Walker in charge. Sighted northbound unscheduled train after party reached the beach. Train passed on unharmed. Party left beach to return to boat after having been ashore an hour. When party was 300 yard from boat, another train came along; but this one was not so lucky. Engine blew up with terrific explosion and all the cars piled up on top of the wreckage.

A 55 pound demolition charge was used as the explosive. This was planted between two ties under the outboard rail. Three dry cell batteries supplied the current for the detonator and a micro switch completed the circuit. The micro switch was placed under the rail in such a manner that the deflection of the rail due to the weight of the train would close it. A test lamp was placed in the circuit for test purposes, which was by-passed when the charge was connected. The dry cells were sealed in a No. 10 can and all connections were taped to prevent moisture from grounding the circuit. Adjustment of micro switch clearance was by means of wedges, on one of which it was mounted. Final clearance was set less than 1/8 inch.

(I) MINES

No mines were sighted.

Frigate patrol was encountered close to the two La Pérouse minelines labeled as possible. It may have been coincidence that their patrol paralleled these lines.

(J) ANTI-SUBMARINE MEASURES AND EVASION TACTICS

There were two phases of antisubmarine measures.

The first phase was normal for a shallow water submarine patrol with three different bombings, one gun attack and two depth chargings. Since traffic moved only during daylight, and well inside the ten fathom curve, the escort deployment used is of particular interest and was very effective. Two DEs and 2 PCs acted as inner screen. A *Terutsuki* DD and plane made up an outer screen. Twice we were spotted, probably by the plane, while attempting to break through this combination, and both times bombed. It is believed that this spotting was due to our hull outline being seen in the shallow water. Both times the DD followed up with depth charging, escorted by the plane. Though armed with long extensive depth charge racks, the DD used only side throwers, the charges from which were set at

50 and 100 feet. A combination of listening and pinging was used by the DD, and his attacks were made at speeds of 10 and 12 knots. This slow speed, as well as the shallow water may account for his failure to use depth charges from his racks.

The depth charge direction indicator proved invaluable as an aid to evasion during all depth chargings and bombings. During our heaviest attack; though acting like a pin ball machine and registering everything including "TILT" it was found to be accurate at ranges outside of 400 yards. These were checked by the CO visually through the periscope and ST ranges were obtained on the depth charge geysers.

Primary evasion on the first pass consisted of attack firing two sets of down the throat shots. When these failed and the DD was close to his dropping point, our screws were revved up to full speed for twenty seconds to indicate a speed increase then slowed to 1/3 speed. This must have been successful for the destroyer commenced dropping ahead of us. When DCDI indicated ahead, scope was raised and counter attack commenced (special report). On his second pass the plane had no bombs left, and again we fired a down the throat salvo. These missed and we evaded using the same full speed tactics. The destroyer dropped astern of us. As he swung for a third pass 5 NAC beacons set at 3 minutes were fired at 1 minute intervals, depth changed to 80 feet and silent speed resorted to. No charges were dropped and we were never picked up again. A hold down bomb was dropped later in the afternoon.

In the La Pérouse area, four *Shimushu* class frigates were used. Three patrolling minefields, one escorting Otomari traffic. When hunting us these paired off. After one was sunk the remaining three hunted together. There was an obvious reluctance on their part to chase or attack us singly. During fog they kept to the ten fathom curve. When alone they hugged the minefields.

While gunning a lugger off Sakayehama were were attacked by two coastal defense guns.

While bombarding Kaihyo To we were attacked by machine gun and rifle fire from the island. The island was defended on its western side by 4 pillboxes, one exposed .50 Cal. machine gun and one 75 mm field piece. The field piece and one pillbox was destroyed. Opposition was silenced after the initial crossfire, by sweeping the island with twin 20 MM, two .50 Cal. and two .30 Cal. automatic guns. Whenever we ceased fire and drew away, the island would again open up with their machine guns.

Two of the luggers encountered counterattacked ineffectively with 37 MM tracer single fire.

The second phase of antisubmarine measures occurred after the carrier strikes on Hokkaido. Only 2 planes were encountered. La Pérouse area remained unchanged.

No countermeasures resulted from rocket assaults or our train demolition work.

In retrospect, our closing experiences, seem to add to the many evidences that the Japs have their backs against the wall.

(K) MAJOR DEFECTS

Hull and Machinery:
1. #1 periscope leaked excessively and it became necessary to repack the lower bearing. The leaks were stopped but the scope turned exceedingly hard. #2 scope would not hold pressure and it was necessary to recharge the scope several times.

2. The superstructure was noisy at submerged speeds of 2/3 and over, particularly the extension rods to MBT stops in #10 blow lines, and external air salvage connections. These were eliminated by using wooden wedges. A vibrating noise around JP head could not be located.

3. Lower packing gland starboard side of SD antenna hydraulic piston rod was repacked.

4. Azimuth head on QB sound equipment stripped threading on outer casing of the QB shafting, due to faulty assembly, temporarily repaired.

5. #4 Outboard exhaust valve gasket – While running the auxiliary generator at full load without running #4 main engine, the outboard exhaust valve gasket was burned out due to insufficient cooling water being discharged through the spray rings by the auxiliary generator salt water system.

6. #4 Main generator – Due to a faulty oil seal ring on the forward bearing, this generator was used for emergency only the last half of the patrol.

7. On #2 Main Engine a six inch crack developed on the inboard side of crankcase, near forward holding down bolt.

Ordnance and Gunnery
1. No casualties, misfires or duds for 40 MM gun, 5 inch gun, or rockets.

(L) RADIO

In general, the operation of radio gear was satisfactory. What few casualties to equipment were experienced were promptly and well repaired by the Chief with the help of the Auxiliary force.

TBL-6. Seven transmissions were made in the area – all of them on 8470 KCS. In each case, more than usual difficulty was encountered in establishing contact. Several call-ups were needed to establish communications on the first three of the transmissions listed below and on the fourth, no shore station could be reached. It was found that an "OP" procedure, used on the first messages, would not be answered and had to be changed to "O." The last several messages were sent with "O" priority initially and no difficulty was encountered.

Message #1 to NPM Received by RDO Pearl.
Message #2 to NPM Received by RDO Pearl.
Message #3 to NPM Recieved by RDO Pearl.
Message #4 to NPM Received by RDO Pearl
Message #5 to NPM Received by RDO San Francisco.
Message #6 to NPM Received by RDO Pearl.
Message #7 to NPM Recieved by RDO Pearl.

RAL-7. This was installed by the U.S.S. *Euryale* before the Barb's departure of Pearl Harbor. It was used on 8470 KCS and, although Jap interference was both strong and invariably exactly tuned to frequency, little difficulty was encountered once contact was established.

RBH-2. Used on the Wolf Pack frequency. Calls were frequently heard and two messages intercepted but reception, due probably to distance only, was very weak.

RAL-5. Reception was better than average on this equipment most of the time except during periods of heavy fog and during the hours of 0600 to 1200, King. It was used on the "P" schedule covering the 9-16,000 KCS frequencies.

VHF-624(A). When the lifeguard assignment was received, this equipment was turned on for a test and the trans-receiver began to smoke heavily. Inspection showed a combination of casualties the cause of none of which could be determined: Both 5U4G filaments in the rectifier were burned out; The Harmonic Amplifier, VT-203(9003), was shorted; burned out were the Condenser, 206-1, and the resistor, 246; the channel-shifting mechanism was inoperative.

Repairs were made, using Radar spares since none were supplied for this installation, and tubes, resistors, condenser and equipment tuned to Channel "A." Communications was established with our aircraft and no difficulty experienced thereafter.

RAK-5. This equipment was used to cover the 500 kcs frequency during lifeguard duty.

VHF-610(A). One attempt was made to use this equipment when communication was established with the U.S.S. Kingfish on SJ radar, but the range (established at 60,000 yards) was too great and the effort was wholly unsuccessful.

Antennas. The newly installed "Spot" antennas were entirely satisfactory and none of the expected difficulty in loading them was experienced. The whip antenna was mainly useful in taking Loran fixes en route to and from patrol; it was not used in the area.

JP Sound. Satisfactory.

WDA-1. Cable trouble developed several times with this equipment and, on one occasion, when it snapped at the stuffing box allowing the ends from the head to fall into the shaft, it appeared that the rest of the patrol would be made without QB sound. An excellent job of repair by the radio Chief and the Auxiliary force saved the day, however. The azimuth circle and yoke were removed, the cables fished out of the shaft and, after fourteen hours of work, the gear was back in use. The difficulty of the job was greatly increased by the damage caused by faulty re-installation during overhaul when the yoke set-screws were not properly located in the shaft receiving holes. This carelessness resulted in the serious burring of the threads both on the yoke and the shaft and was only discovered when repair to the cable was undertaken.

(M) RADAR

SJ. The range indicator was replaced during overhaul, greatly increasing sensitivity. The set suffered no major casualties during the patrol. Operation was highly satisfactory. Second sweep echoes, seldom encountered in the past, were frequent enough to be of navigational value. En route from area transmitter blower motor bearing had to be shimmed into the end ball.

ST. Enough cannot be said regarding the value of this addition to the fire control equipment. However the beat oscillator was found to be quite unstable (tried several 723 A/Bs). This made it hard to keep the unit in tune, and initial ranges several times left much to be desired. On the surface, the ST followed targets out 15% farther than the SJ (probably due to relative antenna heights). A tunable echo box is greatly needed. Optimum tuning conditions were while submerged. To determine the effect of pressure in the boat on the tuning of the beat oscillator, the set was tuned to land and while the operator watched the echoes an inch of pressure was added to the boat. There was no noticeable change in echo height.

SD. The SD-5 was installed during overhaul. This set demonstrated to the satisfaction of all hands its unreliability. During lifeguard duty it would have a good contact on a plane at fifteen to twenty miles and yet show only occasional contact on a flight of planes at five miles.

IFF. The BN and ABK are now controlled from either SD or SJ. Their operation was entirely satisfactory throughout the patrol. The length of the ABK pulses was used to calibrate the pulse duration scale of the AM/SPA.

(N) SOUND GEAR AND SOUND CONDITIONS

Nothing new concerning sound conditions.

(O) DENSITY LAYERS

Very few dives in this area exceeded 150 feet. At the surface, the water varied from 41 to 49 degrees, and was often isothermal to 80 feet, but invariably between 80 and 140 feet the water temperature would drop 10 to 15 degrees.

The cards recorded will be forwarded to the Hydrographic Office.

(P) HEALTH FOOD AND HABITABILITY

Health was excellent with no man hours lost. Our "Doc" proved himself a real doctor by patching up wounded prisoners, removing shrapnel, sewing ligaments and muscles, and treating first degree burns.

The Commissary department, ably led, outshone itself and far surpassed previous patrols.

Habitability was good for this area. Only 5 days were passed submerged, during which the ship sweat[ed] heavily.

(Q) PERSONNEL

How difficult it is to close this chapter of the *Barb*. What wordy praise can one give such men as these. Men who, without the information available to the CO follow unhesitatingly when in the vicinity of minefield so long as there is the possibility of targets. Men who offer half a year's pay for the opportunity to land on Jap land, to blow up a Jap train with a self trained demolition team. Men who flinch not with the fathometer ticking off 2 fathoms beneath the keel. Men who shout that the destroyer is running away after we've thrown every punch we possess and are getting our ears flattened back. Men who will fight to the last bullet and then want to start throwing the empty shell cases. These men are *Submariners*.

(a) Number of men on board during patrol — 75
(b) Number of men qualified at start of patrol — 61
(c) Number of men qualified at end of patrol — 73
(d) Number of men unqualified making their first patrol — 9
(e) Number of men advanced in rating during patrol — 8
(f) Number of men recommended to Squadron for advancement—no vacancy on board. — 5

(R) MILES STEAMED – FUEL USED

	MILES	GALLONS
Pearl Harbor to Midway	1,376	15,040
Midway to Area	2,160	23,620
In Area	8,043	55,415
Area to Midway	2,000	20,850

(S) DURATION

Days Pearl Harbor to Area — 11
Days in Area — 39

Days Area to Midway   6
Days Submerged   5

(T) FACTORS OF ENDURANCE REMAINING

Torpedoes, Rockets, Ammunition   Fuel   Provisions   Personnel
                                   17,000 gals.   30   30

Limiting factor this patrol – Ammunition.

(U) RADAR COUNTERMEASURES

The following are contacts made by the AN/APR and AN/SPA RCM equipment. TN-2 was found to be calibrated four megacycles above TN-1.

Often several contacts appeared in the same vicinity, varying only slightly in frequency, pulse note, or pulse duration.

Excessive pulse duration was indicated in many cases, but calibration of the AN/SPA sweep scale with IFF pulses checked correctly.

Vicinity of:
    42-40 N., 145 E.   305/500/15
                              206/500/23
                              102/500/23

These were thought to be harmonics from the same source, but comparison of pulse shapes and the different times of the contacts as well as dissimilar sweep methods tended to discount this.

102/500/23 was strongest when we were nearest Kushiro. The others appeared to be in the vicinity of Akkeshi Wan.

    153/500/23

This contact was strongest when near 43-10 N., 154-30 E. Possible source Nemuro.

Land based air search type radar, 60-80/500/25-35 was contacted in several localities. Four units of distinctly different characteristics were contacted between 145-00 E., and 146-00 E., 43-10 N.

Vicinity of:
    44-30 N., 145-30 E.   78/500/60

During both passages of Shikoten Suido (43-40 N., 146-30 E.) the above contact was made. Contact was had on the same type of radar during four passages of Kunashiri Suido, possible source Atoiva Misaki.

    198/900 or 1150/20-25

This contact was had while along the north west coast of Kunashiri Shima. At the same time contact was had on 79/500/20. This latter (possibly same station) was strong while in Abashiri Wan, as was contact on 185/1000/20.

Vicinity: 44-30 N., 143-20 E.
   79/500/ 25 – 79/1000/60 – 135/250/13
Vicinity: 46-00 N., 142-20 E. (Possibly Nishi Notoro Misaki)
   95/450–500/40 – 159/650/13 – 75/500/25
Vicinity: 45-50 N., 143-30 E. (Possibly Naka Shiretoko Misaki)
   75/500/25
Vicinity: Cape Patience 49-00 N., 144-40 E.
   79/750/18 – 72/500/25 – 117/1250/8 (Had contact for less than
   a minute.)
Vicinity: 46-50 N. to 47-20 N., 143-30 E. (Airo Misaki) One sweep per min.
   155/500/8-13 – 79/500/13–70 –82/500/100 – 98/500/15
Vicinity: 47-30 N., 142-50 E. (Sakayehama) Had similar contact at 310 Meg.
   76/500/10 – 77/500/20
Vicinity: 48-00 N., 143-50 E. Appeared to be four contacts.
   59/500/25   74–79/500–750/40–70
Vicinity: 48-30 N., 142-10 E. (Shiritori)
   135/1500/8 – 74/500/40 (Irregular fast sweeps)
   99/375/long (had no definite pulse shape. Possibly a beacon.)
Vicinity: 48-50 N., 143-14 E.
   68/1000/25 – (strong sweep)
   95/500/23
Vicinity: 50-00 N, 144-15 E.
79/500/23 (Slow, weak sweeps)
75/500/60 (Appeared not to sweep)

COMMUNICATIONS COUNTERMEASURES

No enemy transmissions were intercepted except those used for.........
Jamming. CW continuous keying was encountered at all times on 8470 kilocycles with occasional additions of voice. Wolf pack frequencies were consistently straddled by voice jamming. While such jamming was found to be exactly on frequency, it was only partly effective in that no difficulty was experienced once communication was established with the stations called.
There were no instances of known enemy deception on this run.

SONAR COUNTERMEASURES

During the duel with the destroyer continuous keying on 17 kilocycles was heard. The frigates encountered keyed on a frequency below 14 kilocycles.

(V) REMARKS

The torpedo has fulfilled its purpose. Its day, in this war, is passing. It is believed that, in the not too distant future, with the anticipated increase in tempo of air strikes, and the lack of air opposition, that lifeguard duties will be taken over, more capably and more efficiently, by PT boats. Thus, those of us, not specially equipped for the last good area, must stagnate and slowly slip into oblivion, or look to a new main battery—rockets. The rocket is not a toy. It's possibilities are tremendous, strategically and tactically, but not beyond comprehension. For the sake of argument let us take only the tactical side, with which the skipper is immediately concerned, and consider it in the light of our meagre experience.

For immediate use the material available to us is the same as used on the LCI(G)[9]. The rocket concerned is the Mk 10 Mod. 0, 5 inch, high capacity, spin stabilized, rocket, carrying an explosive charge of 9.6 pounds. This explosive charge is much greater than that of our 5 inch projectile and really packs a wallop. The Mk 51 launcher used weighs about 75 pounds and holds 12 rockets. It is simple and easy to operate with angle settings of 30, 35, 40 and 45 degrees for ranges of 4,500, 4,900, 5,150, 5,250 yard respectively. Deflection or drift varies from 10 miles[10] right for the closest range to 50 miles right for the farthest range. The rocket rises 4,300 feet in its trajectory. Accuracy is very good with an impact area of 400 yards in diameter. Firing is done electrically from the conning tower. Twelve rockets are fired from a single launcher in 4.5 seconds. Maximum time of flight is 30 seconds. Blast consists of a light shower of small sparks and rocket trail disappears about 20 feet above the hull. The reload crew waited in perfect safety alongside the conning tower fairwater. Reload was accomplished in less than 2 minutes.

Augmenting this set up, the following is recommended. Carry torpedoes only in the tubes. These to be steam torpedoes, so that afterbody space only is required for routining. Remove all torpedo racks and replace them with rocket stowage bins. In this manner well over 2,000 rockets may be carried. One to three banks of six launchers each to be installed forward. Whether these be permanent or portable is a question for material personnel. Permanent pressure proof firing circuit to be installed with deck connections for short portable leads to the launchers. Thus we have a battery firing a salvo of 72 to 216 rockets, depending upon its size. Variations in this are obvious and a matter of experience and need.

On the subject of the approach, it is assumed that all submarines now use a plexiglass PPI plot or its equivalent for accurate inshore navigation. Preliminary

---

[9] LCI(G): Landing Craft, Infantry (Gunnery): The standard landing craft, but fitted with rocket launcher racks and used to lay down a barrage as the troops are hitting the beach. Your editor, having been on the receiving end of numerous attacks by the slightly-smaller Soviet 122 MM rockets in Viet Nam, can attest to the effectiveness of concentrated rocket barrages at disrupting efficient operations.

[10] Original has "miles," but should probably be "mils."

reconnoiter is desirable. An ST check is made for possible definite pips, which may be used in conjunction with TDC for taking the desired attack position. Specific navigational landmarks are noted and plotted for possible TBT–radar approach. If neither of above can be determined or visibility precludes their use, radar navigation alone may be used if target site is suited for its use. Rocket range is preset by the launcher angle and drift is taken care of by variation of ship's head as launchers are line up with ship's head. If greater impact area is desire, launchers may be set at varying angles and ship's head swung during firing.

Normally no opposition will be encountered even when attacking targets protected by heavy coastal defenses. Naturally the attack will be conducted under visibility requirements suited for night surface convoy work. The attack itself approaches the instantaneous. Only a flash will be apparent to shore observers, yet, if the submarine is noticed in the flash, shore gunsights would have extreme difficulty in getting on the submarine. In very dangerous situations the firing key may be closed and the diving alarm sounded simultaneously, observing results through periscope.

Fortunately the Japanese set up presents numerous shoreline targets. Many of these are more suited for submarine assault than surface craft bombardment; or can be more effectively handled by a submarine than a minor task force—notably Hokkaido, Karafuto and the Kurile Islands.

Rockets themselves are self selling, simple and easy to operate. They do not require gunsights. Most of our opposition does.

What tremendous advantages we possess—each submarine a submersible task force. Let's make the rocket our final devastating blow against the Japs with one idea in mind—destroy and pulverize.

Recommended Desirable Features
  (a) High capacity incendiary rocket.
  (b) Increase rocket range to 8,000 yards.
  (c) Design a more rugged launcher and pressure proof rockets.
  (d) Blast deflection into superstructure.
  (e) Rockets to be stowed in metal containers in place of boxes. (We removed the boxes, wrapped the rocket motor in towelling, and stowed rocket projectile and motor separately as a precautionary measure. Projectile and motor are easily and quickly assembled prior to use. Ground band was left on motor until rocket received topside via the scuttle.)
  (f) Some method be devised for more facile scuttle handling.
  (g) Consideration be given to a stern bank of rocket launchers.

2. Area

North coast Hokkaido, Aniwa Wan and Taraika Wan (Patience Bay) was requested as an area in an effort to alleviate the crowded submarine situation by opening up a new area. Much of this area had never been investigated by a submarine and no part of it had been touched since 1943, this in the vicinity of La Pérouse.

Summer coastal steamers were anticipated in Patience Bay and Aniwa Wan with a slight possibility along Hokkaido. Anticipated many sampans in Patience Bay, possible convoys in La Pérouse and daily train ferries from La Pérouse to Otomari. Patrol was to be conducted as usual on the surface until traffic had been established. Minefields were to be avoided by flight, or, in necessity, by diving and paralleling at shallow depth. Four coastal steamers were encountered, however, this traffic is now confined to Otomari alone. Train ferries encountered early in the area must have shifted to Hakodate after the carrier strikes there. La Pérouse–Kurile convoys, now infrequent, make their landfall on Karafuto in the vicinity of Anaiwa Misaki then hug the coast religiously to La Pérouse, travelling only by day. Full moon prevented night attacks on our convoy. Heavy ship, lugger and trawler traffic occurs between La Pérouse and Otomari—at least two ships a day. These are good targets. With fog they should be easy. Without fog, since they travel inside the 10 fathom curve, only a 3 or 4 mile stretch is open to submarine attacks without FM[11]. Sampan and trawler traffic was well below our expectations.

The whole area is shallow, about 30 fathoms with the 10 fathom curve about 4,000 yards offshore. Soundings were taken at 15 minutes outside the 10 fathom curve and continuously when inside. Navigation is simple, but tiring, with continuous coastal running. Weather was much clearer than normal, seas usually less than state one. Typical atmospheric periscope fogging was eliminated by using the anti fog paste (from rescue breathing apparatus) on exterior surfaces.

Karafuto has grown up. There are many factories and coal mines. Perhaps many of the factories the Japanese have said they have moved underground have instead been shifted to this out of the way place. Nearly all towns charted, even on fairly recent Japanese charts, have expanded. There are many suitable rocket and gun bombardment targets. All towns as far north as Shikuka are connected by railroad and highway. POW says trains also go to Chiri, thus connecting the whole of Karafuto. These coastal trains are excellent gun targets, particularly at night, now that our strikes have practically eliminated planes from the area. A hitting range of 2,000 yards can be obtained in several places with 5 fathoms of water beneath the keel. This hourly train traffic should be stopped. Had we known earlier, no train would have gotten by.

---

[11] FM sonar. This late war development was accurate enough, and had sufficient definition, for plotting individual mines and thus could be used to navigate a submarine through a minefield. Only a few submarines were fitted with this gear before the war ended.

3. Torpedoes

19 Mk 18-2 torpedoes were carried[12]. Only 2 hits were obtained. All were fired and tracked normally to the target. All targets for the Mk 18-2 torpedoes were steady course, steady speed. No maneuvers were made by targets to avoid. ST information was used on all attacks except large AK, which was sunk. Injection was low. No duds were apparent. Our firing system was checked after each attack. Ranges were short, tracks and gyros not excessive, and target draft at least twice as great as depth set. Several torpedoes exploded on the beach. Major variation of torpedo speed would not have affected hits in many cases. It is believed torpedoes ran deep, but after thorough study no basis can be made for this other than elimination of all other possibilities. Conviction is so strong in this belief, that it is not too farfetched a consideration to attribute our two hits to erratic runs, from the normal run of these torpedoes. Albeit, with three very successful past runs using Mk 18 torpedoes, our faith is not shaken and we will take them again.

---

12   In addition to the Mark 18 torpedoes listed, *Barb* carried 3 Mark 28 homing torpedoes, and Mark 27 "Cutie" homing torpedoes. The Mark 27 was a 19" "swim out" torpedo, intended to be fired at a depth of 150 feet for use against escorts, and was developed from the Mark 24 air-dropped anti-submarine torpedo. The Mark 28 was a 21" passive-acoustic anti-shipping torpedo. Both were considered experimental at this time and their use was recorded in a separate special report as information on these torpedoes was classified at a higher level than the "Confidential" classification of the patrol reports. Unfortunately, that special report is not available for inclusion here.

FB5/322/A16-3 SUBMARINE DIVISION THREE TWENTY-TWO
                           c/o Fleet Post Office,
Serial: 08   San Francisco, Cal.

CONFIDENTIAL   6 August 1945

First Endorsement to:
U.S.S. *Barb* (SS220) Report
of Twelfth War Patrol.

From: The Commander Submarine Division Three Twenty-Two.
To: The Commander in Chief, United States Fleet.
Via: (1) The Commander Submarine Squadron Thirty-Two.
          (2) The Commander Submarine Force, Pacific Fleet.
          (3) The Commander in Chief, United States Pacific Fleet.

Subject: U.S.S. *Barb* (SS220), Report of Twelfth War Patrol.

    1. The twelfth war patrol of the U.S.S. *Barb*, conducted north of Hokkaido and east of Karafuto during the period from 8 June 1945 to 2 August 1945 is an unparalleled example of daring, planning, and originality, resulting in outstanding achievements. The introduction to submarine warfare, with devastating results, of rockets and saboteur attacks, was but a phase of this remarkable patrol.

    2. Action resumés follow:

    (a) During the first night in the area, radar contact was established on two craft later identified as luggers. Close range gun attacks, delivered at dawn, disposed of both targets in seventeen minutes. This first gun attack demonstrated the worth of the new 40 MM sight yoke.

    (b) During the night of 22 June 1945 *Barb* took station 5,250 yards from the center of the town of Shari and launched twelve rockets as repayment for two aircraft bombs received that afternoon. No fires were started, but all rockets exploded in the center of the city.

    (c) A large wooden trawler, sighted during the early morning of 23 June 1945, was taken under fire from 2,000 yards with 5 inch and 40 mm to determine amount of resistance. *Barb* closed and pin point shooting soon had a large hole at the waterline and fires raging. With a miserly desire to conserve ammunition, the bow wave, at 10 yards, was next used to despatch this target. One prisoner was taken from six volunteers.

    (d) Three days later, under freak atmospheric conditions, sight contact was made on a convoy at forty thousand yards. Convoy consisting of three freighters, a DD, 2 DEs and 2 PCs, could not be closed after submergence, but an attack was made on the seaward escort. This is covered by a special report. After surfacing contact on the convoy was reestablished, but broadsides from twelve thousand yards prevented attack. Tracking continued through the twenty-seventh and twenty-eighth with *Barb* being only on the receiving end. About noon of the twenty-ninth *Barb* was again submerged ahead of the convoy, and in contact. An attack, covered by a special report, was delivered shortly thereafter. At 1320, from a range of 960 yards, three electric torpedoes were fired down the throat, at the DD, for no hits. Unable to go deep, the Commanding Officer had the doubtful pleasure of watching this ship pass almost overhead with side throwers working at the double. Another attack, covered by a special report, was delivered. On his next pass, at 620 yards, three more electrics were fired down the throat for no hits. The Commanding Officer then prudently ordered "deep submergence" of eighty feet while receiving numerous close charges. Five NAC beacons aided escape.

(e) On the morning of 2 July a surface approach was made on the seal rookery at Kaihyo To. In addition a radio station and twenty barracks buildings and warehouses were observed. Bombardment was commenced from 1,100 yards and again pin point shooting resulted. All buildings were systematically destroyed while the 40 MM silenced the opposition and destroyed three sampans. A well planned assault force was called away, but the presence of 4 pill boxes, previously unnoticed, caused a change of plan. One of these was destroyed by a direct 40 MM hit in the aperture.

(f) On 3 July a salvo of twelve rockets was fired at Shikuka and landed "amongst a mass of buildings," but no fires resulted.

(g) Later that day a small coastal freighter was attack. This is covered by a special report.

(h) On 5 July, while submerged, two ships were sighted. The larger was thought to be a Russian and the smaller appeared to be taking advantage of it as an unofficial screen. After approach was under way the larger was identified as enemy and target was shifted. Three electric torpedoes, fired from 1,600 yards on a 95° track, with 15° gyros, resulted in no hits. Ship was swung and two more electrics were fired from the stern tubes for one hit. The ship was stopped. While maneuvering for a third attack the ship was seen to break amidships and sink.

(i) On 8 July a lugger was destroyed by 40 MM fire, but the presence of a plane caused the *Barb* to break off action before the target had finally sunk.

(j) On 10 July an ST approach, close inshore, on two 800 ton AKs resulted in no hits from three electrics fired from 540 yards on a 145° track with 43° gyro angles.

(k) A large diesel sampan was destroyed by gunfire on 11 July within 15 miles of an airbase on Shikotan.

(l) On 12, 13, and 14 July, lifeguard duties were performed for strikes on north Hokkaido.

(m) With five torpedoes left, submerged approach was commenced, during the morning of 15 July, on a large AK and its escorting frigate. Two electrics were fired from 1,240 yards on a 160° track, with 10° gyros at the frigate, ship was swung right and the remaining three torpedoes were fired at the AK from 1,500 yards on a 120° track with gyros at 43°. All torpedoes were set on four feet. No hits were obtained in the AK, but one hit sank the frigate.

(n) A beautifully planned and excitingly executed saboteur attack blew up a heavily loaded train on 23 July.

(o) A triple rocket attack on Shiritori was particularly successful. Large fires and heavy explosions were observed by the entire crew. Some explosions were still occurring, accompanied by thick smoke, when *Barb* returned next day.

(p) A single salvo of rockets, fired at the factories of Kashino on 23 July, landed in the target area, but no fires were started and damage could not be observed.

(q) A sampan was attacked on 25 July, boarded, and then sunk by gunfire.

(r) A sampan was taken under fire a few hours later, in the vicinity of Chiri. One round of 5 inch, following hits by automatic guns sank the sampan, so fire was shifted to the canneries of Chiri. Buildings were damaged, but no fires started. Battle stations were secured for a short period before another sampan was sighted, taken under fire, and sunk. Again, 15 minutes later, another was sighted, then two more. All three were sunk after resorting to starshell in the five inch.

(s) With only automatic ammunition remaining, a devastating gun attack was made on the lumber mill and sampan building yard at Shibetoro. Hits in an oil tank caused fires, which spread and destroyed the mill and all sampans under construction. While observing this destruction another trawler was taken under fire and soon stopped, burning. Two prisoners were taken and the trawler, burning but not sinking, was finally pushed under by ramming at five knots.

3. It is recommended that pressure proof sights with yokes, of make shift design if necessary, but installed on all 40 MM guns as quickly as possible. Nothing can be added to the Commanding Officer's recommendation regarding rockets except the obvious coordinated bombardments.

4. It is a distinct pleasure to the Administrative Division Commander to be officially associated again with this ship and to congratulate them on this, their fifth successive, outstanding patrol.

J.R. Waterman[13]

---

[13] Captain Waterman was, of course, *Barb*'s commanding officer on six of her first seven war patrols.

FC5-31/A16-3   SUBMARINE SQUADRON THIRTY-TWO

Serial: 0107

C-O-N-F-I-D-E-N-T-I-A-L

Care of Fleet Post Office,
San Francisco, California,
13 August 1945.

<u>Second Endorsement</u> to:
U.S.S. *Barb* (SS220) Report of
Twelfth War Patrol.

From: The Commander Submarine Squadron Thirty-Two.
To: The Commander-in-Chief, United States Fleet.
Via: (1) The Commander Submarine Force, Pacific Fleet.
           (2) The Commander-in-Chief, Pacific Fleet.

Subject: U.S.S. *Barb* (SS220) – Report of War Patrol Number Twelve.

    1. Forwarded, concurring in the complete remarks of the Commander Submarine Division Three Twenty-Two.

    2. The twelfth war patrol of the U.S.S. *Barb* adds another glorious chapter to the history of this submarine's wartime operations. This patrol is positively outstanding in all phases due to the expert execution of intelligently conceived planning involving the use of all the usual submarine weapons plus rocket and saboteur attacks.

    3. The recommendations of the Commanding Officer and the Commander Submarine Division Three Twenty-Two concerning the employment of rockets by submarines deserves serious consideration.

    4. It is recommended that the U.S.S. *Barb* be credited with damage to the enemy on her twelfth war patrol as follows.

SUNK

1 – AK Large (EC)	7,500 tons	(Attack No. 2B)
1 – FF *Shimuru* Class Frigate (EC)	1,000 tons	(Attack No. 4A)
2 – MIS Lugger (EC)	200 tons	(Gun Attack No. 1)
1 – MIS Trawler (EC)	150 tons	(Gun Attack No. 2)
1 – MIS Sampan (EC)	50 tons	(Gun Attack No. 4)
1 – MIS Sampan (EC)	50 tons	(Gun Attack No. 5)
1 – MIS Sampan (EC)	50 tons	(Gun Attack No. 6)
1 – MIS Sampan (EC)	50 tons	(Gun Attack No. 7)
2 – MIS Sampan (EC)	100 tons	(Gun Attack No. 8)
1 – MIS Sampan (EC)	50 tons	(Gun Attack No. 9)
1 – MIS Trawler (EC)	100 tons	(Gun Attack No. 10)
Total –	9,300 tons	

In addition three bombardments of shore installations were conducted resulting in the destruction of 20 warehouses, barracks, and 3 sampans, 1 lumber mill, and 35 sampans in building yards. A canning factory was damaged. Four rocket assaults were made on four separate towns with devastating effects.

5. The commanding officer, officers, and crew of the U.S.S. Barb are most heartily congratulated upon the completion of this outstanding patrol and for their remarkable ability, initiative, and spirit in carrying out such successful attacks on enemy units afloat and his shore installations.

K.C. Hurd.

SUBMARINE FORCE, PACIFIC FLEET

FF12-10(A)/A16-3(18)   mr

Serial 02164

CONFIDENTIAL

Care of Fleet Post Office,
San Francisco, California,
30 August 1945.

Third Endorsement to
Barb Report
Twelfth War Patrol.

NOTE: THIS REPORT WILL BE
DESTROYED PRIOR TO
ENTERING PATROL AREA.

ComSubPac Patrol Report No. 855
U.S.S. *Barb* – Twelfth War Patrol.

From:	The Commander Submarine Force, Pacific Fleet.
To:	The Commander in Chief, United States Fleet.
Via:	The Commander in Chief, U.S. Pacific Fleet.
Subject:	U.S.S. *Barb* (SS220) – Report of Twelfth War Patrol (8 June to 2 August 1945).

1. The twelfth war patrol of the *Barb*, under the command of Commander E.B. Fluckey, U.S. Navy, was conducted in the areas north of Hokkaido and east of Karafuto. Except for three days devoted to lifeguard duty this was an offensive patrol. There were no opportunities to rescue aviators.

2. The *Barb* on her twelfth patrol continued her excellent record and turned in another outstanding performance. This patrol is particularly noteworthy for its bold aggressiveness, fine planning, ingenuity, extremely thorough area

coverage, and smart execution. By striking ship and shore installations in rapid succession in different parts of the area, the *Barb* was a constant source of destruction and concern to the enemy. The *Barb*, for the first time in submarine warfare, successfully employed rockets against shore installations. She landed a party of commandos who very effectively wrecked a train. Through smart conservation and use of ammunition plus excellent gun pointing the *Barb* succeeded in inflicting much damage with her five inch guns and automatic weapons.

3. Award of Submarine Combat Insignia for this patrol in authorized.

4. The Commander Submarine Force, Pacific Fleet, takes great pleasure in congratulating the commanding officer, officers, and crew of the *Barb* for this extremely aggressive, smartly conducted and productive patrol which is a very fitting culmination to *Barb*'s illustrious war record. In addition to sinking the shipping listed below, the *Barb* is credited with inflicting the following during this patrol:

(a) Destruction of one railroad train of twelve freight cars, two passenger cars and one mail car by a party of commandos who went ashore and planted a demolition charge which destroyed the train as it passed over the charge[14].

(b) Rocket assaults on the towns of Shari, Shikuka, Kashaiko and Shiritori, the last of which created excessive damage and fires.

(c) Shore gunnery bombardments on the towns of:

(1) Kaihyo To – in which about 20 buildings, warehouses and barracks were destroyed and fifty percent of all structures ruined.

(2) Shibetoro – in which fires were started in fuel tanks with the resulting destruction of a lumber mill, 35 sampans in various stages of construction, three large buildings, and many houses.

(3) Chiri – in which canneries were damaged.

SUNK

1 – Coastal AK (EU)	– 1,000 tons	(Separate Report)
1 – Large AK (EU)	– 7,500 tons	(Attack No. 2B)
1 – FF (*Shiburu* Class) (EC)	– 1,000 tons	(Attack No. 4A)
2 – MIS (luggers, 100 tons each) (EU)	– 200 tons	(Gun Attack No. 1)
1 – MIS (Trawler) (EU)	– 150 tons	(Gun Attack No. 2)
1 – MIS (Lugger) (EU)	– 75 tons	(Gun Attack No. 3)
1 – MIS (Sampan) (EU)	– 50 tons	(Gun Attack No. 4)
1 – MIS (Sampan) (EU)	– 50 tons	(Gun Attack No. 5)
1 – MIS (Sampan) (EU)	– 50 tons	(Gun Attack No. 6)

---

14 *Barb*'s Saboteur Party were the only American combat forces to intentionally land on one of the Japanese home islands prior to the Japanese surrender. In recognition of their accomplishments, all landing party members were awarded the Silver Star medal. This was unusual in that, normally, only the officer in command of the landing party would have received the Silver Star, with the rest of the party receiving a Bronze Star. (Fluckey was of the opinion they should all have received the Navy Cross.)

1 – MIS (Sampan)(EU)	–	50 tons	(Gun Attack No. 7)
2 – MIS (Sampans, 50 tons each)(EU)	–	100 tons	(Gun Attack No. 8)
1 – MIS (Sampan)(EU)	–	50 tons	(Gun Attack No. 9)
1 – MIS (Trawler)(EU)	–	100 tons	(Gun Attack No. 10)
3 – MIS (Sampans, 50 tons each)(EU)	–	150 tons	(During bombardmen of Kaihyo To)
35 – MIS (Sampans, 20 tons each)(EU)	–	700 tons	(During bombardment of Shibetoro)
	Total Sunk	11,225 tons	

Merrill Comstock,
Deputy.

Distribution:
(Complete Reports)

Cominch	(7)
CNO	(5)
Cincpac	(6)
JICPOA	(1)
AdICPOA	(1)
Comservpac	(1)
Cinclant	(1)
Comsubslant	(8)
S/M School, NL	(2)
CO, S/M School, PH	(1)
Comsopac	(2)
Comsowespac	(1)
Comsubs7thFlt (Fwd Echelon)	(2)
Comsubs7thFlt (Rear Echelon)	(2)
Comnorpac	(1)
Comsubspac	(3)
ComsubspacAdComd	(40)
SUBAD, MI	(2)
ComsubspacSubordcom	(3)
All Squadron and Div. Commanders, Pacific	(2)
ComSubOpTrnGrBalboa (Airmail)	(5)
Substrainpac	(2)
All Submarines, Pacific	(1)

E.L. Hynes, 2nd,
Flag Secretary.

United States
04B/89